THE CAMBRIDGE
COMPANION TO
JONATHAN SWIFT

EDITED BY

CHRISTOPHER FOX

University of Notre Dame, Indiana

CAMBRIDGE
UNIVERSITY PRESS

PUBLISHED BY THE PRESS SYNDICATE OF THE UNIVERSITY OF CAMBRIDGE
The Pitt Building, Trumpington Street, Cambridge CB2 1RP, United Kingdom

CAMBRIDGE UNIVERSITY PRESS
The Edinburgh Building, Cambridge, CB2 2RU, UK
40 West 20th Street, New York, NY 10011–4211, USA
477 Williamstown Road, Port Melbourne, VIC 3207, Australia
Ruiz de Alarcón 13, 28014 Madrid, Spain
Dock House, The Waterfront, Cape Town 8001, South Africa

http://www.cambridge.org

First published 2003

Printed in the United Kingdom at the University Press, Cambridge

Typeface Sabon 10/13 pt.   *System* LATEX 2$_\varepsilon$ [TB]

A catalogue record for this book is available from the British Library

ISBN 0 521 80247 4 hardback
ISBN 0 521 00283 4 paperback

CONTENTS

SEAMUS DEANE is Professor of English and the Donald and Marilyn Keough Professor of Irish Studies at the University of Notre Dame, Indiana. He is a member of the Royal Irish Academy, a founding director of the Field Day Theatre, the general editor of the Penguin Joyce, and the author of several books, including *A Short History of Irish Literature*, *Celtic Revivals: Essays in Modern Irish Literature*, *The French Revolution and Enlightenment in England*, and *Strange Country: Modernity and the Nationhood In Irish Writing Since 1790*. Deane has edited the *Field Day Anthology of Irish Writing*, has written four books of poetry and a novel, *Reading in the Dark*. He is completing a new novel and a book on Edmund Burke to be published in the Field Day Critical Conditions series.

MARGARET ANNE DOODY is Professor of English and the John and Barbara Glynn Family Professor of Literature at the University of Notre Dame, Indiana. Her books include *The True History of the Novel*, *Frances Burney: The Life in the Works*, *The Daring Muse: Augustan Poetry Reconsidered*, and *A Natural Passion: A Study of the Novels of Samuel Richardson*. She has edited Frances Burney's *Evelina*, Jane Austen's *Catharine and Other Early Writings*, and L. M. Montgomery's *Anne of Green Gables* (*The Annotated Anne*). Her mystery novel, *Aristotle Detective*, has just been republished and has also been translated into Italian. She is currently working on two books, one on Apuleius and one on Venice.

CAROLE FABRICANT is Professor of English at the University of California, Riverside. She is the author of *Swift's Landscape* (2nd edn., 1995) and has published widely in the fields of Eighteenth-Century Studies, Postcolonial and Gender Studies. She is currently completing an edition of *Swift's Miscellaneous Prose* for Penguin Classics and collaborating on an edition of Swift's *Irish Writings* for St. Martin's Press. She received a Guggenheim Fellowship for her new critical project, "Speaking for the Irish Nation: Problems of Colonial Representation in Eighteenth-Century Ireland."

CHRISTOPHER FOX is Professor of English at the University of Notre Dame, Indiana. He is the author of *Locke and the Scriblerians: Identity and Consciousness in Early Eighteenth-Century Britain* and editor of several books, including *Psychology and Literature in the Eighteenth Century, Gulliver's Travels: Case Studies in Contemporary Criticism, Teaching Eighteenth-Century Poetry*, and co-editor, with Robert Wokler and the late Roy Porter, of *Inventing Human Science: Eighteenth Century Domains*, and with Brenda Tooley, of *Walking Naboth's Vineyard: New Studies of Swift*. He is currently working on a study of Swift and Defoe.

BREAN HAMMOND is Professor of English at the University of Nottingham. He is the author of numerous articles and several books on the eighteenth century, most recently *Professional Imaginative Writing in England, 1670–1740: "Hackney for Bread,"* published by Clarendon Press. His current project is an edition of Vanbrugh for Oxford University Press World's Classics.

IAN HIGGINS is Senior Lecturer in English Literature at The Australian National University in Canberra, Australia. He is the author of *Swift's Politics: A Study in Disaffection*, published by Cambridge University Press, and of several articles on Swift. He has also written on Swift's contemporaries in the Jacobite Diaspora and on radical Whig authors.

J. PAUL HUNTER is Professor of English at the University of Virginia. He has published numerous essays on the eighteenth century and is the author of several books, including *Before Novels: The Cultural Contexts of Eighteenth-century English Fiction, Occasional Form: Henry Fielding and the Chains of Circumstance*, and *The Reluctant Pilgrim: Defoe's Emblematic Method and Quest for Form in Robinson Crusoe*.

PATRICK KELLY is Fellow and Senior Lecturer in Modern History at Trinity College, Dublin. He is the editor of *Locke on Money* for *The Clarendon Edition of the Works of John Locke* and the author of numerous articles. With Aileen Douglas and Ian Campbell Ross, Kelly has co-edited *Locating Swift: Essays from Dublin on the 250th Anniversary of the Death of Jonathan Swift*. He is currently completing a critical edition of William Molyneux's *The Case of Ireland Stated*.

JOSEPH McMINN is Professor of Anglo-Irish Studies at the University of Ulster, at Jordanstown, Northern Ireland. He is the author of several books on Swift, including *Jonathan Swift: A Literary Life* and *Jonathan's Travels: Swift and Ireland*. He is currently working on a longer study of Swift's interest in the "sister arts."

JUDITH C. MUELLER is Associate Professor of English at Franklin and Marshall College, Pennsylvania. She has published articles on Swift and on masculinity in Restoration and eighteenth-century literature and culture in such journals as *English Literary History*.

DAVID OAKLEAF is Associate Professor of English at the University of Calgary, Canada. He has edited Eliza Haywood's *Love in Excess* and published essays on eighteenth-century writers in *SEL: Studies in English Literature, Studies in the Novel, Eighteenth-Century Fiction, Eighteenth-Century Life*, and the *University of Toronto Quarterly*. With Noel Chevalier and Joyce Rappaport, Oakleaf's most recent project is *The Broadview Anthology of Restoration and Eighteenth-Century Literature in English*.

MICHAEL F. SUAREZ, S.J. is Associate Professor of English at Fordham University, New York. His scholarly interests include bibliography and publishing history, the so-called "sister arts" and literature and the history of ideas. Along with a study of Robert Dodsley's *Collection of Poems*, he has co-edited, with Peter D. McDonald, *Making Meaning: Selected Essays of D. F. McKenzie*, and with Michael Turner, *The Cambridge History of the Book in Britain, Volume V, 1695–1830* (forthcoming). His current project is a study of mock-biblical satire from 1660 to 1832.

PAT ROGERS is Professor of English and the DeBartolo Professor of Liberal Arts at the University of South Florida. He is the editor of *Jonathan Swift: The Complete Poems* and the author of numerous books, including *Grub Street: Studies in a Subculture, Literature and Popular Culture in Eighteenth Century England, The Text of Great Britain: Theme and Design in Defoe's Tour*, and *Eighteenth Century Encounters: Studies in Literature and Society in the Age of Walpole*.

MARCUS WALSH is Professor of English Literature at the University of Birmingham. He has co-edited, with Karina Williamson, *The Poetical Works of Christopher Smart*, published by Oxford University Press, and has written extensively on Smart, Swift, Johnson, and Sterne, on the history and theory of editing, and on biblical interpretation and scholarship in the seventeenth and eighteenth centuries. His study of *Shakespeare, Milton, and Eighteenth-Century Literary Editing* was published by Cambridge University Press.

1667 Jonathan Swift born 30 November in Hoey's Court, a fashionable
     area of Dublin.
1673 Enters school at Kilkenny, seventy miles south of Dublin.
1682 Enrolls in Trinity College Dublin and receives a B.A. by "special
     dispensation" or *speciali gratia* in 1686.
1688 The so-called Glorious Revolution and the War of the Two Kings
     (the Catholic James II versus the Protestant William of Orange)
     erupts and Swift leaves Ireland soon afterwards.
1689 Receives employment in Sir William Temple's household at Moor
     Park near Farnham, Surrey and meets eight-year-old Esther
     (or Hester) Johnson, later known as Stella.
1690 Visits Ireland in the year William III defeats James II at the Battle of
     the Boyne.
1691 Returns to Sir William Temple and Moor Park.
1692 Obtains M.A. from Oxford.
1695 Ordained as a priest in Dublin and takes the prebendary of Kilroot,
     near Belfast.
1696 Returns to Moor Park.
1699 In Ireland after Temple's death, where Swift becomes chaplain to
     the Earl of Berkeley and edits Temple's works.
1700 Becomes vicar of Laracor, County Meath and prebendary of
     St. Patrick's Cathedral, Dublin.
1701 In England with Lord Berkeley where Swift publishes his edition of
     the third volume of Temple's *Miscellanea* and his own *Discourse of
     the Contests and Dissentions Between the Nobles and the
     Commons in Athens and Rome*. Esther Johnson (Stella) and
     Rebecca Dingley move to Dublin to be near Swift.
1702 Receives a D.D. at Trinity College, Dublin and becomes The
     Reverend Dr. Swift.

1704 Publishes *A Tale of a Tub, The Battle of the Books,* and *A Discourse Concerning the Mechanical Operation of the Spirit.*

1707 Around the time of the 1707 Union with Scotland, Swift writes *The Story of the Injured Lady* and, in London, meets Esther (or Hester) Vanhomrigh (later known as Vanessa) and the Whig writers, Joseph Addison and Richard Steele.

1708 While in England on Church of Ireland business, writes political and religious tracts, including *A Letter from a Member of the House of Commons in Ireland to a Member of the House of Commons in England concerning the Sacramental Test,* and begins *The Bickerstaff Papers.*

1709 Publishes *A Project for the Advancement of Religion* and, in Steele's *Tatler,* "The Description of the Morning."

1710 Back in England, meets Robert Harley, the new Tory Chancellor of the Exchequer and later Lord Treasurer, secures the so-called First Fruits for the Church of Ireland, and starts writing for the pro-government paper, *The Examiner.* Begins a private correspondence with Esther Johnson and Rebecca Dingley, now called *The Journal to Stella.*

1711 Publishes *Miscellanies in Prose and Verse* which includes *Contests and Dissentions, The Sentiments of a Church of England Man, An Argument Against Abolishing Christianity, A Project for the Advancement of Religion, Meditation Upon a Broomstick, A Letter from a Member of the House of Commons in Ireland,* and *Various Thoughts.* Also publishes *The Conduct of the Allies* as part of the Tory campaign against the Duke of Marlborough.

1712 Publishes *A Proposal for Correcting the English Tongue.*

1713 Becomes Dean of St. Patrick's Cathedral, Dublin and returns to London, where he joins Alexander Pope, John Gay, Thomas Parnell, John Arbuthnot, and Robert Harley (now Earl of Oxford) in meetings of the Scriblerus Club.

1714 Publishes *The Publick Spirit of the Whigs,* which brings a fierce condemnation by the Scottish Lords, and returns to Ireland after the fall of Oxford's government and the death of Queen Anne.

1715 Swift falls under suspicion during the First Jacobite Rebellion, after one of his former associates, Robert Harley, Earl of Oxford, is impeached and imprisoned, and another, Bolingbroke, flees to France.

1720 Publishes *A Proposal for the Universal Use of Irish Manufacture* which lands his printer, Edward Waters, in jail.

1721 Publishes *A Letter to a Young Gentleman, Lately Enter'd into Holy Orders*.

1723 After death of Vanessa, travels extensively through Ireland.

1724 Publishes *The Drapier's Letters* and the government at Dublin Castle offers a reward to anyone who can identify "the Drapier."

1726 Visits England, stays with Pope, and publishes *Gulliver's Travels*. Swift's longest poem, *Cadenus and Vanessa*, published in Dublin and later in London.

1727 Visits England for the last time and stays with Alexander Pope.

1728 Stella dies; Swift publishes *A Short View of the State of Ireland* and begins his collaborative series of papers with Thomas Sheridan in *The Intelligencer*.

1729 Publishes *A Modest Proposal*.

1731 Publishes *The Memoirs of Captain Creichton*.

1733 Publishes *On Poetry: A Rhapsody* and *To a Lady*.

1735 Dublin publisher George Faulkner prints the first four volumes of Swift's *Works*.

1736 Swift writes *The Legion Club*.

1738 Publishes a *A Complete Collection of Genteel and Ingenious Conversation*.

1739 Swift's *Verses on the Death of Dr. Swift* is published.

1742 Swift declared *non compos mentis* (of unsound mind and memory).

1745 Swift dies 19 October and is buried next to Stella in St. Patrick's Cathedral.

ABBREVIATIONS

C   *Correspondence*. Ed. Harold Williams. Oxford: Clarendon Press, 1963–65, 5 vols.

CW   *Correspondence*. Ed. David Woolley. Frankfurt-am-Main: Peter Lang, 1999–. In progress, with four volumes projected, two published at this time.

E   Ehrenpreis, Irvin. *Swift: The Man, His Works, and the Age*. London and Cambridge, MA: Harvard University Press, 1962–83. 3 vols.

JS   *Journal to Stella*. Ed. Harold Williams. Oxford: Clarendon Press, 1948. 2 vols.

P   *Poems*. Ed. Harold Williams. 2nd edn. Oxford: Clarendon Press, 1958, 3 vols.

Poems *Complete Poems*. Ed. Pat Rogers. Harmondsworth: Penguin and New Haven: Yale University Press, 1983.

PW   *Prose Works*. Ed. Herbert Davis *et al*. Oxford: Blackwell, 1939–74, 14 vols.

CHRISTOPHER FOX

Introduction

"When a true Genius appears in the World," Swift wrote, "you may know him by this infallible Sign; that the Dunces are all in Confederacy against him"(*PW* I: 242). He may well have been speaking about himself. After his death, his ghost was said to haunt the aisles of St. Patrick's Cathedral in Dublin, complaining that "The Pamphlets wrote against me, would have form'd a Library."[1] Jonathan Swift (1667–1745) lived a contentious life in a contentious age. The day Swift, an ordained Anglican priest, became Dean of St. Patrick's in 1713, these lines of welcome were said to be posted on the Cathedral gate:

> Look down St. *Patrick*, look we pray,
> On thine own *Church* and Steeple,
> Convert thy Dean, on *this great* Day,
> Or else *God help* the People.[2]

Swift of course invited and sometimes even welcomed this response. He did so because he was first and foremost a political writer, and one who was not afraid to speak truth to power. As a political writer, Swift was a brilliant controversialist with an uncanny ability to become what he attacked and then burrow from within. During his lifetime, political writers were at a premium. Swift lived to see the emergence of the new two-party system in the wake of the so-called Glorious Revolution of 1688 and the explosion of print media after the lapse of the Licensing Act in 1695. These contributed to what Jürgen Habermas has called the "growth of the public sphere."[3] In a new world of opinion-making, writers of Swift's caliber were highly sought after by politicians such as Robert Harley (later Earl of Oxford) who understood the power of the press to shape public perception.[4] As David Oakleaf points out in this volume, in writing for Harley and the Tory administration in the last four years of Queen Anne (1710–14), Swift "attacked what he called faction with a partisan vehemence unsurpassed even in a vehement and partisan age"

(p. 45 below). In the partisan world of party politics, the counter-attacks on Swift were fierce. "Wild Beasts are reckon'd sporting Creatures, and must be kill'd fairly," writes one opponent of Swift in 1714, "but others that are Ravenous and Cruel, are knock'd down...as we can find them. I have an Adversary that claims a Place in the last Class."[5]

Swift's move in the same years to the Tory party, after his early allegiance to the Whigs, was neither forgiven nor forgotten. Francis Jeffrey was still complaining about it a century later. "In public life, we do not know where we could have found any body," he said in 1816, who so "openly deserted and libelled his party." Whatever may be Swift's merits as a writer, "we do not hesitate to say, that he was despicable as a politician, and hateful as a man."[6] Calling this attack on Swift "a sharp, slashing, libelous assault, as if he were in the dock, and somebody had hired a rhetorician to get him hanged," one nineteenth-century commentator would remark: "It is not to be wondered at that Swift has had various treatment. You know he acted in public life with the Tory party; so of course the Whigs assail him."[7] The critic, William Hazlitt, would agree that Jeffrey "does not seem to have forgotten the party politics of Swift" and add that "I do not carry my political resentments so far back: I can at this time of day forgive Swift for having been a Tory."[8] Few showed such tolerance. And the winners – the Whigs, as Herbert Butterfield reminds us – wrote the history.[9] Years after Hazlitt, in the same *Edinburgh Review* in which Jeffrey had written, Macaulay would continue to refer to Swift as "the apostate politician" with "a heart burning with hatred against the whole human race..."[10]

In looking at Swift, it is important to recall this highly politicized early history and the ways in which he was written into it and out of it. Macaulay's comment points to another factor, besides partisan politics, that has shaped and sometimes slanted representations of Swift and his work. This is the author's reputed misanthropy, usually connected with his critique of the then-emerging belief in human benevolence. In Swift's view, human nature was radically flawed from the start.[11] As a moralist, he inherited a tradition that saw human nature itself as inherently self-serving and corrupt, and the original sin, pride, as a "main cause of psychological distortion," of "prejudice, misperception, misunderstanding, and worse, delusion, in one's thinking about oneself and everything else."[12] In a letter to Alexander Pope on September 29, 1725, Swift tied this view to his best-known work, *Gulliver's Travels*: "I have got Materials Towards a Treatis proving the falsity of that Definition *animal rationale*; and to show it should be only *rationis capax*. Upon this great foundation of Misanthropy (though not in Timons manner) The Whole building of my Travels is erected" (C III: 103). Timon of Athens, the subject of works by Lucian and Shakespeare, was the archetypal hater of humankind. In his letter, Swift differentiates his own position from Timon's by arguing that he does not hate specific people; he just does not expect very much from them. Man is not a rational animal (*animal rationale*) but an animal capable of reason (*rationis capax*). Swift would later tell Pope and his friends that "after all I do not hate Mankind, it is vous autres [you others] who hate them because you would have them reasonable Animals, and are angry for being disappointed. I have always rejected that Definition and made another of my own" (*C* III: 118).

Swift's ideas here were not always shared by others, especially those beginning to entertain newer views of human nature. In his time, thinkers such as the third Earl of Shaftesbury were arguing that, far from being selfish and fallen, human nature is basically benevolent. Perhaps the only fall we have experienced is the belief that we are fallen. These ideas would later be developed by writers such as Jean-Jacques Rousseau, who would argue that not people but the institutions that surround them are corrupt. By the middle of Swift's century, the belief in human benevolence began to carry the day, as did a new stress on the importance on the individual. This brought with it a corresponding redefinition of pride. During the eighteenth century, this first medieval sin became the main modern virtue and the cornerstone of the new individualism.

This helps explain one reason why Swift was soon maligned as a misanthrope. In the first full-length critical consideration of the author – *Remarks on the Life and Writings of Jonathan Swift* (1751) – the Earl of Orrery took the newer path and found Swift's satire on human pride and pretense in *Gulliver's Travels* to be "a real insult upon mankind." In the story of the humanoid and grotesque Yahoos in Book IV especially, Orrery says, Swift "has indulged a misanthropy that is intolerable. The representation which he has given us of human nature, must terrify, and even debase the mind of the reader who views it." Though consistent with centuries of Christian belief in original sin, Swift's satire was linked by Orrery instead to a pathological "disposition" that caused the author "to ridicule human nature itself."[13]

Friends of Swift rushed to correct this view, among them Patrick Delany, who argued that far from being a misanthrope, the author of *Gulliver's Travels* managed "to do more charities, in a greater variety of ways...than perhaps any other man of his fortune in the world."[14] Along with giving away much of what he earned to the Dublin poor, Swift left his entire fortune to found the first mental hospital in Ireland, St. Patrick's Hospital (which is still there). As he had said himself:

He gave what little wealth he had,
To build a house for fools and mad:
And showed by one satiric touch,
No nation wanted it so much.

(Poems 498)

Challenging the charge of misanthropy, others would point to Swift's wide circle of friends, both male and female. (As Margaret Doody suggests in this volume, Swift's friendship with women was something Lord Orrery simply could not understand.) Still others would note the love fellow Irish Protestants showed Swift after he had vigorously defended them against English authorities in *The Drapier's Letters* of 1724–25, where he had argued that "in *Reason*, all *Government* without the Consent of the *Governed*, is the *very Definition of Slavery*" (*PW* x: 63). After traveling to London in 1726 to drop off the manuscript of *Gulliver's Travels*, Swift returned home (if the report can be believed) in triumph:

> In his return to Dublin, upon notice that the ship in which he sailed was in the bay, several heads of different corporations, and principal citizens of Dublin went out to meet him in a great number of wherries engaged for that purpose, in order to welcome him back. He had the pleasure to find his friend Dr. Sheridan, in company with a number of his intimates, at the side of the ship, ready to receive him into their boat, with the agreeable tidings that [his friend Stella, who had been ill] was past all danger. The boats, adorned with streamers, and colours...made a fine appearance; and thus was the Drapier brought to his landing-place in a kind of triumph, where he was received on shore by a multitude of his grateful countrymen, by whom he was conducted to his house amid repeated acclamations, of *Long live the Drapier*. The bells were set a ringing, and bonfires kindled in every street.[15]

Somehow, this does not accord with Lord Orrery's misanthrope. But Orrery's view prevailed.

The hostile response to Swift that began to set in from several fronts was reinforced by stories surrounding the tragic circumstances of his last years. In 1742, at age seventy-five, in an action taken by his friends to protect him, Swift was legally declared *non compos mentis* or of "unsound mind and memory." After three more years of deafness and ghastly suffering, Swift died (in Johnson's words) "a driveller and a show."[16] Soon after his death and the publication of Orrery's *Remarks*, Swift came to be pictured as one of his own dark creations, a decrepit and deranged old Strudlbrugg or a dirty and disgusting Yahoo. As Allen Reddick points out, Swift's protracted final illness and death "became a cautionary tale told over and over again" as a moral exemplum and a just punishment for his misanthropy. Focusing on

Swift's own bodily and intellectual decay "provided something of a relief, particularly from the burdens and direction of his satire and his peculiar use of wit." The "insistence and consistency with which moralizing on Swift's protracted illness and death was substituted for discussion of his works is," Reddick notes, "remarkable."[17]

In his chapter in this volume, Seamus Deane would add that focusing on Swift's illness or madness or eccentricity or (more recently) energy has allowed readers to avoid the material and political dimension of Swift's writing, by doing something not unlike what Orrery did, reducing it to the pathological. Even the critic who begins to locate Swift in his "historical circumstances," says Deane, can then imply "that there is in his writings something fierce and repellent the explanation for which must be sought beyond history. This alternative source is Swift's psyche, to which many commentators have claimed special access" (p. 243).

This is particularly true of assessments of Swift as a distinctly *Irish* writer. His writings on Irish matters have tended to be seen as simply "occasions for Swift's satire, rather than objects of it."[18] *A Modest Proposal* (1729) for instance has often been read in complete isolation from its Irish context and reduced to a model exercise in irony or an amusing example of Swift's perversity (or both, ending with the latter). In his chapter in this volume, however, Patrick Kelly shows that this same pamphlet was published in Dublin during the second worst famine in the century, brought about by "the series of bad harvests and severe climatic conditions which had started in 1725 (and would continue to the summer of 1729)" (p. 138 below). Conditions were so dire that Dublin streets were said to be "crowded with living spectres" in search of food: "If they happen to hear of the death of a horse, they run to it as to a feast" (*E* III: 627).

Here and elsewhere in his writing on Irish political economy, Swift does not simply blame the weather for the situation. "As to this country," he wrote Pope from Ireland on August 11, 1729, "there have been three terrible years dearth of corn, and every place strowed with beggars, but dearths are common in better climates, and our evils here lie much deeper. Imagine a nation the two-thirds of whose revenues are spent out of it, and who are not permitted to trade with the other third" (*C* III: 341). As Swift saw it, English colonial restrictions on trade and Ireland's failure to protect herself had compounded a situation so terrible that the only option left the Irish was to sell their own babies – to the butcher. "I have been assured by a very knowing *American* of my Acquaintance in *London*," the narrator of the *Modest Proposal* asserts, "that a young healthy Child, well nursed, is, at a Year old, a most delicious, nourishing, and wholesome Food; whether *Stewed*, *Roasted*, *Baked*, or *Boiled*; and, I make no doubt, that it will equally serve in a *Fricasie*, or *Ragoust*." He offers to "*publick Consideration*" that

> of the Hundred and Twenty Thousand Children, already computed, Twenty Thousand may be reserved for Breed; whereof only one Fourth Part to be Males ... [for] *one Male* will be sufficient to serve *four Females*. That the remaining Hundred thousand, may, at a Year old, be offered in Sale to the *Persons of Quality* and *Fortune*, through the Kingdom; always advising the Mother to let them suck plentifully in the last Month, as to render them plump, and fat for a good Table. A Child will make two Dishes at an Entertainment for Friends; and when the Family dines alone, the fore or hind Quarter will make a reasonable Dish; and seasoned with a little Pepper or Salt, will be very good Boiled on the fourth Day, especially in *Winter*.   (*PW* XII: 111–12)

Other end products could result. The skin for instance could be used to make "admirable *Gloves for Ladies*" or kid gloves (*PW* XII: 112). The modest proposer's scheme of improvement would allow Ireland to be self-sufficient down to the very bone. After promoting his plan and enumerating its many benefits, the proposer concludes with a solemn oath "in the Sincerity of my Heart" that his project is solely intended for "the *publick Good*" and not personal benefit: "I have no Children, by which I can propose to get a single Penny; the youngest being nine Years old, and my Wife past Child-bearing" (*PW* XII: 118).

A reader might ask whose children would *not* be eaten, which calls into question the proposer's own stated disinterestedness. As a satirist, Swift delighted in puncturing inflated claims to purely altruistic acts.[19] The "reasonable Dish" of course seems less reasonable than he suggests; but it is in line with the respectable economic theory that people are the wealth of the nation. The work takes this literally. It also takes a cannibalism charge – directed historically at the native Irish – and turns it back on the English colonial rulers and absentee landlords. These are the real eaters, Swift implies, who are already consuming Ireland and her people, and doing so out of mean self-interest disguised as rational economic policy.

Samuel Johnson observed that the ancients guess, the moderns count.[20] The almost obsessive use of numbers in the above passage and throughout the tract identifies the modest proposer as a modern counter, an economic "projector" in the mode of Sir William Petty, author of such works as *Political Arithmetick* (1690) and *The Political Anatomy of Ireland* (1691). In *A History of The Modern Fact*, Mary Poovey finds Petty's basic "theoretical proposition" to be "that the 'value' of human beings themselves should be figured in monetary, not religious or ethical terms." She also points to

Petty's hope that Ireland itself could become "a kind of laboratory, where... economic 'experiments' could be made to yield usable results."[21]

The modest proposer would agree, on both counts. His plan to turn human beings into saleable commodities demonstrates a concern for what he calls "The Number of Souls in *Ireland*" not the souls in Ireland (*PW* XII: 110–11). In Swift's satire, of course, this experiment will yield no results (or results anyone can live with). The modest proposer's numbers do not add up to reason but to madness; as elsewhere in Swift, benevolence masks a form of brutality. Along with a theory that produces a graveyard, Swift shows Ireland to be the graveyard of theory, the place where projects (including many of his own schemes for improvement) die.[22] Most disconcerting is the deadpan prose, the seemingly neutral, impartial, and quantitative language of the proposal itself, starkly demonstrating what Emer Nolan describes as Swift's ability "to apply polite styles to intractable realities."[23] This contributes to the work's lasting power. At a reopening of Dublin's Gaiety Theatre in 1984, without announcing what he was doing, actor Peter O'Toole read from the *Modest Proposal* and "prompted a mass walk-out of dignitaries." In a newspaper report on the incident, "O'Toole Defends 'Disgusting' Reading," the actor claimed that he wanted to capture Swift's savage indignation by reciting a piece that had "a little something to offend everybody."[24] If this episode suggests anything, it is Swift's ability to literally move an audience hundreds of years after his death.

More could be said about the *Modest Proposal*. But enough has been said to highlight the importance of Irish contexts to Swift's work. A native Dubliner, Swift spent most of his long life there, much of it politically engaged. For that reason, chapters in *The Cambridge Companion to Jonathan Swift* by Carole Fabricant, Patrick Kelly, and Seamus Deane explore, in different ways, the centrality of this experience to the author and his work. Though often unnoticed, Swift's connection with Ireland is also apparent in works written during his residence in England, as Carole Fabricant suggests. She and other contributors also address the vexed issue of Swift's Anglo-Irish identity. Historically, Swift has been variously pictured, on one hand, as an Englishman stranded in Ireland and, on the other, as the first Irish nationalist (or sometimes something in between, a so-called colonial nationalist). In recent postcolonial studies, he has been represented as a voice of liberty and an originator of the so-called "Patriot" cause in Ireland at the same time he has been portrayed as an arch defender of the English Pale and Protestant Ascendancy interests.

We can thus add the Irish patriot and the English colonialist to the often contradictory but consistently contested images we have seen – the apostate politician pilloried by the Whigs, the pathological misanthrope pictured by

Lord Orrery, the mad Yahoo punished for his critique of human pride. Many more "Swifts" would be constructed, some into our own time, often to suit a specific cultural or political purpose. During Cold War days and the 1960s, for example, Swift served the conservative cause as an arch critic of totalitarianism *and* the liberal cause as an arch critic of war and the moneychangers who make a killing on it.

In the opening chapter of *The Cambridge Companion to Jonathan Swift*, Joseph McMinn says that Swift "realized that his life would become as contentious as his work, and that he would be recreated and reinvented by friends and enemies alike" (p. 14). In the ways he pictured himself and his work, Swift also tried (successfully at times, unsuccessfully at others) to control future representations. How else for instance can we account for Swift's long poem, *Cadenus and Vanessa*, describing his relationship with one of the two young women who followed him to Dublin to live out their lives? In what sense was Swift here, as Margaret Doody asks (p. 99), "less of a Priest and more of a Beast"? Swift's relations with and representations of women have generated their own contested set of after-images, among these, the misogynist author of excremental poetry – "Nor, wonder how I lost my wits; / Oh! Celia, Celia, Celia shits"(*Poems* 466) – or the polygamous lover and putative hero of such scandalous tales as the *Memoirs Of the Amours and Intrigues of A Certain Irish Dean* (1728).[25] In recent discussions, feminists have found him both friend and foe. In her exploration of Swift's complex relationships with women – relatives, friends, lovers, and authors – Doody adds significantly to this ongoing debate. Her examination of the manuscript of Swift's own autobiographical statement, "The Family of Swift," opens up new ways of looking at his work.

So does Brean Hammond's chapter on Swift's reading, a subject that has been recently advanced by the collective efforts of an international group of scholars associated with the Ehrenpreis Center for Swift Studies in Germany. Looking at what Swift read does not always help with the more difficult question of what he *did* with what he read, as Hammond notes. But it does help us understand how Swift negotiated his own relation to tradition and to classical, continental, and contemporary writers. Much of Swift's reading was not in what we have come to call "literature" but in history, itself intricately connected, as David Oakleaf adds, to Swift's view of politics. Oakleaf also stresses a point sometimes missed: that Swift's political writing is *always* connected with religion. From his early and brilliant *Argument Against Abolishing Christianity* to his later anti-Presbyterian tracts of the 1730s, Swift defended the established church – particularly the Church of Ireland – with all the resources at his disposal. As Marcus Walsh suggests here, when Swift took his first Church of Ireland post in 1695, "he joined an embattled institution, under severe economic strain, politically dominated by England and the English church hierarchy, struggling to maintain its devotional and pastoral position as a minority group of believers amongst indigenous Roman Catholics and immigrant Presbyterians" (p. 162). Though not always acknowledged or sufficiently understood, Swift's switch to the Tories had much or almost everything to do with the Whigs' endorsement of toleration for religious dissenters in Ireland. This would, Swift believed, destroy the established church in Ireland by tilting the balance of power to the Scots Presbyterians, who had large numbers in the north.[26] Walsh and Oakleaf also note the strong connection Swift saw between church and state, a point that undergirds his conservative views on such issues as toleration and censorship.

Swift's career as a cleric is also connected to his career as a satirist, as Michael Suarez argues. In this context, satire's end is not simply condemnation. Rather, satire makes us think critically, instills or restores an awareness of choices. Suarez also notes the connection between language, religion, and politics which, for Swift, are "not strictly divisible, but all intricately linked as integral parts of human endeavor" (p. 112). This link is also evident in Swift's extensive discussion of language in such works as *A Proposal for Correcting...the English Tongue* (1712) or *A Letter to a Young Gentleman, Lately Enter'd into Holy Orders* (1721). In the latter, Swift tells the young clergyman that "Proper Words in proper Places, makes the true Definition of a Stile" (*PW* IX: 65). The master of the so-called plain style himself, Swift's own prose is often deceptively simple, as Ian Higgins argues, particularly in a highly politicized age. Although Swift "preferred a plain style, he hardly practiced plain statement. Beneath the seeming simplicity of his concise plain style is a challenging complexity." His conservative theory of language "coexists" with a "love of verbal play" that often got him into trouble (p. 149). This was particularly true, as Judith Mueller argues, in his brilliant early satire on abuses in religion and learning, *A Tale of A Tub* (1704). A defense of the established church, the ironic play of wit here led Swift's work to be criticized by a contemporary as "one of the Prophanest Banters upon the Religion of *Jesus Christ*" ever written and its author to be caricatured as an atheist priest.[27] Swift's lifelong fascination with puns and codes and the play of language is culturally and politically inflected, as several contributors suggest. Carole Fabricant points to the number of Irish rhymes in Swift's verse. Ian Higgins sees in Swift's coded language a thread of high Tory Jacobitism. After his association with Harley's Tory ministry, Swift was certainly accused of being a Jacobite, that is, of supporting the ousted Stuarts over the reigning

Hanoverians. Whether Swift was a Jacobite remains a debated issue, as is the precise nature of his allegiance to the Whigs or the Tories.[28]

Historically, Swift the prose stylist has often eclipsed Swift the poet. As several chapters suggest, however, Swift's poetry has been widely read and more influential than often noticed. Margaret Doody for example shows how Swift's octosyllabic form and subjects opened up spaces for later women writers. Carole Fabricant finds a fascinating Irish aesthetic in Swift's poetry, one that differs significantly from Pope's. Brean Hammond discusses Swift's "Beast's Confession to a Priest" as a veritable handbook of Swiftian satire, and his mock use of Ovidian metamorphoses in "A Beautiful Young Nymph Going to Bed" (a poem in which a woman literally takes herself apart). Michael Suarez explores the rich wildness of Swift's *Verses on the Death of Dr. Swift*, an account of his own death and the reaction to it published when he was very much alive. In a wide-ranging chapter, the editor of Swift's poems, Pat Rogers, considers some neglected verse of Swift and looks at it in new ways. As Rogers and other contributors point out, the poetry itself richly repays reading.

Much of Swift's poetry was written late in life, in his sixties, and well after the publication of *Gulliver's Travels* in 1726. This seems to counter Orrery's myth of the deranged old man in the last two decades of his life. As J. Paul Hunter points out here, Swift was highly prolific for many of these years, before age and ailments (particularly his lifelong battle with a condition now called Ménière's Syndrome) got the best of him. Published when he was fifty-nine, *Gulliver's Travels* was a sensation. John Mullan elsewhere notes that over 100 separate editions of *Gulliver's Travels* were published by 1815 and 330 versions after it, making it easily the best-selling work of prose fiction produced in the eighteenth century.[29] Along with its popularity, it also created controversy in an age when – as Hunter comments – "any published text of any significance was immediately identified with some party or ideology and quickly both praised and denounced for whatever its loyalties and implications were perceived to be" (pp. 218–19). Since its publication, Swift's book has continued to generate debate. In our own time, *Gulliver's Travels* has sparked lively discussion among feminists, historians of politics, historians of science, and literary and cultural theorists. Like other writings of Swift, it finds a place in recent critical, cultural, and political debates over Anglo-Irish relations, the role of the Protestant Ascendancy in Ireland, and the nature of political economy, as well as in theoretical discussions of colonialism, modernity, and enlightenment.

If the past is any indication, Swift in the future will remain a controversial and contested figure. It is part of his jagged legacy. His work will no doubt be at the center of emerging debates on such issues as the relations between political and cultural identity, Englishness and Irishness, wealth and scarcity, partition and union, nation and empire. In *The Cambridge Companion to Jonathan Swift*, there has been no attempt to tame the tiger or to soften the disagreements that may exist even among the contributors. This volume does not set out to resolve these disagreements but to introduce Swift and his work, and the cultural debates he has generated, to a new group of readers. The editor and contributors of the *Cambridge Companion* have also tried, insofar as possible, to ensure a broad coverage of Swift's writing, ranging from his earliest to his later works and from the better known to the lesser known. His career as an author spanned nearly fifty years, so it would be unfeasible and impossible to cover everything. It is nonetheless hoped that this *Companion*, whose focus is largely thematic, will offer a way into Swift's writing and into various critical and theoretical approaches at the same time as it contributes new knowledge and raises new questions. Despite the wealth of writing on Swift – reflected only partly in the Selected Bibliography at the end of the book – there is still much to learn. The answers we get will be determined by the questions we ask.

I here thank my student, Dr. Kirsten Sundell, who has worked on this project from the very beginning. For help at various stages, I also wish to thank Beth Bland, Michael J. Conlon, Audrey Cotterell, Christian Dupont, Laura Sue Fuderer, Judith Fox, Geoffrey Fox, Nila Gerhold, Thomas Kaska, Sean Kohl, Joseph McMinn, Ray Ryan, Jim Smyth, and James Woolley.

NOTES

1. Anon., *Dialogue Between Dean Swift and Tho. Prior, Esq. in the Isles of St. Patrick's Church...By a Friend To the Peace and Prosperity of Ireland* (Dublin, 1753), p. 6.
2. [Jonathan Smedley?], *An Hue and Cry After Dr. S—t.* 3rd edn. (London, 1714), p. 23. Smedley, who probably wrote these lines and cites them here, was a longtime Whig opponent of Swift.
3. Jürgen Habermas, *The Structural Transformation of the Public Sphere; An Inquiry into a Category of Bourgeois Society*, trans. Thomas Burger with Frederick Lawrence (Cambridge, MA: MIT Press, 1991), especially p. 58.
4. See especially J. A. Downie, *Robert Harley and the Press: Propaganda and Public Opinion in the Age of Swift and Defoe* (Cambridge: Cambridge University Press, 1979).
5. [Daniel Defoe], *The Scots Nation And Union Vindicated; From The Reflections Cast on Them, In An Infamous Libel, Entitl'd, The Publick Spirit of the Whigs* (London, 1714), p. 3.
6. Francis Jeffrey, quoted in Kathleen Williams (ed.) *Swift: The Critical Heritage* (London: Routledge & Kegan Paul, 1970), p. 316.
7. James Hannay, *Satire and Satirists* (New York: Redfield, 1855), p. 132.

8. Williams (ed.), Swift: *The Critical Heritage*, p. 329.

9. See Sir Herbert Butterfield, *The Whig Interpretation of History* (London, 1931; reprinted New York: Norton, 1965).

10. Thomas Babington Macaulay, quoted in Donald M. Berwick, *The Reputation of Jonathan Swift 1781–1882* (New York: Haskell House, 1965), p. 56.

11. On this point, see especially Claude Rawson, "The Character of Swift's Satire: Reflections on Swift, Johnson, and Human Restlessness," in Rawson (ed.) *The Character of Swift's Satire: A Revised Focus*, (Newark: University of Delaware Press; London and Toronto: Associated University Presses, 1983), p. 21.

12. Frederick M. Keener, *The Chain of Becoming: The Philosophical Tale, The Novel, and a Neglected Realism of the Enlightenment* (New York: Columbia University Press, 1983), p. 79.

13. John, Earl of Orrery, *Remarks on the Life and Writings of Jonathan Swift, Dean of St. Patrick's Dublin*, 3rd edn. (London, 1752), pp. 120–21, 117, 41.

14. Patrick Delany, *Observations Upon Lord Orrery's Remarks On the Life and Writings of Dr. Jonathan Swift* (London, 1754), pp. 7–8.

15. Thomas Sheridan, *The Life of the Rev. Dr. Jonathan Swift* (London, 1784; rpt. New York: Garland, 1974), pp. 260–61.

16. Samuel Johnson, *The Vanity of Human Wishes*, in *Samuel Johnson: The Major Works*, ed. Donald Greene (Oxford: Oxford University Press, 1984), p. 20, line 318.

17. Allen Reddick, "Avoiding Swift: Influence and the Body," in Aileen Douglas, Patrick Kelly, Ian Campbell Ross (eds.) *Locating Swift: Essays from Dublin on the 250th Anniversary of the Death of Jonathan Swift, 1667–1745* (Dublin: Four Courts Press, 1998), pp. 150–52.

18. Robert Mahony, "The Irish Colonial Experience and Swift's Rhetorics of Perception in the 1720s," *Eighteenth-Century Life* 22 (1998), 63–75, especially 63.

19. Christopher Fox, "The Myth of Narcissus in Swift's *Travels*," *Eighteenth-Century Studies* 20 (1986–87), 17–33, especially 30.

20. See Samuel Johnson, *A Journey to the Western Islands of Scotland*, ed. Mary Lascelles (New Haven and London: Yale University Press, 1971), p. 98: "To count is a modern practice, the ancient method was to guess..."

21. Mary Poovey, *A History of The Modern Fact: Problems of Knowledge in the Sciences of Wealth and Society* (Chicago and London: University of Chicago Press, 1998), pp. 131, 123.

22. Elsewhere, Patrick Kelly notes that the *Modest Proposal* shows Swift's recognition that the conventional mercantilist economic theory of the time "had nothing to offer for the solution of Ireland's appalling problems." This recognition of the inapplicability of conventional theory to poorer countries like Ireland was, Kelly adds, a starting point for George Berkeley's later economic thought. See Kelly's " 'Conclusions by no Means Calculated for the Circumstances and Conditions of *Ireland*': Swift, Berkeley and the Solution to Ireland's Economic Problems," in Douglas, Kelly, Ross (eds.) *Locating Swift*, pp. 47–59, especially pp. 49, 56.

23. Emer Nolan, "Swift: The Patriot Game," *British Journal For Eighteenth-Century Studies* 21 (1998), 39–53, especially 53.

24. *Toronto Globe and Mail* (October 28, 1984), quoted in Anne Cline Kelly, *Jonathan Swift and Popular Culture: Myth, Media and the Man* (New York and London: Palgrave, 2002), p. 185.

25. For an account of the polygamous lover and the many other "Swifts" that have been generated, see Kelly, *Jonathan Swift and Popular Culture*, especially p. 75.

26. On Swift and the northern Presbyterians, see Christopher Fox, "Swift's Scoto-phobia," *Bullán: An Irish Studies Journal* 6 (2002), 43–66.

27. [William Wotton], *A Defense Of The Reflections Upon Ancient and Modern Learning ... With Observations upon The Tale of a Tub* (1705), reprinted in A. C. Guthkelch and David Nichol Smith (eds.) *A Tale of A Tub*, 2nd edn. (Oxford: Clarendon Press, 1958), p. 324. Wotton's attack on Swift is also a response to Swift's attack on him in a defense of Sir William Temple in *The Battle of the Books*, published with the *Tale of a Tub* in 1704.

28. See Ian Higgins' larger study, *Swift's Politics: A Study in Disaffection* (Cambridge: Cambridge University Press, 1994); for disagreement, see J. A. Downie, "Swift and Jacobitism," *English Literary History* 64 (1997), 887–901. On Swift as a Whig or a Tory, see J. A. Downie's *Jonathan Swift: Political Writer* (London: Routledge & Kegan Paul, 1984) and F. P. Lock, *Swift's Tory Politics* (London: Duckworth, 1983).

29. According to Mullan, the only close rival in the century is Defoe's *Robinson Crusoe*, with 70 different published editions by 1800 and 300 after it, excluding translations. See John Mullan, "Swift, Defoe, and Narrative Forms," in Steven N. Zwicker (ed.) *The Cambridge Companion To English Literature 1650–1740* (Cambridge: Cambridge University Press, 1998), pp. 250–75, especially p. 252.

1

JOSEPH McMINN

Swift's life

It is difficult to give an account of Swift's life without talking of the ways in which it has been represented. This does not mean that his life is merely "textual," that whatever facts or certainties shared by his biographers are of less significance than the competing interpretations which they provide. Rather, it means that any account should acknowledge the history of Swiftian biography. That history was itself anticipated and imagined by Swift, who realized that his life would become as contentious as his work, and that he would be recreated and reinvented by friends and enemies alike. The extent to which a literary work reflects, betrays, or conceals its author is an issue which concerned Swift as much as it has concerned his biographers.

Two main interpretative difficulties present themselves to contemporary Swiftian biography. The first relates to the very limited sources available for an understanding of Swift's childhood. Biographers have been forced to depend upon a single autobiographical text by Swift for the writer's earliest years, *Family of Swift*, written in late middle age (*PW* v: 187–95). The second lies in the way Swift's autobiographical fictions, especially his poems, distance themselves from their author: most of Swift's extensive writings were published anonymously or pseudonymously, thereby rendering the question of authorship, and the reliability of personal views expressed in those writings, quite complex. His reliance on a variety of different voices has usually made it difficult for critics and biographers to "match" the life and the work.

The history of biographical writings on Swift shows us that biography can have vicious as well as idealistic sources of inspiration. Before the twentieth century, very few of those writings would come close to what we now might understand as literary biography, a study which sought to understand the complex and causal relation between life and work. According to John Updike, literary biography has only one proper objective, the elucidation of artistic creation. The rest is gossip.[1] For better or worse, most of the early biographical writings were personal reminiscences with little systematic interest in Swift's work beyond *Gulliver's Travels*, and were determined to either revile his memory or, by way of overreaction to such libelous portraits, idealize him as a tragic, if odd, genius.[2]

Several biographical accounts of Swift appeared shortly after his death. The most notorious of these, one which has had a profound, if unlikely and disproportionate, influence upon all subsequent biography is Lord Orrery's *Remarks on the Life and Writings of Jonathan Swift* (1751). This volume is what has come to be known as a "Judas-biography," an attack on Swift by someone who once claimed the writer as a close friend. Generally dull and malicious, Orrery nevertheless seems to have created a version of Swift's personality which has proved almost indestructible if not irrefutable, one which, according to Orrery himself, explains the unwholesome and unedifying character of his writings. Orrery also seems to be responsible for that critical maneuver in Swiftian biography which believes that *Gulliver's Travels* best exposes the "real" Swift.

The idea that Swift's writings, especially *Gulliver's Travels*, mirrored Swift's personality, and did so in ways which confirmed the author's mental sickness, proved almost unshakeable throughout the nineteenth century, with savage *ad hominem* attacks by Macaulay and Thackeray. Even Sir Walter Scott, who produced one of the first scholarly editions of Swift, tried to excuse parts of *Gulliver's Travels* by reference to the author's "incipient mental disease."[3] Sir William Wilde, in *The Closing Years of Dean Swift's Life* (1849), suggested that Swift's apparent insanity was confused with a serious physiological condition, one which was confirmed in 1882 by J. C. Bucknill, who demonstrated that Swift had suffered all his life from Ménière's Syndrome, a disorder of the inner ear first identified by the French neurologist, Prosper Ménière, in 1861. After more than a century of polite superstition about Swift's eccentric behavior, and its presence in his writings, it seemed that a rational explanation was now available.

This more scientific understanding of Swift eventually entered into what is now considered to be the most authoritative and most sympathetic modern biography of Swift, that by Irvin Ehrenpreis.[4] This monumental work draws heavily on two principal sources for its information and interpretation, the scholarly annotated editions of Swift's correspondence, prose, and poetry which began to appear in the early decades of the twentieth century, and the emergence of a biographical model influenced by Freudian psychoanalysis. Faced with a biographical legacy of hostility to Swift, Ehrenpreis made it very clear from the outset of his project that he wanted to demythologize that legacy. (Controversially, he ignored a well-researched study by Denis Johnston which claimed that *Family of Swift* was designed to conceal the writer's illegitimacy.)[5] Other modern biographers, such as David Nokes, believe that fictions constructed about Swift's life are an important element of any attempt at biographical understanding.[6]

In the preface to the third volume of the biography, which deals with Swift as Dean of St. Patrick's, Ehrenpreis makes his attitude to Swift resolutely clear: while acknowledging Swift's "notable eccentricities of behavior," he insists that Swift was "fundamentally rational and self-possessed" (E III: xiii). Like all good biographers, however, Ehrenpreis realizes that a degree of speculation is inevitable, even desirable, in the recreation of a life, its motives, and its obsessions. Faced with the "notable eccentricities" of Swift's behavior towards women, he is quite explicit about his recourse to psychoanalytical theory – "Much of my discussion of Stella and Vanessa is speculation based on Freudian psychology or on inferences drawn from a few data" (E III: 416). These imaginative speculations about Swift's relations with women are based on his reading of *Family of Swift*. Ehrenpreis is convinced that a childhood trauma lies behind the seeming strangeness of Swift's sexual relations and his fictional representations of the human body. Richard Ellmann, one of the most distinguished of modern biographers, argues that before Freud, childhood and its secrets did not seem to preoccupy biographers; after Freud, however, there is no denying them.[7]

According to Swift's own account, his ancestry was pure English, with his parents coming over to Ireland during the Restoration. Whether he was illegitimate or not, he writes of a father, also called Jonathan, who served as a steward in the Law Courts of Dublin, and who died before the son was born on November 30, 1667, in the parish of St. Werburgh, close to St. Patrick's Cathedral. Some of the details about his earliest years, even though they may disguise certain unspeakable facts about the circumstances of his birth, suggest that a formative experience was that of loss and insecurity. In an extraordinary passage of the *Family of Swift*, he writes of having been abducted by his nurse at the age of one, taken by her to England, and only returned to his mother at the age of three. Swift's mother, it seems, soon returned to England, entrusting her son to the care of one of the boy's several uncles, Godwin Swift. One fact is clear, and seems to have had a decisive influence on his later sense of proud self-reliance – growing up without his parents, the young Swift depended on the kindness of strangers for many years before he could establish any form of independent life.

The picture of Swift's life becomes clearer, and the evidence less dependent on Swift himself, once he enters education. At the age of six, Swift was enrolled at one of the best schools of its kind in Ireland, Kilkenny College. This school was reserved for children of the Church of Ireland, and gave Swift an excellent educational start. He finished school at the age of fourteen, and in April 1682 entered Trinity College Dublin. His academic record there was unexceptional, and his poor disciplinary record seems to have been the reason for the award of a degree *speciali gratia* ("by special dispensation"), a minor humiliation which Swift noted in his autobiographical fragment. The final stages of Swift's university life were passed under the threat of war, when Prince William of Orange was crowned King of England. Once it was clear that the final showdown between King James II and King William of Orange was to take place in Ireland, the authorities of Trinity advised students to leave the city until the impending conflict was over. Swift left Dublin at the close of 1689 and headed for his mother's home in Leicester, soon after which he would take up his first job, as a secretary to Sir William Temple, one of England's most distinguished diplomats, now living in retirement at Moor Park in Surrey. Out of this connection would come some of Swift's most enduring attachments and preoccupations. Swift's literary career begins here.

For Ehrenpreis, Sir William Temple becomes the father whom Swift never knew. The decade which Swift spent at Moor Park, a period which included a couple of return-visits to Ireland, helped to shape several distinctive features of his later literary career.[8] One of those features was Swift's self-image as a public servant betrayed and disappointed by a corrupt, irrational political system. Swift's new home, which included an extensive library of the classics, also inspired his earliest attempts at creative writing. Six lengthy poems survive from these years, one of them in praise of King William, but none displaying the sense of irony and humor which would soon become his hallmark. Apart from the inculcation of classical tastes in the literary arts, Moor Park also introduced Swift to the young girl who would remain his closest friend until her death nearly forty years later. This was Esther Johnson, aged eight when Swift first met her, daughter of one of Temple's housekeepers, and named "Stella" by the older Swift.

On two occasions during his apprenticeship at Moor Park, Swift felt obliged to leave his new employer, only to return after an unsuccessful attempt to create a different life in Ireland. The first departure for home came after only a year with Temple, when Swift started to suffer from fits of what he termed "giddiness," wrongly believing that the English climate had badly affected his system. This was the onset of Ménière's Syndrome. A year spent back in Dublin saw no relief, and he returned to Temple. The next departure involved one of the most fateful decisions of Swift's life. Following a family tradition of which he was aggressively proud, Swift decided to become a clergyman. Sorry to be abandoning the protective sphere of Temple's influence, but determined to secure some kind of independent career, Swift came back to Ireland and was ordained a priest at Christ Church Cathedral in

Dublin in January 1695. Until his death, fifty years later, Swift would defend the Church of Ireland against all comers. Any attempt to understand Swift which ignores his religious career and loyalties misses possibly the single most important element of his life, a touchstone for his outlook on most issues.

In the spring of 1695, then aged twenty-seven, Swift took up his first clerical appointment, the parish of Kilroot, County Antrim, situated ten miles north of Belfast. The religious and political character of Kilroot, an isolated and neglected outpost of Anglicanism surrounded by a thriving settler community of Scottish Presbyterians, seems to have affected Swift's prejudices and convictions deeply. Out of this isolation, however, came his first great satire on religious matters, *A Tale of a Tub*. Swift's lifelong fear and hatred of religious non-conformists was born directly out of his experience in the north of Ireland, where he was reminded of the fact that Protestantism was a church divided, unevenly, between his own High-Church Anglicanism and a host of dissenting Protestant sects, the largest of which was Presbyterian. Swift's Church of Ireland was the state church, part of the Anglican establishment, whose religious and political authority was enshrined in law: non-conformists, or dissenters, were those Protestants who did not accept the theological authority of the Church of Ireland. Under penal legislation, a Sacramental Test Act was introduced in Ireland in 1704, by which dissenters were excluded from public office unless they acknowledged the authority of the Anglican church. Swift supported this law throughout his life, and opposed all English appeals for "toleration" of dissent. He was equally resolute in his support of penal laws against the Roman Catholic majority.

One of the lesser-known, but significant, women in Swift's life appears during his time at Kilroot. This was Jane Waring (nicknamed "Varina" by Swift), daughter of a well-to-do family with important business interests around Belfast. Swift's correspondence confirms that he proposed marriage to Jane Waring, which she declined on the grounds that he was still financially insecure. An indignant Swift took immediate advantage of a call from Temple to rejoin him in Surrey, where he was convinced his talent and ambition could find expression.

After this abortive attempt to live as an independent clergyman, Swift now settled down once again at Moor Park, where he continued work on *A Tale of a Tub*. Temple, his benefactor of many years' standing, his rescuer from the Irish fiasco, died in 1699, and Swift was appointed as literary executor of his extensive memoirs and correspondence. Still the literary servant, Swift completed this editorial task in honor of Temple, and published the work in London over the next couple of years. He took advantage of his editorial position to make his name better known, through a signed dedication of the volumes to King William. Temple's death was certainly a watershed for Swift, who was now determined to rise in the clerical world while making good use of his anonymous literary talents.

When trying to understand the relation between Swift's religious vocation and his literary ambition, we need to remind ourselves that writing was an amateur passion which often served Swift's religious and political convictions. He sometimes made money from his work, but he saw himself as a kind of literary public servant. His writings regularly advocated, or satirized, political and religious beliefs, but as a clergyman he thought it unseemly and improper that he should ever write for financial gain.

The new century began with Swift taking up his second clerical appointment, a distinct improvement upon Kilroot. In 1700 he became vicar of Laracor, County Meath, a small parish outside the town of Trim, about thirty miles from Dublin. He was now in a more comfortable and secure living, closer to the centers of political and clerical power. In the previous year he had also found a new job as private chaplain to the Earl of Berkeley, a Lord Justice of Ireland. In a move which was to frame Swift's emotional life for many years to come, Esther Johnson and her companion, Rebecca Dingley, themselves no longer tied to Temple's estate, crossed the Irish Sea and settled in Dublin.

Swift's literary career began to take distinctive shape during the first years of the eighteenth century, when he was in his mid-thirties. He now wrote directly about major national issues, hoping thereby to secure attention and advancement. His first serious intervention was the anonymous appearance in London in late 1701 of an allegorical pamphlet, *A Discourse of the Contests and Dissentions Between the Nobles and the Commons in Athens and Rome*, which addressed one of the great political controversies of the day, the attempt by the Tories to impeach Whig ministers who had questioned the monarch's handling of foreign policy in Europe. While in London on business with the Earl of Berkeley, Swift had revealed his authorship of the pamphlet to certain of those Whig ministers, notably Lord Somers. Swift's involvement with this controversy, seemingly as a defender of Whig ideology, raises one of the major political issues of his career, especially since he would soon become chief propagandist for the Tories. In so far as the Whigs were seen as the most enthusiastic supporters of King William's victory over King James, and of the new political settlement based on contractual government between monarch and parliament (upon which the political security of Protestants in Ireland depended), Swift would have been sympathetic to their cause: but Whig advocacy of greater legal toleration for dissenters, contrasted with traditional Tory defense of the supreme authority of the Anglican church, seems to have decided Swift's later change of allegiance.

Even though the Tories still included a Jacobite element loyal to the defeated Stuart monarchy, they seemed to Swift the more trustworthy religious allies.

Three years later, in the spring of 1704, Swift published an anonymous set of satires in London which would transform his career, usher in what he later recalled as the best years of his life, and demonstrate the most remarkable satirical talent ever witnessed in the contemporary English literary scene. This was *A Tale of a Tub*, to which was attached *The Battle of the Books* and *The Mechanical Operation of the Spirit*. The volume was pointedly dedicated to Lord Somers. The *Tale* became Swift's first best-seller, going into three printings in its first year. Its satire on divisions within Christianity, written from conservative convictions but in imitation of theological extremism, seemed to many who could not follow its ironies a vindication of the religious fanaticism it intended to expose. Reluctantly, Swift later attached a scathing "Apology" to a new edition, stressing that the author's purpose was the celebration of "the Church of England as the most perfect of all others in Discipline and Doctrine." Not for the last time would Swift's ironical, often grotesque, methods of representing irrationality be taken as a revelation of his own madness. The parasitical nature of parody ensured that many readers would identify and confuse the beliefs within the text with those of the author.

During this decade, we can see Swift feeling his way into new circles of potential patronage and influence, all the while trying to balance or reconcile his steadfast religious principles with the deceptive, changing world of political faction. He began to sense that a career in London was now a strong possibility, but his fascination with such a prospect led him to underestimate the ways in which the question of Ireland could frustrate his ambition and recall him to first principles. In 1707 he was appointed by his ecclesiastical superior in Dublin, Archbishop King, to negotiate the remission of government taxes, called the First Fruits, upon the church, and soon discovered that the Whigs whom he had earlier defended would only offer a *quid pro quo* which he and the Irish church would find unacceptable. These long drawn-out, and humiliating, negotiations confirmed Swift's unconditional loyalty to his church, and his lifelong sense of the fatal difference in religious culture between England and Ireland. The Whigs would remove the tax on the church if it agreed to encourage legal toleration for non-conformists. With the full backing of his superiors, Swift rejected any trade-off between the rights of the established church and the ambitions of those he distrusted. He began to write anonymous polemical pamphlets on the matter, such as *The Story of the Injured Lady* (written in 1707, but not published until 1746), the first of many writings in which he attacked England's colonial behavior towards Ireland, not as one who wished for any kind of separation, but as a loyal subject who demanded equal rights.

By the summer of 1709, it was clear that his mission on behalf of the church had failed and, after a long visit to his mother in Leicester, he took the boat home to Ireland. There he devoted a good deal of his time to the material improvement of his Laracor vicarage. In May 1710, he received news that his mother had died. This must have completed Swift's sense of the end of an era, at which point he had no longer any close family connection with England; his first foray into the world of London politics and literature seemed to have been his last. This, however, proved to be one of several false endings in the dramatic pattern of his life, one which would soon be replaced by the years of his greatest political, if not literary, triumphs.

In the autumn of 1710, Swift sailed back to England, having been asked by the Church of Ireland to make fresh representations about the First Fruits. The Whig government was not as secure as it had been when Swift had made his first unsuccessful inquiries, and it was now hoped that someone, either Whig or Tory, would be more sympathetic. In the general election of October, the Tories were swept back into favor and power, and Swift found a very willing listener in the new Chancellor of the Exchequer, Robert Harley. This time the suggested *quid pro quo* offered a remarkable exchange of favors, one which could not compromise Swift's religious convictions. In return for the remission of the taxes, Swift was invited to become the Tory party-writer, in effect, a propagandist. In the space of a few months, Swift's life was transformed. The vicar of Laracor assumed editorial control of the Tory weekly, *The Examiner*, from which position he lashed the Whigs, portrayed the Tories as the "natural" party of England and truest friend of the Anglican church, and over a period of eight months devoted his anonymous articles to justifying Tory strategies to end the war with France and to secure peace in Europe. Swift was now the most powerful journalist in England, someone whose job included public clarification and justification of British foreign policy. His most substantial and effective contribution to a policy which was determined to resolve the War of the Spanish Succession was *The Conduct of the Allies*, published by the government in November 1711, which sold over ten thousand copies in two months. Few students of Swift read these kinds of writings now, seeing them as somehow unlikely and untypical productions of a satirical genius. Yet a political triumph such as *The Conduct of the Allies*, which helped prepare public opinion for the Treaty of Utrecht within two years, was then seen as characteristic of this most political of writers.

Now part of the inner circle of the political administration, Swift's social life included visits to Windsor Castle, dinners with cabinet ministers, and an intimacy with London's political elite which convinced him that he was finally enjoying the fruits of principled service to the nation. The three years he spent working for the Tories are perhaps the best-documented years of his life, thanks largely to the extensive correspondence which survives from those years. The most remarkable element in this correspondence is the *Journal to Stella*, so-called by editors who finally assembled these sixty-five letters by Swift to Esther Johnson and Rebecca Dingley, giving them a detailed and dramatic account of his life in London. Alongside its documentary value as a diary of London life, the *Journal* is a very special source of biographical information, revealing Swift's daily routine, his reading habits, his health, and his changing sense of identity. The *Journal to Stella* records several new friendships, including one with a young woman, Esther Vanhomrigh, whom he later called "Vanessa," and who would soon develop a secretive, passionate attachment to Swift. Not long after they met, Swift wrote *Cadenus and Vanessa*, the longest poem in his literary career, in which he reflects upon their relationship, praising Vanessa's outstanding beauty and intelligence, but sounding wholly bemused that he should be the object of her youthful desire. Most of the poem is devoted to self-deprecatory reflections, and to those reasons which do not allow Cadenus to respond to Vanessa's love. The poem has often been seen as a fictional piece of autobiographical reasoning close to Swift's true feelings for Vanessa, helping to explain some of his ambiguous and fearful dealings with both Stella and Vanessa.

Another important friendship begun in these years was with Alexander Pope. If Swift was England's greatest prose-stylist of the period, then Pope was arguably her most celebrated poet. Both writers came to political prominence through their identification with the Tory achievement of peace in Europe. Pope's *Windsor-Forest* (1713) had celebrated the justice and reason of English policy, and Swift's authorship of articles for *The Examiner* and *The Conduct of the Allies* was now public knowledge. The two writers shared a similar satirical talent, and quickly established a friendship which would last until death. Pope introduced Swift to a sympathetic group of writers who would form the Scriblerus Club, an informal gathering of like-minded talents which included John Gay, Dr. John Arbuthnot, and Rev. Thomas Parnell. The Club's plan for a shared project, a mock-biography of an intellectual pedant, one Martin Scriblerus, seems to have been overtaken by yet another political crisis, this time one which would reverse the fortunes of the Tories and all those, like Swift, who were identified with their administration.

The two leaders of this administration, Robert Harley, now Earl of Oxford, and Henry St. John, now Viscount Bolingbroke, Secretary of State, began to quarrel amongst themselves, and the Whigs pushed their seeming opportunity. Swift hoped that his patrons in the party would reward him with a suitable and worthy clerical promotion before they lost their powers of recommendation in the political storm which lay ahead. Ultimate power over clerical appointments lay with the monarch, and on this occasion Queen Anne apparently decided that the author of *A Tale of a Tub* was not the kind of person who should grace an English bishopric. A deeply disillusioned Swift was told that he had been offered the deanery of St. Patrick's in Dublin.

Swift rode north once again to catch the boat from Holyhead in Wales. Once home, he went straight to Laracor, from where he wrote to Vanessa in the manner of one who had seen enough of politics, and had now decided on a dignified retirement. He would only return to England, he added, if asked. This provisional rather than absolute resolution betrays Swift's fixation with politics and his temperamental inability to ignore public affairs. After only three months, he was indeed asked by friends in London to return, a request which satisfied pride as well as principle. Being told he was appointed Dean of St. Patrick's felt like a sacking; being asked to assist former heads of government restored his abeyant sense of ambition.

His final, public contribution to the fading cause of the Tories was an extended pamphlet, *The Publick Spirit of the Whigs*, which attacked what it characterized as the treasonable character of the rising opposition party, while delivering a savage caricature of its leading literary advocate, Richard Steele. The Tory position seemed quite hopeless, however, and Swift decided he could do no more. Before he returned to Ireland, he stayed with a friend in Berkshire to prepare himself for yet another arduous journey home. While there he wrote what Pat Rogers describes as one of his "most important and revelatory" poems, "The Author Upon Himself," which casts a critical eye over his years with the Tories (*Poems* 670). Like so many of his autobiographical writings, especially those in poetic form, the poem is cast in biographical mode, as if Swift is studying someone else. Swift's banishment, we are told, is the deliberate outcome of jealousy and betrayal on the part of those close to the queen. The poem strongly suspects that the queen's decision to send him back to Ireland was due to willful misrepresentation of his purpose in *A Tale of a Tub*. The poem concludes with a self-portrait of stoical dignity, "By faction tired, with grief he waits a while, / His great contending friends to reconcile. / Performs what friendship, justice, truth require: / What could he more, but decently retire?" (*Poems* 165). The poem can be viewed as an *apologia pro vita sua*, a classic form of self-vindication. While preparing to travel home, Swift heard that the Earl of Oxford had been dismissed by the queen, who died shortly after, on August 1, 1714, leaving the way open for the Whigs to return to power. Swift hurried home, and would not see England again for twelve years.

For nearly six years after taking up his new post as Dean, Swift wrote and published very little: this is one of the rare quiet periods of his life. Yet we know from his correspondence that he devoted a great deal of his time and energy to the responsibilities of his new position as guardian of a great, but impoverished, cathedral. He also made several new and lasting friendships, the most significant of which were with two other clergymen, Rev. Patrick Delany, who would later write one of the earliest biographies of Swift, and Rev. Thomas Sheridan, whose son would do the same. Swift now began to travel extensively in Ireland. Horse-riding he considered a vital form of exercise, part of a deliberate and daily health-regime which he hoped would offset the debilitating effects of his relentless dizzy spells and nausea. That Swift should have defied and overcome such constant physical suffering through an extraordinary body of creative work is a testament to his powerful mental energy.

Swift's increasing knowledge of Ireland resulted in a series of passionate and daring tracts which account for his later reputation as a patriotic writer. The first of these was *A Proposal for the Universal Use of Irish Manufacture* (1720), an anonymous pamphlet urging greater Irish economic self-reliance through a boycott of English imports, whose spirited irony includes the famous observation that the Irish should burn everything from England "except their People and their Coals" (*PW* IX: 17). This provocative appeal which, like so many of the Irish pamphlets, questioned English interference in Irish affairs, was quickly charged with being "false, scandalous, and seditious" (*E* III: 129). The legal case against it, however, was finally dropped. Four years later, a controversy over similar economic matters led to Swift's most renowned intervention in Irish affairs. Swift wrote a series of seven pamphlets, later collected as *The Drapier's Letters*, in which he assumed the persona of a Dublin tradesman who denounced an English scheme to introduce a new copper-coinage for Ireland. What began as a minor economic and diplomatic miscalculation on the part of London was transformed by Swift's Drapier into a fundamental issue of national sovereignty. In the fourth letter of the campaign, the Drapier made his famous rhetorical appeal to Ireland's sense of national dignity:

> The Remedy is wholly in your own Hands; and therefore I have digressed a little, in order to refresh and continue that *Spirit* so seasonably raised amongst you; and to let you see, that by the Laws of GOD, of NATURE, of NATIONS, and of your own Country, you ARE and OUGHT to be as FREE a People as your Brethren in *England*. (*PW* x: 63)

This sounds like a revolutionary, at least a rebellious, call to national action (and so the Whig authorities at the time interpreted it), but in reality Swift's rhetoric believed that it served fundamental, conservative truths about Ireland's constitutional rights. This pamphlet was also declared seditious, a reward was offered to anyone who could reveal the author, and the printer was jailed. Swift seemed to be living dangerously, but popular support amongst the Protestants of Ireland (to whom the pamphlet was implicitly addressed) was so unified and determined that the government abandoned the scheme to introduce the new coinage. An enterprising young Dublin publisher, George Faulkner, quickly assembled five of the pamphlets and published them as *Fraud Detected: or, The Hibernian Patriot*. This was the high-point of Swift's Irish career, and the Dean was hailed as a "national" hero. Swift was now beginning to take a unique kind of literary revenge on the Whigs who had contributed to his earlier humiliation, and in so doing was beginning to give English-speaking Ireland a new sense of a separate identity, one which would enter into the mainstream of later Irish nationalism.

Now that he saw his future lying in Ireland, Swift began to see England much more critically, as a power which had deeply marked his own fortunes, as a system of government which did not seem so benign from an Irish perspective. What makes Swift's reflections on Anglo-Irish relations so dramatic is that he takes everything personally: he knew most of the major figures of power and influence, and he had served a system he now subjected to personal scrutiny. Old Tory friends, some of whom were now revealed as Jacobite sympathizers, were in serious political and legal difficulties, if not in physical danger: Oxford had been impeached, and Bolingbroke had fled to the Pretender's court in France. The new Dean was convinced, with some justification, that his mail was being intercepted and read. The unsuccessful Jacobite rising of 1715 in Scotland had convinced the Whigs that a military threat remained, and that Tory sympathizers had to be watched closely.

In early 1722, Swift had written a long letter to Pope which is of significant biographical interest. This was not an ordinary letter (in fact, it was never posted), but an intimate and studied form of self-explanation and self-vindication. The letter reviews his years with the Tories from the perspective of what it calls this "plot-discovering age," and counters the multiple misrepresentations of his behavior and belief with a systematic declaration of his political principles (*PW* IX: 33). Throughout the letter, Swift makes it clear that as a public-spirited writer he always felt a responsibility to expose corruption and hypocrisy, as well as the right to do so. This self-portrait of a virtuous writer who works to maintain a range of contractual liberties, not least that between the artist and the public, is an uncompromising defense of his political integrity, one which is keenly aware that his reputation is contestable. Misrepresentation and misattribution, he realizes, are inevitable but inexcusable reactions to an art which is satirical and parodic, confusing the message with the messenger.

The greatest personal alteration in Swift's private life during these early years at the Deanery results from the presence in Dublin of both Stella and Vanessa. We know from Swift's letters to Vanessa that he was constantly anxious that she might embarrass him socially, since Dublin society had become used to the reality of Stella and Mrs. Dingley as friends of the Dean. There are several strong hints, but no real evidence, that Swift secretly married Stella during this period, in order to prove his loyalty to her, and to convince Vanessa of the impossibility of any such bond with her. A substantial correspondence between Swift and Vanessa remains, in which her frustration and desperation are made clear. In June 1723, however, this complex scenario came to a tragic end when Vanessa died, aged thirty-four.

Since 1721, Swift had been writing a work which would become synonymous with his name, *Gulliver's Travels*. He had put it aside during the Drapier's pamphlet-war, but had now completed the manuscript, which he was determined to see published in London. He chose to deliver the work through intermediaries, and to create an elaborate authorial fiction to conceal his identity. In March 1726, he traveled to London, where he stayed with Pope at Twickenham. Once his text was delivered, and friendship renewed with Pope, he returned home to Dublin to await the outcome. *Gulliver's Travels* was published in October, and was an instant and extraordinary success, soon as celebrated in Europe as in England.

Early interest and controversy centered on the object and identity of satirical allusions to contemporary figures in the tale. Gulliver's travels may have taken him to several "Remote Nations," but many readers noticed that the period of his travels was almost contemporary with Swift's experiences of England. Even though there was clearly a difference between Swift's views and those of Gulliver, for readers familiar with Swift's writings there was a disturbing congruence between them in certain episodes. For example, many of the political principles held dear by the King of Brobdingnag are almost identical to those outlined by Swift in his 1722 "Letter to Pope." The ways in which biography enters into and complicates the narrative is unpredictable, and should be followed with circumspection both by those who see the texts as autobiographical and by those who reject any reflective relation between the two.[9]

King George I died while Swift was in London in 1727. This time there was no hope of a Tory comeback, and no likelihood of a new English position for Swift, now almost sixty. In any event, Ireland had become his home, and the loyalties, if not the affections, of his old age were firmly with his birthplace. While preparing to return, he was sent the distressing news that

Stella was seriously ill. In September, weighed down by the prospect of her probable death, Swift made his way, for the last time, out of England. Stella lived for only a couple of months longer, and died in January 1728, aged forty-six. Swift was devastated by her loss but, typically, began to compose a biographical tribute, describing her as "the truest, most virtuous, and valuable friend, that I, or perhaps any other person ever was blessed with" (*PW* v: 227). There had been many false endings in Swift's earlier days, but this was not to be one of them. The loss of Stella undoubtedly made Swift take stock of his own life, and it is in this somber period that he composed his autobiographical fragment, *Family of Swift*.

In the final decade of his literary career, Swift became both retrospective and anticipatory about his life and work, and collaborated on several projects by which he hoped to shape his reputation and legacy. The first of these was his cooperation with Pope on a series of volumes, to be called *Miscellanies*, which would publish their selected works. Another was a collaboration with Thomas Sheridan on *The Intelligencer*, a weekly paper which began in May 1728 and ran until the following December, in which the two friends could indulge whatever topics took their fancy, serious or lighthearted. *The Intelligencer* also included a reprint of one of Swift's final series of pamphlets on the Irish economy, *A Short View of the Present State of Ireland*, which had appeared earlier that year. This broadside attacked those who, despite the evidence, declared Ireland to be a prosperous country under a benign administration. Recurrent famine, widespread poverty and misery amongst the native peasantry, the failure to create a more self-reliant economy, and the landlords' moral complacency are the principal targets of Swift's anger. The unnatural distortion of the human economy presented itself in shocking form in *A Modest Proposal* (1729), in which Swift's nameless projector calmly offers, and systematically defends, a solution to the crisis – that the children of the poor be cannibalized. Well prepared for any objections to his scheme, the projector turns against his readers, reminding them of their failure to respond to earlier proposals, which we can recognize as Swift's own over many years.

A remarkable feature of Swift's old age is the revitalization of his poetry: as his prose seemed to decline in ambition and novelty, his poetry took a qualitative and even quantitative leap forwards. Pat Rogers points out that most of Swift's longest poems, and some of the best he ever wrote, were composed in the 1730s, when Swift was in his sixties (*Poems* 37–40). Two kinds of verse from this period have an important bearing on Swift's biography.

The first of these is a group of poems which, like *Gulliver's Travels*, have often been used to speculate upon the sanity and health of Swift's outlook.

These poems, often described as "scatological," include "The Lady's Dress-ing Room" (1732) and "A Beautiful Young Nymph Going to Bed" (1734), poems in which romantic or idealistic versions of female beauty are displaced by voyeuristic portraits of female intimacy designed to shock and revolt readers through graphic, often grotesque, imagery. For those who already saw Swift as mad or misanthropic, such verses confirmed earlier charges of misogyny against the Dean. The "scatological" poems later seemed to provide psychoanalytical criticism with abundant evidence of various forms of dysfunction and neurosis, textual proof of Swift's own distorted sexu-ality. Moralistic as well as "scientific" critics have been attracted to these verses, with biographers such as Middleton Murry describing them as "so perverse, so unnatural, so mentally diseased, so humanly *wrong*."[10] In a famous defense of both Swift and the poems, Norman O. Brown argues that the psychoanalysts, and not Swift, were insane.[11] Brown, taking his cue from Freud's writings on great artists, praises Swift for his imaginative, pre-scientific understanding of the nature of repression and sublimation, pointing out that art is often as effective as science in uncovering such strange per-versions of what is considered normal. Like Ehrenpreis, Brown credits Swift with a degree of intelligent understanding and mastery of his emotions, and rejects the charge that the scatological poems expose Swift's own perversion or neurosis.

The ability and the need to distinguish between, if not separate, the writer and the work becomes one of the leading motifs in what is arguably Swift's most famous poem, *Verses on the Death of Dr. Swift* (1739). The several versions of this lengthy poem have always fascinated critics and biographers because it is not just another *apologia*, but also an explanation of his own personality and artistic method. The eternal problem, still unresolved, is the extent to which the poem is autobiographical.

The poem is a daring anticipation of biographical speculation, one in which Swift imagines what people will say about him once they learn of his death. The poem's inspirational epigraph, from Rochefoucauld, suggests that relief rather than pity is our true response to the misfortune of others (that is, relief that the misfortune did not happen to us). The opening lines provide a gloss on this skeptical view of benevolence which goes straight to the heart of Swift's self-defense, "As Rochefoucauld his maxims drew / From nature, I believe 'em true: / They argue no corrupted mind / In him; the fault is in mankind" (*Poems* 485). Looking back over those who have misrepresented his life and work, looking forward to those who will surely continue to do so, Swift uses the character of an anonymous witness, "One quite indifferent in the cause" (*Poems* 493), to create a heroic self-portrait which systematically counters all myth and legend about the man. Swift, we hear, always acted for the public good, stood up for Irish liberty, never compromised his principles, wrote impersonal rather than spiteful satire, and "Was cheerful to his dying day" (*Poems* 498). As usual, Swift concedes nothing to posterity. Any attempt to understand Swift has to take into account such unique autobiographical versions, even if they function as self-serving fictions which anticipate the same by others.

For those who doubted the sincerity of the final lines of *Verses on the Death of Dr. Swift*, in which the speaker commends Swift's public legacy of a new lunatic asylum for a nation badly in need of such a facility, the writer proved true to the poem's pledge – most of Swift's personal fortune was donated to establish St. Patrick's Hospital, which opened in 1746 and which remains to this day. In the last few years of his life, Swift stayed within the deanery, where he continued to write letters and receive visitors concerned about his health. Despite a long history of chronic illness, Swift outlived most of his closest friends, including Addison, Harley, Congreve, Archbishop King, Arbuthnot, and Sheridan: he even outlived Pope, by one year. In May 1742, a committee of guardians was appointed to care for him, after he had been declared "of unsound mind" (but not insane), and unable to care for himself. Three years later, on October 19, 1745, Swift died and was laid to rest, according to his own instructions, in the middle aisle of St. Patrick's Cathedral. On the wall nearest his grave was erected a marble plaque whose famous epitaph preserves Swift's final challenge to an imagined future: "Here lies the body of Jonathan Swift, Doctor of Divinity and Dean of this Cathedral Church, where savage indignation can no more lacerate his heart. Go, traveller, and imitate if you can one who strove with all his might to champion liberty." For the last time, Swift defiantly asserts the terms in which his life might be posthumously understood.

Allen Reddick has suggested that the myth of Swift's madness was an attempt to explain away a literature that defied, and offended, conventional morality and taste. The myth-makers viewed Swift's life, and especially his final physical and mental deterioration, as "a cautionary tale," his insanity as "divine retribution for a life misspent."[12] After Foucault we can now perhaps better understand the purpose, if not the persistence, of a myth which reduces Swift's writings to such a damning diagnosis. The fact that Swift was a clergyman would also help to explain a great deal of the outrage and incomprehension which fueled this myth.

In emphasizing the essentially Irish, rather than English, character of Swift's life, Ehrenpreis has probably offered another important clue to the hostility shown towards Swift amongst many English commentators. Even though Swift's own sense of national loyalty seems that of an English settler, his Irish background and experience help explain a great deal about his rhetorical rage. In his 1720 *Proposal*, he had argued that English injustice in Ireland would drive anyone beyond reason, and quoted scripture to illustrate his point, "Oppression makes a wise Man mad." Radical protest could be safely dismissed by government as an incomprehensible and uncivilized rant: Swift knew this strategy only too well, since he had employed it himself for much of his life.

NOTES

1. John Updike, "One Cheer for Literary Biography," *The New York Review of Books* 4 (February 1999), 3–5.
2. See Kathleen Williams (ed.) *Swift: The Critical Heritage* (London: Routledge & Kegan Paul,1970), pp. 1–29; Harold Williams, "Swift's Early Biographers," in James Clifford and Louis A. Landa (eds.) *Pope and his Contemporaries* (New York: Oxford University Press, 1949), pp. 114–28; David Berwick, *The Reputation of Jonathan Swift 1781–1882* (New York: Haskell House, 1941), pp. 18–29.
3. Williams (ed.) *Swift: The Critical Heritage*, p. 24.
4. Irvin Ehrenpreis, *Swift: The Man, His Works, and the Age*, 3 vols. (London and Cambridge, MA: Harvard University Press, 1962–83).
5. Denis Johnston, *In Search of Swift* (Dublin: Hodges Figgis, 1959).
6. David Nokes, *Jonathan Swift, A Hypocrite Reversed* (Oxford: Oxford University Press, 1985), pp. viii–ix.
7. Richard Ellmann, *Literary Biography* (Oxford: Clarendon Press, 1971).
8. A. C. Elias, Jr. *Swift at Moor Park: Problems in Biography and Criticism* (Philadelphia: University of Pennsylvania Press, 1982).
9. Irvin Ehrenpreis, "Personae," in Carroll Camden (ed.) *Restoration and Eighteenth Century Literature* (Chicago and London: University of Chicago, 1963), pp. 25–37.
10. John Middleton Murry, *Jonathan Swift* (London: Jonathan Cape, 1954), p. 440.
11. Norman O. Brown, *Life Against Death: the Psychoanalytical Meaning of History* (Middletown, CT: Wesleyan University Press, 1985), pp. 179–201.
12. Allen Reddick, "Avoiding Swift: Influence and the Body," in Aileen Douglas, Patrick Kelly, Ian Campbell Ross (eds.) *Locating Swift: Essays from Dublin on the 250th Anniversary of the Death of Jonathan Swift, 1667–1745* (Dublin: Four Courts Press, 1998), pp. 150–66.

2

DAVID OAKLEAF

Politics and history

Frequently remembered as the legendary Irish patriot who rallied his people against Robert Walpole's corrupt English regime, Swift cut his teeth as a political writer – no other phrase seems appropriate – in the service of English administrations. Defending the nation against self-interested coffee-house factions, he proved a thoroughly partisan enemy of party and faction. Asserting that he understood neither party labels nor the passions they aroused, he represented himself as a judicious independent while allying himself first with the Whigs and then with the Tories. A brilliant polemicist, he crafted for general readers deeply interested in politics a body of writing that now tests the scholarly mettle of specialists in remote partisan squabbles.

No wonder Swift mordantly satirizes political writers in his great narrative satires. *A Tale of a Tub* savages hacks who write for rival factions, as he would soon do. *Gulliver's Travels* opens when Lemuel Gulliver is thirty-eight, just a little older than the Swift who published *A Tale of a Tub* to impress potential Whig patrons and only a little younger than the Swift who began editing the Tory *Examiner* in 1710. In Gulliver's perpetual surprise that self-serving pettiness dominates court politics, Swift surely recalls his own political naiveté. Since Gulliver too wants to eliminate party and faction, Swift as surely recollects his own vanity of authorship when Gulliver complains that "after above six Months Warning, I cannot learn that my Book hath produced one single Effect according to mine Intentions" (*PW* XI: 6).

Yet we cannot ignore the activity Swift viewed so ironically. Politics were too important to him, and he was perhaps too important to politics. In what follows, I suggest some continuities, quickly outline Swift's turbulent career as a propagandist, and then consider two different ways of asking, "How can we read this writing?" Asked one way, the question means something like this: "What do Swift's political tracts mean in their original partisan context?" This question provokes illuminating but contradictory answers that represent Swift as some kind of Whig or Tory. Asked another way, however, the question addresses not what Swift said but the fact that he was saying it: "What does it mean that Swift engaged in this activity?" In answers to this question, Swift looks less like a man apart, a turncoat or principled ideologue. He resembles other writers of his generation, the talented men and women who scented opportunity in the inescapable dissensions between Whig and Tory.

Three patterns recur throughout Swift's career as a political writer. First, political convictions foster but also test personal loyalties. Whig or Tory, Swift offered his considerable writing abilities to an uncommonly literate older man of formidable intellect, a powerful minister who coordinated public opinion for his party, and he then befriended remarkably capable fellow writers. In support of the Whigs, he especially addressed John, Baron Somers, and although the ties did not survive his defection, he formed strong friendships with Joseph Addison, Richard Steele, and other Whigs. In his Tory phase, his political "father" was Robert Harley (called Oxford after being elevated to the peerage as Earl of Oxford). His Tory friends included both the statesman and writer, Henry St. John (later Viscount Bolingbroke), and John Arbuthnot, the impressive man of letters who was the Queen's physician.

Second, Swift *always* writes as a clergyman serving a state church of which the monarch is head. To most people that arrangement seemed essential to political stability. Although a few people had hoped, at the Restoration, for a church structure sufficiently loose to include most Protestants, the church "by law established" made few concessions to those it blamed for the Civil War. Firmly episcopal in structure, it created a group of dissenters, Protestants disenfranchised for their opposition to church government by bishops. To evade restrictions, a few dissenters qualified themselves for public office by sometimes taking communion in the Church of England (or Anglican church), a hotly contested practice called occasional conformity. Staunchly Protestant, the church also disbarred Roman Catholics from office, and when the Catholic James II threatened the Restoration political settlement by appointing Catholics to various offices, he provoked the Glorious Revolution of 1688, forfeiting his throne to the Dutch Protestant William of Orange and Queen Mary. In 1701, Parliament passed an Act of Settlement restricting the throne to Protestant heirs. (Loyalists to the Catholic Stuart heir, or Pretender, were called Jacobites from the Latin for "James.") Since this arrangement was at once religious and political, charges of Popery or godlessness invariably accompany accusations of absolutism or republicanism. As Swift notes in *Examiner* No. 25 (January 25, 1711),[1] Tories are routinely accused by their opponents of supporting "*Popery, Arbitrary Power*, and the *Pretender*." Just as routinely, Whigs are accused of "Views towards a *Commonwealth* [republic], and the Alteration of the *Church*" (*PW* III: 69).

Third, Swift invariably adopts an Irish perspective on English politics. This is obvious in the opposition tracts he wrote in Ireland, but it is also true of the government tracts he wrote in England. For he served not the Church of England but the Church of Ireland; that is, the Anglican church established by law in Ireland. He went to London in 1707 as an agent of the Irish church whose task was to secure, through his political connections, the remission of the First Fruits for the Church of Ireland. These were church taxes which Henry VIII had confiscated but which Queen Anne had recently restored to the Church of England, creating a fund for poor clergy that was known as Queen Anne's Bounty. The Church of Ireland wanted the same benefit. With him, Swift carried a visceral hostility to dissent uncommon among his English Whig associates. It was born of his early experience as a minister in the north of Ireland, where Roman Catholics were thoroughly subjugated but Presbyterian congregations flourished while the established church languished.

These continuities did not hold Swift on a straight path. He caught the eye of the great with *A Discourse of the Contests and Dissentions Between the Nobles and the Commons in Athens and Rome* (October 1701), an anonymous tract defending an out-going Whig administration impeached by a Tory House of Commons. Written "in a few weeks," it missed its occasion when Lords Portland, Oxford, Somers, and Halifax were acquitted. Bolstered with a generalizing final chapter, it appeared while Swift was safe in Ireland and promptly ran through two editions. When Swift returned to England in 1702, he acknowledged authorship with "the vanity of a young man" (*PW* VIII: 119). He dedicated *A Tale of a Tub* (1704) to Lord Somers, publishing it when he had renewed hopes for his patronage. Writings courting Whig favor include *A Famous Prediction of Merlin* (1709) – a poem with a prose commentary – and his preface to the third volume of Sir William Temple's *Memoirs*. In *A Letter from a Member of the House of Commons in Ireland to a Member of the House of Commons in England, Concerning the Sacramental Test* (1708), Swift expresses his Irish antagonism to measures sympathetic to Dissent as well as the commitment to the established church also evident in *A Project for the Advancement of Religion and the Reformation of Manners* (1709).

Swift's powerful Whig friends did not secure the remission of the first fruits for him, however, and when he returned to England from Ireland in 1710, they were losing power. Received coolly by Lord Godolphin but courted by Robert Harley, the shrewd leader of the Tory majority in the Commons, Swift lampooned Godolphin in a poem, "The Virtues of Sid Hamet the Magician's Rod" (October 1710). In November, Swift assured his archbishop that Queen Anne would extend her bounty to the Irish church. Recognizing that gratitude offered a surer hold than anticipation alone on Swift's loyalty, Harley had secured his ally. From November 2, 1710[2] until June 1711, Swift edited *The Examiner*, a weekly Tory paper stating the ministry's position for a readership of squires and rural clergymen. (For other audiences, Harley employed other propagandists, notably Daniel Defoe, coordinating his various writers to achieve his political ends.) Swift's change of allegiance was complete.

As Examiner and then chief Tory propagandist, Swift elaborated a few themes in a series of brilliantly reductive essays. Exploiting contemporary anxiety about the growing power of speculative capital, he disparaged the Whigs as a subversive faction serving the treacherous forces of godlessness (dissent) and credit. He rallied support for the Tory government's policy of extricating Britain from the War of the Spanish Succession, a protracted foreign commitment financed by land taxes and alarming levels of government borrowing. He insisted that avarice tainted even the Duke of Marlborough, a national hero for his spectacular military success. After a general early tract, *The Sentiments of a Church of England Man* (1711), Swift addressed particular occasions in a variety of forms. His masterpiece, *The Conduct of the Allies* (November 1711), questioned the integrity of England's continental allies, exploiting English war-weariness to mobilize opinion behind the Tory policy of negotiating for peace despite allied resistance. It was anticipated or bolstered by *A New Journey to Paris* (September 1711), which defended poet-diplomat Matthew Prior; *Some Remarks upon the Barrier Treaty* (February 1712), which commented on an earlier Whig treaty; *Some Reasons to Prove that No Person Is Obliged by His Principles as a Whig to Oppose Her Majesty or Her Present Ministry: In a Letter to a Whig-Lord* (June 1712); and *A Letter from the Pretender to a Whig-Lord* (July 1712), which provocatively reversed the Whig association of the Tories with Jacobitism.

Swift was relentlessly partisan and staunchly pro-Harley. In *Some Remarks upon a Pamphlet, Entitled a Letter to the Seven Lords of the Committee Appointed to Examine Gregg* (August 1711), he insinuated that a Frenchman who had stabbed Harley was doing just what the Whigs wanted. Alarmed by a Parliamentary set-back, he criticized the Queen's confidante, the Duchess of Somerset, in *The Windsor Prophecy* (December 1711), a mock-prophecy foretelling Whig defeat. He urged extreme Tories to tolerate Harley's moderation in *Some Advice to the October Club* (January 1712). In two poems and a prose lampoon – "An Excellent New Song, Being the Intended Speech of a Famous Orator against Peace" (December 1711), "Toland's Invitation to Dismal, to Dine with the Calves-Head Club" (June 1712), and "A Hue and Cry after Dismal" (July 1712) – Swift attacked the Tory Earl of

Nottingham, who had voted with the Whigs against the Tory peace negotiations in exchange for Whig support for an Occasional Conformity Bill. In another poem, "The Fable of Midas" (1712), he again attacked Marlborough's avarice. In *A Letter from My Lord Wharton to the Lord Bishop of St. Asaph* (July 1712), he mocked a Whiggish bishop by ironically impersonating the Earl of Wharton, a politician he disparaged in his *History of the Last Four Years of the Queen* (1713; pub. 1758) as "overrun with every Quality which produceth Contempt and Hatred in all other Commerce of the World" (*PW* VII: 10). (Since Swift despised Wharton as a Lord Lieutenant of Ireland more sympathetic to dissent than to the church, Irish animosities energize this English satire.) In *The Importance of the Guardian Considered* (November 1713) and *The Publick Spirit of the Whigs* (February 1714), he denounced the comprehensive dullness of his compatriot and former friend Richard Steele. Now Member of Parliament for Stockton, Steele was raising fears of a threat to the Protestant Succession.

In the dying days of the Ministry he served, Swift was rewarded with the deanery of St. Patrick's, a place in the gift of the Lord Lieutenant of Ireland. Many felt, as Swift did, that his services merited even more. Unfortunately, *A Tale of a Tub*'s apparent irreverence and *The Windsor Prophecy*'s attack on one of her intimates apparently determined Queen Anne never to prefer the ambitious champion of the Irish church who coveted English deaneries in her gift. In *Gulliver's Travels*, Swift recapitulates his position as a bumbling servant punished for his unclean expedients: when Gulliver puts out a palace fire by urinating on it, he wins not gratitude but the Queen of Lilliput's anger. This may be Swift's most ironic comment on his brilliant career as a government propagandist.

But what does Swift's political writing mean? Partisan discourse invites partisan readings, so we can first ask whether, or in what sense, Swift was a Whig or a Tory. It is hard to save appearances while rationalizing Swift's political convictions, so rival answers of comparable authority compete for acceptance. In his incisive survey of Swift's English political writing, F. P. Lock reads Swift as Whiggish by nurture but Tory by nature.[3] An underlying rugged pessimism – the gloom of a Tory satirist?[4] – emerges more clearly in Lock's Swift as political experience abrades the Whiggish opinions common among the Irish Protestant establishment and cultivated by Swift's former patron, Sir William Temple. According to J. A. Downie too, a brilliant scholar of Harley's press strategies, Swift's apparent inconsistency masks a profound consistency. Downie's Swift is a crag unmoved by seismic shifts of the surrounding rock. Downie emphasizes Swift's unease with political labels, his occasional references to Revolution principles, and his awareness that modern Tories resembled old Whigs: "I AM not sensible of any material

Difference there is," wrote Swift in *Examiner* No. 33 (March 22, 1711), "between those who call themselves the *Old Whigs*, and a great Majority of the present *Tories*" (*PW* III: 111). Downie's Swift is an Old Whig, a supporter of principles of the Glorious Revolution. As Whig and Tory positions changed around him, he found himself neither Whig nor Tory in the terms of Queen Anne's reign.[5]

Although these views command wide assent, other scholars are fomenting revision. Ian Higgins rejects both Downie's sturdy Whig and Lock's relatively comfortable Tory for a more radical Tory. Swift's political writing commonly reacts to an immediate occasion, as Edward Said has observed,[6] and Higgins sensibly distrusts any tidy fit between writer and party ideology. Despite their rhetoric, political parties are commonly coalitions addressing urgent challenges. A new challenge can divide such factious groupings on tactics or even principle. Certainly nothing fretted Swift more than the intense competition for power between two Tories, Harley and St. John.

Higgins privileges the brute fact that the authorities scrutinized Swift's correspondence for signs of Jacobitism after the Tory ministry fell. They may simply have suspected his correspondents, of course, but so many of Swift's Tory allies opened lines of communication with the Stuart Pretender in France that "Tory" meant "Jacobite" for a half century after the accession of George I. Evidence of Whiggishness for Downie, Swift's reluctance to call himself a Tory could just as easily reveal Jacobite prudence: fearing prosecution for treason, any sensible Jacobite might do the same. Whatever configuration we conjecture for the bedrock, Higgins suggests, we can approach Swift's writing only over the boggy ground of Jacobitism.[7]

Such contradictory readings form the most precise engagements to date with Swift's political thought. Every reader of Swift's politics must place him somewhere on this contested terrain. The Gilbert-and-Sullivan principle that everyone is naturally a Whig or a Tory provides scant comfort, however, for anyone disentangling the intractable political alignments behind the obvious antagonisms.[8] John Somers and Robert Harley both came from dissenting backgrounds, and Harley like Swift began as a Whig but later found himself a Tory. Of course, Harley was a Tory politician who distrusted political parties, a Tory who could employ both Swift and the decidedly Whiggish Defoe. But that hardly makes the simple party label more illuminating. Political labels puzzled even contemporaries.

Named by their enemies for Irish outlaws, the Tories are often thought of as the monarch's party. But in complex circumstances, a common "principle" can lead to opposed actions. While some Tories supported the royal prerogative to the point of becoming Jacobites, Hanoverian Tories like Swift staunchly supported the Protestant succession. Tories had overwhelmingly supported the 1701 Act of Settlement that established Hanoverian succession. Although "passive obedience" was widely regarded as Tory doctrine, many Tories felt, as Swift argued in *Examiner* No. 33 (March 22, 1711), that subjects owed their obedience not to the monarch personally but to the supreme legislative power, the compound entity sometimes called the crown-in-parliament. In *The History of the Four Last Years of the Queen*, therefore, Swift dismisses with real exasperation Louis XIV's "absurd Notion...of a Divine Right annexed to the Proximity of Blood, not to be controuled by any humane Law" (*PW* VII: 150). Swift's position is not obviously Tory, but Louis' monarchist prejudice was impeding the peace the Tories were negotiating. From Swift's point of view, the French were straining at a gnat the English had swallowed in 1688.

In the rough and tumble of parliamentary politics, Tories readily opposed the king if their other oxen were being gored. A Tory attack on William III's exercise of his royal prerogative in foreign affairs, for example, provoked Swift's Whig counter-attack, *A Discourse of the Contests and Dissentions Between the Nobles and Commons in Athens and Rome*. Although William had acted well within his rights, otherwise royalist squires resented both overseas adventures and peacetime standing armies – costly expedients that kept taxes high. Tim Harris argues from their shifts of stance that Stuart Tories were not primarily royalist and potentially absolutist. Rather, they were authoritarian, "conservative legal-constitutionalists, deeply committed to the rule of law and the Anglican Church."[9] In his view, even the Glorious Revolution, that touchstone of Whig principle, has a Tory cast!

Derisively named for Whiggamores, fanatically anti-papist Scottish Covenanters, Stuart Whigs too formed fluid allegiances. Nominally champions of dissent, Whigs were generally not hostile to the Test acts that discriminated against Roman Catholics as well as dissenters, and they had softened their original anti-episcopalian rhetoric after the Glorious Revolution, for bishops sympathetic to them found places in the church hierarchy.[10] And though they nominally championed the authority of parliament or "the people" in opposition to royal tyranny and Popery, Whigs could align themselves with the crown, as Lord Somers did in a tract he wrote on behalf of the Junto Whigs after the House of Commons imprisoned five Kentish petitioners in 1701.[11] A "Country" opposition to a patronage-based government could unite Whig representatives of town corporations with Jacobite squires. The elastic term "Whig" could describe any patronage-based administration, including not only the Whig Junto Swift defended and then defected from but also the durable Whig oligarchy headed by Robert Walpole. It could describe both nostalgia for a stern agrarian virtue grounded in an idealized past and a forward-looking mercantile ethos like Defoe's, an ethos that associated political freedom with commerce, progress, and politeness. Indeed, the historian J. G. A. Pocock locates a tension between agrarian and mercantile elements at the heart of Whiggism.[12] In brief, the terms "Whig" and "Tory" were each contested by mutually hostile and self-divided groups. Each encompassed an array of opinions too broad to fix the political positions of Swift or one of his contemporaries.[13] Neither aligns cleanly with a modern political party or with one of the political impulses we loosely call radical and conservative.

Harris argues that contemporary factions divide most consistently not over royal authority but over attitudes to dissent. This division fractures both the gentry and the established church. Observing their opportunistic alliances, some members of the church treat dissent and Rome as the dual faces of a common foe. On this principle, Jack (dissent) is frequently mistaken for Peter (Catholicism) in Swift's *Tale of a Tub*. Yet others solidly within the church sympathized with their persecuted fellow Protestants outside it, directing the loaded if hazy charge of Popery against practices within the Church of England as well as against Rome. Apparently cohesive groups like the gentry and the church are as self-divided as political parties.

Such tensions have led some readers to view Swift as an amalgam, a Whig in politics and a Tory in religion.[14] In "Memoirs, Relating to That Change Which Happened in the Queen's Ministry in the Year 1710," Swift describes his political views in a way that might seem to support such an assessment:

> I talked often upon this subject with Lord Sommers; told him, that, having been long conversant with the Greek and Roman authors, and therefore a lover of liberty, I found myself much inclined to be what they called a Whig in politics; and that, besides, I thought it impossible, upon any other principle, to defend or submit to the Revolution: But, as to religion, I confessed myself to be an High-churchman, and that I did not conceive how any one, who wore the habit of a clergyman, could be otherwise... (*PW* VIII: 120)

Clearly aware that popular opinion aligned the high-church position with the Tories, Swift nevertheless avoids calling himself a Tory. Positioning himself as a high-church Whig who supports both pillars of the political settlement, he sounds remarkably like one of Harris' conservative legal-constitutionalists.

Swift's not uncommon position seems inconsistent only if we accept the political stereotypes Swift did so much to foster. Since negative advertising, as we now call it, is as old as the influence of public opinion on politics, Swift thoroughly derided the Whigs once he agreed to defend a Tory government to an audience of squires. He represented the Whigs as a narrow monied interest opposed to the stability of land, as if Tory landlords commonly spurned speculative profits. Since they often sympathized with Dissent, he further denounced them as godless. In *Examiner* No. 38 (April 26, 1711), for example, he slyly refers to "Those among the *Whigs* who believe a G O D." In No. 34 (March 29, 1711), he insists, perhaps sincerely, that his political caricature is not "Satyr" but clear-sighted penetration into a faction's designs (*PW* III: 140, 117). Yet Swift was just as prone to stark caricature, and just as hostile to dissent, when he wrote as a Whig. The stridency of the rhetoric on both sides betrays an impulse to polarize along clean lines a complex and consequently unpredictable political situation.

We find familiar, even reassuring, a bipartisan competition for political power that is mediated by public opinion. In the aftermath of a destructive civil war, however, many saw only a threat to social order in the fierce partisan quarrels that provoked so many tendentious pamphlets. In the early 1690s, an English merchant deplored England's fragmentation: "The Kingdom of England is made up of Papists and Protestants. The Protestants are divided, and of late years distinguished by the name of Tories and Whigs."[15] Swift too lamented religious and ideological divisions. In his "Thoughts on Religion," he wrote that "Every man, as a member of the commonwealth, ought to be content with the possession of his own opinion in private, without perplexing his neighbour or disturbing the public" (*PW* IX: 261). He so cherished this view that in *Gulliver's Travels* he assigned a similar opinion to the wise King of Brobdingnag (*PW* XI: 131). Yet in London he joined a community of writers, men and women with more talent than income, who sought preferment by voicing political opinions. We must ask what it means that Swift engaged so vigorously in an activity he so distrusted.

This paradoxical situation was exhilarating. Parliament had allowed the Licensing Act to lapse in 1695 so that it could appeal to public opinion without first seeking a license to publish. In the resulting paper wars, rival pamphlets contested controversial issues, sometimes from politically radical or free-thinking positions. Since skilled writers found themselves in demand, the struggle to control opinion fostered a remarkably vibrant community animated by competitive emulation among the wits. Baron Somers and Robert Harley, the political leaders to whom Swift appealed, were astute managers who quickly grasped the possibilities of public opinion and organized writers to support their parties. The circle around Somers and the Whigs in 1708 included William Congreve, like Swift a graduate of Kilkenny College and Trinity College, Dublin. Congreve already had his brilliant theatrical career behind him, but Swift also encountered a circle of writers who, like him, were still making their names and their fortunes. They included Richard Steele, the poet Ambrose Philips, and Joseph Addison, with whom Swift formed an intense friendship. Addison shared his reserve but won Whig preferment with a deftness he must have envied.

Swift and Addison associated closely with Steele, whose *Tatler* (April 12, 1709–January 2, 1711) became the model for many subsequent eighteenth-century periodicals. Traces of the friends' interaction include poems and hints Swift contributed to *The Tatler*, notably his "Description of the Morning" and the pen name "Isaac Bickerstaff, Esq.," which Steele took from Swift's papers mocking the astrologer John Partridge. When Addison traveled to Ireland in 1709–10 as Secretary to the Earl of Wharton, the new Lord-Lieutenant of Ireland, Swift and Addison continued their friendship even though Swift resented Wharton's sympathy with dissent. This is the level at which Swift's shift of political allegiance to Robert Harley mattered. Although he violated no political principle dear to him, he achieved remission of the first fruits and gained the political influence he sought only by placing himself in opposition to his Whig friends. He tried to put these friendships above the political strife that had fostered them, but he failed. He long protected Steele, for example, although he eventually attacked him with his customary partisan ferocity: "you are to suppose a Lad just fit for the University," he claims in *The Importance of the "Guardian" Considered*, "and sent early from thence into the wide World...He hath no Invention, nor is Master of a tolerable Style" (*PW* VIII: 5–6). Above all, he deeply regretted his estrangement from Addison, a consequence of political differences that grieved and bewildered both men.

Among the Tories, Swift found a similar community. Ironically adopting a view opposite to his own, as he so often did, he celebrates his new associates in *Examiner* No. 26 (February 1, 1710): "there is one Thing never to be forgiven [Harley]; that he delights to have his Table filled with *Black-Coats* [clergymen], whom he useth as if they were *Gentlemen*." He adds that St. John "hath clearly mistaken the true Use of *Books*, which he has thumbed and spoiled with Reading, when he ought to have multiplied them on his Shelves: Not like a great Man of my Acquaintance, who knew a Book by the Back, better than a Friend by the Face, although he had never conversed with the former, and often with the latter" (*PW* III: 80). Swift so valued these friendships that he was slow to recognize the destructive rivalry between Harley and St. John. Unwavering in his loyalty to Harley, he was nevertheless fascinated by the charismatic St. John. Before making Swift his principal propagandist, in fact, Harley firmly reminded him who was in charge: he eased him from editorship of *The Examiner* for pursuing a line too close to St. John's extreme Toryism.[16]

Notwithstanding its unavoidable strains, the union of literature with secular power in a community of wit gratified Swift's deepest longing. In the

John Bull pamphlets, a series of Tory tracts after Swift's own heart, his friend and collaborator John Arbuthnot domesticated the War of the Spanish Succession as a ruinous lawsuit involving rural neighbors.[17] In the same spirit, Swift would later literalize the issue of the standing army, presenting Gulliver in Lilliput as a one-man expeditionary force whose appetite threatened to bankrupt the kingdom.[18] This stimulating combination of politics with play likewise attracted Alexander Pope, John Gay, and others who joined Swift, Harley, and Arbuthnot in the Scriblerus Club, the social and literary collaboration most often associated with Swift. When Harley's ministry disintegrated, the friends were scattered but the friendships survived. Their collaborations and correspondence provide enduring records of personal ties formed and tested by the political trials of the day.[19]

Friends and antagonists alike grappled with a discourse that both fostered and fragmented community. Since they expressed solidarity in collaborative publications or found themselves unexpectedly opposed in print, their friendships were public as well as private. J. G. A. Pocock characterizes their discourse as inherently ambiguous:

> Swift, Davenant, Defoe – to go no further – were found in differing company at different times of their lives; and . . . these changes of front are best explained not by attempting to assess questions of commitment and consistency, venality and ambition, but by recognizing that they were employing a highly ambivalent rhetoric, replete with alternatives, conflicts, and confusions, of which they were very well aware and in which they were to some extent entrapped.[20]

This uncertain ground has become familiar to literary scholars. Historians of the novel note that contemporary discourse oddly confounds news (narratives allegedly true) with novels (narratives apparently fictional). They relate such questions of truth to the status of inconsistencies evident when ostentatiously wealthy stock traders and merchants jostle with impoverished offspring of the gentry. They scrutinize the changing legal status of authorship within this baffling discourse. They scrutinize the links among the emerging amatory novella, female personifications of authorship, and conventionally female personifications of Lady Fortune and credit.[21] After all, political writers like Aphra Behn and Defoe wrote the earliest novels, creating from this ambivalent public rhetoric the typically modern literary form that mediates between public and private selves. No wonder Swift parodies the new form so incisively in the first-person narrative he attributes to Lemuel Gulliver. The literary and political interpenetrate.

Educated in a common classical tradition, friends and antagonists shared the conviction that led Shakespeare to explore power in both English and Roman history plays. English writers assumed that classical history illuminated English history, just as ancient historians had assumed parallels between the histories of Greece and Rome. Swift adopts the parallel history in *A Discourse of the Contests and Dissentions between the Nobles and the Commons in Athens and Rome* (1701). Although a modern editor notes that Swift distorts his evidence, Swift asserts, "I am not conscious that I have forced one Example, or put it into any other Light than it appeared to me, long before..."[22] Since his distortions would be as apparent to his original readers, Swift is not being disingenuous. Gentlemen gradually and thoroughly acquired their classical learning not as a scholarly accomplishment but to illuminate the present by the light of the past. Similarly, the poets Rochester and Pope both imitate Horace by finding contemporary equivalents for ancient situations. Like his appeal to "a Sincere *Roman* Love of our Country,"[23] Swift's literary form locates him in the mainstream of English political debate.

Even Swift's image of himself as a principled man independent of politics draws on a classical precedent. Cato the Younger, the Roman embodiment of incorruptible republican virtue, appears in the "*Sextumvirate*" of worthies Gulliver admires in Glubbdubdrib (*PW* XI: 196). He also inspired a pair of Whig masterpieces. Addison's tragedy *Cato* (1713) was staged to associate the out-of-power Whigs with incorruptible virtue in exile, but Tories cheered too. In the 1720s, John Trenchard and Thomas Gordon wrote *Cato's Letters* to criticize the standing army and corruption, twin evils that seemed the two faces of a single evil. The South Sea Bubble, a devastating stock market crash that ruined many investors, had made the danger of a corrupt monied interest all too palpable. Swift parts from this Cato on attitudes to the church, but his Tory opposition to Walpole's government shares a common idiom with Trenchard and Gordon.

The differences that divided Swift and Addison are consequently discursive, more literary and temperamental than ideological. In the battle between the Ancients and Moderns, Swift is an Ancient. Author of *The Battle of the Books*, he locates wisdom, virtue, and authority in the classical past, lamenting humanity's subsequent degeneration. Firmly in the Whig camp that situates political virtue in the agrarian past symbolized by Cato, he identifies the political nation with the Tory squires to whom he addressed *The Examiner*. Addison, by contrast, is a Modern. He celebrates the cultural refinement that results from increased commerce, praising even credit. In *The Spectator*, he represents the political nation as a club. Mr. Spectator associates with both the country squire Sir Roger de Coverley and the eminent London merchant Sir Andrew Freeport, not to mention a member of the Inner Temple, an army captain modeled on Steele, and (occasionally) a clergyman conspicuously less truculent than Swift. As calculated for a political end as Swift's Examiner,

Addison's Mr. Spectator relies on politeness to contain differences of class and conviction within a flexible, shared discourse.

Where Swift divides to conquer, that is, Addison incorporates in order to subdue. Swift brilliantly masters a demotic political style, but the *Discourse* betrays his congenital intolerance for wits slower or Latin shakier than his own. His vigorous English prose brandishes Latin tags with an aggressive exuberance that anticipates *A Tale of a Tub*. Inevitably, he reminds even scholarly readers how narrowly birth and privilege inscribe the charmed circle about those few who can properly rule – or who can write with any propriety about public affairs. By contrast, Addison, like Trenchard and Gordon, thoroughly domesticates Cato in English. He prefers the dialogue to the lecture, making even literary criticism a supple instrument for building social consensus.[24] A gentlemanly discourse not confined to gentlemen, Addison's style proves an ideal instrument for "the management of a system of public finance by a class of great landed proprietors."[25] Addison strategically blurs the social boundaries that Swift sharpens.

Swift and his contemporaries shaped and were shaped by the public sphere, the emerging social institutions and practices through which public opinion is created. These institutions include journals and periodicals, clubs and coffee houses, various combinations of political agents or booksellers with printers or even with the hawkers of anonymous broadsheets; in brief, everything associated with the dissemination and social reception of "information," especially its public debate. These emerging institutions are no more neutral than the bipartisan politics that they eventually contain and legitimate. Flattering himself outrageously in *Examiner* No. 22 (January 4, 1711), Swift impersonates a Whig reader frustrated by the journal's independence of party: "But nothing is so inconsistent as this Writer; I know not whether to call him a Whig or a Tory, a Protestant or a Papist" (*PW* III: 53). Unhappily, this pose of impartiality is itself a partisan ploy. However desirable an independent press might be, *The Examiner* was directed at a Tory readership by a Tory government.

Political leaders relied on writers to mold public opinion because parliamentary debates could not be published. The voices crying most loudly for public attention served a fierce, partisan competition for parliamentary power. The Addisonian exchange of ideas in a coffee house provides a gentrified model of this turbulent discourse. Swift experienced, and evidently relished, something more like the slanging match before an indefinitely postponed brawl. When ministries changed, even cabinet ministers feared disgrace and imprisonment. St. John fled to France when the Tory administration that Swift served finally disintegrated. Impeached for treason, Harley spent two years in the Tower of London before he was acquitted by his peers in July 1717. The writers who served them were more vulnerable still. Notoriously, Defoe had been pilloried and imprisoned in 1703 for writing *The Shortest Way with the Dissenters*. The charges against her were later dismissed, but Delarivier Manley, who replaced Swift as editor of *The Examiner*, had been arrested and charged after she published *The New Atalantis* (1709), a scandal romance satirizing powerful Whigs. Responding to complaints, the queen put a price of £300 on the head of the anonymous author of *The Publick Spirit of the Whigs*, which Swift had written for Her Majesty's Government. Even a writer who polished the Speech from the Throne could face arrest for something he had written.

For a writer of modest means, the promise of power and preferment offset the known risks. Even hirelings paid by the piece – the anonymous, barely literate hacks satirized in *A Tale of a Tub* – could eke out a living by their wits. Writers who could catch the mood of the town could combine a decent living with the exhilarating exercise of power. Defoe and Manley won influence as well as money, and the rewards were still greater at the upper level represented by Swift and Addison. When Swift brilliantly impersonated Isaac Bickerstaff to make the astrologer John Partridge a public laughingstock, he was flaunting his power in a medium newly opened to his talents and thereby raising his market value. By remaining a Whig, his former friend Addison eventually became an Under-Secretary and then Secretary of State.

Swift frequently registers his ambivalence towards the contentious discourse within which he established his power and authority. When he dismissed the Whigs in *Examiner* No. 26 (February 1, 1711) as "a routed Cabal of hated Politicians, with a dozen of Scribblers at their Head" (*PW* III: 78), he was himself the chief scribbler for a Tory administration. Long editor of *The Examiner* and still a propagandist, he sneers in *The Importance of the "Guardian" Considered* that "Mr. *Steele* publishes every Day a Peny-paper to be read in Coffee-houses, and get him a little Money. This by a Figure of Speech, he calls, *laying Things before the Ministry*, who seem at present a little too busy to regard such Memorials" (*PW* VIII: 12). For he scrupulously distinguished his own services from those of a lower order of hacks. Hence his insulting reference to Steele's need for money or the condescending sympathy with which he elsewhere spoke of his ally Manley. As a gentleman, Swift did not work for pay and was offended when Harley, early in their association, offered him £50. However, he did hope that his powerful friends would acknowledge his considerable services by offering him preferment in the church. He wanted what Lord Peterborough called "a Lean Bishoprick, or a fat Deanery" in England (*C* I: 219). He became Dean of St. Patrick's Cathedral, Dublin – second best, but still a prize.

Swift and his less fortunate associates were all propagandists, professional writers rewarded for perplexing their neighbors and disturbing the public with opinions.

However convincingly he impersonates and parodies political hacks, Swift reflects on the power of the press only locally. His *History of the Last Four Years of the Queen* reads like an *apologia* for the ministry he served. He inscribes an absolute boundary between Tory and Whig, disinterested landed virtue and self-serving venality. In *The Conduct of the Allies*, he strategically circumscribes public debate within narrow limits:

> IT is the Folly of too many, to mistake the Eccho of a *London* Coffee-house for the Voice of the Kingdom. The City Coffee-houses have been for some Years filled with People, whose Fortunes depend upon the *Bank, East-India*, or some other Stock: Every new Fund to these, is like a new Mortgage to an Usurer, whose Compassion for a young Heir is exactly the same with that of a Stockjobber to the Landed Gentry. At the Court-End of the Town, the like Places of Resort are frequented either by Men out of Place, and consequently Enemies to the Present Ministry, or by Officers of the Army . . .
>
> (*PW* VI: 53)

Swift brusquely dismisses the self-serving parasites who throng a locality as narrow as their self-interest. These stock jobbers, parliamentary placemen, and army officers profit when high taxes and reckless borrowing against anticipated revenues finance an expensive war. Swift identifies himself with the nation itself, which he embodies in the landed gentry whose estates can be beggared by unscrupulous usurers ready to lend money to spendthrift heirs.

Most characteristically of all, Swift here distinguishes voice from echo, his own speech from his enemies' chatter. Swift's religion can make modern readers uncomfortable. When he writes as a clergyman, he so often addresses inescapable duties, clerical prerogatives, or parish revenues. Yet he thought his church came as close as possible to the primitive church. The Protestant minister of the Church Militant surely confesses his conviction that he serves only the living Word. In politics, this conviction conferred Swift's certainty but deafened him to the plurality of voices even within his own party. He seems never to have grasped that his colleagues' differences of opinion – including the delays and disagreements with which Oxford and Bolingbroke greeted the manuscript of *The History of the Four Last Years of the Queen* – are themselves the very stuff of history. A brilliant parodist, he rejected the inevitable plurality of political discourse even as he mastered it. The voice of his nation, he attacked what he called faction with a partisan vehemence unsurpassed even in a vehement and partisan age.

NOTES

1. I treat dates as if the year began on January 1 rather than March 25, or the so-called Old Style; for Swift, this date was January 25, 1710.
2. Originally No. 14 but numbered 13 in subsequent collections, which omit the original No. 13, Atterbury's defense of hereditary right; see Frank H. Ellis (ed.) *Swift vs. Mainwaring: The Examiner and The Medley* (Oxford: Clarendon Press, 1985), p. lxx.
3. F. P. Lock, "Swift and English Politics, 1701–14," in Claude Rawson (ed.) *The Character of Swift's Satire: A Revised Focus* (Newark: University of Delaware Press; London and Toronto: Associated University Presses, 1983), pp. 127–50.
4. Louis I. Bredvold's enduring phrase; see "The Gloom of the Tory Satirists," in James L. Clifford and Louis A. Landa (eds.) *Pope and His Contemporaries: Essays Presented to George Sherburn* (Oxford: Clarendon Press, 1949), pp. 1–19.
5. The argument of J. A. Downie, *Jonathan Swift: Political Writer* (London: Routledge & Kegan Paul, 1984).
6. Edward Said, "Swift as Intellectual," *The World, the Text, and the Critic* (Cambridge, MA: Harvard University Press, 1983), p. 78.
7. Ian Higgins, *Swift's Politics: A Study in Disaffection* (Cambridge: Cambridge University Press, 1994).
8. See the song that opens Act II of *Iolanthe, Complete Plays of Gilbert and Sullivan* (New York: Modern Library, 1940), pp. 266–67, where the poles are Liberal and Conservative.
9. Tim Harris, *Politics under the Later Stuarts: Party Conflict in a Divided Society 1660–1715* (London and New York: Longman, 1993), p. 119.
10. *Ibid.*, pp. 155–56.
11. Of course, Somers also exploits radical Whig arguments (see *ibid.*, pp. 168–69).
12. See J. G. A. Pocock, "The Varieties of Whiggism from Exclusion to Reform: A History of Ideology and Discourse," in *Virtue, Commerce, and History: Essays on Political Thought and History, Chiefly in the Eighteenth Century* (Cambridge: Cambridge University Press, 1985), pp. 215–310.
13. David Nokes, *Jonathan Swift: A Hypocrite Reversed* (Oxford: Oxford University Press, 1985), p. 57.
14. See J. A. Downie, *Jonathan Swift: Political Writer*, p. 81; Swift, *PW* VIII: 120.
15. Thomas Papillon, quoted in Craig Rose, *England in the 1690s: Revolution, Religion and War* (Oxford: Blackwell, 1999), p. 63.
16. J. A. Downie, *Robert Harley and the Press: Propaganda and Public Opinion in the Age of Swift and Defoe* (Cambridge: Cambridge University Press, 1979), pp. 137–38.
17. For John Arbuthnot's political writings, see Alan W. Bower and Robert A. Erickson (eds.) *The History of John Bull* (Oxford: Clarendon Press, 1976).
18. See Christopher Fox, Introduction to *Gulliver's Travels*, ed. Fox (Boston and New York: Bedford Books and St. Martin's Press; London: Macmillan, 1995), p. 5.
19. The scope and nature of these relationships is the subject of Patricia Carr Brückmann's *A Manner of Correspondence: A Study of the Scriblerus Club* (Montreal and Kingston: McGill-Queen's University Press, 1997); on backgrounds, membership, and actual meetings, see the introduction to *Memoirs*

of the *Extraordinary Life, Works, and Discoveries of Martinus Scriblerus*, ed. Charles Kerby-Miller (1950; reprinted New York: Russell & Russell, 1966).

20. J. G. A. Pocock, *The Machiavellian Moment: Florentine Political Thought and the Atlantic Republican Tradition* (Princeton: Princeton University Press, 1975), p. 446.

21. See Lennard J. Davis, "News/Novels: The Undifferentiated Matrix," *Factual Fictions: The Origins of the English Novel* (New York: Columbia University Press, 1983), pp. 42–70; Michael McKeon, *The Origins of the English Novel 1600–1740* (Baltimore and London: Johns Hopkins University Press, 1987), chapter 4; Brean S. Hammond, *Professional Imaginative Writing in England, 1670–1740: "Hackney for Bread"* (Oxford: Clarendon Press, 1997); Catherine Ingrassia, *Authorship, Commerce, and Gender in Early Eighteenth-Century England: A Culture of Paper Credit* (Cambridge: Cambridge University Press, 1998).

22. *A Discourse of the Contests and Dissentions between the Nobles and the Commons in Athens and Rome*, ed. Frank H. Ellis (Oxford: Clarendon Press, 1967), pp. 161–62, 116; this edition cited throughout.

23. *Ibid.*, p. 127.

24. See Terry Eagleton, *The Function of Criticism: From "The Spectator" to Post-Structuralism* (London: Verso-New Left Books, 1984), pp. 29–43; see also Hammond, *Professional Imaginative Writing in England*, pp. 145–91.

25. Pocock, "The Varieties of Whiggism," p. 218.

3

CAROLE FABRICANT

Swift the Irishman

The most revealing aspects of Swift's relationship to Ireland are the contradictions at its very core, suggested by his own often conflicting statements about his place of birth and the antithetical attitudes he expressed about his native land, as well as by the widely divergent views about him put forward by readers over the years, their disagreements often hinging on whether they locate him in a primarily Irish or English context. This chapter, while recognizing the significance of the latter context, will explore the many reasons why Swift cannot be understood apart from his multi-varied ties to Ireland. There is room for disagreement about the precise nature and meaning of these ties, but there can be no disputing the fundamental connection itself – a kind of umbilical cord which, though sometimes perversely denied or concealed, was never severed and in fact greatly strengthened during the final quarter-century of his life. Ireland did not simply provide an inert background for Swift's life; it was an integral part of his identity, an essential ingredient in the way he viewed the world, an indispensable thread in the recurring patterns and textures of his writings. A man exceptionally sensitive to his immediate surroundings in all their concrete detail and steadfastly refusing to turn a blind eye to the material conditions of his existence, Swift settled into Dublin life with the whole of his being, fully inhabiting the spaces of St. Patrick's Cathedral and the surrounding area, known as the Liberties, with a physical as well as intellectual presence that demanded not only acknowledgment but also active engagement.

Ireland has long been a land known for the emigration or self-exile of its greatest writers, and during Swift's time, for the frequent and lengthy (often permanent) departures of its "absentees": a term referring principally to the wealthy landlords reviled by Swift, but one also applicable to the literary figures – William Congreve, Richard Steele, George Farquhar – born and raised in Ireland, who left to seek their fortunes across the water. But in Swift, Ireland could boast of one of its least peripatetic native sons, one who wound up spending over fifty years on its soil and who could look upon those

48

who came and went with alternating scorn and humor, portraying them as "Birds of Passage" and as "Soldiers who quarter among [the Irish] for a few Months" and then depart, like hit-and-run seducers of young women (C III: 77). To be sure, Swift might himself have become one of these "Birds of Passage" had he obtained the preferment in England he clearly hoped for during the lengthy periods he spent there from 1689 until the year 1714, when he returned to Ireland for good. But speculating now about how Swift's life might have been different is pointless, for the fact remains that Swift (like the Fairfaxes in Andrew Marvell's poem, "Upon Appleton House") "made destiny his choice" and came to actively embrace the varied roles that Ireland offered him: as churchman, pamphleteer, political activist, and general thorn in the side of the very establishment upon which his own position as Anglican dean depended. In what follows I want to consider Swift in three interrelated contexts – the personal, the political, and the literary – each of which underscores the reasons why it is impossible to understand either his life or his writings apart from Ireland.

The personal dimension

Details of his childhood are rather scant. What we do know, however, underscores the contradictions that were to shape the rest of his life. He grew up as part of a privileged Anglo-Irish Protestant community though with little means of his own and thus in a state of financial dependency, in a city deemed the center of the English Pale in Ireland, the site of the main institutions of Protestant power, but one also boasting a bicultural society marked by a substantial presence of native Irish scholars, merchants, and servants.[1] With the financial assistance of his uncle, Swift attended the prestigious Kilkenny School, located about seventy miles southwest of Dublin, and in the spring of 1682 entered Trinity College, Dublin, a prominent Anglo-Irish establishment where his academic performance proved far from distinguished but nevertheless earned him a B.A. degree. Just at the time he was attaining adulthood (1688–89) and facing crucial decisions about his future, the widespread turmoil following upon the so-called Glorious Revolution – the bloody civil war in Ireland between the supporters of the Catholic James II, who had been forced to relinquish the throne, and his chosen successor, the Protestant William of Orange (King William III) – caused a large number of Protestants to flee to England, Swift among them.

The following dozen years were dominated by Swift's complicated, often frustrating relationship with the noted Whig diplomat and man of letters Sir William Temple, who took him on as his personal secretary, and by Swift's decision in 1694 to take holy orders, which resulted in his first church living in Kilroot, a bleak, Presbyterian-dominated area just north of Belfast.[2] So disillusioning was this experience that Swift soon returned to Moor Park, Temple's Surrey estate, continuing there until his patron's death in 1699. However creatively productive this sojourn was for him – the composition of his early masterpiece, *A Tale of a Tub*, dates from this period – it proved barren in terms of the career preferment he hoped for, and he again returned to Ireland, where he was presented to the vicarage of Laracor, about thirty-five miles east of Dublin, which (unlike Kilroot) offered Swift enough room and fertile soil to cultivate a much-cherished garden and supplied him with a congenial Anglican community, centered in the nearby town of Trim.

In the decade between 1704 and 1714, Swift shuttled between Ireland and England as an emissary of the Church of Ireland and later, as chief propagandist for the Tory ministry. Entries from the *Journal to Stella* (1710–13) – written to Esther Johnson, whom Swift had met as a young girl at Moor Park and who later became his intimate companion after moving to Dublin – attest to the fact that this was indeed a heady time for Swift, when he was as close as he ever would be to the corridors of power. At the same time, the *Journal* reveals Swift's continual frustration at the secret machinations of those in whose interests he labored, as well as a deepening mistrust of even his closest allies, who he wryly noted "call me nothing but Jonathan; and I said, I believed they would leave me Jonathan as they found me" (*JS* 193–94). The later entries in particular express his growing disillusionment with London politics and society, coupled with the desire to be back among his friends and willow trees in Ireland. Nostalgia is not a quality we normally associate with the staunchly anti-romantic and unsentimental Swift, but there are places in the *Journal to Stella* for which that word seems most appropriate: "Oh, that we were at Laracor this fine day! the willows begin to peep, and the quicks to bud... Faith that riding to Laracor gives me short sighs, as well as you. All the days I have passed here, have been dirt to those" (*JS* 220; 302). Passages like these remind us that if Swift's stays in England rendered him susceptible to the enticements of a permanent settlement there, they also impressed upon him the sacrifices such a settlement would entail by making him acutely conscious of what he would be leaving behind in Ireland.

When Swift sailed back to Ireland in September 1714 after the death of Queen Anne and the fall of the Tory ministry, he returned to a country in which (except for two lengthy visits to England in 1726 and 1727) he would spend the rest of his long life. He now began his tenure as Dean of St. Patrick's Cathedral in Dublin, an office he would hold for the next three decades and which, though falling short of his earlier career ambitions, he succeeded in molding to his own specifications and transforming into a springboard for the many activities that would immortalize his name. It was here that Swift made his mark through his exertions on behalf of the area's struggling middle and working class composed of shopkeepers, merchants, and weavers, whose economic welfare was being systematically undermined by English trade restrictions, and through his generous if harshly unsentimental acts of charity toward the poor who continually streamed through the neighborhood. It was here as well that Swift undertook to reshape his immediate environs to reflect more of his own personality, cultivating a two-acre orchard near the Deanery, sardonically named "Naboth's Vineyard," where he planted a variety of fruit trees and native elms. Increasingly, Swift came to recognize the Deanery and its larger urban setting as a place of comforting familiarity where he could find resources sufficient for his needs. As he explained to a London friend in 1734: "I have here a large convenient house; I live at two thirds cheaper than I could there, I drink a bottle of French wine my self every day ... I ride every fair day a dozen miles, on a large Strand, or Turnpike roads; You in London have no such Advantages" (C IV: 268). So closely did Swift come to be associated with St. Patrick's and its environs that he could playfully claim the status of "absolute Lord of the greatest Cathedral in the Kingdom" (C IV: 171) and dub himself "absolute monarch in the *Liberties*, and King of the Mob," an epithet lent credence by the recognition accorded him by others in the neighborhood.[3] For example, when in June 1734 he came upon a group of disgruntled weavers in search of imported goods to confiscate and exhorted them to disperse, they immediately did so, "crying out, Long live Dean Swift, and Prosperity to the Drapier [a famous persona he had adopted some years earlier]"(PW XIII: xxix).

Thus the popular view of Swift living out his years in Ireland as a disgruntled exile, filled with bitterness at his entrapment in a hateful land and constantly obsessing about his "glory days" in England, requires drastic modification. Although he maintained a lifelong correspondence with a handful of English friends and in various writings expressed a sense of loss and regret at the turn of events that necessitated his departure from England in 1714, once back in Ireland Swift set about improving rather than merely bemoaning the situation at hand, resuming old friendships and developing new ones. Within a short time his circle of acquaintance had expanded to include people from all walks of life. The majority of these were persons who, born and raised in Ireland, considered that country their home and were concerned to make a contribution to its well-being – people like the clergyman Robert Grattan, whose unabashed embrace of his Irish birthright Swift celebrated in his poem, "To Charles Ford Esq. On his Birth-day": "Can you on Dublin look with scorn? / Yet here were you and Ormonde born. / Oh, were but you and I so wise / To look with Robin Grattan's eyes: / Robin adores that spot of earth, / That literal spot which gave him birth" (*Poems* 255). The poem affectionately refers to Swift's "favourite clan," the Grattans and their cousins, the Revs. John and Daniel Jackson – all loyal, down-to-earth companions with whom Swift was able to share convivial dinners and humorous exchanges of verse. This varied circle of friends included individuals who afforded Swift important links to Irish culture, including Anthony Raymond, Rector of Trim, an antiquarian scholar fluent in the Irish language, who embarked on an English translation of Geoffrey Keating's celebrated history of Ireland; Patrick Delany, Chancellor of Christ Church and St. Patrick's Cathedrals, who served as patron to the last of the great Irish bards, Turlough Carolan; and Thomas Sheridan, scholar and schoolmaster both in Dublin and in county Cavan, where he opened his humble residence, "Quilca," to Swift for extended visits. From a native Irish family of Protestant converts with strong Gaelic roots, Sheridan in many ways typified the kind of friends Swift surrounded himself with: of modest birth and circumstances, intellectually gifted but missing out on career advancement due to a lack of political connections, identified with the country's patriotic opposition to England's colonial rule, and acutely conscious of the ambiguities of the (Hiberno-) English language, thus delighting in puns and other verbal *jeux d'esprit*. Among the most intimate of Swift's companions despite a relationship marred by periodic misunderstandings and rifts, Sheridan became a collaborator of Swift's on *The Intelligencer* (1728–29), a periodical that in part turned a spotlight on Ireland's dire social and economic conditions, and was the patriarch of a famous family whose members never forgot their connections to Ireland.[4]

Swift's life and activities in Ireland extended well beyond Dublin. While others among his acquaintance traveled to Europe, visiting sites identified with aesthetic refinement and cultural capital, Swift never set foot on the Continent but instead made Ireland his arena of travel, exploring large areas of a country he complained was as little known and alien-seeming as Mexico or Lapland to most Britons. Satisfying a passion for horseback-riding, he regularly rode the length of the Strand along the island's eastern seacoast up to Howth Castle in the north and Dún Laoghaire in the south. He took delight in visiting friends both near and far from Dublin, such as Charles Ford at Woodpark, about fourteen miles outside of the city on the road to Trim; the Rochforts at Gaulstown, forty miles west of Dublin in county Westmeath; and the Achesons at their country estate, Market Hill, located in the northern county of Armagh. These and other habitations were sites of often protracted visits by Swift over the years, many figuring in his literary activities. Sheridan's Quilca, for example, inspired a number of Swift's *jeux d'esprit*, and served as his retreat in the spring and summer of 1725 when completing the manuscript of *Gulliver's Travels*, while Market Hill became the subject of over a dozen semi-autobiographical poems.

Extended trips on horseback in 1722 and 1723 – the first, through the northern province of Ulster; the second, through southern and western parts of the country – provided additional materials for both prose and verse recreations of the Irish landscape. Swift was no scenic or picturesque traveler – his descriptions of what he saw (like his assessments of Ireland's economic conditions) tended toward the harsh and bleak, as typified by his comments on Tipperary as "a bare face of nature, without houses or plantations; [with] filthy cabins, [and] miserable, tattered, half-starved creatures, scarce in human shape" (C IV: 34). Nevertheless, his descriptions served to underscore the importance of eye-witness accounts, tacitly making the case for Ireland's worth as an object – even more, as a *subject* – of empirical examination and study. Swift's own travels in Ireland no doubt fueled his insistence that the only way to truly know Ireland was to "ride round the Kingdom, and observe the Face of Nature, or the Faces of the Natives" (PW XII: 10), rather than having to depend upon hearsay or propaganda.

To be sure, Swift never entirely resolved his ambivalent feelings towards his native land. Even as he admitted to one correspondent that he was "a Teague, or an Irishman, or what people please" (C IV: 229), he was characterizing himself to another as "an obscure exile in a most obscure and enslaved country"(C IV: 468). And well after his emergence as Ireland's model patriot during the Drapier controversy, he was still capable of painting Ireland as a land of "fools" and "knaves" (*Poems* 330) and expressing a desire to be buried in Wales instead (C V: 35). Yet, ultimately, Swift bequeathed virtually all of his money to Ireland – most notably, for the construction of St. Patrick's Hospital – and gave very specific directions for his body's interment in St. Patrick's Cathedral, underneath a Latin epitaph he himself composed, which linked his name forever with Ireland.[5] Swift's ambivalence, then, is most meaningfully understood in light of his lifelong struggle to come to terms with his Irish birthright.

The political dimension

The question of Swift's precise place in the Irish nationalist tradition has generated a good deal of debate. Addressing this question, we might begin by looking at a few of the more significant examples of Swift's activism on Ireland's behalf, which is usually dated from 1720, when the first of his anti-colonialist pamphlets appeared in print. Well before this, however, there were indications of Swift's resentment of Ireland's position vis-à-vis England. *The Story of the Injured Lady*, written in 1707 (though remaining unpublished in Swift's lifetime), portrays the link between England and Ireland as an economically and sexually abusive relationship. The specific occasion, the

Union of England and Scotland, provides the work with its central theme and metaphor but at various points becomes eclipsed by the more vivid account of the severe injuries sustained by the Lady at the hands of her oppressive lover over the years – a chain of abuse beginning at a time predating the Union, hence demanding attention in its own right: "I was undone by the common Arts practised upon all easy credulous Virgins, half by Force, half by Consent, after solemn Vows and Protestations of Marriage. When he had once got Possession, he soon began to play the usual Part of a too fortunate Lover, affecting on all Occasions to shew his Authority, and to act like a Conqueror" (*PW* IX: 5). One year later, in *A Letter Concerning the Sacramental Test*, written as though by a member of the Irish House of Commons addressing an English counterpart, Swift included a paragraph striking for the bitter sarcasm it directs at the lopsided power relationship between the two countries: "If your little Finger be sore, and you think a Poultice made of our *Vitals* will give it any Ease, speak the Word, and it shall be done; the Interest of our whole Kingdom is, at any Time, ready to strike to that of your poorest *Fishing Town*" (*PW* II: 114). Anticipating the cannibalistic relationship of the later Irish tracts, this depiction, like that of *The Story of the Injured Lady*, is consistent with the more general perception conveyed in Swift's later writings of the yawning abyss that exists between the powerful and the powerless, exemplified by Gulliver's recognition that "*Poor* Nations are *hungry*, and *rich* Nations are *proud*; and Pride and Hunger will ever be at Variance" (*PW* XI: 246). That Swift, at the time he wrote these earlier pieces, was still hoping for a permanent settlement in England did not prevent his sense of identification with an exploited and oppressed Ireland, though it did create an ironic tension and a doubleness of perspective which we can now appreciate as among the most distinctive features of Swift's writing.

In the years immediately following his return to Ireland in 1714, Swift fell afoul of the Whig authorities, who falsely suspected him of Jacobitism (that is, endorsing the claim to the throne made by the so-called "Old Pretender," son of the ousted James II) and hence treated Swift as a potential traitor, opening his mail in search of incriminating evidence and generally keeping him under close surveillance. This treatment fueled Swift's adversarial relationship with dominant elements of the Anglo-Irish establishment and contributed to his emergence as an eloquent spokesman for the "Irish interest," which insisted upon Ireland's equality with England under the British Crown, hence its possession of the same political and legal rights. Here as elsewhere, Swift's personal resentment was transformed into a political position that went far beyond (though it never completely canceled out) the personal, contributing to an ideology of forward-looking activism as well as of disgruntled reaction. It is the former that characterizes *A Proposal for the*

Universal Use of Irish Manufacture (1720), which boldly calls for an Irish boycott of English goods, urging the House of Commons to declare anyone who wears imported silks or other fashionable materials from abroad "an *Enemy of the Nation*" (*PW* IX: 16). As in other works, this tract is firmly rooted in the specifics of time and place – to the point of having had its publication orchestrated to coincide with the celebrations of King George I's sixtieth birthday – even as it embodies a surplus of utterance that spills over the particular occasion to embrace other political issues. Starting with a particular instance of inequitable treatment – England's restriction of Ireland's trade as a result of the Woollen Act of 1699 – the tract almost immediately begins expanding its focus until its subject becomes nothing less than Ireland's enslavement in all its many guises and manifestations: one that has "reduced the miserable *People* to a *worse Condition* than the *Peasants* in *France*, or the *Vassals* in *Germany* and *Poland*" (*PW* IX: 21). Continuing the imagery of sadistic exploitation and mutilation in earlier works, the *Proposal* analogizes Ireland's plight to that of Ovid's Arachne, a young virgin whose superior weaving skills provoked an envious Pallas to decree that she forever spin and weave out of her own bowels: "For the greatest Part of [Irishmen's] *Bowels and Vitals* is extracted, without allowing [them] the Liberty of *spinning* and *weaving* them" (*PW* IX: 18).

Incorporating ideas from John Locke's *The Second Treatise of Government* (1690) and William Molyneux's *The Case of Ireland's being Bound* (1698), Swift's *Proposal for the Universal Use of Irish Manufacture* challenges the validity of any law "*to bind Men without their own Consent*," invoking the "general Opinion of *Civilians*" and the model of limited government in support of its argument (*PW* IX: 19). Fueling this challenge was the Declaratory Act passed several months earlier for the explicit purpose of "better securing the Dependence of the Kingdom of Ireland upon the Crown of Great Britain" (*PW* IX: x). The principle laid down in the *Proposal*, of government by the consent of the governed, although technically being applied only to the right of the Anglo-Irish class to enact laws for Ireland, is the kind of universal axiom that by definition transcends sectarian boundaries, containing the seeds of a much more radical claim for self-determination by Irishmen of all classes and religious denominations. By invoking this principle, Swift was in effect helping to lay the groundwork for a much broader nationalist movement that would begin to emerge shortly after his death, albeit one very far from his thoughts when he was writing this tract. Even without this broader intention, however, Swift expands the idea of Irish victimization well beyond the parameters of the Protestant ruling class by depicting Ireland's oppression through the figure of downtrodden rural tenants – many of them among the poorest of the country's denizens and a large number of them (like the French peasants with whom they are compared) Catholic.

By the time Swift came to write *The Drapier's Letters* three years later, he had had a good deal of experience as a local agitator and political pamphleteer, not to mention as a satirist whose adoption of different personae gave him access to perspectives and modes of speech that might not otherwise have been available to him. All these experiences stood him in good stead when he took on the role of "M. B. Drapier" in response to the developing crisis surrounding a patent obtained by an Englishman, William Wood, to mint halfpence for Ireland. Although the country was in fact suffering from a serious money shortage, the project provoked immediate and widespread opposition for several reasons: the large amount of coinage it authorized, far in excess of what the country needed; the absence of safeguards to ensure the intrinsic worth of the coins; the perception that the patent was obtained through political graft, having passed into Wood's possession after a £10,000 payoff to George I's mistress, the Duchess of Kendal; and smoldering resentment at Ireland's inability to mint its own money. Although not among the first to protest, the Drapier soon became a focal point for the resistance against the coinage scheme. Reading the seven *Letters* that comprise this body of tracts, we can understand why.

Each *Letter* presents the issues in a lucid, forceful, and engaging manner, especially appropriate to the specific individual or group being addressed while also appealing to a broader readership. The *First Letter*, for example, which directs its polemic "To the Shop-Keepers, Tradesmen, Farmers, and Common-People of Ireland," sets forth the situation in simple language capable of being understood by those with little education, on whom complex legal or constitutional arguments would be lost: "I will therefore first tell you the *plain Story of the Fact*; and then I will lay before you, how you ought to act in common Prudence, and according to the *Laws of your Country*" (*PW* x: 4). Targeting an audience whose horizons are defined by the everyday struggle for survival, the Drapier represents the adverse effects of accepting Wood's halfpence in terms of concrete deprivations in their daily lives, warning that they would have to pay at least two hundred of these debased coins for "a Yard of Ten-penny Stuff" and that "any Person may expect to get a Quart of Two-penny Ale for Thirty Six of them" (*PW* x: 11, 12). The *Third Letter*, addressed "To the Nobility and Gentry of the Kingdom of *Ireland*," replaces these mundane details with an examination of the precise terms of Wood's patent and a refutation of the Report of the Committee of the Privy Council in England which found in Wood's favor. Obviously directed at a more literate group than the addressees of the *First Letter*, this epistle focuses on a world of documents in need of careful analysis, inhabited by those with the ability to understand textual and stylistic nuances. For this audience the Drapier can elaborate upon the complexities of the "Doctrine of *Precedents*" (*PW* x: 40), just as he can strategically play upon his readers' sense of entitlement as members of a high social class who assume equality with their English brethren: "Were not the People of *Ireland* born as *free* as those of *England?* . . . Am I a *Free-man* in *England*, and do I become a *Slave* in six Hours, by crossing the Channel?" (*PW* x: 31).

The *Fourth Letter*, "To the Whole People of *Ireland*," is the most radical and potentially subversive of the Drapier's tracts. Indeed, its publication resulted in the offer of a reward of £300 for turning its author in to the authorities – an offer that went unclaimed despite the widespread knowledge of the Drapier's real identity. Obviously addressing a much broader audience than previously, one defined as a unified national entity rather than as a particular class or trade, the Drapier combines the concrete detail of the *First Letter* with the more conceptual and analytic points of the third to deliver an incisive attack on Wood's coinage scheme and a rousing call to defeat it. Throughout the piece he spotlights the firm consensus of opinion about the halfpence among Irishmen of all walks of life, depicting the opposition to Wood as "universal" (*PW* x: 61). The unanimity emphasized in this *Letter* was at once an actual historical phenomenon and a rhetorical construct, designed to call into being an autonomous nation that alone could give meaning to such a show of loyalty and solidarity. Here as elsewhere, Swift's calls for unity are informed by the conception of patriotism that he increasingly urged as a model of conduct for his fellow countrymen. Thus he has the Drapier justify his involvement in the Wood's halfpence affair by explaining why even "a Tradesman hid in Privacy and Silence should *cry out* when the Life and Being of his Political *Mother* are attempted before his Face" (*PW* x: 89).

The identification of Ireland rather than England as the Anglo-Irishman's "political mother" demonstrates that Swift's advocacy of Ireland's interests cannot adequately be described by the term "colonial nationalism," used to characterize the attitudes held by a small group of Anglo-Irish elite, whose patriotic exertions on behalf of Ireland extended only to affirming their own rights as Irish Protestants of English origin.[6] To be sure, the Drapier rebuts the malicious rumor that the opposition to Wood's halfpence was an Irish Catholic plot by asserting, "it is the *True English People* of *Ireland*, who refuse it" (*PW* x: 67). Nevertheless, Swift's outlook extends beyond the boundaries of a narrowly defined "colonial nationalism" to embrace a more expansive vision, one that undoubtedly assumed the continued hegemony of the Anglo-Irish elite but that also makes room for a range of other groups in Irish society – the "People of all Ranks, Parties, and Denominations" who are "convinced to a Man" of the fraudulence of Wood's coinage scheme (*PW* x: 60), the "great Numbers of Farmers, Cottagers, and Labourers" with whom the Drapier converses in his travels around the country (*PW* x: 16), and those whom the Drapier extols as "my faithful Friends the common People"(*PW* x: 88). While the Drapier's legal and constitutional arguments for Ireland's parity with England tend to promote the interests of the Anglo-Irish ruling class, his diatribes against the disastrous consequences of Wood's halfpence on the Irish economy speak to the interests of a much broader segment of the population, showing particular sensitivity to the hardships of those in the middle and lower ranks of society, and to a rural as well as an urban populace. A similar sensitivity is expressed in *The Intelligencer*, No. 19 by the Swiftian persona "A. North," described as "a Country Gentleman, and a Member of *Parliament*," who laments his own growing economic problems but goes on to note, "But the Sufferings of me, and those of my Rank, are Trifles in Comparison of what the meaner Sort undergo"(*PW* xii: 54).

Swift puts even further distance between himself and "colonial national-ism," predicated as it was on the identification of the Anglo-Irish with their English peers, by ending the *Fourth Drapier's Letter* with an insistence upon the linguistic and experiential gulf separating the English on the one hand, and the Irish conceived as an undifferentiated national group on the other. Thus, referring to reports that the English Prime Minister, Robert Walpole, has given the Irish an ultimatum, "*either [to] take [Wood's] Half-pence or [to] eat our Brogues*" – the latter term signifying rude shoes made of untanned hide, commonly worn by the rural and lower classes in Ireland (though no doubt also punning on "brogue" as the distinctive dialect of the Irish) – the Drapier assures his readers these reports must be false since "I am confident Mr. *Walpole* never heard of a *Brogue* in his whole Life" (*PW* x: 67, 68). Like James Joyce's Stephen in *A Portrait of the Artist*, reflecting on the word "tundish" and its incomprehension by the college dean, "a countryman of Ben Jonson's," the Drapier focuses on "brogue" as a term that clearly sepa-rates the English from the Irish, constituting a distinctive marker both of Irish existence, and of English ignorance about that existence.[7] Though in actu-ality the Anglo-Irish elite would have had little use for "brogues" – whether on their feet or their lips – Swift deftly appropriates the commonest objects of the lowliest inhabitants of the kingdom as symbols of the Irish nation as a whole, assuring his readers, "we are perfectly safe from [Walpole]; and shall…be left to possess our *Brogues* and *Potatoes* in *Peace*" (*PW* x: 68). The image of the Irish patriot as brogue wearer and potato eater is perhaps Swift's boldest contribution to the struggle against Wood's halfpence, under-scoring the extent of his identification with a larger, more inclusive Ireland than the one embraced by others of his class.

Swift never again achieved the dramatic success and tumultuous acclaim attendant on his role as the Drapier, but in the years following the defeat of Wood's patent (officially revoked in August 1725) he continued to produce large numbers of political tracts dealing with every aspect of Ireland's affairs, including *A Short View of the State of Ireland* (1728) and his brilliantly sardonic satire, *A Modest Proposal* (1729). It was during this period that the image of Swift as "Hibernian Patriot" began to be actively fostered by many within the Anglo-Irish (as well as native Irish) community. Sheridan, for example, reprinted the *Short View* in *The Intelligencer*, No.15 with an introduction proposing that statues honoring the Drapier be erected throughout the country; and the Dublin printer George Faulkner put out an edition of *The Drapier's Letters* in 1725 under the title, *Fraud Detected: or The Hibernian Patriot*.[8] Such examples point to the way that Swift's association with Ireland became transformed into myth even in his own lifetime.

The problem with this myth-making is that it tends to gloss over both the ambivalence of Swift's relationship to Ireland, evident even in his final years, and the contradictions inherent in his simultaneous roles as Irish patriot and as member of a ruling-class institution complicit in England's colonialist oppression of Ireland. At the same time, the figure of "the Hibernian Patriot," firmly rooted as it is in the specific writings and actions of the Drapier-Dean, provides insight into a crucial aspect of Swift's identity – one that he himself came to embrace (however reluctantly) as his chief hope of immortality. Thus the *Verses on the Death of Dr. Swift*, while describing his post-1714 life in Ireland as an "exile," also reveals his awareness that to future generations his name would be inseparable from the nation he spent so much energy and ink defending: "'The Dean did by his pen defeat / An infamous destructive cheat. / Taught fools their interest to know; / And gave them arms to ward the blow. / Envy hath owned it was his doing, / To save that helpless land from ruin'" (*Poems* 496). If this passage perpetuates Swift's mythic status as "Hibernian Patriot," it simultaneously affirms the reality of a life capable on many levels of sustaining it.

Some would deny Swift a place in the Irish nationalist tradition because of his religion and class affiliation. Such a position is based on an oversimplified, monolithic model of nationalism that posits the existence of a single group who alone can speak for the nation in a "pure" way. Nationalism, however, has a nasty habit of manifesting itself in a messy, contradictory body of attitudes having little to do with purity of identity or sentiment, as often as not constituting a distorted mirror image of the very colonialism it opposes. Joyce, acutely conscious of this irony, had no hesitancy about including a number of Protestants in his list of Irish patriots from the eighteenth century onward.[9] It would thus be more accurate to say that Swift did indeed express an early form of Irish nationalism, though one mediated through his own implication in certain levels of what we might call the "internal colonialism" of the Protestant Ascendancy, and made ironic by the fact that the very idea of Ireland as an independent nation completely separate from England was not historically available to Anglo-Irishmen at the time. What *was* available was the idea of Ireland as an autonomous kingdom, enjoying full equality with England under the British crown, and this Swift urged with all the rhetorical power at his disposal. Moreover, he stretched this idea to its outermost limits, locating the victims of England's oppression not only within but also outside of the Pale: in those western and rural regions inhabited by "Tenants; who live worse than *English* Beggars," and "Families of Farmers, who pay great Rents, living in Filth and Nastiness upon Butter-milk and Potatoes, without a Shoe or Stocking to their Feet" (*PW* XII: 11, 10). The Drapier's invocations of a "liberty" defined in the broadest terms, as "*a Blessing, to which the whole Race of Mankind hath an Original Title*" (*PW* X: 86), point towards a conclusion they were not yet able to articulate: that the rights and privileges of nationhood cannot be reserved for a small segment of society while being denied to the rest.

The literary dimension

There are some authors – Jorge Luis Borges and T. S. Eliot come to mind – whose writings derive their distinctive style and coloration from factors other than specificity of place. Then there are others whose writings cannot be separated from the shapes, textures, and political struggles of a particular land and landscape. Swift unquestionably belongs in this latter category, with both the form and the content of his works reflecting the historical accident of his Irish birth as well as the later personal and political commitments of his life in Ireland. Not only do most of his occasional tracts deal directly with Irish affairs, but so also do many works we now think of as "literary." Take, for example, *A Modest Proposal*, the brilliant satire now often read exclusively for its formal or rhetorical qualities, but originally one of a number of political tracts Swift wrote in 1729 in response to Ireland's worsening economic conditions, highlighted by a severe famine. As a parody of the many fatuous proposals for dealing with the problem put forward by writers who had little understanding of the situation, *A Modest Proposal* must be understood as a profoundly occasional work in form as well as content, mocking – and through that mockery exemplifying – a specific, temporally defined sub-genre while simultaneously translating into comically surreal terms the tragically real situation of Ireland as a country being "eaten up" by the colonialist policies of England and forced, in the extremity of its condition, to adopt its own form of cannibalism for its very survival. The very "literariness" of the work functions as a scathing critique of any stance of detachment, aesthetic or otherwise, in the face of prevailing horrors, necessarily implicating the aloof, analytic eye of the literary critic along with the cold mathematical calculations of the Modest Proposer. Other prose satires now apt to be classified as 'literature' also operate as commentaries on the contemporary Irish scene. "The Last Speech and Dying Words of Ebenezer Elliston" (1722) – like *A Modest Proposal* a parody of a popular sub-genre of the day, the published "Last Words" of criminals sold on the day of their execution – makes use of general satiric conventions and devices while announcing on the title page its inextricable ties to a particular historical moment: the actual punishment of Ebenezer Elliston, "*Executed the Second Day of* May, 1722" (*PW* IX: 37). The occasionality of this piece, as a response to the growing problem of urban crime, is underscored in a note to the 1735 edition of Swift's *Collected Works* ("*About the Time that this Speech was written, the Town [Dublin] was much pestered with* Street-Robbers..." [*PW* IX: 37n.]). Another prose satire, *An Examination of Certain Abuses, Corruptions, and Enormities, in the City of Dublin* (1732), while incorporating many of the generic conventions found in Swift's earliest satiric pieces, shares much in common with the later tracts through its mocking commentary on aspects of post-1714 Ireland – in this case, the political paranoia of the Whig administration in its exaggerated fear of the danger posed by Tories and suspected Jacobites. As its title suggests, the *Examination* offers a close (not to mention wildly comic) look at the contemporary scene, interspersing mock-allegorical devices and a running satire on the problem of false interpretation with the distinctive sights, sounds, and (not least) smells of Dublin street life in the 1720s and 1730s.

Swift's poetry likewise often takes the concrete conditions and surroundings of his life as its subject. It is filled with descriptions of his Dublin environs as well as references both to specific events and to the everyday miseries and absurdities of Irish life. In shifting our attention from his prose works and polemical pieces to his poetry, we do not therefore move from the political to the aesthetic sphere, but rather from one mode of response to the immediate circumstances of his existence to another. Some verses explicitly serve as companion pieces to his prose tracts, such as the more than a dozen poems relating directly to Wood's halfpence. A number of prominent public figures in Ireland, epitomized by the despised Chief Justice William Whitshed, condemner of the Drapier's printer, inhabit Swift's verse, turning it into a recurring reflection on the institutions of authority and quality of governance in Ireland. "On the Irish Bishops" (1732), for example, gives voice to the more general resentment of the lower clergy at the privileged position of those in the upper echelons of the church hierarchy, most of them Englishmen who had obtained their posts through influential connections in London: "Our bishops puffed up with wealth and with pride, / To hell on the backs of the clergy would ride" (*Poems* 499). In "Aye and No: A Tale from Dublin" (1737), Swift takes satiric aim at the highest churchman in the land – Hugh Boulter, Archbishop of Armagh and Primate of All Ireland – for his stand on monetary issues and for his cosy relationship with the Whig establishment in England. The poem ends with Swift conveying a none-too-subtle threat against Boulter in his capacity as "king of the mob": "'It's a pity a prelate should die without law; / But if I say the word – take care of Armagh'" (*Poems* 560). Nor were the clergy of Swift's own rank (especially if they were English-born) immune to his subversive wit: in "An Excellent New Ballad: or The True English Dean to be hanged for a Rape" (1730), the satiric target is Thomas Sawbridge, Dean of Ferns, who was prosecuted for raping a young woman but acquitted – according to Swift, only because he succeeded in buying her off (C III: 405). This single instance of physical rape is made to function as an implicit metaphor of England's all-encompassing "rape" of Ireland, perpetuated through its control of Irish employments whereby "Our church and our state dear England maintains" (*Poems* 447). Swift turns his scathing mockery from religious to political institutions in *A Character, Panegyric, and Description of the Legion Club* (1736), which transforms Dublin's grand new Parliament House on the north side of Trinity College Green into a madhouse inhabited by an assortment of traitors, idiots, and fools: "Let them, when they once get in / Sell the nation for a pin; / While they sit a-picking straws / Let them rave of making laws; / While they never hold their tongue, / Let them dabble in their dung" (*Poems* 551).

Perhaps even more interesting than their thematic links to Ireland are his verse's formal and linguistic connections to it. "An Excellent New Ballad" is only one of a number of broadsides and ballads, making use of popular tunes such as "Packington's Pound," which demonstrate Swift's ties to a popular satiric tradition: one that includes the seventeenth-century English anti-Puritan *Rump Songs* and *Poems on Affairs of State* but that also reflects the more specific influence of Irish culture, with its emphasis on oral and musical expression, and its dependence on cheap print technology as a means of literary production and distribution. As a writer involved in a wide network of both friendly and adversarial relationships to the many balladeers, poetasters, and printers who plied their trade in the capital city, Swift developed his poetic craft amidst the raucous energies and colorful babble of Dublin's Grub Street. It is thus not surprising that his verse is informal and down-to-earth, appealing more to common readers than to the literati, and often featuring the humblest members of society, such as the street hawkers who inspired his "Verses Made for the Women Who Cry Apples" and the half-deranged beggar Molyneux, who became the wily "Mullinex" of several satirical poems of the 1720s. "An Excellent New Song upon His Grace Our Good Lord Archbishop of Dublin" (*Poems* 278–80) specifies the "singer" as "Honest Jo, one of His Grace's Farmers in Fingal" (that is, Finglas, a parish north of Dublin) and employs dialect words – "yoke," a Kentish word for both a measurement of land and a manor, and "bailie," a Scottish term for a bailiff or sheriff – which call attention to non-standard English practices and, by implication, those geographical areas, like Ireland, which retained their own distinctive mode of expression. By the same token, "An Epilogue to a Play for the Benefit of the Weavers in Ireland" (1721) contains lines rhyming "savers" and "weavers" (*Poems* 228): a specifically "Irish" rhyme based on a pronunciation of "weavers" then no longer used in England, though it continued to prevail in Ireland. What Pat Rogers terms "a certain pervasive 'Irishness' of diction" in the verse (*Poems* 37) is even more apparent in "The Yahoo's Overthrow; Or, The Kevin Bail's New Ballad" (1734), set to the popular tune of "Derry Down." A comic attack on Richard ("Booby") Bettesworth, a sergeant-at-law who made bodily threats against Swift, this ballad figuratively (and, so concrete and vivid is its detail, almost literally) drags Bettesworth through the streets of Dublin by a neighborhood gang – the "Jolly boys of St. Kevin's, St. Patrick's, Donore, / And Smithfield" (*Poems* 539) – led by the same subversive Swift glimpsed in "Aye and No: A Tale from Dublin." Emphasizing the sheer force of street justice as opposed to the empty rhetoric and illusory justice of the legal system, "The Yahoo's Overthrow" combines colorful proverbial sayings ("leap of a louse") and colloquial terms having precise local associations ("skip," short for "skip-kennel," signifying a footman or lackey but also, more specifically, a college-servant or scout at Trinity College, Dublin) with lively street slang: "We'll colt him through Kevin, St. Patrick's, Donore, / And Smithfield, as Rap was ne'er colted before; / We'll oil him with kennel, and powder him with grains, / A modus right fit for insulters of deans" – the last two lines offering another example of a specifically Irish rhyme.

Swift's Irishness as a writer is most obviously exemplified by "The Description of an Irish Feast" (1720), which was adapted by Swift after having been translated out of the original Irish, presumably by the author himself, Hugh MacGauran, at Swift's behest. Under its Irish title "Pléaráca na Ruarcach," the poem was set to music by the famous Gaelic harpist Turlough Carolan, who, according to oral tradition, personally regaled Swift with his rendition of the "Pléaráca" at the Deanery. Swift's poem brilliantly conveys a sense of the anarchic energy and mayhem of the feast hosted by "O'Rourk" (the Irish chieftain Brian O'Rourke, who rebelled against the English in 1580) through its clipped five-syllable line, its vividly animated detail, and its onomatopoeic effects: "They dance in a round, / Cutting capers and ramping, / A mercy the ground / Did not burst with their stamping, / The floor is all wet / With leaps and with jumps, / While the water and sweat, / Splishsplash in their pumps" (*Poems* 222). The poem makes liberal use of dialect words (such as "ramping" for "romping"), Irish words ("Usquebaugh," literally "water of life," for "whiskey"), and Anglo-Irish terms ("madder," for a wooden drinking vessel) to produce a kind of babble which linguistically mirrors the physical pandemonium described in the verse. The acts of translation running through the poem constitute, not a process of conversion from one single, unified linguistic system to another, but an opening up to the heteroglossic features of both spoken and written language in a multi-lingual culture in which "many forms of English and many forms of Irish...rubbed against and influenced each other."[10]

Swift's lifelong indulgence in all forms of word-play, including puns, riddles, and invented languages, needs to be understood within the context of this kind of culture, where words could have dual (or more) meanings and often functioned on several different levels at once, creating the possibilities for both linguistic plenitude and semantic confusion. His punning contests with Sheridan in particular resulted in polylingual concoctions that played upon Latin, Greek, French, English, Irish, and Hiberno-English verbal constructions, producing also an invented language, "Latino-Anglicus," used in a series of humorous verses. It is not surprising, then, that a number of Swift's prose pieces take language as their main subject: for example, *A Discourse to Prove the Antiquity of the English Tongue*, which is not (as the title might lead one to believe) a serious attempt to vindicate the superiority or purity of the English language but on the contrary, a satiric subversion of such an attempt, featuring a ludicrously ethnocentric and chauvinistic persona who concludes that "the Greeks, the Romans, and the Jews, spoke the language we now do in England; which is an honour to our country that I thought proper to set in a true light" (*PW* IV: 239). In essence an extended punning joke, the *Discourse* parodies philological scholarship through a series of mock-etymologies according to which the Greek warrior Achilles got his name from "*A Kill-Ease*, or destroyer of ease" and Abraham had that name bestowed on him because "he was a man (in the Scotch phrase, which comes nearest to the old Saxon) of *a bra ham*; that is, of a brave strong ham" (*PW* IV: 233, 239). Similar kinds of word-play occur in *A Modest Defence of Punning*, a work that not only supports the use of puns but is itself an ingenious embodiment of such usage, incorporating Anglo-Latin, Greek, Spanish, and French terms into a series of English word games that continually remind its readers of the multiple interpretative possibilities of words.

Perhaps the most interesting of these prose works are *A Dialogue in [the] Hibernian Style between A and B* and *Irish Eloquence* (*PW* IV: 277–79), two short pieces that demonstrate Swift's familiarity with the language spoken by the Irish planter class: those English or Scottish settlers who took over forfeited lands in the seventeenth century and cultivated the soil while they "planted," or founded, a colony. These texts' wide linguistic range includes colloquialisms, dialecticisms, and vulgarisms of English usage, as well a variety of words and idioms ("sowins," "garrawns," "spawlpeen," "lend me a loan," "how does he get his Health?") taken from Irish usage.[11] Although the main purpose of these pieces seems to be to ridicule the planters' language, it is possible to view them in a less judgmental light, as evidence of Swift's fascination with non-standard English and with regional variations in expression. This fascination belies the common misconception of Swift as a maligner of the Irish language and as one who advocated its eradication, which is based largely on a partial statement taken out of context from the following passage: "It would be a noble achievement to abolish the Irish language in this kingdom, so far at least as to oblige all the natives to speak only English on every occasion of business, in shops, markets, fairs, and other places of dealing" (*PW* XII: 89). The point of this passage is not that the Irish language should be wiped out but that English should be promoted in the carrying on of all business transactions – a proposal consistent with the interests of the emerging Catholic middle class, whose success in the marketplace depended on a knowledge of English. Tellingly, the idea of abolishing the Irish language is also advocated in a satiric piece, *On Barbarous Denominations in Ireland*, which notes the existence of "an odd provincial cant… sometimes not very pleasing to the ear" in England rather than in Ireland, and which locates the main problem with the Irish brogue not in its inherent qualities but in the prejudiced reception it invariably elicits, regardless of "whether the censure be reasonable or not" (*PW* IV: 281). The proposal to translate Ireland's "barbarous denominations" into supposedly civilized English undergoes further satiric subversion by being presented as a project "for the sake of the English lawyers," who cause confusion in parliament by butchering the pronunciation of Irish names.

The works discussed above provide additional context and meaning to the more well-known instances of Swift's word games and invented languages, such as the "little language" he uses when writing to Esther Johnson in *The Journal to Stella*: "and zoo must cly Lele and Hele, and Hele aden. Must loo mimitate pdfr, pay? Iss, and so la shall. And so leles fol ee rettle" (translated by the *Journal*'s first editor as, "And you must cry There, and Here, and Here again. Must you imitate *Presto* [Swift], pray? Yes, and so you shall. And so there's for your letter") (*JS* 210). Swift's identification of this private language with oral communication ("when I am writing in our language I make up my mouth just as if I was speaking to you" [JS 210]) emphasizes its contrast with the world of print and writing that characterized Swift's life in London as editor and pamphleteer for the Tory ministry. It is a contrast that operates on several levels, differentiating private expression from public statement, eccentric language usage from formal, officially sanctioned rhetoric – as well as, in a number of important ways, Ireland from England.

We might think of Swift's complex, often inconsistent attitudes towards language in terms of the "Tory anarchism" (the contradictory combination of authoritarian and libertarian tendencies) that George Orwell ascribed to him, the "Tory" side reflected in his efforts, best exemplified by his *Proposal for Correcting the English Tongue* (1712), to "fix" the English language and purge it of all eccentric or non-standard vocabulary, the "anarchist" side delighting in colloquial and dialectal forms of speech, in made-up vocabularies, and in all those aspects of language most susceptible to variation and change.[12] These antithetical strains can be understood in light of the contradictions of Swift's identity as an Anglo-Irishman, with his "anarchistic" attitude toward language embodying the Irish side of his linguistic views and practices – that part which was by definition a divergence from the (Anglo-centric, imperial) norm, hence automatically perceived as aberrant.

Invented languages play a large role in *Gulliver's Travels*, where the protagonist repeatedly finds himself shipwrecked on strange lands whose inhabitants speak in unfamiliar tongues he must learn for purposes of basic survival. Fortunately, Gulliver turns out to be quite a cunning linguist, quickly mastering the fundamentals of these alien languages and even becoming an expert translator. The "Tory" Swift appears here in those passages, especially in Part III, that satirize modern language experiments as well as in the recurring protests against a continually changing language, underscored by Gulliver's discovery, upon each of his returns to England, that his countrymen's "old Dialect was so altered, that I could hardly understand the new" (*PW* XI: 7). At the same time, Swift's "anarchistic" proclivities imbue Gulliver's world with a linguistic as well as geographic expansiveness – with a delight in word-play and verbal experimentation, whether in the "Master Bates" trap set for the reader at the outset (*PW* XI: 19–20) or in the foreign yet sometimes teasingly familiar or onomatopoeically inflected words spoken by Gulliver's various hosts. Terms like "Hekinah Degul," "Tolgo Phonac," and "Quinbus Flestrin" flow lovingly off Gulliver's tongue, tying him to his creator as an aficionado of non-standard-English modes of expression. This avoidance of monologism occurs in the generic as well as the linguistic sphere, with the work resisting clear-cut classification by incorporating a variety of literary forms, including the picaresque, travel narrative, spiritual autobiography, utopian fiction, and satire.

Given that the composition of *Gulliver's Travels* dates from the same period as *The Drapier's Letters*, it is not surprising that the satire shares a number of themes with Swift's Irish tracts, and even includes a fictive version of the successful resistance to Wood's patent in its account in Part III of the Lindalinians' revolt (*PW* XI: 309–10). The most pertinent example is Gulliver's contradictory role as an often enthusiastic participant in the British colonial enterprise – he is a ship's surgeon on various trading expeditions to the East and West Indies – who ultimately rejects colonialism with a scathing denunciation that substitutes Britain's brutal conquest of overseas territories for its harsh oppressions in Ireland:

> Ships are sent with the first Opportunity; the Natives driven out or destroyed, their Princes tortured to discover their Gold; a free Licence given to all Acts of Inhumanity and Lust; the Earth reeking with the Blood of its Inhabitants: And this execrable Crew of Butchers employed in so pious an Expedition, is a *modern Colony* sent to convert and civilize an idolatrous and barbarous People. (*PW* XI: 294)

The colonial's brutal encounter with the (racial and cultural) other, which lies at the heart of this passage, is imaginatively transformed into the black humor of Gulliver's encounter with the species of Yahoo, whom he initially reviles as an "ugly Monster" (*PW* XI: 224) but in whom he shortly thereafter, to his indescribable "Horror and Astonishment," discerns "a perfect human Figure" (*PW* XI: 229–30). Similar such moments of loathing and self-recognition recur elsewhere in Swift's writings, enacting his own conflicted feelings about the native Irish and his relationship to them. His tracts periodically echo Gulliver's revulsion of the "monstrous" Yahoos through their depictions of the native Irish – "those animals" that outwardly resemble their two-legged counterparts in England, though "differing in their notions, natures, and intellectualls more than any two kinds of Brutes in a forest" (*PW* XII: 65). At the same time, the tracts contain examples in which Swift, like Gulliver, acknowledges his resemblance to the Yahoo and thus, in effect, recognizes his own "monstrosity" – even more to the point, his own "savagery" reflected through colonial eyes. As Swift notes in the *Fourth Drapier's Letter*, the English "look upon us as a Sort of *Savage Irish*, whom our Ancestors conquered several Hundred Years ago: And if I should describe the *Britons* to you, as they were in *Cæsar's* Time, when they *painted their Bodies, or cloathed themselves with the Skins of Beasts*, I should act full as reasonably as they do" (*PW* X: 64). When Gulliver is placed in a box and "carried about for a Monster" by the Brobdingnagian farmer (*PW* XI: 97), or when he is examined as a weird specimen by the three eminent scholars at the Brobdingnagian court and proclaimed to be a "*Lusus Naturæ*" or jest of nature (*PW* XI: 104), he undergoes a process of objectification that may be seen to "hibernicize" him, turning him into an alien creature upon whom others can project their own biased, ethnocentric assumptions. In this sense Gulliver embodies the conflicted identity of an Anglo-Irishman, lost in a world where the familiar has become strange and where he is caught between the roles of master and slave, civilized being and savage.

In one other important way does *Gulliver's Travels* reveal its links to an Irish author and context. Its episodic, fragmented structure, composed of voyages that differ from one another formally as well as thematically, ex-emplifies a stylistic trait characteristic of Swift's writings, reflective of a tex-tual preoccupation with unruly particulars or disjunctive elements rather than with their harmonious resolution – an insistence on the primacy of the part over the whole. Throughout his career, Swift produced texts made of up fragments and calling attention to their incompleteness, starting with his earliest satire, *A Tale of a Tub* (1704), and illustrated by his partiality for certain kinds of literary forms such as the journal, the picaresque, and works made up primarily or wholly of dialogue and snippets of conversa-tion. Swift's *oeuvre* also includes literal fragments – the few short sections of a projected *History of Britain* that was never finished, for example, and his autobiographical piece *The Family of Swift*, a fragmentary account of his lineage and early life which ends abruptly at age thirty, with no prospects (or closure) in sight. The fifty-six lines of Swift's "Allusion to the First Satire of the Second Book of Horace" ("A Dialogue between an Eminent Lawyer and Dr. Swift") represent only one-third of the length of Pope's *Imitation* of the same poem. That Swift looked to Horace as a literary model indicates an aspiration he shared with the English Augustan poets to situate himself as a writer in the learned, classical tradition. At the same time, his imitations of only portions of Horatian texts suggest his marginality to this tradition, and have the effect of casting an ironic perspective on contemporary neo-classical assumptions about the importance of artistic unity. If Pope in effect fashioned himself as "the English Horace," Swift might be thought of as an "Irish Horace," one who specifically inscribed his paraphrase of "Horace, Book I, Ode XIV" to Ireland – "Poor floating isle, tossed on ill fortune's waves" (*Poems* 291) – and used the Horatian ode as a vehicle for rallying Irish patriotism in its resistance to British colonialist oppression.

These distinctive aspects of Swift's style can be understood in part as man-ifestations of what we might call an "Irish aesthetic": a decentralized, anti-organic mode of writing that implicitly challenged eighteenth-century British aesthetic hegemony, especially its insistence on the integrated wholeness of a work of art and its promotion of *concordia discors*, the overriding unity of discordant elements – precepts well-suited to a nation that was increasingly becoming the imperial center around which a constellation of ethnically and culturally diverse colonies revolved.[13] Such a sense of nationhood and imperial inclusiveness would find its consummate aesthetic expression in Pope's description of *Windsor-Forest* (lines 13–16), where potentially warring elements converge, "Not *Chaos*-like together crush'd and bruis'd, / But as the World, harmoniously confus'd: / Where Order in Variety we see, / And where, tho' all things differ, all agree."[14] In Pope's aesthetic as well as ideological formulations, particulars are given their due but ultimately subordinated to a single, all-encompassing structure of truth, beauty, and (not least) power. Hence Pope's assertion that "'Tis not a *Lip*, or *Eye*, we Beauty call, / But the joint Force and full *Result* of *all*" (*Essay on Criticism*, lines 245–46); and hence also his paean to the British empire at the end of the *Epistle to Burlington*, where the Earl of Burlington's invincible command over the realms of both art and nature is hailed for producing "Imperial Works... worthy [of] Kings" (line 204). Swift's rejection of the consolidation and closure implicit in Pope's "Order in Variety" is registered in writings that foreground the anarchic autonomy of rambunctious elements and free-floating fragments. Although the latter can at times have a negative valuation, pointing up Ireland's lack of internal coherence and sectarian strife, they can also – as "The Description of an Irish Feast" vividly shows – represent a sensuous concreteness and individualistic spirit impervious to the homogenizing technologies of Britain's global domination.

By the early 1730s, Swift's reputation as a writer had grown to the point where there was interest in making his entire body of work available in print. Given Swift's ties to Dublin's literary circles, epitomized by his friendship and patronage of the gifted young Dublin-born poet William Dunkin, there were compelling arguments for an Irish edition, despite the fact that most of his previous work had been published in London. Among those eager to put out such an edition, and thereby displace the Englishman Benjamin Motte as Swift's main publisher, was the young Irishman George Faulkner, whom Swift called "the Prince of Dublin Printers" (*C* IV: 222). Periodic disavowals notwithstanding, Swift became an active collaborator in Faulkner's 1735 edition, providing materials to be included and helping to ensure the accuracy of its content. The importance of this edition is that it presented Swift's works as part of a consciously and thoroughly Irish production, in effect making him into a writer inseparable from Dublin life and letters. Swift recognized and quietly embraced this fact even as he continued to express the desire to have such an edition published instead in England – not least because the copyright protections available to English authors and printers did not extend to their Irish counterparts. No doubt another reason was his never entirely suppressed wish to be a writer speaking from the center of civilization rather than from its margins, which created a deep ambivalence towards "being published in so obscure and wretched a country" as Ireland (C IV: 322). Swift's acute awareness of the power of cultural hegemony must on some level have intensified this aspiration even as it simultaneously made him realize its unworthiness. Just as he had earlier longed to become England's official Historiographer Royal but wound up becoming instead an unofficial historian of Irish affairs, so in later years he was moved by the temptation to situate himself in the pantheon of great British writers immortalized in definitive London editions, but ultimately welcomed his status as the author of works to be forever associated with a Dublin printer and a distinctively Irish edition. Defending the latter edition in a letter to Motte, Swift underscored its political significance as an anti-colonialist gesture, doing in the cultural arena what *The Drapier's Letters* had done in the political one. Declaring himself "incensed against the Oppressions from *England*" and with "little Regard to the Laws they make," Swift defiantly defends acts of civil disobedience in both the political and literary spheres, asserting that just as he has encouraged Irish merchants to ignore England's trade restrictions and export their wool to whatever countries they wish, so too he would encourage Irish booksellers "to sell your Authors Books printed here, and send them to all the Towns in *England*, if I could do it with Safety and Profit" (C IV: 494). Deane Swift, writing to thank his cousin for the gift made him of the edition, foregrounded its political dimension by identifying its contents with the fostering of a patriotic spirit and a commitment to resist tyranny. As he promised his benefactor, "I shall from this moment enlist myself under the conduct of Liberty's General; and whenever I desert her ensigns, to fight under those of Tyranny and Oppression, then, and not till then, will I part with those books which you have so highly honoured me with . . . that I may never afterwards be reproached either by the sight of them, or the remembrance of the donor" (C v: 134).

In the years that followed, a long line of readers would similarly associate Swift's writings with Irish patriotic and pro-liberty sentiments. Even those who declined to interpret them as a clarion call to arms in defense of the mother country often saw them as part of a literary tradition rooted in the Irish soil, expressive of a quintessentially Irish wit and word-play. It is no coincidence that Swift appears as a tantalizing presence throughout Joyce's fiction and as the ghost who continually haunts Yeats, revealing himself to the poet alternately as a perversely mocking specter and as the noble embodiment of Protestant Ireland.[15] The contradictions inherent in Swift's Anglo-Irish identity remind us that we cannot characterize either the man or his work in any simple fashion, but they also allow us to appreciate the many ways in which Swift was an Irish writer, speaking in a variety of tongues while simultaneously delighting in and striving to tame the instabilities of language, and uttering denunciations with a verbal ferocity which, like the invective of the old Irish *file*, the poet purportedly capable of rhyming rats to death, became a fearsome weapon against the seemingly endless supply of fools and knaves who got trapped in his crosshairs.[16]

NOTES

1. A useful overview, "Gaelic Dublin in the Eighteenth Century," is provided in Alan Harrison, *The Dean's Friend: Anthony Raymond 1675–1726, Jonathan Swift and the Irish Language* (Dublin: Edmund Burke Publisher, 1999), chapter 2.
2. For Swift's relationship to Temple and his life at Moor Park, see *E* 1: 91–149; 169–82. For Swift's unhappy experience in Kilroot, see Louis A. Landa, *Swift and the Church of Ireland* (Oxford: Clarendon Press, 1954), pp. 15–24.
3. Swift's self-characterization appears in *Memoirs of Laetitia Pilkington*, ed. A. C. Elias, Jr., 2 vols. (Athens and London: University of Georgia Press, 1997), vol. I, p. 35. Despite Elias's conjecture (vol. II, p. 411) that Pilkington was "putting words into Swift's mouth" here, the epithet is entirely consistent with others of Swift's semi-ironic portrayals of himself vis-à-vis Ireland, both in letters and in poetry.
4. Sheridan's grandson was the celebrated playwright, Richard Brinsley Sheridan. For a discussion of the Sheridan family within a specifically Irish context, see Fintan O'Toole, *A Traitor's Kiss: The Life of Richard Brinsley Sheridan* (New York: Farrar, Straus and Giroux, 1997).
5. See *The Collected Poems of W. B. Yeats* (New York: Macmillan, 1966), p. 241; and J. Paul Hunter, p. 236 below.
6. In this connection, see D. George Boyce, *Nationalism in Ireland*, 3rd edn. (London and New York: Routledge, 1995), pp. 94–122.
7. See Joyce, *A Portrait of the Artist as a Young Man*, ed. Seamus Deane (New York: Penguin, 1993), p. 205.
8. See Swift and Sheridan, in *The Intelligencer*, ed. James Woolley (Oxford: Clarendon Press, 1992), p. 174.
9. See, for example, "Ireland, Island of Saints and Sages" (1907), in Ellsworth Mason and Richard Ellmann (eds.) *The Critical Writings of James Joyce* (Ithaca: Cornell University Press, 1959), pp. 161–62.
10. See Andrew Carpenter's Introduction to Carpenter (ed.) *Verse in English from Eighteenth-Century Ireland* (Cork: Cork University Press, 1998), p. 3.
11. See Introduction to *A Dialogue in Hybernian Stile Between A & B & Irish Eloquence*, ed. Alan Bliss (Dublin: The Cadenus Press, 1977), pp. 42–49; the quoted terms are from this edition.
12. See George Orwell, "Politics vs. Literature: An Examination of *Gulliver's Travels*," in *Shooting An Elephant and Other Essays* (New York: Harcourt, Brace & World, 1950), pp. 53–76.

13. I mean to apply this characterization of an "Irish aesthetic" specifically to prose writing and poetry. Drama raises a different set of aesthetic and stylistic (as well as ideological) issues.

14. Quotations from Pope are from *The Twickenham Edition of the Poems of Alexander Pope*, ed. John Butt, *et al.* 3rd edn. (New Haven: Yale University Press, 1966).

15. Swift is evoked at the very outset of *Finnegans Wake* and pervades the rest of the novel (as he does, somewhat less overtly, in *Ulysses*). For Yeats' obsessive fascination with Swift, see his play, *The Words upon the Window-pane*, where Swift appears to the participants in a séance as both a madman and "the chief representative of the intellect of his epoch." In Richard J. Finneran (ed.) *The Yeats Reader* (New York: Scribner, 1997), pp. 225–40, especially 239.

16. For a discussion of the savage satire of the early Irish poets and their reputed ability to rhyme rats (or human enemies) to death, see Robert C. Elliott, *The Power of Satire: Magic, Ritual, Art* (Princeton: Princeton University Press, 1966 [1960]), pp. 18–48; and Vivian Mercier, *The Irish Comic Tradition* (Oxford: Clarendon Press, 1962), pp. 105–16.

4

BREAN HAMMOND

Swift's reading

Are great works of imaginative literature, such as *Gulliver's Travels*, made out of life, or are they made out of other books? In 1919, T. S. Eliot published a landmark essay entitled "Tradition and the Individual Talent," arguing that the true worth of a writer was not to be found in "those aspects of his work in which he least resembles anyone else," but rather that "the most individual parts of his work may be those in which the dead poets, his ancestors, assert their immortality most vigorously."[1] Eliot's anti-romantic account minimizes originality and foregrounds hard work. Artistic achievement results from consciousness of the past, of cultural history. Literature is made of other literature, Eliot contends, more surely than it is made out of life experience. Readers of Swift might feel, perhaps should feel, that the antithesis is a false one. Nevertheless, Eliot's argument is persuasive enough to suggest that investigating the way in which a major writer modifies, and is modified by, pre-existing literary traditions, can be a valuable approach to the creative work. Our most direct source of knowledge here must derive from what Swift himself read. Accordingly, the first section of this chapter will be concerned with the books that Swift read, and with his way of reading them. The second section will focus more generally on what he made of what he read.

How do we know what Swift read? Swift himself drew up a list of the reading he undertook in a single year, from January 7, 1696/7 to January 7, 1697/8, while he was working as Secretary to Sir William Temple at Moor Park.[2] This was probably not a typical year, because at that time he was assembling the materials for *A Tale of a Tub*, one of the two satirical prose works upon which his enduring reputation rests. Later, Swift was to describe himself as at the height of his powers during this period, and certainly, the *Tale* seems to be the work of an omnivorous reader, not to say a polymath. Thirty-three titles are listed in the reading list, some worth considering in a little more detail, because they provide a fair indication of Swift's enduring interests.

He read his way through Homer's *Iliad* and *Odyssey*, the *Satyricon* of Petronius Arbiter (the Roman writer who flourished in the first century AD, and whom we might term a "novelist"), the whole of Horace ("9 volumes," Swift records, as if to make the point that he did not skimp), Virgil twice and Lucretius no less than three times. Cicero's *Epistolae* and the first volume of the Stoic-influenced writings of Aelian complete his reading of classical texts. Works of ancient and recent history and travel writing figure just as prominently, however, as do works of the imagination – if, indeed, that is a valid distinction. Swift read Diodorus Siculus, who penetrated the mysteries of the ancient Mediterranean peoples and told the story of the Macedonian empire; and Cyprian and Irenaeus amongst the early fathers of the church. His reading in modern history is, however, amongst the most significant and revelatory material on the list. Paolo Sarpi's *History of the Council of Trent* was first published in Italian in 1619, but Swift probably read Nathaniel Brent's English translation of 1676. Since Sarpi's book was a very powerful critique of the Council's failure to integrate new Protestant ideas into traditional Catholic doctrine during the period of its session (1545–63), the *History* was a considerable bulwark to Protestantism. Gilbert Burnet's *History of the Reformation of the Church of England*, of which the first two volumes were published in 1679 and 1681, was so also: a recent historian's analysis of Burnet is that he was "one of the first English historians to understand the importance of causation, and the need to explain great religious movements not solely by reference to religion itself or to the actions of individuals."[3] Swift loathed Burnet, however, and we will return to him.

Perhaps the most surprising feature of Swift's annual reading list is that there are very few works by recent writers in English. There are two works of synoptic and recent history by Sir William Temple, but Temple was after all his boss; two volumes of Jeremy Collier's *Essays Upon Several Moral Subjects* very recently published, and an epic poem recently published by the king's physician, Sir Richard Blackmore's *Prince Arthur*. Blackmore was, almost from the outset, a target for mockery amongst the wits; and it is difficult to imagine that Swift read this for any other reason than to mine it for infelicities and absurdities – lines like "With strutting Teats the Herds come lowing home" from book II. Spotting the omission of recent imaginative writers from the list enables us to make some wider points about Swift's library and his reading preferences. Apart from the handlist already mentioned, three inventories exist of Swift's library: a catalogue made in his own hand of the books he owned in August 1715; a manuscript catalogue of what was on his shelves taken by Dr. John Lyon in October 1742 and cross-checked nearly two years later (presumably to prevent purloining) when Swift's mental competence was under investigation; and a published catalogue of the books that went under the hammer when his library was sold after his death in February 1746. All of these confirm that Swift's library was not primarily that of a literary man: by which sensational remark, I mean that Swift did not energetically collect the writings of contemporary imaginative writers – the works of the myriad poets, playwrights, and fiction-writers with whom we can either prove or presume he was familiar from other sources – those being primarily his published works and his correspondence. Heinz J. Vienken has made the most recent analysis of the contents of Swift's library, and although he shows that the 657 volumes sold in the 1746 sale actually represent the writings of some 1,961 separate authors, his further analysis does nothing to dilute the claim that Swift's interests – at least as far as those are represented by book acquisition – are not those of the professional imaginative writer. Vienken calculates that "the library contains 358 historians, 120 theologians, 43 medical writers, 33 legal authors, and 29 diplomats."[4] If we were to compare Swift's library with that of, say, Henry Fielding, or even his close friend Thomas Sheridan (at whose country residence in Quilca, County Cavan, Swift completed the writing of *Gulliver's Travels*), this impression of Swift as not first and foremost a literary man, is underscored. Sheridan owned far more books than Swift did in total – the sale of his books in Dublin in 1739 had 1,040 lots – and his collection of literature recently published, and literature in various European languages, was far superior. Swift's library is particularly rich in French authors, whereas quite a few of the English authors he owned were those he could not avoid owning because they were presentation copies from the writers themselves. Henry Fielding's library represents an excellent point of comparison. Fielding's library, though well-stocked in the classics and in works of legal history that were his specialist interest, testifies to his immersion in the English dramatic and literary tradition, and in the cut-and-thrust of the contemporary publishing world. To select just one or two obvious examples: Fielding owned Dryden's plays and much of his poetry, whereas although Swift assuredly knew some of Dryden's work, he did not rate him highly enough to own a copy. Or take Shakespeare. Fielding owned the 1747 Warburton edition and the 1748 Hanmer, and it is known that he was entirely familiar with Theobald's Shakespeare. An anecdote handed down by Swift's young admirer Laetitia Pilkington is indicative of Swift's comparatively careless attitude to book-collecting:

> When I read any thing peculiarly charming, I never forgot it, and ... I could repeat not only all [Swift's] Works, but all *Shakespear*'s, which I put to this Trial; I desir'd him to open any Part of it and read a Line, and I would engage to go on with the whole Speech; as we were in his Library, he directly made the Experiment: The Line he first gave me, he had purposely pick'd out for its singular Oddness:

Put rancours in the Vessel of my Peace. Macbeth.

I readily went on with the whole Speech, and did so several times, that he try'd me with different Plays. The Dean then took down *Hudibras*, and order'd me to examine him in it, as he had done me in *Shakespear*; and to my great Surprize, I found he remember'd every Line, from Beginning to End of it.[5]

As Pilkington's modern editor, A. C. Elias, points out, however, there is no copy either of Shakespeare or of Butler to be found in any of the library lists. Particularly in the case of Samuel Butler, this is very odd. Arguably, Shakespeare was not an especially important influence on Swift, but a fundamental premise of all criticism of his poetry is that Butler's "3-part burlesque epic *Hudibras* (1663, 1664, 1678) pioneered the colloquial, comic 8-syllable rhymed couplet form which Swift perfected in his great poems of the 1730s."[6] In Fielding's library there is a good collection of seventeenth- and eighteenth-century drama, most of the major poets (he has *Hudibras* in an up-to-the-minute annotated 1744 edition), many of the works of topical writers (Addison and Steele, Mrs. Manley, Defoe, Charlotte Lennox, Francis Coventry, Samuel Richardson, John Dennis, James Thomson, Nicholas Rowe), and books of general cultural interest, such as Petty's *Political Arithmetick*, Hogarth's *Analysis of Beauty* or Hume's *Philosophical Essays*, that the reader who wants to preserve a broad intellectual conspectus would have on his shelves. In all of those respects, Swift's library offers a contrast. For those who think of Swift primarily as the author of *Gulliver's Travels*, it might be salutary to consider the energy he must have put into reading twelve folio volumes of Cardinal Caesar Baronius' *Annales ecclesiastici* (a mind-numbingly dull history of the Popes published in Antwerp in Latin between 1612 and 1629), annotating several volumes in barbed and witty Latin:[7]

Baronius 7.525:	Swift:
Vos qui hujusmodi narrationibus	Those who delight in this narrative
delectamini Attendite	pay attention
Inter quos ego non sum	Amongst whom I am not one.

And this leads us into the question of Swift's way of reading, for which his books are particularly valuable evidence. Again there is a contrast to Fielding. Frederick and Anne Ribble, recent cataloguers of Fielding's books, make the excellent point that his library bears witness to its owner's intellectual tolerance.[8] Even-handedly, Fielding read both Catholic and non-conformist controversialists, as if trying to understand both sides of an argument, and the nature of the compromise that Anglicanism represented. Swift did not read even-handedly, or to find "beauties" in what he read. Swift read adversarially.

Several of the surviving books from his library carry furious marginal comments, in wholesale contrast to the light markings that point up memorable passages in the margins of Fielding's books and Pope's. One such marked-up copy is featured on the 1696/7 reading list, Lord Edward Herbert of Cherbury's *The Life and Raigne of King Henry the Eighth* (1649). Swift's own copy of this book survives in the Rothschild Library in Trinity College, Cambridge, one of more than twenty volumes belonging to him now to be found in that collection. The copy is fiercely annotated in Swift's own hand. Clearly, Swift cared for neither the author nor the subject. Henry VIII is represented by many Protestant historians, by Burnet for example, as the founder and spiritual leader of English Protestantism. To Swift, he was a vicious and cruel tyrant who persecuted alike those who denied his supremacy and those who denied the basic tenets of the Catholic church, the monarch responsible for weakening the church and its power by making over church lands to laymen after dissolving the English monasteries, upsetting the balance of power between church, nobility, and commons, and gratifying his lust.[9] A few of Swift's marginal glosses are reproduced in the table below, just to give the perfervid flavor of his interaction with what he read:

258	Mistris Bolen whether she ... had rather be that Lords Wife than a Kings Mistris [crossed out]	Whore
391	he would have been glad not to be compell'd to such violent courses;	Nature alone compelled him
468	the King ... commanding the said Sir John Nevil to be put to death at York. Shortly after followed the Countess of Salisbury's Execution	Dog, Villain, King, Viper, Devil Monster
574	That concupiscence which in some is vice, – in others a necessity of nature.	as men go to Stool so he was damnably laxative
575	To conclude; I wish I could LEAVE HIM IN HIS GRAVE.	And I wish he had been Flead, his skin stuffed and hangd on a Gibbet, His bulky guts and Flesh left to be devoured by Birds and Beasts for a warning to his Successors for ever. Amen.

Even more spectacular are the annotations Swift made on a copy of Gilbert Burnet's *History of His Own Time*, published in two volumes in 1724 and 1734, which survives in the library of Lord Lansdowne in Bowood House.

This copy belonged to his friend John Lyon, and Swift had to apologize for disfiguring it when he returned it, which must have been after 1739 because one of his marginal notes refers to that date. Lyon gifted the book with Swift's penciled notes to Lord Shelburne, first Marquis Lansdowne, in 1768. There is a particular pleasure in being able to trace such an intimate and specific set of connections between a great writer and his reading processes; and in this case, there is also significant knowledge to be gained from the activity. Burnet's "grand narrative" in compiling his history is to vindicate the coming over of William of Orange as a knight on a white charger, carrying out a providential plan to rescue England from the tyrannical domination of a Catholic monarch who had declared himself above parliament and the law: and to glorify his own personal role in that. Burnet dwelt in grimly circumstantial detail upon the royal birth in 1688, advancing the view that there were two stillbirths before a third child was smuggled into the birthing chamber in a warming-pan; and considering, with a particularity that not even the Clinton prosecution could match, the question of what part of the queen's belly her lady-in-waiting was permitted to feel, and how close exactly to her nipples milk marks were found upon her linen. With all of this Swift is impatient: he clearly does think that James II had a legitimate heir. The overall effect of Swift's marginalia is to oppose the thrust of Burnet's account in vindicating the Revolution. He is antagonized by Burnet's self-satisfaction and vanity in presenting himself as at the center of events, and anti-Scottish remarks pepper the notes, Burnet being a Scot. Swift's settled prejudice is that the Prince of Orange always intended to become king, even before he was invited to take the throne. In his marginal note to p. 782 of Burnet's *History*, for example, where Burnet quotes William as saying that he "went to England with no other intentions, but those he had set out in his declaration [in which he did not claim the throne]," Swift writes: "Then he was perjured; for he designed to get the crown, which he denied in the declaration" (*PW* v: 228). Many of Swift's marginalia are Jacobite in sympathy, reverential towards Charles I and implacably hostile to William III. For Swift, then, the historian whom Fielding called in his last novel *Amelia* "almost the only English Historian that is likely to be known to Posterity, by whom he will be most certainly ranked amongst the greatest Writers of Antiquity," was a canine Scottish falsifier whose brand of Protestantism could not be trusted.[10] Here is a case where close attention to Swift's patterns of reading and to his marking-up of a book can reveal something secret and intimate about his political allegiance and the nature of his Protestantism.

The first section of this chapter has been necessarily somewhat technical, in describing and evaluating Swift's library and his reading habits. We now have to consider the more speculative question of what Swift did with his reading and with the literary traditions he inherited. The books Swift owned at various points in his life are an indispensable starting-point to considering how his reading might have shaped his creative imagination, but they are no more than that. Probably every single reader of this chapter will have books on the shelves that s/he has not read and never intends to, and so, doubtless, did Swift. If a remark he made in a letter to Pope and Bolingbroke is to be taken at face value, Swift was not comfortable in libraries, places that reminded him of the insignificance of any individual author: "I hate a crowd where I have not an easy place to see and be seen. A great Library always makes me melancholy, where the best Author is as much squeezed, and as obscure, as a Porter at a Coronation."[11] A *Tale of a Tub* is an instance of how Swift's seeming erudition might lead us to false conclusions. It is a prose work apparently steeped in the dark, mysterious writings of cabbalists, occultists, Rosicrucians, and other sects even more obviously on the lunatic fringe; but as his reading list shows, the only such book he actually read at the time was Nicolas de Montfaucon de Villars' *Le Comte de Gabalis, ou Entretiens sur les Sciences Secrètes* (Paris, 1671), a popularization of Rosicrucian lore which, according to Alexander Pope, "both in its Title and Size is so like a Novel, that many of the Fair Sex have read it for one by mistake."[12] Virtually everything Swift needed to know about the alchemists and the mystics he could have gleaned from Louis Moréri's *Great Historical, Geographical, and Poetical Dictionary*, to the 1694 London edition to which he subscribed. Although the *Tale* has running gags that poke fun at the shorthand methods to which hacks resort in gaining erudition – digests, indexes, reviews – there is an additional layer of irony in that Swift probably resorted to them himself: "What remains therefore, but that our last Recourse must be had to large Indexes, and little Compendiums? Quotations must be plentifully gathered and bookt in Alphabet; To this End, tho' Authors need be little consulted, yet Criticks, and Commentators, and Lexicons, carefully must" (*PW* I: 93). Vienken puts at some 1,400 the number of authors indirectly referred to or inferable from Swift's published writings, additional to those contained in his library, thus indicating that analysis of his library has its shortcomings.[13]

So who are the authors that were most important to Swift? Who had most bearing on his major imaginative writing? Pat Rogers, recent editor of Swift's poetry, gives the following answer:

> His borrowings derive chiefly from Latin rather than Greek sources, and the three most common sources are Virgil, Ovid, and Horace. Indeed, the two poems of the ancient world which bit most deeply into his consciousness were

plainly, on this evidence, the *Aeneid* and the *Metamorphoses*. Among earlier English poets, the key texts include *Paradise Lost, Hudibras*; the works of Cowley; and certain areas of Dryden, notably the translations, the odes, and the panegyrical poems. As for contemporary poetry, the obvious echoes are those of Prior's *Alma*; Gay's *Trivia* and *Fables*; and the major works of Pope, above all, *The Rape of the Lock*.

(*Poems* 25)

I would endorse Pat Rogers' view that although Swift alluded to a vast range of writers throughout his work, there was a relatively small canon that truly mattered to him. For the major prose, we would want to include Lucian, Rabelais, and Cervantes – the last especially in view of fascinating recent evidence that Swift actually embarked upon a translation of *Don Quixote* in the 1730s and probably had a hand in writing a preface for it.[14] With respect to Lucian (the second-century Greek writer of comic prose dialogues), interest in an older view that Swift's engagement with him is mediated through a complex tradition of Renaissance "Menippean" satire that might include Erasmus' *Praise of Folly* (1511), More's *Utopia* (1516), Burton's *Anatomy of Melancholy* (1621–51), and Rabelais' *Gargantua and Pantagruel* (1532–34) is currently reviving. Aesop's fables transmitted via the *Fables Choisies* of Jean de La Fontaine (1668–94), surprisingly omitted from Rogers' list, is clearly an important influence on many of Swift's poems cast as beast fables, such as "The Beasts' Confession to the Priest" (written in 1732 though published in 1738, a poem that is a veritable thesaurus of Swiftian preoccupations), and has a wider formative effect upon his imagination. There is a copy of the *Fables* in the 1715 library list, and Swift still had it in his library when he died. Hobbes and Bacon are the philosophers who stimulated Swift's creative energies, usually in a satirical direction tinged nevertheless with grudging admiration, and he knew Locke. There are writers who were very important to Swift because they were writers he loved to hate, and I would put both Dryden and Defoe into that category. Two of Swift's most important early prose satires are immersed in the so-called Ancients/Moderns controversy. In the final decade of the seventeenth century, the intellectual world was split over the question (or perhaps, non-question!) whether the ancient writers had completed the stock of human wisdom and there was nothing new under the sun, or whether, on the contrary, modern writers had new things to say and intellectual progress was a valid concept. *A Tale of a Tub* and *The Battle of the Books* are populated with writers who exemplify those "ancient" and "modern" positions. For *Gulliver's Travels*, the major influences were probably relatively ephemeral travel books and reports of the more bizarre experiments carried out in the Royal Society. William Dampier's *A New Voyage Round the World* might deserve a special mention, because

Swift possessed a copy of the third (1698) edition and it is mentioned by him in the "Letter from Captain Gulliver to his Cousin Sympson" prefixed to Faulkner's 1735 edition of the *Travels*. Beyond that, literary detective work has unearthed hundreds of local possibilities, of which I would mention only two or three, texts that are now not at all well known but in my view have a more than local – approaching a structural – shaping influence on significant aspects of Swift's writing. They are Marvell's *The Rehearsal Transpros'd* Part 1 (1672), the influence of which upon the *Tale* is now coming to be accepted and a copy of which Swift owned, Charles Cotton's *Scarronides*; or *Virgile Travestie* (1664–65), that he also owned and that he had asked an Irish poet-friend, William Dunkin, to revise or rewrite, and John Dunton's *A New Voyage Round the World; or, A Pocket Library* (1691). This third is a bizarre production that Swift assuredly did not own, but Dunton's chronic use of digression, supreme indifference towards the reader, constant self-referentiality, interruption, word-play, and linguistic alteration, as well as the travel-literature outer shell, makes it a suggestive model for the kind of semi-literate, manic proto-novel that the *Tale* and *Gulliver's Travels* were attempting to kill in the womb. This is a point I will pursue at the close of my chapter.

For the present, we pick up the point made in the first section, that an examination of Swift's library would not encourage us to think that he was primarily a literary man. One suspects that his ambition was not so much to write *Gulliver's Travels* as to write a history of his own times less relentlessly Whiggish than Burnet's. This instinct can be developed further. Swift was a career clergyman, not a professional author who hoped to gain a living by exploiting his wits and his pen; and he lived most of his life in Ireland, not in England. These two facts gave him both an elevation over, and an estrangement from, the London literary scene. He never knew quite what was going on in literary London, but he could not bring himself much to care. In the preface to "The Beast's Confession to the Priest," probably written by Swift, he comments acidly on this:

> I compute, that London hath eleven native fools of the beau and puppy kind, for one among us in Dublin; besides two thirds of ours were transplanted hither, who are now naturalized; whereby that overgrown capital exceeds ours in the article of dunces by forty to one; and what is more to our further mortification, there is not one distinguished fool of Irish birth or education, who makes any noise in that famous metropolis, unless the London prints be very partial or defective; whereas London is seldom without a dozen of their own educating, who engross the vogue for half a winter together, and are never heard of more, but give place to a new set. (*Poems* 508)

Perhaps this is one reason (if reasons are what we need) why Swift's writing is so rich in what formalist critics might call "alienation techniques," devices that make the familiar strange and the strange familiar. In his use of inherited literary traditions, Swift is probably the most subversive writer in his, or possibly in any, literary period. What he takes from Virgil or Ovid, he takes to turn on its head, or to deploy in a less-than-reverential fashion. One obvious example is the poem "A Beautiful Young Nymph Going to Bed" (1734), where the pastoral tradition is used as a spine upon which to hang the putrefying flesh of city street life; and where the poem dramatizes a parodic Ovidian transformation. Instead of, for example, Daphne turning into a laurel tree, this poem has a woman literally take herself apart and become a heap of prosthetic parts lying on the floor. The poem is haunted by fear that its comedy tries to fend off, fear that a prostitute, resorting to cosmetic concealments, might be so soulless as to have no self at all.

We might select, as a case-study in miniature, Swift's use of Virgil. The 1696/7 list tells us that Swift read Virgil twice in that year, and we can glean from the library lists that he owned five Virgils in three different editions. There is no overlooking Virgil's importance to Swift. But how, precisely, does he deploy Virgil? In the poem "A Description of a City Shower" (1710), describing the behavior of London citizens during a gradually intensifying rainstorm that finally gathers overtones of the biblical Flood, there is a structural set of allusions to the first book of the *Georgics* (lines 483–86 and 533–38), but mediated through Dryden's translation; and also to the storms that occur in the *Aeneid* II and IV, the latter the very significant one that drives Dido and Aeneas into the cave where they behave badly. Brendan O'Hehir's analysis of the borrowings asserts that their effect is to impart moral significance to a dark vision of the city as a modern Sodom. This he derives from the fact that the flooding of the Eridanus in Georgics I and the rainstorms in the *Aeneid* all betoken or prognosticate civil strife and disaster. The topography of Swift's poem is particularly associated with excessive filth or venality. The poem upholds, and does not mock, the standards of the heroic tradition, deriving from Virgilian sources an understated moral standard that was one expectation of the georgic genre. For Roger Savage, however, the relationship between georgic and mock-georgic is expressed in a different key. London is not a sink of degradation – there is nothing apocalyptic going on here; it is just that the modern city and one's language for describing it fail to live up to the classical ideals of civilization and its descriptive formulae. Neither Savage nor O'Hehir would agree with Swift's most prominent recent biographer, Irvin Ehrenpreis, that the poem adds up to "a cheerful acceptance of the urban scene," but they probably would concur that "while there is an element of satire in the poem, it is directed not against Virgil, of course, but against his English imitators, especially Dryden"(*E* II: 387, 384).[15] Why, though, are they so sure that the poem is not directed against Virgil? Swift, as we have seen, was entirely familiar with, and owned the 1670 edition of, Charles Cotton's *Scarronides; or, Virgile Travestie: a Mock-Poem on the First and Fourth Books of Virgil's Aenaeis in English Burlesque*, where there is as scurrilous and ludicrous a version of the Dido and Aeneas episode as it is possible to imagine. At issue here is the "depth of cut" in Swift's use of the mock-georgic and mock-epic. How close does he get to cutting off the branch upon which he is sitting? It is difficult to read Cotton without becoming aware of an inherent ludicrousness in Virgil's epic treatment of the coupling of a soon-to-be jilted mistress and her unfaithful lover, pushed into a conveniently dark cave by bad weather. And although it is some-times thought that the irony of "mock-heroic" was directed only at modern living and writing, leaving the classical world unscathed, it is more convinc-ing to argue that English mock-genres cut in both directions. They under-mined both the modern and the ancient behaviors that came within their reach.

The nettle is now out there to be grasped. Writing a piece on Swift's reading is a peculiarly self-conscious activity because at very many points in his writing, Swift has great sport with those who ply the critical trade.

> It were much to be wisht, and I do here humbly propose for an Experiment, that every prince in Christendom will take seven of the deepest Scholars in his Dominions, and shut them up close for seven Years, in seven Chambers, with a Command to write seven ample Commentaries on this comprehensive Dis-course. I shall venture to affirm, that whatever Difference may be found in their several Conjectures, they will be all, without the least Distortion, manifestly deducible from the Text. (*PW* I: 117–18)

A Tale of a Tub is in its physical presentation a satire on the then current state of bookmaking. Its virgin reader is faced with an initial catalogue of treatises by the same author even before he or she has had an opportunity to savor this one. There follows an "Apology" that seems to be largely but not entirely helpful and straightforward, then a postscript to the "Apology" commenting on the appearance of a new set of notes that we are assured are "utterly wrong" (so why include them?) and mystifying the question of au-thorship. The Dedication to Lord Somers is written by someone posing as a bookseller-publisher who does not, it appears, understand simple Latin and whose methods are identifiably those of the hack, dwelling more lovingly on the physical processes and strategies of writing than is at all comfortable. On the other hand, this dedicator seems to score some good points about the rhetoric of current book dedications and brings off a good compliment.

There follows a mysterious statement by the bookseller to the reader further complicating the question of authorship. "The Epistle Dedicatory to his Royal Highness Prince Posterity" makes the point that Posterity will trouble itself very little over most of the literary productions of the current age: and in this brief letter, a swarm of ephemeral, venal, pointless writers buzzes into the reader's ken – though the specific names mentioned, Dryden, Nahum Tate, Dennis, Bentley, Rymer, and Wotton, do not actually fit the generalized picture of the scribbler. When the preface and the tale proper finally get under way, there is a relentless concern with reading strategies: interpretation, allegorizing, the dangers inherent in prying beneath the surface of things, the need to remain superficial, insanity as the consequence of unbalanced reading or interpretation, the respects in which unauthoritative embellishment upon basic and simple tenets can lead to fanaticism – this concern is so extreme and the points are so insistently made, that it has led some readers to the view that Swift's writing has at its core "a question about the very idea of the reading mind as authority."[16] Clive T. Probyn has argued forcefully that Swift's writing is an anticipation of postmodern deconstruction and of the theories of recessive meaning, abdication of authorial and textual intention, and infinitely regressive parody (Probyn prefers the term "palimpsest" because "parody" implies something specified that is parodied) that deconstruction brings in train. Terry Castle has taken a similar line with respect to *Gulliver's Travels*; and under the influence of such charismatic critics, the "postmodern Swift" has been launched.[17] Robert Phiddian's highly nuanced and sensitive account of how Swift's parody works takes full account of the fact that there are actually very many of Swift's works where there is no difficulty at all in seeing beyond the narrator to the historical Swift and to a set of positions that this historical Swift wishes to advance.[18]

A study of Swift's reading, and of Swift reading, finally resolves itself into the study of reading Swift. Not everyone agrees that the processes of reading Swift are quite as vertiginous and endlessly ramificatory as the above descriptions suggest. Some good advice from Claude Rawson on how to read *Gulliver's Travels*: "It is more useful to think not of a continuous shifting persona but of a continuously shifting interaction between the surface voice and at least one other behind it: If you really want to stay more or less on the rails you must concentrate on the point being made, not on who is making it."[19] This advice occurs as the culmination of an important argument that Rawson is making about the nature of the first-person narrator in *Gulliver's Travels*, an argument that brings out more clearly, perhaps, than any discussion of local reading difficulties the full subversive potential of Swift's use of inherited forms. It is usual to find *Gulliver's Travels* included as part of a history of the modern English novel. Rawson contends, however, and I agree with him, that it is "neither 'modern' nor...a novel...I think it a fair guess that Swift wouldn't be too hospitable to the idea that his book resembled, or would be included in collections with, *Robinson Crusoe*, or *Pamela*, or *Tristram Shandy*."[20] Rawson's analysis shows that Gulliver's voices, in their changes and counterchanges, "are those of an authorial irony, not of a novelistic character or narrator. And the irony demands, not that the reader should be wholly captured by the illusion (as might be the case either in a novel, or in a hoax), but that he should be aware that irony is in fact taking place."[21] In neither the *Tale* nor *Gulliver's Travels* are there the narrative techniques or the ideological commitments that went into the furthering of the novelistic project in eighteenth-century writing. In both, indeed, there are sustained parodies of those techniques and commitments. Swift sensed instinctively the cooperation of new amatory-realistic fiction with progressive crosscurrents of "modern" thinking that he feared and despised. He had read Defoe, but he did not want him on his shelves.

NOTES

1. T. S. Eliot, "Tradition and the Individual Talent" (1919), in *Selected Essays* (London: Faber and Faber, 1972), p. 14.
2. This was first printed by Thomas Sheridan in his *Life of Swift* (London: 1784).
3. John Kenyon, *The History Men: the Historical Profession in England since the Renaissance*, 2nd edn. (London: Weidenfeld and Nicolson, 1993), pp. 34–40, especially p. 40.
4. Heinz J. Vienken, "Jonathan Swift's Library, his Reading, and his Critics," in Christopher Fox and Brenda Tooley (eds.) *Walking Naboth's Vineyard: New Studies of Swift* (Notre Dame, IN: University of Notre Dame Press, 1995), pp. 154–63, especially p. 154.
5. *Memoirs of Laetitia Pilkington*, ed. A. C. Elias, Jr. (1748–54), 2 vols. (Athens and London: University of Georgia Press, 1998), vol. I, p. 55.
6. *Ibid.*, vol. II, p. 435.
7. A selection of the annotations to Swift's copy of Baronius are printed in *PW* XIV: 16–35. My example is cited on p. 34.
8. Frederick G. and Anne G. Ribble, *Fielding's Library: an Annotated Catalogue* (Charlottesville: Bibliographical Society of the University of Virginia, 1996), p. xxxiii.
9. The marginal glosses to Cherbury are printed in *PW* V: 247–51.
10. Henry Fielding, *Amelia*, ed. Martin C. Battestin (Oxford and Middletown, CT: Clarendon Press and Wesleyan University Press, 1967–83), p. 256.
11. *The Correspondence of Alexander Pope*, ed. George Sherburn, 5 vols. (Oxford: Clarendon Press, 1956), vol. III, p. 29.
12. Pope writes this in the introductory "Letter to Mrs. Arabella Fermor" that precedes the 1714 version of *The Rape of the Lock*.
13. Vienken, "Jonathan Swift's Library," p. 159.

14. See A. C. Elias, Jr., "Swift's *Don Quixote*, Dunkin's *Virgil Travesty*, and Other New Intelligence: John Lyons' 'Materials for a Life of Dr. Swift,'1765," *Swift Studies* 13 (1998), 27–104.

15. Brendan O'Hehir, "The Meaning of Swift's 'Description of a City Shower,'" *English Literary History* 27 (1960), 194–207, reprinted in David M. Vieth (ed.) *Essential Articles for the Study of Jonathan Swift's Poetry* (Hamden, CT: Archon, 1984), pp. 107–21; Roger Savage, "Swift's Fallen City: A Description of the Morning," in Brian Vickers (ed.) *The World of Jonathan Swift: Essays for the Tercentenary* (Cambridge, MA: Harvard University Press, 1968), pp. 171–94, especially p. 187.

16. Clive T. Probyn, "Swift and Typographic Man: Foul Papers, Modern Criticism, and Irish Dissenters," in Richard Rodino and Hermann J. Real (eds.) *Reading Swift: Papers from the Second Münster Symposium on Jonathan Swift* (München: Wilhelm Fink, 1993), pp. 25–43, especially p. 29.

17. Terry J. Castle, "Why the Houyhnhnms Don't Write: Swift, Satire and the Fear of the Text," *Essays in Literature* 7 (1980), 31–44.

18. Robert Phiddian, *Swift's Parody* (Cambridge: Cambridge University Press, 1995).

19. Claude J. Rawson, "Gulliver and Others: Reflections on Swift's 'I' Narrators," in Rudolf Freiburg, Arno Löffler and Wolfgang Zach (eds.) *Swift: the Enigmatic Dean: Festschrift for Hermann Josef Real* (Tübingen: Stauffenburg, 1998), pp. 231–46, especially p. 244.

20. *Ibid.*, p. 231.

21. *Ibid.*, p. 236.

5

MARGARET ANNE DOODY

Swift and women

Swift's relationships with women have been subject to comment since his own day, and have evoked speculation and (sometimes) derision among his critics since the days of Lord Orrery. Swift's connections with women are sufficiently complex, and women were his associates in some of the most important ventures of his career.

Early life and family connections

Swift's incomplete autobiography, attempted relatively late in life, indicates what Swift thought of the women in his family. The autobiography is obviously a special sort of document, revealing Swift attempting to create a satisfactory paternal and male line. Swift, who (like David Copperfield) was what we strangely call a "posthumous child," had not known his father, so there is a particular poignancy in this endeavor to create a paternal line and a "Family," beginning with the first sentence "the Family of the Swifts was antient in Yorkshire." Any money often seems to have come – and remained – with the women whom the Swift males married. The man whom Swift terms "The Founder" of the Irish branch of the Swifts married a rich woman "by whom he got a very considerable estate, which however she kept in her own power, I know not by what artifice, and it hath been a continuall tradition in the family that she absolutely disinherited her onely Son Thomas for no greater cause than that of robbing an orchard when he was a boy."[1] To this account, Swift adds one of his odd marginal notes, amplifying the unpleasantness of this heiress: "She was a capricious ill-natured and passionate woman, of which I have been told severall instances." This story begins to sound like *Castle Rackrent*. Later, Thomas Swift married another heiress as Swift recounts; recollecting this lady's portrait in another of his telling side-margin comments, he says she "seems to have a good deal of the Shrew in her Countenance."[2]

The picture of the Swift males that arises from this autobiographical fragment's view is a representation of rather Shandean misfits, powerless against
the formidable control exerted by their disagreeable females. The worst marriage of all would seem to be that of Swift's father and his mother Abigail,
née Erick:

> The marriage was in both sides very indiscreet, for his Wife brought her hus-
> band little or no fortune, and his death happening so suddenly before he could
> make a Sufficient establishment for his family: – And his Son (not then born)
> hath often been heard to say that he felt the consequences of that marriage not
> onely through the whole course of his education but during the greatest part
> of his life.[3]

This account, which indirectly leads us to believe that Jonathan was an
only child, begotten shortly before his father took hasty leave of this world,
completely ignores Swift's older sister, Jane. (Possibly Swift was jealous of
Jane, if only for the simple reason that the sister had been acquainted with
her paternal parent.) In so finely resenting his parents' marriage, and the ill
effects of it on his own life, Swift seems to find an admissible way of wishing
that he had never been born. His mother would seem (by implication) to be
one of the succession of controlling women – plain-featured and shrewish –
who married into the Swift family. Abigail Swift also took control of Swift's
life, primarily by making it happen. One wonders if he ever quite forgave
his mother her original sin of bringing him into the world.

The statement regarding his parents' marriage is immediately followed by
Swift's compressed account of his birth, an account which immediately runs
into the strangest episode in Swift's childhood:

> He was born in Dublin on St. Andrews day, and when he was a year old,
> an event happened to him that seems very unusuall; for his Nurse, who was
> a woman of Whitehaven being under an absolute necessity of seeing one of
> her relations, who was then extremely sick, and from whom she expected a
> Legacy, and being at the same time extremely fond of the infant she stole him
> on Shipboard unknown to his Mother and Uncle, and carryed him with her
> to Whitehaven, where he continued for almost three ['two' crossed out] years.
> For when the matter was discoverd, His Mother sent orders by all means not
> to hazard a Second voyage, till he could be better able to bear it. The Nurse
> was so carefull of him that before he returnd he had learnt to spell, and by the
> time that he was three year old he could read any chapter in the Bible.[4]

The paragraph is even odder in the manuscript than it looks in print (*PW*
v: 192). One can see that Swift forgot to write "born," and had to stick
the word in above the line, so the sentence first began "he was in Dublin
on St. Andrews day" – as if Swift could omit the messy business of being

born altogether and concentrate on Dublin and the male saint whose "day" it was. Swift also makes a shot at putting down a birth year, but scratches it out, in unusual indecisiveness. The episode of the Nurse of Whitehaven introduces us briefly to the only woman spoken of with any affection in this whole truncated autobiographical document; this is also the first time in this document that any of the male–female relationships mentioned have entailed any affectionate feeling, and, aside from the friendship of Dr. South to Thomas Swift's second son (of whom he was an "intimate friend"), it is the sole example of any strong positive emotional connection. The woman of Whitehaven is defended on pragmatic grounds for her decision to go home to Yorkshire – that she was expecting a legacy from the sick man displays her prudence, not a venal nature. Swift is involved in explaining and defending her action, and her action leads to success – the nurture of the Nurse leads to the child learning his letters and being able to read the Bible. This passage is antipathetic to the Freudian reading of the relationship of the male child to civilization. According to Freud, the male child is consoled for his inability to possess the mother by being offered male culture and civilization, abstraction, religion, and literacy. Swift's version of his acculturation links it to the absence of the mother – but to the presence of the mother-substitute, the "nurse" who nurtures civilization and spelling.

When on the other hand Swift enters into his masculine heritage, the patrimony of learning, he represents himself as doing abominably badly, both at the school at Kilkenny where his uncle sent him and a little later at the "University of Dublin" (Trinity College). He claims he was unhappy (even, he implies, cripplingly unhappy) because of his relations' ill treatment of him:

> he was so discouragd and Sunk in his Spirits, that he too much neglected his Academick Studyes, for which he had not great relish by Nature...So that when the time came for taking his degree of Batchelor...he was stopped of his Degree, for Dullnesse and Insufficiency, and at last hardly admitted in a manner little to his Credit, which is called in that College Speciali gratia, And this discreditable mark, as I am told, stands upon record in their College Registry.[5]

This dismal account is, as Irvin Ehrenpreis has shown us, highly exaggerated as far as external facts are concerned.[6] But this account of depression rings true to subjective experience. Swift always had too low an opinion of his innate abilities; some part of him never felt quite worthy of the great masculine heritage of culture and Latinate literacy.

In his mature years, Swift could be furiously antagonistic to anyone whom he judged guilty of betrayal, especially within familial relations. This probably explains the amazingly vituperative tone taken towards the daughter of his distant relative Mrs. Swanton when that widow turned to the Dean for advice as to what to do with her daughter who had fled the parental home, taking her clothes with her. Swift, believing the girl has been enticed by "some beggarly rascal, who would pass for a Gentleman of fortune," advises the mother to cast her off entirely, if the daughter still refuses to come home.

> Let her know, in plain terms, that you will never have the least correspondence with her, and when she is ruined, as will certainly be the case, that you will never see her . . . and if she will run into destruction with her eyes open, against common sense, and the opinion of all rational people, she hath none to blame but her self; And that she must not expect to move your compassion some years hence with the cryes of half a dozen children at your door for want of bread. (C IV: 178–79)

This letter of 1733 shows Swift's more "savage" aspects. The advice to the mother to repeat her entreaties to the girl to come home is sound, but the fantasia of the future starving children is revengeful, novelistic in its style of realism (one wonders if Swift had recently been reading Defoe's *Roxana*, in which the guilty heroine's five children come crying for bread to the door of their relatives when their mother gets rid of them). Here Swift reacts to the motif of betrayal by taking – and even overtaking – the mother's part. He reacts with a certain fear to the dauntless exhibition of sexuality on the part of the disobedient girl who, in going off with her false "Gentleman," shows how easily duty and gratitude can be cast aside. It is strange that Dean Swift as Christian counselor should urge a mother to be the kind of disinheriting shrew he seems to detest among his ancestresses. What is even more surprising is that Swift by 1733 had acted the part of the "beggarly rascal" of a Gentleman more than once. He had enticed three young women to leave their respective mothers and come with him, and in two of these cases he was successful.

The story that Swift told himself about his relationship to the first women in his life is fraught with disappointment, anger, need, and rejection. His mother is in one of the lines of the self-sufficient shrews, a distant and rejecting woman with too much control who did not need him. She never tried to live near him or seemed greatly concerned for his welfare. The adult Swift knew about his mother's poverty, but emotionally she seemed self-sufficient, apparently finding her son superfluous. The unnamed Nurse of Whitehaven offers care and concern. These two female "Characters" emerge in different corners of Swift's writing. In *Gulliver's Travels*, to take probably the most sustained and overt instance, the Empress of Lilliput who objects to the vulgarly physical Gulliver's copious and inappropriate urination is one of Swift's negative "mothers." The Queen of Brobdingnag is a nicer version of a negative mother, large and controlling but not cold – as long as she is entertained by a creature she considers a harmless unimportant toy. The old female horse who arrives late to tea because her husband has happened to pass away – but who is otherwise undisturbed – may be on one hand a Stoic ideal, but on the other she represents a satiric reproach to women who seem to survive their husbands' deaths quite nicely, as Swift's own mother had done, and Temple's sister Lady Giffard, and Mrs Vanhomrigh, among other acquaintances. Gulliver's little nurse Glumdalclitch, on the other hand, seems a meditation, wholly or partly unconscious, upon the Nurse of Whitehaven. There was always an ideal nurse somewhere in the back of Swift's mind. Sometimes he himself takes that role.

Swift's own unusual family situation, his want of money, and his persistent misery in regard to all of his relations make it the more natural that he would regard marriage with extreme caution. In his service as secretary to Sir William Temple, he encountered a substitute father who met some emotional needs while adding to anxieties. In Temple, too, Swift saw as a model a man who was surrounded by bright and interesting women, including his wife Dorothy and his sister Martha, the vivacious widow Lady Giffard. Temple's household included a housekeeper, Mrs. Johnson, and her daughters Ann and Hester ("Hetty"). Hetty was a child of eight years when Swift first arrived; Swift served as her tutor. His later life may have been an effort to recreate to some extent the emotional life of Moor Park, with himself acting the part of the middle-aged man of letters and man of the world as Temple had first seemed to him. Unlike Temple, who still used the language of libertine gallantry and whose own life had not been peculiarly marked by chastity, Swift boasted of his own cold temper, indicating to male friends that he found it relatively easy to master sexual inclination. But these boasts (if one can call them that) or defensive professions of coldness and chastity are inspired by charges of flirtation, and he does seem to have engaged in what looked like flirting (or worse) with two young ladies of Leicester. One of these girls, Elizabeth Jones, was a relative of his mother's. Whenever Jonathan visited his mother in Leicester he seems to have got into trouble by paying too particular or too gallant attentions to a girl. Relatives feared he might throw himself away in a poor marriage, disregarding the opportunities offered by his connection with Temple. Swift in a letter to a friend in early 1692, in reaction to certain rumors about him, is contemptuous of those who have "Ruind their selves" in bad marriages, including those young men who "are too literal in rather marrying than burning & entail misery on

themselves & posterity by an over acting modesty." The young Swift boasts
of his own restraint:

> I confess I have known one or two men of sence enough, who inclined to frolicks
> have marryed & Ruind themselves, out of a maggot; But a thousand Household
> thoughts, w[hi]ch always drive matrimony out of my mind, whenever it chances
> to come there, will I am sure fright me from that, Besides that I am naturaly
> [sic] temperate, and never engaged in the contrary, which usually produces
> those effects.

While denying carnal connection he registers contempt for the gossips:

> I shoud not have behavd my self after the manner I did in Leicester if I had not
> valued my own entertainment beyond the obloquy of a parcel of very wretched
> fools which I solemnly pronounce the inhabitants of Leicester to be.
> (Letter to Revd. John Kendall, February 11, 1691/1692, CW 1: 4–5)[7]

Swift is consistent in entertaining a dislike of marriage, of associating it –
even among his own ancestry – with "ruin" and unhappiness. Yet he could
never do without women's society. As a young man Swift may well have
seemed to "wretched fools" the accomplished flirt or designing scapegrace
that he thought he was not. His relationships with women in his mature years
(relationships which have puzzled many observers of his life) are always
and even primarily variations on friendship – whatever else they may be.
That Swift actually could consider women as friends, however, marks him
as unusual for his time (and even, to some extent, for ours). Although there
are a number of digs at women's physicality and sexuality in his work, there
are fewer than we would expect from a major satirist. He rarely tackles the
easier targets of the anti-feminist satiric tradition. Not woman's physical
nature but her capacity to be heartless and unsympathetic is what arouses
his rage. Yet, at times at least, he is also willing to estimate the extent to
which women's conduct is the result of masculine cultural prescription. He
is capable of odd sympathies.

All his life, Swift was to make friends with women, and he valued the
social pleasure afforded by the company of women. This value shows itself
early, in his friendship with Lady Elisabeth, daughter of the Earl and Count-
ess of Berkeley, in whose household Swift served as chaplain. The jocular
Lady Betty (fifteen years old when she knew him) exchanged puns and jokes
with Swift, and remained fond of him. They renewed acquaintance later in
London, when she was Lady Betty Germain, and Swift wrote a brilliant light
poem in praise of Lady Betty's companion Biddy Floyd. Female friendships
tend to win his support. Swift had evidently helped young Lady Betty at a
difficult time, when her young sister Penelope died in 1699. Later, in 1733,

Lady Betty paid for a monument to this deceased sister, which Swift installed in St. Patrick's Cathedral with an inscription written by himself. Swift also knew Anne Finch (Lady Winchilsea); his poem "Apollo Outwitted" (*Poems* 100–02) is in comic praise of her.

Perhaps Swift appreciated female society all the more because it dispensed him from the usual heavy drinking associated with male bonhomie, a masculine activity for which Swift seems to have had no taste at any time in his life. His addiction was to coffee. Not only do we modern readers associate Swift with women and coffee taken together, we can see that he does so too. He bought his cousin Patty Rolt a coffee roaster costing three shillings in May 1709, as noted in his accounts (*E* 1: 303). Laetitia Pilkington gives us a comic view of Dean Swift making coffee for her:

> the Dean set about making the Coffee; but the Fire scorching his Hand, he called to me to reach him his Glove, and changing the Coffee-pot to his Left-hand, held out the Right one, ordered me to put the Glove on it, which accordingly I did; when taking up part of his Gown to fan himself with, and acting the character of a prudish Lady, he said, "Well, I do not know what to think; women may be honest that do such Things, but, for my part, I never could bear to touch any Man's Flesh – except my Husband's, whom perhaps, says he, she wished at the Devil.".[8]

Swift associates sexual jest with the coffee, at the same time enjoying and playing with his travesty role as the coffee-maker and, as it were, hostess of the moment, developing that role into the "prudish Lady" in a transitory but surprising riff.

Since the eighteenth century, references to drinking coffee in Swift's letters to "Vanessa" have been seen (rightly, in my view) as a code phrase for having sexual intercourse, but such interpretation can be repudiated, as it has been by some editors and biographers, precisely because Swift obviously did so often enjoy coffee and conversation with an attractive or interesting woman. Such moments may have allowed him to bring out the "feminine" side of himself.

Varina and Stella

The big and by now unavoidable questions regarding Swift and women have all had to do with his sexual life – or lack of it. He proposed marriage early in life, perhaps in a desperate half-effort to establish a home for himself and some security. The courtship (if it can be called that) of Jane Waring took place when Swift was isolated and unhappy in Kilroot, looking after what was really a set of badly-off parishes in a bleak country, largely populated by Dissenters, on the shore of Belfast Lough. Jane and her recently widowed mother seem to have been living in Belfast at the time. Jane was refreshingly Anglican, the daughter of a clergyman, the former Archdeacon of Dromore. With Jane, Swift could enjoy a style of conversation at a far remove from the boorishness and hostility that seemed to surround him in Presbyterian Kilroot. Jane was an attractive young woman in delicate health. Ehrenpreis acutely notes that Jane "became the first of the three frail, fatherless, first-born young women to whom he successively attached himself" (*E* 1: 165). Swift, who had a habit of altering language and presenting nicknames, called Jane "Varina" in a twist on "Waring"; the new nickname also puns with "Verena" meaning "truth." Swift's proposal to Varina was contingent on the demand that she agree to forsake her mother, of whom Swift disapproved morally – or perhaps socially.

Swift himself never seems to have gone wife-hunting in higher or at least wealthier classes, although this course was open to many an ambitious young man. Varina had attracted him during his dismal time in the north of Ireland, but that was before his return to England and his renewed and mature friendship with Esther Johnson. When in 1700 Varina tried to revive the relationship and get him to come to the point of marrying, he was able to evade her. Varina had after all pleaded earlier against marriage, citing her poor health and his low income. Neither of these factors had altered, as Swift reminded her in a forceful and somewhat cruel letter. He also challenged her with her fitness to be the ideal wife, of a meek sort as defined by the conduct books:

> Have you such an inclination to my person and humour, as to comply with my desires and way of living, and endeavour to make us both as happy as you can? Will you be ready to engage in those methods I shall direct for the improvement of your mind, so as to make us entertaining company for each other, without being miserable when we are neither visiting nor visited? Can you bend your love and esteem and indifference to others the same way as I do mine? . . . Have you so much good-nature as to endeavor by soft words to smooth any rugged humour occasioned by the cross accidents of life? . . . These are the questions I have always resolved to propose to her with whom I meant to pass my life; and whenever you can heartily answer them in the affirmative, I shall be blessed to have you in my arms, without regarding whether your person be beautiful, or your fortune large. Cleanliness in the first, and competency in the other, is all I look for.   (Letter to Miss Jane Waring, May 4, 1700, *CW* 1: 35–36)[9]

The demands he places on Varina as a wife are not unreasonable according the standards of the day, but to put them so baldly, so briskly, and in such an uncompromising, rapid-fire manner seems like a deliberate attempt to elicit the answer "No." The ending is even more directly insulting. If she is good enough to be meek and docile and keep clean, he will overlook the fact that she not only brings no dowry but also lacks beauty. Swift could rightly calculate that no woman of any wit or wisdom could accept such a proposal; at the same time, he is virtuously free of the charge of jilting her. We can believe his other statement to Varina, "neither had I ever thoughts of being married to any other person but yourself" (CW I: 33). The thought of marriage seems to have given Swift severe qualms. It is not sexuality that disgusts him so much, but, rather, marriage in itself, coupledom, the designed production of children, mechanical and enforced and inescapable intimacy. Swift always associates marriage with loss – including his own parents' marriage, which had better not have happened. Apparently, marriage is in Swift's eyes a sort of vampirish exchange, as heterosexual liaisons are in Henry James' *The Sacred Fount*. Marriage diminishes and exhausts one or the other member of the dismal partnership. His father died of it. Either he will kill the delicate Varina or she will stifle him. Beneath the cruelty of this letter to Varina one can sense a rising panic, an effort to ward off disaster. The disaster that Swift obscurely feared could not be averted by choosing to marry a beautiful woman with money. It could be averted by engaging in a close association with a woman that did not entail marriage.

When Swift undertook the post of secretary to Sir William Temple at Moor Park, he had met young Esther (or Hester) "Hetty" Johnson, whose widowed mother was a protégée of Temple. In 1699 Temple died. In 1701 Swift was again in England, and again met with Miss Johnson, who was now in the service of Lady Giffard, though still in company with her mother and her old friend, the unmarried Rebecca Dingley. Ehrenpreis thinks that Swift schemed to get Hester Johnson to go back to Dublin to live (in effect though not overtly) with him, and that he came to England with this idea in mind, though he admits Swift represents matters otherwise (E II: 66). Swift himself stresses that he advised Hester Johnson to make the move for financial reasons – he rationally pointed out that Hester's meager inheritance would not go far in England and would allow a much higher standard of living in Ireland, where rents were low and interest rates high. Sir William Temple had left Hester Johnson a lease of lands in Morristown, in County Wicklow, so in making the move she could be closer to the Irish source of income (JS I: 74). It is evident from his own account books that Swift himself contributed fifty pounds a year towards Hester's support – no small matter in those early years when his own income was not large. To assume, as Ehrenpreis does, a sexual relationship already consummated, and deep-laid plans made as early as 1699, is to assume too much. Ehrenpreis is on more solid ground when he points out that in the cases of all three of the young women with whom he was to be closely connected (Jane Waring, or "Varina"; Hester Johnson, or

"Stella"; and Esther Vanhomrigh, or "Vanessa"), Swift made it a condition
of receiving their affection that the woman separate herself from her mother
(E II: 66–67). The deficiencies Swift suspected, perhaps unjustly, in Mrs.
Waring seem to have been moral. Hester Johnson's mother Bridget was thoroughly respectable, but her origins were low, and her status (as a housekeeper) not high. (Her name also sounds suspiciously Roman Catholic.)
Hester – witty, good-looking, conversible, and intelligent – would seem of
higher rank if her mother were absent. So Swift at age thirty-four was able
to persuade Hester Johnson, who was only twenty, to come to Dublin. Or
perhaps she persuaded him that she and Rebecca should go to be with him.
Swift and Hester were never to live together, and the *convenances* were preserved by the constant presence of Rebecca Dingley, who appears in history
as Hester Johnson's dependent, and served as her "humble companion," as
that age termed such a role. Rebecca was a relative of Sir William Temple but
had no means of her own; her only inheritance from her father amounted
to fourteen pounds a year. Rebecca was not good-looking and not particularly gifted; Deane Swift said she was about fifteen years older than Hester
(around Swift's age, in fact) (JS I: xxvii). To be getting on in years, plain,
respectable, and poor – these are not splendid qualities in a woman but they
are very good in a companion for a young woman, what Thackeray's Becky
Sharp calls "a sheep-dog."[10] But Rebecca Dingley has been seen largely from
a conventional masculine view according to which the real and only "love
affair" (of whatever sort) is between Stella and Swift, with Rebecca serving only as a docile veiling. It may be that the three-cornered relationship
was considerably more complicated than that. Jonathan Swift himself does
not describe the relationship of Rebecca and Hester as one of servitude or
necessity but as a matter of choice on Stella's part. She contracted an intimate friendship with another lady of more advanced years. Hester Johnson
may well have found real pleasures and solid satisfactions in her "intimate
friendship" with the devoted Rebecca that were just as important to her as
(though different from) the pleasures and satisfactions of her relationship
with Swift.

Certainly, without the presence of Rebecca Dingley, who supplied re-
spectability and reputation to the ménage in Ireland, the new arrangement
would not have been possible. Swift may still have thought, as he did in
Leicester, that he "valued his own entertainment beyond the obloquy of a
parcel of very wretched fools" (CW I: 4–5), but prudence demanded care
for his own reputation and Hester's. This time he outfaced the gossips with
unusual care. Swift was anxious to have it believed that he never saw Hester
without a third party being present, and that he never saw Hester in the
early morning "except once or twice in a journey." He was also very open

about the fact that there *was* a constant friendship between himself and Hester Johnson, and in the main his stratagems for making Dublin swallow this unusual arrangement was largely – not entirely – effective. (There was, however, more gossip than Swift himself realized and even he had to recognize that one report was circulating according to which a particular little boy was the offspring of himself and Hester. After Vanessa's death there were anonymous printed scurrilous reports of the relations between Dean Swift and both Hester Vanhomrigh and Esther Johnson.)[11] Esther Johnson was received by Dublin society, including Anglican clerical society, and was often invited to parties and visits. In writing his letters to Esther, Swift communicated officially with both herself and Rebecca alike. Even the "little language," the baby-talk he invented for their informal conversation, included the oft-used term for both, "MD" [my dears], and he addresses the two women alike in terms such as "little dears," "young women," "sirrahs." Swift kept in constant touch when he was absent from Dublin, and the *Journal to Stella*, letters from the period of his longest absence from Hester since she had come to Ireland, is the result. This work is invaluable to us as a picture of Swift's life and personality, as well as of English and Irish politics in the heyday of the Tories under Queen Anne during 1711–12.

The letters in the *Journal to Stella* show how much of Swift's serious and playful thought was elicited by Esther, and how much her presence meant to his mind. It is transparent to the reader (who was never meant to come into the picture as a fourth party, although Rebecca was always to make a third) that – despite the official double addressee – the letters are truly addressed to Esther. Swift has given her the magical and romantic name of Stella, arising out of the resemblance of the words Hester or Esther to the Greek *aster* (star) and the English "star." A star is beautiful and distant, unavailable, as inaccessible to love as a "bright particular star" in the firmament, as Shakespeare's Helena says of Bertram in *All's Well*.[12] "Stella," the Latin word for "star," is also the name under which Sir Philip Sidney disguises the identity of his beloved in the famous sonnet cycle *Astrophil and Stella* – "Star-Lover" and "Star." Swift (who comically names himself "Presto") is both comic clown and romantic lover, fated poet and dreamer, like his romantic Elizabethan predecessor. Some elements of Elizabethan poetry are to be found in Swift's poems, transmogrified by context but not ruined. The phrase "the Angel-Inn" which supplies the central image and the central conceit of one of the very best of Swift's poems, "Stella's Birth-Day 1721," has an Elizabethan ring which helps to convince us of the possible idea of sustainable and enduring richness and beauty, even though Stella's face, like a real inn sign, is growing more worn with age:

Now, this is Stella's Case in Fact;
An Angel's Face, a little crack't;
(Could Poets or could Painters fix
How Angels look at thirty six)
This drew us in at first to find
In such a Form an Angel's Mind.

(P 734–35, lines 15–20)

The clichéd comparison of a beloved woman with an angel is transformed by the intermediate and material image of the hospitable inn and its very physical sign. The inn itself is active, not passive, it gives energetically in its hospitality, and is not a silent lodestone for praise.

In Swift's poems to Stella, the elements of the love language and its own comic awareness of its own absurdity – already found in Philip Sidney – are shrewdly mixed with Swift's own humor, mock-self-idolizing pseudo-flippancy – an art partly borrowed from the mob of gentlemen who wrote with ease, the Cavalier poets of Charles II's time. This apparently artless art accompanies and even enables a personalized plain language that can convey the material reality and day-to-nature of a deep affection. Swift's poems to Stella deserve credit as original love poems, a literary kind in which the eighteenth century is hardly rich. They are new inventions in the poetic language of love.

The letters that we know as the *Journal to Stella* show us that the conversation between Swift-Presto and Esther-Stella is an intimate conversation, despite the constant official presence of Rebecca as a third party. Swift expresses to Hester some of his deeper and less categorizable feelings, his unconscious or subconscious self, with an intimacy in which self-consciousness is not really an issue:

Morning. Morrow, little dears. O, faith, I have been dreaming; I was to be put in prison, I don't know why, and I was so afraid of a black dungeon; and then all I had been enquiring yesterday of Sir Andrew Fountain's sickness I thought was of poor Stella. The worst of dreams is, that one wakes just in the humour they leave one.

(JS 1: 152)

In this 1711 entry his own anxiety about himself, his feelings of loss and entrapment, can be alluded to by his giving an account of his dream (a very feminine thing to do), and he himself catches his own anxiety and decodes it as focusing not on Sir Andrew, nor even on both of the two women he officially addresses, but on Stella herself. That he has a friend dying makes him fear to lose her. So he works more visibly and energetically at the game of turning absence into presence:

[Anthony Henley] desired lord Herbert to tell me, I was a Beast for ever after the order of Melchisedec. Did you ever read the Scripture? It is only changing the word *Priest* to *Beast*. – I think I am bewitched to write so much in a morning to you, little MD. Let me go, will you? And I'll come again to night in a fine clean sheet of paper; but I can nor will stay no longer now; no, I won't, for all your wheedling: no, no, look off, don't smile at me and say, pray, pray, Presto, write a little more. Ah! you're a wheedling slut, you be so. (*JS* 1: 152)

Here the addressee is obviously singular, and "MD" becomes singular also, matching "wheedling slut." There are two levels of play here, one the simple conjuration of absence into presence, and the other creating a present scene of sexual suggestiveness. A promise to come again in the evening "in a fine clean sheet" is usually a promise of something more carnal than an epistle, and Swift has just been talking about the way the London people are using puns these days. Is he going to be less of a Priest and more of a Beast? There is no need for definition in these epistles, both deliberately and unconsciously (so it would seem) playful and multiplex. Does such suggestive intimacy denote a foregone conclusion? Even in his playful suggestive moments, however, Swift is playing games of infinite deferral. Intimacy means that nothing precise has to happen, or happen precisely on schedule. He could probably relax with Stella because he knew that no further demands on him would be forthcoming – and knew that the other intimacy between the addressee and second party of "MD" would take care of any feelings that might otherwise turn in his direction and entrap him.

Whether it is necessary to fathom the exact nature of relationships between other people, or inspect the sheets to see if there are signs of intercourse, is arguably both rude and unnecessary. Yet so much ink has been spilt on Swift's relations with women that anyone tackling the subject is really required to come down on some side of the question. It is my belief that the relationship between Stella and Swift was deep and included strong sexual feelings but that it was never physically consummated. Letters, puns, etc. were safety-valves for Swift's sexuality which was to be directed to this odd version of a neo-Platonic relationship that would give each of them the autonomy that he or she so craved. The plot of marriage is for Swift a story of loss and entrapment. He was so fond of Stella that it may well have seemed unthinkable to put both her reputation and her health into the danger of pregnancy – and in the eighteenth century, practically bereft of contraception, pregnancy would have been a likely outcome with a female partner as young as Stella was at the outset of her life in Dublin. Stella's pregnancy would have blown up Swift's reputation and allowed scandalized enemies to get him removed from the cathedral and possibly even from the clergy (as he had no powerful backers). This does not mean, however, that the relationship in intensity, complexity, and emotional satisfactions did not seem to both parties as strong as what we usually mean by "an affair" – and a good deal more lasting than most. Swift supplied the masculine element in Stella's life and she supplied the feminine in his, but they were both free to adopt other elements, Stella being more "masculine" in wit and judgment and her own desire for autonomy, Swift allowed to be more "feminine" in confession of fears and dreams and absurdity.

Swift also is permitted in such a relationship to indulge what might be called the "motherly" part of himself. He not only flirts with Stella, he fathers her (in offering her good advice, masculine reading, etc.). And he mothers her too – in care for her health, in offering nurture. Swift often saw himself as a kind of mother; in a letter to his cousin he compares his fondness for his own writings to the Aesopic baboon who gloats over the beauty of her children.

> I have a sort of vanity, or Foibles, I do not know what to call it...that I am overfond of my own writings...I find when I writt what pleases me I am Cowley to my self and can read it a hundred times over...I know farther, that I am wholly in the wrong, but have the same pretence the Baboon had to praise her Children, and indeed I think the love in both is much alike, and their being our own offspring is what makes me such a blokhead [sic].
>
> (Letter to Thomas Swift, May 3, 1692, CW I: 110)

This allusive self-image links up interestingly with the portrait of the monkey in Book II of *Gulliver's Travels*, the pet beast who picks Gulliver up and tries to feed him. That story in turn seems related to a legend that Swift knew:

> John Fitz-Thomas, afterwards Earl of Kildare, then an infant, was in the Castle...when there was an alarm of fire. In the confusion...the child was forgotten, and when the servants returned to search for him, the room in which he lay was found in ruins. Soon after a strange noise was heard on one of the towers, and on looking up they saw an ape which was usually kept chained, carefully holding the child in his arms. The Earl afterwards, in gratitude for his preservation, adopted a monkey for his crest, and supporters, and some of his descendants, in memory of it, have the additional motto of "Non immemor beneficii."[13]

The author, Charles William Fitzgerald, Duke of Leinster, includes a variant version of this story, now related to the ancestors of the Earls of Desmond, in which the ape is more mischievous, though this "tame baboon or ape" responds to the loneliness of the newly orphaned infant, after its father is killed in battle, by carrying it around the battlements and bringing it back in safety.[14] The author firmly substantiates the Kildare legend as Swift's source: "When Dean Swift was writing 'Gulliver's Travels', he had quarrelled with the Earl of Kildare, and in order to vex him, introduced into his story the part in which his hero is carried off and fed by the Brobdinagian [*sic*] ape."[15] In both these monkey stories, the baboon or ape is replacing an absent parent, and seems to act chiefly the mother's part, in compensation for loss of attendants or paternal parent. In the first story, which includes the alarm of fire (how like Lilliput!), the monkey as adoptive parent acts the kind of rescuing role that was congenial to Swift's own notion of his relation to other people – more especially people of the opposite sex.

There is a monkey-mother in Swift – parodied by himself later in *Gulliver's Travels*, Book II, when the gigantic monkey tries to adopt Gulliver and feed him. Stella, like Swift's writings, is his monkey-daughter – or son. She can be daughter, son, parent, friend, even *princesse lointaine*, and yet again almost part of his flesh – but never mistress or wife. Swift took some sort of vow to himself never to marry, and obviously kept it, though that caused him some difficulty. He had no mental model for himself married, just as he had literally no visible model of a parental marriage, not even a bad marriage. The story that Swift and Stella married on her deathbed may be true, but it has never been perfectly authenticated. It has been suggested that Swift and Stella could not consummate their love because of the bar against incest – as Swift believed both he and Stella were really the progeny of Sir William Temple – but that seems mere romancing on the part of Prince Posterity.

Vanessa

In the winter of 1707 Swift went to England. Hester Johnson and Rebecca Dingley came to London as well (it was to be their last expedition to their native land), but they returned sometime in 1708. At this time Swift evidently either made or confirmed the friendship with the Vanhomrigh family, whom he probably had known in Dublin. That family consisted of Mrs. Vanhomrigh and her four children. Mrs Vanhomrigh was a widow. Her husband, a Dutch immigrant who had died in 1703, had been a commissary for the Williamite army in Ireland, and a rich man; he had become Lord Mayor of Dublin. The Vanhomrigh widow had money and spent it; in London Mrs. Vanhomrigh took an attractive lodging near St. James' Square. The family had many attractions, not least the beauty and taste of their eldest daughter Hester, whom Swift first called by the babyish name of "Mishessy." Swift in his letters frequently speaks of going to play cards at "Mrs. Van's." In 1709, when he was back in Ireland, Mishessy wrote to him. Swift represents his first interest in the girl as paternal and tutorial; he advised her what to read, talked to her, and told her to take care of her health. To the half-orphaned young woman he was – perhaps – a substitute parent. But it is more likely that

"Mishessy," however young, did not think of him that way; twenty-year-old Hester Vanhomrigh and forty-one-year-old Swift seemed to be forming a friendship and a connection not to be categorized by the common rules of packs of idiots. In *Cadenus and Vanessa* Swift makes Cadenus (or *Decanus*, the Dean) teach the girl that inner virtue makes one secure against all foes, that one can be good without conforming:

> That common Forms were not design'd
> Directors to a noble Mind. (*P* 706)[16]

At first at least, Swift was doubtless pleased to have someone else on whom to exercise his monkey-mother talents, someone to eat an orange with, and scold gently for her lack of exercise. But something else was going on, which Swift could not ignore. He consciously began to drop out from his letters to Stella references to going to Mrs. Van's, even though, as biographers note, the other evidence such as the diary notes in his account books show that he went to the Vanhomrighs very frequently. Swift has lost the upper hand in the relationship with Hessy Vanhomrigh – she writes him worrying about *his* health, turning the tables. On leaving England, Swift had tried to shake off thoughts of Vanessa, but on his return in 1710 they became much closer, even as the Vanhomrigh family fortunes were declining. Vanessa-Hessy (now twenty-three years old) was much more likely to be certain of what she wanted. On evidence provided by Swift himself, she would invite him alone into her bedroom. It seems safest to say that she wanted him and that he wanted her in the same way – but not at the outset. His own youthful determined abstention from full sexual activity may have given Swift an overabundance of confidence in his virtue, and thus in his ability to engage in questionable experiments with both himself and Vanessa.

But it may be more truly said that these were experiments that both parties wished to perpetrate, and their experiments, however crude, belong also in the history of our endeavor to create equal rights for women, our long and still incomplete experiment to see how and in what ways members of the two (there are supposedly only two) sexes may live and work together and appreciate each other without making the relationship gel into the old connection of man and wife or the official comic liaison of man and mistress. Both of these latter connections were decidedly unfavorable to the woman in Swift's day – and not much better in our own. (The flood of ridicule and vituperation aimed at Monica Lewinsky in the late 1990s was equal to anything that eighteenth-century scurrility could produce.) How could Swift consummate a relationship with a young woman whom he admired? In (probably) 1713, Swift wrote *Cadenus and Vanessa*, a poem dealing with this question, a comic-serious work in praise of a woman – a new style of heroic epistle and mock-Ovidian narrative. Venus creates a perfectly intelligent, beautiful, and virtuous woman to answer the men's complaints that women of their day are inferior. The fact that men – and their female peers – cannot appreciate Venus' grand achievement turns the tables against the males, but leaves the beautiful heroine at a loss:

> Both Sexes, arm'd with Guilt and Spite,
> Against *Vanessa*'s Pow'r unite;
> To copy her, few Nymphs aspir'd;
> Her Virtues fewer Swains admir'd:
> So Stars beyond a certain Height
> Give Mortals neither Heat nor Light.
> (lines 438–43)

Vanessa, like Stella, is a Star, above the reach of mortals, and thus doomed to solitude unless like a goddess herself she take refreshment in an odd and unequal union. Vanessa, finding no kindred spirits among her male contemporaries, turns to Cadenus (anagram of *Decanus* or Dean), despite his age and awkwardness and general unfitness for the amatory role. She is the victim of Cupid who shoots her while she is reading Cadenus' "Poetick Works." The author has the success a poet of love-elegies might dream of, arousing a beautiful girl even though his own poems are not poems of passion, and her passion is unexpected and even unwelcome. He enjoys the role of tutor that she gives him and is slow to see the danger. She attributes, he believes, "Imaginary Charms" to the aging man of forty-four. His endeavors to undeceive her and to break off are argued down by the young woman herself, who becomes in turn "The Tutor; and the Pupil, he" (line 807). It is the lady who takes the lead in urging that their union become sexual. Cadenus pleads that Friendship is the highest type of love, and thus she should be content with that. But the ending is deliberately and tantalizingly unclear. Who won?

> But what Success *Vanessa* met,
> Is to the World a Secret yet:
> Whether the Nymph, to please her Swain,
> Talks in a high Romantick Strain;
> Or whether he at last descends
> To like with less Seraphick Ends;
> Or, to compound the Business, whether
> They temper Love and Books together;
> Must never to Mankind be told,
> Nor shall the conscious Muse unfold.
> (lines 818–27)

The conscious Muse did eventually unfold the story, however, in releasing before the end of the century some of the letters between Swift and Hester Vanhomrigh. Mankind was curious to hear more about the business at the time, particularly once Hester Vanhomrigh with her sister Mary (Moll or "Molkin") moved to Ireland. Hester ran away from her mother to be with Swift, a lot like the disobedient girl of whom Swift the Dean so heartily disapproved, the girl who ran away from her mother with a "rascal" in 1733. Hester took a house (perhaps inherited) at Celbridge, about eleven miles outside of Dublin. Swift warned her that if she came they could not often be in each other's company:

> If you are in Ireld while I am there I shall see you very seldom. It is not a Place for any Freedom, but where every thing is known in a Week, and magnifyed a hundred Degrees. These are rigorous Laws that must be passed through: but it is probable we may meet in London in Winter, or if not, leave all to Fate, that seldom cares to humor our Inclinations.
>
> (Letter to Esther Vanhomrigh, August 12, 1714, C II: 123)

Swift conducted the relationship with a caution that makes him seem harsh and mean – probably did so to himself, even as it did to Hester, who had to struggle on largely alone through her sister's decline and sudden death and her own worsening health. Yet the letters, however enigmatic in some respects, are undeniably the letters between lovers who have consummated their relationship. Hester had got under Swift's skin, she had made him descend from the "Seraphick" and had moved through his defenses with her dedicated persistence – a little like Joy Davidman with C. S. Lewis. Horace Walpole was the first outside reader to crack the code of "drinking coffee", upon reading Swift's *Letters* in Hawkesworth's edition: "I think it plain he lay with her...you will see very plainly what he means by coffee.".[17] Harold Williams, mid-twentieth-century editor of Swift's letters, is as horrified as Elrington Ball, an earlier twentieth-century editor of Swift's correspondence, and cries out against Walpole's "sinister interpretation" (C II: 351, note 3) – but, however crude Walpole may seem, he was perfectly right. Swift and Hester Vanhomrigh did not, however, enjoy many meetings, even in the warmest heyday of their love, 1720–21 (interestingly, the very period which elicits one of Swift's best birthday poems to Stella, the "Angel-Inn" piece). It seems likely that Swift and Esther Vanhomrigh combined pleasures by drinking coffee together at intervals during long afternoons in bed, making up for lost time with endearments and recreation. The couple had to be content with long intervals without this release and pleasure: "the best Maxim I know in this life is, to drink your Coffee when you can, and when you cannot, to be easy without it...thus much I sympathize with you that

I am not chearfull [*sic*] enough to write, for I believe Coffee once a week is necessary to that" (Swift to Hester Vanhomrigh, July 13, 1722, C II: 430). If all that Swift wanted in order to feel cheerful was a drink made of roasted Arabian beans, that had always been available more than once a week; it is something more important that will not be available even once a week.

To be on coffee-drinking terms with a woman was always to Swift a sign of relaxation, of restful and playful coming home. Reading these letters – which, unlike the *Journal to Stella* were never meant for a third party – one can even find oneself imagining what Swift was like in bed, a rude imagining at which moral consciousness may well revolt. Swift, like Abelard, can carry an erotic charge. Like Abelard he also has that gift of memory which means much to a woman: Swift offers a catalogues of *topoi* sacred to their love that he urges Vanessa to recall:

> What would you give to have the History of Cad – and – exactly written through all its steps from the beginning to this time...It ought to be an exact Chronicle of 12 Years; from the time of spilling the Coffee to drinking of Coffee, from Dunstable to Dublin with every single passage since. There would be the chapter of the Blister, the Chaptr [*sic*] of Madm [*sic*] going to Kensington... the Chaptr [*sic*] of the Wedding with the Adventure of the lost Key. Of the Strain, of the joyfull Return two hundred Chapters of madness. The Chaptr of long walks. The Berkshire Surprise. Fifty Chapters of little Times: The Chaptr of Chelsea...The Chaptr of hide, and whisper. (August 12, 1720, C II: 356)

No wonder this letter made Esther happy:

> you make me happy beyond expression...it would be to [*sic*] much to once to hope for such a history if you had laid a thousand pound that I should not understand your letter you had lost it tell me sincerely did those curcumstances [*sic*] crowd on you or did you recolect [*sic*] them only to make me happy [?].
> (C II: 357)

They understood each other's codes too well for either to fear – or hope – that the other did not understand. Swift always lived a life of secrecy and codes where love was concerned. Hester Vanhomrigh died, in Ireland in 1723, young and alone. Swift's sorrow goes unrecorded. But it is possible that the loss of one beloved gave Swift an extra impetus towards recklessness, which allowed him to dare the government in writing *The Drapier's Letters* in 1724. Perhaps a certain despair gave him renewed personal courage, so that he did not care too much if he went to prison, or even if he were executed. Swift received new powers of audacity and even of vision which led him through *The Drapier's Letters* to the world-vision of *Gulliver's Travels*. And in his most famous book, Gulliver, the repressed and wilfully "virtuous," is a parody of Swift's virtuous persona.

Swift and women writers

Swift did not escape gossip about his liaisons, real or supposed, during his own lifetime. But neither did he escape censure for his friendships with women in general. The list of female friends and associates should include such talented aristocrats as Mary Pendarves (née Granville) an animated correspondent who was to marry Swift's friend Patrick Delany; her friend Anne Donellan; and the unhappy Frances Kelly, whose interesting mixture of unhappy home life, beauty, and a fatal complaint may have aroused in Swift in 1733 some reminiscence of the feelings he had ten years earlier felt for Vanessa.[18]

John Boyle, Earl of Orrery in his *Remarks on the Life and Writings of Dr. Jonathan Swift* (1752) remarks with fascinated hostility on Swift's friendships with women:

> You see the command which SWIFT had over all his females; and you would have smiled to have found his house a constant seraglio of very virtuous women, who attended him from morning to night, with an obedience, an awe, and an assiduity, that are seldom paid to the richest, or the most powerful lovers; no, not even to the grand Seignior himself.[19]

On this companionship, "these foolishly-trusted women," Orrery chooses to blame Swift's publication of "many pieces, which ought never to have been delivered to the press": "He communicated every composition as soon as finished, to his female senate."[20] Swift was in effect too fond of women, not misogynistic enough. With something like envy, Orrery notes his attractiveness to women even when he is not offering them the inducement of sexual pleasure – though Orrery has to sexualize the Addisonian "little senate" into a sexual enclosure, a paradoxical "seraglio."

Orrery does not refer to the parallel influence of Swift upon the women. The noble lord seems determined to ignore the fact that Swift's "female senate" or seraglio was composed largely of writers. It is not the least surprising aspect of Swift that he actively encouraged a number of women to write. He not only encouraged Mary Barber (1690–1757) but introduced her to the public, when he wrote the dedicatory epistle prefixed to her *Poems on Several Occasions* (London, 1734). When she was hard up, Swift not only donated money directly but also offered the manuscript of *Polite Conversation* with full rights of publication for her own benefit. Mary Barber's own poems show the influence of Swift, in their playfulness, their adoption of "low" circumstances and moments for important and teasing sayings, as when she ridicules male costume as tyrannical and damaging.[21] Barber's contempt for authority and custom, including public English and masculine custom, evidently appeals to Swift, as does her power to satirize:

> They [Barber's poems] generally contain something new and useful, tending to the Reproof of some Vice or Folly . . . She never writes on a Subject with general unconnected Topicks, but always with a Scheme and Method driving to some particular End; wherein many Writers in Verse, and of some Distinction, are so often known to fail. In short, she seemeth to have a true poetical Genius.[22]

Like other women writers of the period, Barber seems to have found in Swift's own verse style a valuable model. Most English poets, including Pope, employed the large and serious iambic pentameter which was the standard English line for serious verse. Swift in the main prefers iambic tetrameter, the short impish line, which perfectly suits the adoption of a colloquial manner, and is itself a statement of lack of pretension. The rhymed iambic pentameter assumes a public ideal, a public language, and a public self. Women writers of this period cannot adopt that kind of public persona, because they really know that they do not have a public persona at all. They have to start with the private self and invent a public voice. Swift's kind of quick, colloquial, impudent rhyming flies into our ears, as it were, as a kind of heckling of the grand tradition and the public male persona – we hear the sound of an interjection from an unexpected and unwelcome quarter. Women writers, especially poets, knew themselves to be always officially unexpected and unwelcome – they had to find a means of expression reflecting the impudence and "sass" that it took to speak at all. Swift offered all these usable qualities, and gave them a practical model for their own tough impishness.

At the same time, Swift himself is an artist in describing the commonplace domestic sphere – he can make much of making butter or going to the privy. And he presents himself as odd – even as comical, as he certainly does in *Cadenus and Vanessa*, in which the aging and ungraceful Decanus is also embarrassed, the comic object of desire rather than in the usual male position of the active desiring subject looking at an object. And Swift is most unusual in presenting in the figure of "Vanessa" a woman who is attractive because of her intellectual gifts, rather than in spite of them. That fact was not lost on other women writers, as indeed it has not been lost on women of our own time. Female critics have been perhaps surprisingly sympathetic to Swift. Ellen Pollak observes that he could find no ending to *Cadenus and Vanessa* because his culture allowed for no female types save for docile or shrewish wives, longing old maids, and frivolous or foolish whores – none of which seemed to have anything to do with Esther Vanhomrigh or his view of her.

Pollak asks "how could he pay tribute to a woman within the confines of a language and a logic by whose terms she was either fallen or unloved?"[23] That Swift's portrait of an able and lively woman was sufficiently distressing in itself is visible in Orrery's peevish comments. All Orrery wants to see in Vanessa is a frivolous and foolish female: "Vanity makes terrible devastation in a female breast. It batters down all restraints of modesty... VANESSA was excessively vain."[24]

Swift, unlike Orrery, does not try to shut women up. It is then not so surprising that a little group of Irish women writers formed an important part of Swift's personal circle. All the members of Swift's seraglio of writing women, including Mary Davys, Laetitia Pilkington, Constantia Grierson, and Mary Barber, identified themselves as Irish, and felt a certain kind of Irish patriotism, for which Swift was a rallying point. Patriot women in times of crisis get more license to speak out, and Swift – especially the later Swift of *The Drapier's Letters* and after – was an admirable representation of speaking up. All of these women might be described as "self-made." Even if married, they usually had to work at some point in their lives to earn a living. They were "low" in birth and underbred and terrifically energetic and ambitious. They are an unusual group, energetic, self-reliant and witty. Swift's influence can be seen in the writings of all of these, and in the works of other women.[25] He fell out with both Lady Mary Wortley Montagu and Laetitia Pilkington (for very different reasons), but in their skilled adventurous and comic verse they show what they have learned from him. Swift's influence extended to writers best known for prose works. He is an influence on Hester Thrale, both in verse and prose. Frances Burney's verse squibs show that she knows Swift's verse, and a conversation with Samuel Crisp in 1774 about a mock book of etiquette shows how well she has absorbed *Polite Conversation*. "'I intend to Dedicate it to Miss Notable,' answered I."[26]

Swift is one of the partners taken in by the women writers when they wish to censure the false idealization of women, the demand that a romantic life should exist apart from the physical; he shares their suspicion that women are being socially used. Swift attracts because he does not ignore dirt, even the dirt of the kitchen and the mop and the outhouse, and because there is the insistent, unmarmoreal, perishing physicality which alone (so Swift seems to think) engages and ensures the reality of affections.

An investigation of the facts dispels notions we might pick up from Lord Orrery or Middleton Murry that Swift is deeply offensive and must be abhorrent to women.[27] Feminist women, and women writers of all sorts, have almost always found him helpful, and even likeable, as is seen in Erica Jong's presentation of Swift in her novel *Fanny*.[28] A writer like Orrery may disgust us, because he writes of women as if they were not quite real. It is that unreality that Swift dismisses so energetically. Women are not goddesses or angels, nor inferior beasts – they are human beings living in bodies in space and undergoing like the men the ravages and opportunities of time. We always catch Swift in the flow of time, reacting to a particular situation, day, or event.

Everything that Swift did in relation to women and nearly everything that he said to or of them can be used to make him appear a failure. He is always engaged in living, seldom heading for the dry uplands of abstraction. Jonathan Swift was evasive and prickly, perhaps cold and unreasonable in some ways, but he really was an adventurer in human relations, and a comic hero of love – in contrast to his comic Gulliver, who not only shows himself inexpert at human relations, as Swift often was, but also dodges human relations in a way that Swift finally does not. Swift is really on the side of the angels in whom he does not quite believe.

NOTES

1. Trinity College Library MS 1050, 2–3. I am grateful to the Librarian of Trinity College manuscript collection for allowing me to look at this manuscript. A version of it with the title *Family of Swift* appears in *PW* v: 187–195.
2. Trinity College Library MS 1050, 2, 3.
3. *Ibid.*, 3.
4. *Ibid.*, 3–4.
5. *Ibid.*, 15.
6. For comments regarding Swift's progress and grades at college, see *E* I: 57–62, 279–83, 284–85.
7. When complete, Woolley's edition will be a source superior to Ball's or Williams'. For one thing, he is more faithful to Swift's actual orthography. Traditionally, editors of great men's letters have cleaned up the writing of the male heroes, while leaving their female correspondents' letters in their raw imperfection, thus often creating or endorsing a greater educational and cultural gap than was truly the case.
8. Laetitia Pilkington, *Memoirs of Mrs. Laetitia Pilkington...Written by Herself. Wherein are occasionally interspersed, All her Poems; with Anecdotes of several eminent Persons*, 3 vols. (Dublin and London, 1749–54; Garland reprint, New York and London, 1975), vol. I, pp. 50–51.
9. All editors of this letter have to rely on the printed version of 1768. Woolley comments: "So far as it is possible to tell, Jane Waring's moment of decision had come and gone in 1696" (*CW* I: 143, note 4).
10. "'Rawdon,' said Becky...'I must have a sheep-dog...I mean a moral shepherd's dog...A dog to keep the wolves off me...A companion.'" See William Makepeace Thackeray, *Vanity Fair* (Harmondsworth: Penguin Books, 1987), pp. 444–45.

11. A pamphlet makes "Polidore" (Swift) an habitual lecher, a rake : "*Polidore . . .* was from his Youth amorously inclined; never with less than two Intrigues upon his Hands." See *Some Memoirs of the Amours and Intrigues of a Certain Irish Dean*, 3rd edn. (London 1730), p. 2. In his self-exculpatory Preface to the Reader, the author of this squib takes a tone of chaste rebuke:

> It's true he was a Man of Gallantry, and so are some of our best _____.
> My Design is only to caution Ladies who may meet with Persons of the
> same Disposition as this gay Man, to take care how they proceed, tho' the
> Person has a Black Garment for his Protection. But I shall enlarge further
> on this Subject in the following Sheets, and shall only leave them to guess
> at the person who bears the chief Part there, by bidding 'em think of V——
> in a celebrated Poem: Every Body who ever heard the Character of the
> Dean, will not be surpris'd to find him seldom with less than two or three
> Intrigues at a Time . . .   (A3v–A4r)

12. "'Twere all one / That I should love a bright particular star / And think to wed it, he is so above me. / In his bright radiance and collateral light / Must I be comforted, not in his sphere": see Helena's soliloquy in *All's Well that Ends Well*, I. i. 87–91 in *Oxford Shakespeare*, ed. Susan Snyder (Oxford: Clarendon Press, 1993), p. 83.

13. Charles William Fitzgerald, Duke of Leinster, *The Earls of Kildare and their Ancestors: From 1057 to 1773* (Dublin: Hodges, Smith & Co., 1857), p. 20.

14. "Thomas Fitz Maurice was only nine months old when his father and grandfather were slain at the battle of Culian, in 1261. The child was at Tralee, and on his attendants rushing out alarmed at the intelligence, he was left alone in his cradle, when a tame baboon or ape took him up in his arms and ran with him to the tops of the tower of the neighboring Abbey. After carrying him round the battlements and exhibiting him to the frightened spectators, he brought the infant back to its cradle in safety. Thomas was, in consequence, surnamed 'An Apagh' (in Irish) . . . or 'The Ape.' He, however, was ancestor to the Earls of Desmond." See *The Earls of Kikdare*, p. 21.

15. *Ibid.*

16. *Cadenus and Vanessa* was first published in 1726, three years after Esther Vanhomrigh's death, and then was more formally presented in *Miscellanies. The Last Volume* (1727). The date of 1713 is educated guesswork, if practically universally agreed upon. Swift did not publish the poem in Vanessa's lifetime, and it could be asked if he showed good taste, kindness to the dead, or good judgment in publishing the poem in his own lifetime.

17. "There is one to his Miss Van Homrigh, from which I think it plain he lay with her, notwithstanding his supposed incapacity, yet not doing much honour to that capacity, for he says he can drink coffee but once a week, and I think you will see very clearly what he means by coffee." See *Correspondence of Horace Walpole*, ed. W. S. Lewis (New Haven and London: Yale University Press, 1941), vol. x, pp. 218–19. Walpole, the staunch Whig, dislikes Swift, the Tory who was so disrespectful of Sir Robert Walpole, and "Horry" does everything he can to diminish him; here he certainly misreads in asserting that Swift could only perform sexually once a week, whereas what Swift is saying is that sex at least once a week is necessary to sustain cheerfulness – and laments that he thus cannot

be cheerful at present. One can see that Swift's long attempt at sexual abstention had led to unfriendly rumors about his "capacity"; it was persistent madness on his part to suppose that there was any way of escaping scandal.

18. As Williams notes, Mary Pendarves thought Miss Kelly had outdistanced herself in winning Swift's heart : "I have given up the trial with Kelly; her beauty and assiduity have distanced me...At present she is disabled, poor thing...but the Dean attends her bedside: his heart must be old and cold indeed, if that did not conquer" (C IV: 155–56).

19. John Boyle, Earl of Orrery, *Remarks on the Life and Writings of Dr. Jonathan Swift. In a Series of Letters*, 3rd edn. (London, 1752), p. 83.

20. *Ibid.*

21. See Mary Barber, "Written for my Son, and Spoken by him at his first putting on Breeches," in *Poems on Several Occasions* (London, 1734), pp. 13–16.

22. Barber, *Poems on Several Occasions*, pp. vi–vii.

23. Ellen Pollak, *The Poetics of Sexual Myth: Gender and Ideology in the Verse of Swift and Pope* (Chicago and London: University of Chicago Press, 1985), p. 151.

24. Orrery, *Remarks*, p. 70.

25. I am here repeating an argument made in an earlier article, "Swift among the Women," *Yearbook of English Studies*, 18 (1988), 68–92.

26. *The Early Journals and Letters of Fanny Burney*, ed. Lars Troide (Oxford: Clarendon Press, 1990), vol. II, p. 49. Also see *The Early Diary of Fanny Burney*, ed. Annie Raine Ellis (London, 1907), vol. I, pp. 324–26.

27. John Middleton Murry is especially disturbed by the excremental poems: "Nevertheless, it is not his direct obsession with ordure which is the chief cause of the nausea he arouses. It is the strange and disquieting combination of his horror at the fact of human evacuation with a peculiar physical loathing of women... [Swift's] animus against women became more and more disproportioned, vituperative and shrill." See Murry, *Jonathan Swift*, reprint (London, 1954), p. 439, p. 441.

28. "Just as I had rever'd Mr. Pope for his Poetical Works so 'twas the Reverse with Dean Swift: my Admiration grew, first from my knowing him, then from the Splendour of his works...he was a slighted Lover of Mankind, one who lov'd not wisely but too well." See *Fanny, being The True History of the Adventures of Fanny Hackabout-Jones* (New York: Signet, 1981), pp. 228, 235.

6

MICHAEL F. SUAREZ, S.J.

Swift's satire and parody

The key concept for understanding Swift's satire is not a rhetorical precept about persona, but a deeply held principle about what it means, in Swift's view, to be a person. For Swift, language, religion, and politics are not strictly divisible, but are all inextricably linked as integral parts of human endeavor. The serious business of Swiftian satire is that it invites (or provokes) the reader to be critical: that is, to judge. Most often, the judgments that Swift's satires ask us to make go well beyond straightforward condemnation of the work's obvious target; rather, we are led to form a series of deeper judgments about language, religion, and politics, and about the operations of human vice and virtue that govern these activities in others and in ourselves.[1] The comic exuberance and imaginative plentitude that often characterize Swift's satirical writings should not blind us to the fact that Swift, though never moralistic, is a relentlessly moral writer. Even when being self-denigrating about its aesthetic qualities, Swift himself is adamant about the purpose of his work: "I have been only a Man of Rhimes, and that upon Trifles," he writes, "yet never any without a moral View" (C IV: 52). This "moral view" pervading Swift's writings in both poetry and prose is not about adherence to a set of pious ordinances, but is deeply concerned with how people act as linguistic, religious, and political beings.

This chapter is divided into five parts. The first identifies wisdom and critical discernment as the allied goals of Swift's satires, and reflects on the potentially problematic nature of the author's own pronouncements about his role as a satirist. The second section identifies two kinds of parody – what Swift calls "transplanting" and "personation" – and considers both as integral parts of his satirical program. Continuing this theme, part three demonstrates how Swift employs negative examples – often by means of parody – rather than positive precepts, as his principal didactic method. Part four is an extended discussion of a single satire, highlighting the importance of language and the relationship between satiric parody and the fictions he creates. Finally, a brief coda returns to the moral purpose of Swiftian satire as equipping its readers to see through the world's deceits.

"There are two Ends that Men propose in writing Satyr," observes Swift in *The Intelligencer* (1728), "private Satisfaction" and "a *publick Spirit*, prompting Men of *Genius* and Virtue, to mend the World as far as they are able." Taking up the first of these two motives for satire, he ironically defends the satirist's right to censure corruption: "I demand whether I have not as good a Title to Laugh, as Men have to be Ridiculous, and to expose Vice, as another hath to be Vicious." Moving to the second of the "two Ends," he comments, "But if my Design be to make Mankind better, then I think it is my Duty" (*PW* XII: 34). Writing four years later, Swift advocates a similarly two-fold purpose of satirical writing in his correspondence: "You see *Pope, Gay*, and I use all our Endeavours to make folks Merry and wise" (*C* IV: 53). Although Swift's formula is a commonplace of his day, it is nevertheless not amiss to ask ourselves, what is this wisdom that is the fruit of Swiftian satire? Does it not go beyond assenting to Swift's particular identifications of viciousness and folly? Does it not mean learning to read the world so that one knows how properly to discriminate, how to judge what is worthy of praise and what is deserving of blame?

A particularly instructive example of Swift's pedagogical ambitions may be found in *An Epistle to a Lady* (1733, also sometimes known simply as *To a Lady*). Much of this long poem is Swift's version of the classical *recusatio* (or "refusal"), a Hellenistic trope – enthusiastically adopted by Horace, Propertius, Virgil, and other Roman authors – in which the poet declines to commemorate a patron or public figure in a lofty manner. Swift's persona questions the "Lady" who has asked him for a panegyric, "Would you have me change my style?" and mockingly suggests that he could "Quote you texts from Plutarch's *Morals*; / Or from Solomon produce / Maxims teaching wisdom's use" (*Poems* 521). Instead, satire – even the gentle kind reserved for friends (what he called "raillery") – is Swift's true *métier*.[2] At the end of the poem – after sharply satirizing Walpole, the court, and even the king – he explains to the woman (Lady Acheson) that he would like his art to

> Make you able upon sight
> To decide of wrong and right;
> Talk with sense whate'er you please on;
> Learn to relish truth and reason.

If she would only allow the critique of his satire to enter and warm the torpor of her "frigid brain," then "we both should gain our prize: / I to laugh, and you grow wise" (*Poems* 521–52).

Wisdom, fostered by satire's stimulation of critical awareness, is the gift that Swift would most wish his readers to receive. Such wisdom includes the ready discrimination of bad from good, the ability to think and to use language well, and the intellectual maturity that delights in genuine understanding. As the poet himself indicates, this gift must come from the dynamic of satire, rather than from maxims, no matter how sagacious the authors who formulated them. His art will, he hopes, "Give your head some gentle raps; / Only [to] make it smart a while" (*Poems* 521). It certainly seems probable that Swift, an inveterate lover of puns (*PW* IV: 205–10, 231–39, 257–66, 271–75; E I: 40–41; E II: 189–91, 447; E III: 125), was playing on two senses of "smart" that were current in his day, signifying both "hurt" and "intelligent" or "adept." By means of this word-play, he underscores the notion that satire, for all its comic laughter, must lead us to the painful knowledge of the world's falsity and of our own shortcomings.

Swift's surviving remarks about the nature and purpose of satire are unsystematic, fragmentary, and frequently subject to misinterpretation because articulated by a persona or taken out of context.[3] Readers have often failed to notice, for example, that in many of his statements on satire Swift closely follows Horace, who always made it a point to show that he did not take either himself or his vocation too seriously. For example, Horace dismissively claims that his satirical versifying is merely an avocation akin to the way other men take up boxing, or riding horses, or even heavy drinking.[4] In addition, students of Swift would do well to consider that the Dean's observations about the satirist's intentions, frustrations, and the apparent futility of his endeavors come from a sworn enemy of positivism and pride (*PW* I: 1, 6, 10, 29–32, [140], 151; *PW* III: 141; *PW* IV: 243; *PW* XI: 5–8, 339, 342; *PW* XII: 23–25, 33–35; C III: 102–03, 117–18; *Poems* 419, 493, 497, 518–21). His comment to Charles Ford, "I have finished my Travells . . . they are admirable Things, and will wonderfully mend the World," exhibits an appropriate sense of accomplishment tempered by the ironic pragmatism so characteristic of his world-view (C III: 87).

Similarly, Gulliver's ironic indignation in his letter to his cousin Sympson, "instead of seeing a full Stop put to all Abuses and Corruptions . . . Behold, after above six Months Warning, I cannot learn that my Book hath produced one single Effect according to mine Intentions," not only manifests the protagonist's false perceptions and distorted self-regard, but also reflects Swift's realistic understanding of satire's limits (*PW* XI: xxxiv). Moreover, his repeated strategy of predicting that even the lash of satire will not effect desperately necessary reforms is not only a humility *topos* to be expected from the satirist (e.g. Persius, Juvenal), it is also an ultimate indictment, implying that one's adversaries are so depraved as to be incapable of amendment.

We are indeed fortunate that Swift persisted as a satirical writer, even as his declarations about the satirist's calling and the effectiveness of his works were much less optimistic and self-important than those of Dryden, Pope, and many of his other contemporaries.[5]

In Swift's satirical writings, there is a dual movement which is at once destructive and constructive. Much attention has been paid to the destructive element, to attacks on the "targets" of the satires – Grub Street hacks, Whig politicians, absentee landlords, greedy projectors, malevolent clerics, etc. – but not enough thinking has been done about the constructive elements that are present even in the darkest Swiftian satires. Often, the positive dimension of a satirical work is rather simplistically treated as the intended reform of the person or persons being ridiculed, but Swift, ever the moral realist, does not appear to have entertained serious expectations of producing genuine amendment in those whom he directly assailed in his satirical writings. (*The Drapier's Letters* [1724–25], in contrast, is a result-oriented polemic intermittently employing satirical stratagems, rather than a sustained work of satire.) Writing in *The Examiner* for April 26, 1711 (No. 38), Swift suggests that the idea of satire shaming the guilty into reform "may be little regarded by such hardened and abandoned Natures as I have to deal with." Accordingly, he directs his attention to those who could be harmed by the reprobate: "but, next to taming or binding a Savage-Animal," he continues, "the best Service you can do the Neighborhood, is to give them warning, either to arm themselves, or not come in its Way" (*PW* III: 141). The purpose of satire for Swift, then, is less the reformation of the target, who is typically too foregone or ill-disposed for amendment, and more about the moral education of the reader.

The satirical program of *A Tale of a Tub* (published in 1704), for example, extends far beyond the rather simple tasks of ridiculing Wotton or exploiting simplistic notions about the follies of modernity. The *Tale* is a deliberately complex and nuanced document that makes considerable demands upon its readers, inviting them to a process of discovery – both in the ordinary meaning of the word and in its forensic sense of a sifting through the evidence provided by one's adversary. The relationships of the individual parts to the whole must be carefully weighed, the various arguments analyzed, and the parodies examined. In the midst of much laughter, the work must be deciphered by means of the careful scrutiny of textual particulars. The *Tale* enacts the complexities of the reader's confrontation with modernity in order to foster the very kinds of discernment that such an encounter demands. For all the negativity of Swiftian satire, these works require a positive act of critical perception, a genuine discovery, if they are to be adequately understood.

The constructive content of the satires, therefore, is not directed towards Swift's "villains," but towards his audience. (As we have observed in *An*

Epistle to a Lady, however, Swift's use of "raillery," a form of mild satirical exhortation through playful ridicule, comic banter, and friendly teasing, is an important exception to this truth.) *A Modest Proposal* (1729), for example, could hardly be an attempt to reform either projectors or landlords; rather, Swift is boldly striving to expose a pervasive and dehumanizing instrumentality, to change the way his readers think about Ireland and its people. Yet, readers of the satires will readily perceive that the positive content in the form of moral precepts, sagacious adages, or even urgent admonitions is almost completely absent from these works. Instead, the constructive element in Swift's satirical writings is the active fostering of moral discernment, leading readers to develop their critical acumen about the workings of vice and folly – venality, ignorance, vanity, pride, dereliction of duty – in others as well as in ourselves. Swift refuses to offer any overarching textual authority in his satires because such a presence would forestall the kind of moral discrimination that these writings are meant to set in motion. A persistent goal of the satires, then, is to educate our capacity for critical reflection on the human condition and, hence, to enlarge our capacity for humanity.

Swift is commonly recognized as one of the greatest writers of Menippean satire, a form named after Menippus of Gadara (3rd century BC), which emphasizes combining parody with satire and mixing together several different kinds of discourse in a single work. True to the inheritance he received from Menippus and his successors (among them: Varo, Seneca, Lucian, Petronius, More, Erasmus, and Rabelais), Swift's satires are typically vigorous literary hybrids produced by juxtaposing and combining multiple discursive forms.[6] Satiric parody, the appropriation of another's discourse to generate ridicule, usually works in one of two ways: either by transposition of the source-text into the new work to alter its original meaning, or by close imitation which exaggerates those features of the source-text most worthy of censure.[7] Swift himself regularly employs these two parodic techniques; not surprisingly, he calls the reader's attention to both methods in *A Tale of a Tub*. Writing in the persona of a literary hack, Swift satirizes the alleged cleverness of his ideological enemies by observing the transience of their wit and its susceptibility to parody. The hack writer notes how easy it is to "injure...Authors by transplanting." He asserts that "nothing is so very tender as a Modern piece of Wit...which is apt to suffer so much in the Carriage" and "which, by the smallest Transposal or Misapplication, is utterly annihilated" (*PW* I: 26). Swift's satires are replete with parodic "transplantings," "carriages," and "transposals" which recontextualize their source-texts in order to expose them to ridicule. Although the *Tale* and *Gulliver* furnish the richest fund of this kind of parody, *Verses on the Death of Dr. Swift* provides a remarkable example which we will examine below in some detail.

Swift also calls attention to his most common form of parody: close imitation to expose aspects of the text and its maker to ridicule. In the "Apology" he added to the fifth edition of a *Tale* in 1710, he offers the following observation: "*There is one Thing which the judicious Reader cannot but have observed, that some of those Passages in this Discourse, which appear most liable to Objection are what they call Parodies, where the Author personates the Style and Manner of other Writers, whom he has a mind to expose.*" (*PW* 1: 3). Later in the same work, Swift also adds a footnote: "Here the Author seems to personate *L'Estrange, Dryden*, and some others, who after having past their Lives in Vices, Faction, and Falsehood, have the Impudence to talk of Merit and Innocence and Sufferings" (*PW* 1: 42). Emphasizing that parody is akin to mimicry or impersonation, Swift acknowledges that "Style and Manner" are vital aspects of his art. Yet, as the second passage clearly shows, Swift's agenda of satiric exposure is by no means restricted to superficial blemishes or stylistic eccentricities, but rather is directed at what he regards as substantial shortcomings in the authors' characters and in the substance of their thought.

Parody and emulation, highly characteristic modes of eighteenth-century writing, are both forms of evaluative appropriation: emulation is an act of homage, and satiric parody, as its reverse is a strategy of disparagement. In both cases, the transformed source-text is exhibited as an example for the reader's aesthetic and ethical consideration, but in parody this display provides a *negative* example, a making explicit of what is defective in the original work. Thus, parody functions as a form of demonstration that is not refutable by ordinary kinds of argument, an exhibition or conspicuous display, a parading of what is degenerate or inane. Emulation communicates the strength, worth, virtue, and power (in Latin, *virtus*) of the text. Conversely, parody flaunts the work's deformity, faultiness, corruption, and defectiveness (in Latin, *vitium*). Of course, these terms are not merely linguistic, stylistic, or literary; they are also inescapably ethical because the social exchanges that reading and writing necessarily entail are vital to the responsible conduct both of our interior and of our public lives. In Swift's world-view, "virtue" and "vice" can never be exclusively textual or solely aesthetic.

Parody exposes habits both of language and of mind; it is almost never merely about style, but rather seeks to reveal the underlying errors and defects in what is seemingly sensible. Accordingly, in Swift's parody, rhetorical, literary, political, religious, and philosophical conventions and presuppositions are laid bare; this anatomizing strips the parodied work and the mind that created it of any claims to being worthy of approbation. Swift's parodies

typically lead the reader to perceive the prideful systematizing, the dangerous absolutism, the logical flaws, and the damaging misperceptions of his
adversaries. Thus, parody acts not merely as a criticism of particular forms
of discourse, but as a critique of the attitudes and subject positions that
generate and relish such discursive forms.

Remarkably, Swift uses parody not only to assail others, but also to implicate himself in his satires.[8] Perhaps the most well-known example is the
self-mockery found in *Verses on the Death of Dr. Swift* when the persona
claims about the Dean, "But what he writ was all his own" (*Poems* 493, line
318). Swift stole this line almost verbatim from Sir John Denham's poem,
On Mr. Abraham Cowley (1667); "what [Swift] writ" was therefore most
certainly not "all his own." Recontextualizing Denham's tribute by inserting
it into his own writing and, thus, radically altering its meaning is a miniature and magnificent instance of Swiftian parody. Swift's ploy is both comic
and clever, but it is much more. His parodic "transplanting" of Denham's
line ("Yet what he wrote was all his own") also calls into question the authority and the reliability both of the persona and of the poet himself as he
self-consciously stages his own death and ironically orchestrates the varying
fortunes of his posthumous reputation. The appropriation of a line about
originality and its transposition into this context ingeniously parodies the
very idea that any author could write what was "all his own," and thus may
be understood as ridiculing Denham.

Sir John had appeared earlier in Swift's career as a character in the culture
wars he satirically depicted in *The Battle of the Books* (comp. 1697; pub.
1704); "a stout *Modern*," Denham was slain by a spear-wielding Homer,
the venerable general of the Ancients' cavalry (*PW* 1: 157). Swift, who hated
the "Modern" notion that an author's productions need not benefit from the
great writings of the "Antients," insisted that broad humanistic learning was
essential for a writer; his own satires, with their multiple parodies, are mas-
terworks of intertextuality and testify to the extent of his reading. In addition, Swift's satiric parody may also be aimed at Dryden, whom Swift seems
to have held in perpetual contempt. The second book of Dryden's famous
translation of the *Aeneid* includes a line that *he* took word-for-word from
Denham (2.763). Swift's theft from Denham thus recalls Dryden's act of bla-
tant arrogation, ironically aligning Swift and Dryden as fellow "thieves" and
confirming the absurdity of Denham's notions about originality and literary
invention. Moreover, the issues that Swift's parody ingeniously raises about
the possibility of writing what is entirely one's own are delightfully complicated still further by a darker aspect of Sir John's literary career. Because
Denham's writings were so uneven in quality, several of his contemporaries
accused the wealthy poet of having bought his most famous works from

other authors, a charge that Swift maliciously refers to in a footnote he wrote for the *Battle* (*PW* I: 157).[9]

Swift's seemingly simple parodic gesture in *Verses on the Death of Dr. Swift* clearly operates on a variety of levels: he uses parody to cast doubt upon the several layers of discourse in his valedictory poem, to ridicule ideas of authorial independence and "pure" originality, and to mock one of his own most characteristic practices as a writer – the miniature parody itself parodies Swift's parodic genius. In addition, because Denham's poem is an elegy for a great poet, Swift's creative theft calls attention to his elegiac enterprise and mischievously raises the possibility that the poet's authorship of his own death song invalidates whatever claims he makes for himself. Because the author uses his textual authority to call into question his own trustworthiness, the reader of the line, "what he writ was all his own," is presented with a dilemma not unlike that of the person who is told by another, "everything I say is a lie." Even in Swift's stanzas on his own demise, then, satiric parody is a source of comic playfulness, forceful irony, and cunning ridicule (directed at others and at himself) – all of which contribute to the effectiveness and the artful appeal of his satire. As this one example may suggest, *Verses on the Death of Dr. Swift*, with its multiple ironies and complex satirical inflections, makes considerable demands upon the critical faculties of its readers. Once again, what Swift's parody requires from its audience is not the mere recognition of a source-text, but a thoroughgoing re-cognition, or re-thinking, of the issues that his parodic appropriation of another's discourse so skillfully raises for our consideration.

Hints towards an Essay on Conversation, which Swift probably composed while working for the Tory ministry in London (1710–14), though not a satire, provides the attentive reader with an important insight into the work-ings of his mind. "Most Things, pursued by Men for the Happiness of publick or private Life," he explains, "our Wit or Folly have so refined, that they sel-dom exist but in Idea," and have become so complicated in the minds of those who think seriously about them, "that for some thousands of Years Men have despaired of reducing their Schemes to Perfection." Cutting through such lofty and unserviceable abstractions, Swift proposes a practical method instead: "it seemeth to me, that the truest Way to understand Conversation, is to know the Faults and Errors to which it is subject, and from thence, every Man to form Maxims to himself whereby it may be regulated" (*PW* IV: 87). Rather than supply a ready-made system of precepts to be observed, he makes the reader mindful of what should be avoided. "[I]t will be nec-essary," Swift continues, "to note those Errors that are obvious, as well as others which are seldomer observed, since there are few so obvious or acknowledged, into which most Men, some Time or other, are not apt to run" (*PW* iv: 88). Once readers have these negative examples before them, Swift affirms, they will be well able to make their own determinations as to how they should conduct themselves. Perceiving what not to do, they will have the understanding necessary to know what they should do without the help of positive rules formulated by an external authority.

Intriguingly, this pattern of enumerating negatives is found in Swift's own guidelines for himself. In a list of resolutions headed "When I come to be old" that the thirty-two-year-old Swift made to direct his future behavior, no fewer than sixteen begin "Not to. . . ." The sole positive provision is, "To desire some good Friends to inform me wch of these Resolutions I break, or neglect, & wherein; and reform accordingly" (*PW* i: [xxxix]). Not surprisingly, Swift's satires repeatedly employ a similar method, using a potent mixture of irony, parody, and comedy to exhibit and ridicule things that are bad as if they were good. False encomiums, spurious rules, mock panegyrics, ignorance masquerading as learning, vanity wearing the false colors of humility, debased particulars displayed as noble universal truths – these are the typical means by which Swift parades a series of "Faults and Errors" before his readers. Almost nowhere in his satires, however, does he establish positive maxims as guides to correct behavior, preferring instead to leave such formulations to his audience. *Directions to Servants in General* (published in 1745), for instance, is full of false counsels which are really instances of what should not be done. The footman, for example, is instructed, "In order to learn the Secrets of other Families, tell your Brethren those of your Master's; thus you will grow a favourite both at home and abroad, and [be] regarded as a Person of Importance" (*PW* xiii: 34). *Polite Conversation*, a work discussed at some length in the fourth part of this chapter, similarly exhibits a series of gross conversational faults and fatuous patterns of mind as the epitome of refinement. Again and again in Swift's writings, the egregious is ironically exhibited as the exemplary.

"Directions for a Birth-day Song" (1729), a satire on the royal birthday odes of the poet laureate, Laurence Eusden, repeats this pattern: Swift enumerates as "the laws of song" those qualities that make the birthday poems at once empty and cloying:

> Thus your encomiums, to be strong,
> Must be applied directly wrong:
> A tyrant for his mercy praise,
> And crown a royal dunce with bays:
> A squinting monkey load with charms;
> And paint a coward fierce in arms.
> (*Poems* 388, 391)

The satire in *Advice to a Parson* (1732) follows much the same pattern; the persona claims that ignorance, insolence, immorality, and flattery are requisite for advancement in the church. Similarly, *On Poetry: A Rapsody* (1733) chronicles the art's debasement and modern impoverishment.

Even in his non-satirical works, Swift typically proceeds by parading negative examples. In *Maxims Controlled* [that is, contradicted] in Ireland," Swift sought to lay out "certain Maxims of State, founded upon long observation and experience, [and] drawn from the constant practice of the wisest nations," only to demonstrate that they did not apply to contemporary Ireland because of its particular political, social, and economic circumstances (*PW* XII: 131). Arguing for the importance of attending to the specific conditions that operate in any given situation, he wrote derisively of the "innumerable errors, committed by crude and short thinkers, who reason upon general topics, without the least allowance for the most important circumstances, which quite alter the nature of the case" (*PW* XII: 131). Although Swift decided, after he had written some 2,000 words, not to publish *Maxims Controlled*, its argument not only underscores his general distrust of aphorisms and precepts, but also highlights his intellectual commitment to the necessity of bringing to the fore and scrutinizing the specific details that have a bearing on "the nature of the case." Obviously, these two aspects of his thought are strongly interrelated and have no small bearing on his practices as a satirical writer.

Spurning generalities, Swift's satire dwells richly in a carefully constructed world of particulars which have two principal imaginative sources: the fictions he creates – most often, a persona writing from a specific perspective and situation – and the parodic treatment of his adversaries' language, practices, and ideas.[10] Working in synergy, Swift's fictions and parodies construct a network of details leading readers to the repeated exercise of their critical judgment. Parody is a central means by which Swift foregrounds the relevant aspects of his adversaries' attitudes and beliefs. It is, moreover, the primary tool he uses to diagnose and display their defectiveness. Recall once again what Swift envisioned would take place in the reader of his catalogue of conversational transgressions: each reader "is to know the Faults and Errors to which [conversation] is subject, and from thence, every Man to form Maxims to himself whereby it may be regulated" (*PW* IV: 87).

Parody is one of the chief means by which Swift sets out his store of carefully chosen negatives so that the reader may, first, identify the errors of mind and morals that produced them and, second, devise his or her own response to what has been anatomized and exposed to ridicule. Occasionally, however, Swift's parodies, like his satiric fictions, take on a life of their own as the exuberance of his inventiveness predominates and vivifies the satire by

\means of an excess which serves no clear instrumental purpose. It is not only in these extreme cases, however, that we should be reminded of a primary function of parody in his writings: it allows Swift – a lover of language who could hear books talking to him (*PW* IV: 253) – to revel in his gift for "personation," to laugh, and to have fun. Readers of Swift's satires should gratefully do the same.

A central reason why parody plays such an important role in Swift's satires is his conviction that both the manner in which we use language and our ability to judge the words of others are vitally important aspects of the moral life. Swift's longstanding commitment to reforming abuses in popular discourse is reflected in a series of publications spanning most of his active years. In his *Tatler* essay for September 28, 1710 (No. 230), Swift assails "the continual Corruption of our *English* Tongue" resulting from "Ignorance" and "false Refinements," pleading instead for "that Simplicity which is the best and truest Ornament of most Things in human Life" (*PW* II: 174, 177). He continues his campaign in *Hints toward an Essay on Conversation* (composed around 1710 and published in 1763), *A Proposal for Correcting... the English Tongue* (1712), and a *Letter to a Young Gentleman, Lately Enter'd into Holy Orders* (1720). His greatest labor in this regard, however, is *A Complete Collection of Genteel and Ingenious Conversation...*, commonly known as *Polite Conversation*. Swift began this satire on the abuse of language and the senselessness of the gentry in 1704 and worked on it intermittently over the course of more than thirty years. Finally published in 1738, it was among the last of his satirical works to appear in print.

Parody is the principal device that drives Swift's satire in the three dialogues on display. Swift's antithetical persona, Simon Wagstaff, has compiled the dialogues to represent his view of all that characterizes truly polite conversation. The reader might therefore reasonably expect to encounter shining examples of wit, tact, restraint, eloquence, and learning, but none of these qualities is present. Instead, each dialogue is a tissue of proverbs, colloquialisms, clichés, and catch-phrases that manifest the superficiality, ignorance, vanity, selfishness, and pride of the interlocutors. The following exchange is typical:

> *Lady Smart* Miss, I hear that you and Lady *Couplers*, are as great as Cup, and Can.
> *Miss Notable* Ay, as great as the Devil, and the Earl of *Kent*.
> *Lady Sm.* Nay, I am told you meet together with as much Love, as there is between the old Cow and the Hay-Stack.
> *Miss.* I own, I love her very well; but there's Difference betwixt staring and stark mad. (*PW* IV: 196)

Swift's parody is remarkable not only for the sheer number of banalities he has managed to string together, but also for the effectiveness of the social satire that it produces. The characters in the dialogues – two lords, two ladies, a knight, a colonel, and a younger unmarried couple – routinely use fashionable slang, mispronounce ordinary words, and proudly report inane remarks that they have made in previous conversations as outstanding instances of wit. At times, Swift's text reveals the speakers to be vulgar and crass. Sir John, for example, explains the custom of hospitality at his estate: "Why, Faith, at *Christmas* we have many Comers and Goers; and they must not be sent away without a Cup of good Christmas Ale, for fear they should p[i]ss behind the Door." Lady Smart replies, "I hear, Sir John has the nicest Garden in England; they say, 'tis kept so clean, that you can't find a place where to spit" (*PW* IV: 185). Decorum and propriety are nowhere in evidence. When offered some cheese, Lady Answerall exclaims, "Lord, Madam, I have fed like a Farmer; I shall grow fat as a Porpoise: I swear, my Jaws are weary with chawing" (*PW* IV: 187).

Such parodic exaggeration highlights the stupidity of talking without thinking, of speaking without having anything to say. By a procession of negative examples, the work comically forces the reader to consider the relationships between language, thought, and manners. The ruling class should provide examples of duty, rectitude, and cultivated civility (for example, Sir William Temple or Lord Cateret), but the dialogues dramatically expose their absence as lords and ladies pass the time in idle chatter and stay until three o'clock in the morning playing cards. Their lives, like their speech, are a sequence of meaningless clichés. As before, Swift provides no precepts for his readers, but leads them to the truth by displaying its opposite. The conversations, though genial, are the fruit of vanity, selfishness, ignorance, and pride rather than of that humane urbanity and consideration which constitute genuine politeness in the upper classes. Like actors on a stage, the characters' pat responses and mindless banter suggest that they live in a simulacrum of reality, a farce in which they are driven by the scripted lines they deliver. Both their speech and their lives are overdetermined by feckless convention. Intellectually and morally vapid, the interlocutors' insistent preoccupation with the superficial gradually reveals them to be people of no substance. Despite their wealth, the linguistic deformity they exhibit manifests the impoverishment of their lives. They are made to look ridiculous because they neither say what they mean nor mean what they say.

The persona who presents these dialogues to us as the epitome of politeness is one "Simon Wagstaff": dissolute, vain, uneducated, profane, interested in fashion and the card table, a self-professed "Modern," and a Whig. Swift's antithesis, Wagstaff speaks approvingly of swearing and gambling, of free-thinking and atheism, of King William III and Bishop Burnet, and of Moderns and Maids of Honour at court. Taking a cue from Pope, Swift has his persona praise such "dunces" as Charles Gildon, Ned Ward, John Dennis, Colly Cibber, and Lewis "Tibbalds," while criticizing Pope, Gay, Arbuthnot, and Edward Young, all of whom were Swift's friends. Wagstaff's smug and self-serving "Introduction to the following Treatise," which is half the length of the "Treatise" itself, repeatedly reveals his lack of judgment about language, politics, religion, and the proper conduct of private and public life. Typically for Swift, these interrelated failings culminate in Wagstaff's revelation of his colossal ignorance about the value of his work and his personal worthiness. Incapable of forming a judicious understanding of himself, he cannot judge the world correctly. In one particularly masterful passage, Wagstaff informs the reader about the honors he presently expects to receive and the prospect of his future glory:

> If my favourable and gentle Readers could possibly conceive the perpetual Watchings, the numberless Toyls, the frequent Risings in the Night, to set down several ingenious Sentences... which, without my utmost Vigilance, had been irrevocably lost for ever: If they would consider, with what incredible Diligence, I daily, and nightly attended, at those Houses where persons... of the most distinguished Merit used to meet, and display their Talents: With what Attention I listened to all their Discourses... I say, if all this were known to the World, I think it would be no great Presumption in me to expect at a proper Juncture, the publick Thanks of both Houses of Paliament, for the Service and Honour I have done to the whole Nation, by my single Pen.
>
> ALTHOUGH I have never once been charged with the least tincture of Vanity... I will venture to say, without Breach of Modesty, that I, who have alone, with this Right Hand, subdued Barbarism, Rudeness, and Rusticity; who have established, and fixed for ever, the whole System of all true Politeness, and Refinement in Conversation; should think my self most inhumanely treated by my countrymen, and would accordingly resent it as the highest Indignity, to be put on the Level, in Point of Fame, in after Ages, with *Charles* XII. late King of *Sweden*.
>
> AND yet, so incurable is the Love of Detraction... that I have been assured... how some of my Enemies have industriously whispered about, that one *Isaac Newton*, an Instrument-Maker... and afterwards a Workman in the Mint... might possibly pretend to vye with me for Fame in future Times.
>
> (*PW* IV: 121–22)

Highly reminiscent of the prefatory matter to *A Tale of a Tub*, written some forty years earlier, Swift's parody of the self-congratulatory authorial introduction reminds the reader that hubris is the epidemic disease of modernity.

As with most of Swift's satires, we must ask ourselves how the fiction of *Polite Conversation* (Wagstaff and his project) is related to the parody or parodies (the dialogues), if we are to take the full measure of its meaning. Wagstaff's failure is one of judgment. His absurdly fulsome self-appraisal reveals not only his presumption and vanity, but also his lack of perspective. Like the interlocutors in the dialogues he records, he is too self-absorbed to perceive the truth about himself or his world. Wagstaff's injudicious appraisal of what is genuinely polite in matters of discourse is of a piece with his approval of atheism, his moral laxity, and his unreflective preoccupation with modern convention. Judgments about language, about religion and politics, and about the worth of one's endeavors cannot be partitioned, Swift's satire insists, because forms of language are inextricably linked to forms of life, and the words one chooses for oneself and approves of in others are necessarily an integral aspect of how one elects to live. The coherence of linguistic parody and social satire in both Wagstaff's "Introduction" and the dialogues together demonstrate that, for Swift, discursive acts – Wagstaff's writing, the gentry's speaking, and our reading – are not merely adjuncts of thought, but rather are themselves essential critical performances among the many judgments that constitute our lives as moral beings.

Parody almost always engenders in the reader a heightened consciousness of language and of the conventions governing its deployment. When, as in the dialogues, the parody is expressly about the everyday forms of language that govern common social interactions – the morning visit, the dinner conversation, and talk over tea – then the effect on the reader's awareness is further intensified. Again using parody to parade the execrable as if it were excellence, Swift raises questions about contemporary notions of politeness, challenges the alleged superiority of the ruling class, and ridicules conversation manuals and other "how-to" books offering shortcuts to genuine cultural attainments. Crucially, he demonstrates not only the close connection between style and manners, but between language and morals.

In addition, Swift surely satirizes himself in his creation of Wagstaff as such an obvious alter-ego, and parodies his own schemes for linguistic reform – especially as advanced in *A Proposal for Correcting . . . the English Tongue* – in his production of a spurious exemplar that will fix "for ever, the whole System of all true Politeness, and Refinement in Conversation" (*PW* IV: 122). Swift was obviously deeply pleased about having finally completed a work he had begun more than thirty years ago. He had struggled over it intermittently and even despaired of ever being able to complete it (*C* III: 219, 293, 439), but eventually he had produced a masterpiece. One way of understanding the excessive claims of Wagstaff, then, is to see them as a comic displacement of Swift's own pride. His parody delights in its own excess as he strings together so many proverbs, catch-phrases, and clichés with admirable facility; like Wagstaff, Swift seems to revel in the fact that he has so seduously recorded them all and finally found a way to put his efforts on display. Although he was among the most rhetorically self-conscious and linguistically judicious writers of his generation, Swift does not fail to implicate himself in the satirical program of *Polite Conversation*. Perhaps he did not let himself escape in the hope that we too might be moved to exercise our capacity for judgment with greater truthfulness – and recognize ourselves in satire's revealing glass.

"I look upon myself, in the capacity of a clergyman," explained Swift, "to be one appointed by Providence for defending a post assigned me, and for gaining over as many enemies as I can" (*PW* IX: 262). Accordingly, Swift wages a satirical campaign against laziness of mind and passive acceptance by repeatedly exposing the implications of his adversaries' writings, attitudes, pronouncements, and policies. Swift's satires are in some senses akin to the coney-catching pamphlets of the sixteenth and seventeenth centuries which – even as they delight in felonious energies – expose crime, reveal a vocabulary of deceit, and alert their readers to the snares awaiting them in the wide world. The coney-catching pamphlets, with their professed purpose of "discovering cozenage" (that is, revealing the deceits of common thieves, crooked gamesters, and smooth-tongued confidence men), both entertained readers and ostensibly equipped them to go about more safely in the midst of villainy. Swift's satires, though they belong to a different rhetorical universe, have an analogous function. One crucial difference, however, is that the coney-catching pamphlets invariably assume that it is always an external force that misleads the victim, whereas Swift's works inevitably are written with an acute awareness that the dupe is perfectly capable of deceiving himself. Although many of Swift's satires are occasional productions written to address specific instances of irresponsibility, ignorance, vanity, or vice, the texts suggest that the deeper problem to be addressed is the gullibility of humankind.

Swift did not live long enough to hear the words of John Philpot Curran's "Speech on the Right of Election of the Lord Mayor of Dublin" (1790), though its most memorable sentence captures the *raison d'être* of his satirical writings: "The condition upon which God hath given liberty to man is eternal vigilance; which condition if he break, servitude is at once the consequence of the crime, and the punishment of his guilt." Swift's satires promote a vigilance against the stratagems of those who would abridge the liberty of living in the truth. Again and again, Swift strives in his satirical writings to help his readers "to arm themselves," to heighten their awareness of the flimflammery that is pandemic in the modern world (*PW* III: 141). Living in the midst of con-men who would gull the public for their own ends – Marlborough, Wotton, Shaftesbury, Hobbes, Walpole, court ladies, advocates of religious enthusiasm, projectors – Swift uses parody to reveal the workings of their confidence games and to establish in his readers a salutary wariness. This is one clergyman who insists that we not take things on faith. (Revelation, belonging to a different order of truth, would constitute an exception for the doctrinally orthodox Swift.) Even commonly held truths, he recognized, were often rooted in partial knowledge and shared misperceptions. Swiftian satire, with its lack of determinate authority and its often multiple ambiguities, attempts to foster critical discernment and to cultivate in its readers the art of disbelief.

NOTES

1. On reader implication in Swift's satires, see Frank Boyle, *Swift as Nemesis* (Stanford, CA: Stanford University Press, 2000).
2. For an excellent discussion of this much misunderstood form, see John M. Bullitt, "Swift's 'Rules of Raillery,'" in Harry Levin (ed.) *Veins of Humor, Harvard English Studies* 3 (Cambridge, MA: Harvard University Press, 1972), pp. 93–108.
3. For a corrective to this last problem, see Philip Harth, "Swift's Self-Image as a Satirist," in Hermann Real and Heinz J. Vienken (eds.) *Proceedings of the First Munster Symposium on Jonathan Swift* (Munich: Wilhelm Fink, 1985), pp. 113–21, which situate Swift's famous letters of September 29 and November 26, 1725 (*C* III: 102–05, 116–19) both as responses to Pope's remarks and as fulfilling traditional rhetorical roles.
4. Horace, *Satires* 2.1, lines 24–29.
5. See P. K. Elkin, *The Augustan Defence of Satire* (Oxford: Clarendon Press, 1973), pp. 71–117 and 185–201.
6. For a useful catalogue of the many kinds of discourse in Swift's most popular work, see Roger Lund, "Parody in *Gulliver's Travels*," in Edward J. Reilly (ed.) *Approaches to Teaching Swift's Gulliver's Travels* (New York: Modern Language Association, 1988), pp. 81–88.
7. For a helpful history and its relation to satire, see Margaret A. Rose, *Parody: Ancient, Modern, and Post-Modern* (Cambridge: Cambridge University Press, 1993).
8. See, for example, Andrew Varney, "Swift on the Causes of War: An Instance of Self-Parody," *Notes and Queries* 35 (233) no. 2 (1988), 181–83.
9. See T. H. Banks, Jr. (ed.) *The Poetical Works of Sir John Denham* (New Haven and London: Yale University Press, 1928), p. 49.
10. See Jean-Paul Forster, *Jonathan Swift: The Fictions of the Satirist* (Berne: Peter Lang, 1998).

7

PATRICK KELLY

Swift on money and economics

As a commentator on the politics and social relations of his age it would have been hard for Jonathan Swift to ignore economic circumstances. The later seventeenth and early eighteenth centuries saw a commercial revolution in the British Isles, transforming patterns of trade – both foreign and domestic, raising living standards, and permeating human relationships with commercial values. On its heels came the financial revolution associated with the European wars of the 1690s, with the emergence of an embryonic stock market, and the growth of new forms of credit both public and private, developments which would culminate a quarter of a century later with the world's first stock market boom and crash in the South Sea Bubble and Mississippi Company debacle of 1720. The financial innovations to which the Wars of Grand Alliance gave birth led to the establishment of new forms of wealth and a class of financial interests, known as the "moneyed men," who challenged the hitherto established predominance of the landed gentry and aristocracy.[1] These developments transformed the world of politics, creating opportunities – sometimes rather questionable ones – for enrichment for wider circles than the financiers themselves and bringing into existence forms of wealth that were not merely intangible but to many people barely comprehensible.[2] Amongst those drawn into in such activities were leading ministers and military commanders. In the later stages of the War of Spanish Succession even the Duke of Marlborough, England's greatest general since the Hundred Years War, came to be seen as putting self-enrichment through war before the interests of his country, corruption for which he was memorably satirized by Swift, along with his inordinate political ambition, in *The Conduct of the Allies* in 1711.[3]

Yet if manifestations of this transformation of British society between the Restoration and the 1720s commanded the attention of Swift as a writer, what we now call economics (in the narrower sense) supplied the subject of his pen in a more direct fashion in the 1720s and 1730s. Six years after his return to Ireland following the death of Queen Anne in 1714, Swift

128

produced the first of a series of specifically economic writings in *A Proposal for the Universal Use of Irish Manufacture* (1720) and for the next decade and a half wrote frequently on Ireland's economic problems and their solution. The 1720s were a time of general economic difficulty in Ireland, marked by three periods of particular crisis. The first, initiated by the Mississippi crash and South Sea Bubble in 1720, gave birth to proposals for a national bank, initially accepted – though ultimately rejected – by the Irish parliament. The second, and best known, was the 1723–25 controversy over the patent granted to the Wolverhampton metal manufacturer, William Wood, to produce copper halfpennies and farthings to supplement Ireland's grossly inadequate currency system, and the third was the culmination of successive years of harvest failure and famine from late 1727 to mid-1729 which led to Swift's most notorious economic pamphlet, *A Modest Proposal for Preventing the Children of Poor People in Ireland, from being a Burden to their Parents* (1729). Thereafter his economic writings were limited to a number of short tracts, mostly dealing with issues which he had raised earlier; though economic questions, in the form of currency management and the plight of the poor, figured among the very last of the works which Swift himself was responsible for publishing.[4]

Once regarded as a reliable depiction of conditions in early eighteenth-century Ireland, Swift's economic writings, however powerful their rhetorical impact, command less credibility amongst historians today.[5] Compared with the works of Thomas Prior, Arthur Dobbs, and David Bindon in the 1720s, to say nothing of George Berkeley's *Querist* of 1735–37, Swift's economic productions come across as strong on assertion and weak on sustained economic argument. Yet to dismiss them as undeserving of attention is to fail to understand both the nature of their significance for Swift and their very considerable impact on Irish economic discourse of the day. Moreover, beyond the major economic works, *Proposal for the Universal Use of Irish Manufacture*, *The Drapier's Letters*, *A Short View of the State of Ireland*, and the *Modest Proposal*, Swift deployed economic arguments in other pamphlets – not primarily thought of as economic pieces, such as *Some Arguments against Enlarging the Power of the Bishops* (1723).[6] In these works, Swift often displays a capacity for analysis superior to his better known economic pamphlets, which is further revealed in pieces that remained unpublished in the author's lifetime, such as the *Answer to Several Letters from Unknown Persons* (written in 1729). His reasons for failing to publish works of so great interest for his economic ideas seem to have varied from political strategy, as in the case of *The Seventh Drapier's Letter* (*An Humble Address to Both Houses of Parliament*, 1725), to a growing despair of such writings having any impact on Ireland's problems, as in the case of pieces from the late 1720s, like *A Proposal that all the Ladies and Women of Ireland should appear constantly in Irish Manufactures* (written in 1729). Failure to publish these pieces emphasizes Swift's concern with the practical impact of what could be said to ameliorate problems which as he grew older seemed to be incapable of rational solution. This despair throws into relief the two contexts in which Swift wrote: the first, the wretched circumstances of Ireland which impelled him, contrary to his earlier resolution to avoid comment on public issues, to produce the *Proposal for the Universal Use of Irish Manufacture* in 1720. The second was the extraordinary flowering of economic publications in the Ireland of the 1720s and 1730s after two decades of near silence on the subject, a flowering initiated by the appearance of Swift's pamphlet.

After two decades of modest but fluctuating prosperity occasioned by sustained demand for Irish agricultural produce on the Continent, the quarter century following the South Sea Bubble of 1720 proved extremely harsh.[7] Eighteenth-century Ireland was a largely undeveloped agricultural economy supporting a landlord class, significant numbers of the more prosperous of whom resided outside the country. Those forms of production for which the country seemed best suited, exporting cattle to Britain and the manufacture of woollen cloth for export, had been debarred by English legislation in the later seventeenth century. The linen industry which English mercantilist policy had sought from the 1690s to substitute for the manufacture of woollens was largely in the north, where the bulk of the population, though Protestant, were Scots-descended Presbyterians. Provision for the Catholic masses was often inadequate and, especially in times of difficulty, vagrancy and begging assumed proportions which seemed beyond Ireland's capacity to sustain. The 1720s and 1730s were particularly unfortunate in that the international market for Irish agricultural produce was generally slack, while the country also experienced severe bouts of famine. The second worst period of famine in the century occurred towards the end of the 1720s, which though less acute than that of 1740–41, cast a long shadow over the 1730s. Bad harvests from 1725 to 1728 led to starvation, vagrancy, riot, increased emigration to North America especially from Ulster, and a general decay of trade that the improved harvests of 1730–32 were not sufficient to pull the country out of. Arrears of rents could not be paid off; difficulties occurred in the linen trade, and the fall in population from the late 1720s was not made good. The major private bank failure of Burton and Falkiner in 1733 disrupted the credit and currency system, and poor harvests were again experienced from 1733 to 1736. Small wonder then that public attention both within and outside parliament turned to consideration first of how the immediate crisis might be coped with, and then to the longer-term issue of how to break through stagnation and increase the employment opportunities of the masses.

In addition, early eighteenth-century Ireland suffered the further disadvantage of a highly dysfunctional currency system. Prices, including the rating of gold, silver, and base metal coins, were expressed in an Irish money of account, which differed in value from sterling. Since 1701 the ratio between the currencies had been 13:12, that is an English shilling piece was rated at 13d Irish (giving an exchange par of 108.33 for silver). However, there were no Irish coins as such, adapted to reckoning in the national money of account – a state of affairs ill-suited to a commercial economy.[8] Instead the circulating medium consisted of English gold and silver coins, together with foreign gold and silver pieces current at rates established by government proclamation. As a result it was generally difficult, and sometimes impossible, to match prices expressed in the Irish money of account in round numbers of English or foreign coins. In addition the official rating of foreign coins consistently undervalued the main currency, metal silver. This bimetallic imbalance ensured that when bullion outflows occurred because of adverse trade balances, the country experienced a severe restriction of its main circulating medium. The problems of the 1720s and 1730s chiefly derived from two factors. First, the failure to rate foreign coins in strict proportion to their metallic content gave rise to disparities which affected gold more extensively than silver. Second, when the gold – silver ratio had been changed in Britain in 1717 with the reduction of the guinea from 21s. 6d. to 21s. od., no corresponding readjustment was made in Ireland. As a result silver was now seriously undervalued in terms of gold, while various foreign gold coins, particularly large denomination Portuguese pieces, were overvalued in proportion to the guinea.[9] Furthermore, Ireland was also chronically short of small change; the lowest denomination English silver piece in general circulation was the sixpence, and provision for smaller sums had to be effected with base coin. The supply of copper money was seriously inadequate, being the product of various concessions to patentees going back to the 1690s and much of the surviving copper consisted of below intrinsic-value pieces known as "Raps" (many of which were counterfeits).[10]

Concern over the deficiencies of the currency lay behind the first two politico-economic crises of the 1720s, namely the bank project of 1720–21 and the Wood's halfpence affair of 1723–25. The bank project was intended to create a national bank with private shareholders, on the model of the Bank of England, that would stimulate credit and promote liquidity in the crisis following the collapse of the South Sea Bubble in England in 1720. Subsequent reaction led the promoters to change their original proposal for a joint stock bank into a land bank, which it was hoped would prove more acceptable to parliamentary opinion. Despite initial enthusiasm, combined fears of stock-jobbing and political corruption eventually killed off the bank project, while strongly worded resolutions from both houses of the Irish parliament effectively blocked the revival of proposals for a national bank in Ireland for more than a decade.[11] Other than private bankers' notes, there was little interest in developing forms of paper-credit in Ireland – in striking contrast to the remarkable creativity in this respect of the American colonies. The Wood's halfpence project had, till overtaken by broader political controversy, been an attempt to provide for additional small change through the production of halfpence and farthings by an English patentee, though without the safeguard of enforced redemption for silver imposed on earlier copper issues, and inadequate control of the volume of coin to be minted. Its credibility was undermined by a national campaign raising fears of the scheme as a plot to drain Ireland of its remaining gold and silver, and as an attack on the country's political liberties. Though an indignant British ministry was finally forced to withdraw Wood's patent, the need for small change persisted as did the problems over gold and silver ratios and the composition of the circulating currency.[12]

The three decades following the publication of Swift's *Proposal for the Universal Use of Irish Manufacture* in 1720 were a period of astonishing fecundity for economic literature in Ireland. According to Henry Wagner's 1907 bibliography of Irish economics, more than two hundred titles, ranging from single broadsheets to tracts of over 100 pages, appeared between 1720 and the second, much revised edition of Berkeley's *Querist* in 1750.[13] Among the notable works of pens other than Swift's were Lord Molesworth's *Some Considerations For the Promoting of Agriculture And Employing the Poor* (1723); David Bindon's *Some Reasons Shewing the Necessity the People of Ireland are under, for Continuing to refuse Mr. Wood's Coinage* (1724) and *An Essay on the Gold and Silver Coin Current in Ireland* (1729); Thomas Prior's *List of the Absentees of* Ireland ... *With Observations on the Present State and Condition of That Kingdom* (1729), and his *Observations on the Coin in General* (1729); Arthur Dobbs's *Essay on the Trade and Improvement of Ireland* (two parts, 1729 and 1731); the first edition of George Berkeley's *Querist* (three parts, 1735–7); Samuel Madden's *Reflections and Resolutions for the Gentlemen of Ireland* (1738), and David Bindon's translation of Jean François Melon's *Essai Politique sur le Commerce* of 1734 (with notes adapting it to Irish conditions) in 1738. Yet none of these writers even came near the volume of Swift's published output in these years, let alone the sheer bulk of what he chose to retain in manuscript. Calculating the total number of items which Swift published on economics is complicated by a number of disputed works, but those accepted without challenge amount to some twenty titles, ranging in size from over twenty pages in the *Prose Works*, down to single broadsheets. Furthermore, it is clear that Swift consciously projected his economic writings as a coherent corpus, frequently referring back to his earlier works, even when on political grounds it would seem to have been prudent to have avoided making such connections. For instance, *The Fifth Drapier's Letter* virtually acknowledged authorship of *A Proposal for the Universal Use of Irish Manufacture*, while the reissue of *A Short View of the State of Ireland* in *The Intelligencer*, No. 15 claimed to come from the pen of the Drapier, and on the title page of *A Scheme for Giving Badges to Beggars* under the vignette of the author as "Dean of St Patrick's" appears the legend "M. B. Drapier."[14]

Swift's first economic pamphlet, *A Proposal for the Universal Use of Irish Manufacture, In Cloaths and Furniture of Houses, &c. Utterly Rejecting and Renouncing Every Thing wearable that comes from England*, was produced in late May 1720, and chiefly reflects concern for the predicament of the Dublin weavers, to whose problems he would return more than once in the next decade and a half.[15] Though presented in a far from systematic manner, the work introduces many of the major themes in Swift's later writings, together with the personal and national prejudices that color his approach to the solution to Ireland's problems – such as the castigation of female vanity. A further significant element in the *Proposal* is Swift's conviction of the uniqueness of Ireland's economic problems and his concern to ensure that the remedies adopted should not be unthinkingly appropriated from English writers but be properly suited to Irish conditions.[16] His starting-point is the paradox that conditions which make for prosperity elsewhere, such as a large population, natural fertility, and plenty of safe harbors, have failed to produce similar results in Ireland. To Swift, this refutation of general experience proceeds from two circumstances, both linked to Ireland's colonial predicament; namely, her subordination to English commercial interests, compounded by the perverse inclination of her own population at all levels from landlords, to tradesmen, to the rural poor, to act constantly against their long-term interests in the hope of immediate gain. In the face of England's prohibition on the export of Irish woollens, Irish landlords have abandoned tillage in favor of sheep-raising, thus pushing up the price of corn and forcing its import from England, and becoming dependent on illegal wool exports to France. Disruption to the French economy from "the present fluctuating Condition of the Coin," that is the Law scheme (fatally damaged that very month by the hostility of the financiers and Paris *Parlement*) threatens ruin unless alternative markets can be found (*PW* IX: 16).

Swift's solution (to which he would constantly return) is to urge national action to promote domestic consumption of Irish products in place of foreign imports, starting with resolutions to this effect from both Houses of Parliament, and a public-spirited determination "never to appear with one single *Shred* that comes from *England*." After raising the spectacle of the pleasure that the idea of Irish men and women celebrating his birthday *"universally clad in their own Manufacture"* (*PW* IX: 16) will undoubtedly cause George I, Swift goes on to assert "that Ireland would never be happy *'till a Law were made for* burning *every Thing that came from* England, *except their* People *and their* Coals," a remark whose offensiveness he seeks to temper by attributing it to "the late Archbishop of *Tuam"* (*PW* IX: 17). Such touches are characteristic of Swift's economic writing, where commonplace propositions such as the proposal for import-substitution are raised to a level of political provocation far from appropriate to the advocacy of new economic policy. And though Swift purported to be astonished by the government prosecution of his printer, Edward Waters, in which Chief Justice Whitshed asserted that the work was a Jacobite provocation, his economic pronouncements (including actions such as raising a black flag on St. Patrick's steeple to protest against the devaluation of gold in 1737) continued to affront official sensitivity to the end (*PW* IX: 25–27; *E* III: 860). The 1720 *Proposal* goes on to blame dishonest shopkeepers and manufacturers for damaging the reputation of Irish goods, while irony resurfaces with the suggestion that the real reason for England's concern at Irish misery is the loss of the profits which she expects to draw from her Irish dependency. After a final attack on the graspingness of Irish landlords, Swift concludes with a brief allusion to a project for erecting a bank in Ireland (*PW* IX: 21–22).

The scheme for establishing a national bank in Ireland that originated in 1720 provided the next occasion of Swift's economic pamphleteering. The bank project was partly occasioned by the company flotation boom sparked off by the initial success of the South Sea Company, but its association with the collapse of the Bubble and the loss of capital which this brought about in Ireland prejudiced public opinion against the bank. However, the precise extent of Swift's contribution to the bank debate has proved hard to unravel. Most confidently identified as his personal work are the two burlesques, *The Wonderful Wonder of Wonders* and *The Wonder of All the Wonders*, which are of little economic interest other than as evidence of Swift's hostility to the scheme. Somewhat more significant are the group of pamphlets attributed jointly to Swift and his friends, notably *Swearer's Bank, Or Parliamentary Security for a New Bank* (1721), which proposes raising capital for a bank through enforcing the act providing financial penalties for cursing and swearing. This paper represents Swift's first resort to sustained parody of contemporary economic projectors' style, a genre which he would turn to far greater impact in *A Modest Proposal* and the *Answer to the Craftsman* (1731).[17] More effective as a refutation of the economic case for the bank is *A Letter from a Lady in Town to her Friend in the Country, Concerning the Bank*. In this, the jargon-ridden pronouncements of a dubious-seeming bank promoter are contrasted with the objections of "a certain LORD to whom I have the Honour to be Related" on the grounds of lack of security, the recent crashes in Britain, France, and Holland, and the economic and social insignificance of the subscribers to the bank (*PW* IX: 301).

Swift's next venture into economic writing was prompted by the Wood's Halfpence scheme, a project widely regarded as a threat to Ireland's already too-vulnerable economy. While his intervention in the form of *The Drapier's Letters* is considered elsewhere in this volume in relation to his role as a Hibernian patriot and political pamphleteer, it must be emphasized that the episode constituted the main basis for contemporaries' view of Swift as a champion of colonial resistance to Britain (*C* IV: 226–28; *C* V: 165–68). In economic terms the affair is noteworthy for the unique success of popular resistance in Ireland, forcing the British government to withdraw a policy on which it had embarked; indeed, it probably constituted Walpole's greatest domestic political set-back as chief minister up to the forced withdrawal of his Excise scheme in 1733. The nub of the project was the patent granted to the Wolverhampton metal manufacturer, William Wood, to produce 360 tons of copper halfpence and farthings to supply small change for the Irish economy, with a face value of £108,000. Fortunately for Walpole, the full background in the form of the sale of the patent to Wood by the original beneficiary, George I's mistress, the Duchess of Kendal, did not emerge at the time.[18] Wood's project became public knowledge in Ireland in 1722, when the viceroy the Duke of Grafton was rumored to have undertaken to foster the scheme in order to obtain royal favor. Opposition to the new copper coin was thus well established before Swift became drawn into writing on the topic, though no mention of the subject is to be found in his letters in 1723. An important inquiry into the scheme was undertaken by the Irish parliament in the autumn of 1723, and both houses drew up addresses calling for the withdrawal of the patent. The public perception of the eventual withdrawal of Wood's halfpence as largely the work of Swift, a view not without some foundation though easily exaggerated, would ensure that his future pronouncements on Ireland's economic problems were treated with an extraordinary degree of respect by the populace at large and exasperated concern by the Dublin administration.[19]

As subsequent *Drapier's Letters* appeared, political concerns and patriotic rhetoric eventually came to predominate over economic considerations, while much of what Swift wrote on the economic plane was parasitic on other works that appeared in the controversy, notably David Bindon's highly sophisticated *Some Reasons Shewing the Necessity the People of Ireland are under, for Continuing to refuse Mr. Wood's Coinage* (1724). In the first of the series, *A Letter to the Tradesmen, Shop-Keepers, Farmers, and Common-People of Ireland*, published in February 1723/4, Swift assumes the persona of a moderately prosperous shopkeeper anxious to instruct his neighbors on the threat which the new copper money presented to the Irish economy, and the means that were available to avoid the danger through resolute common action. In identifying the solution to the problem as lying in the hands of the Irish themselves, Swift once more advocates a course of action such as he had called for in the *Proposal for the Universal Use of Irish Manufacture*, though the idea of a boycott of Wood's coin had already been urged by Archbishop King in 1723.[20] Swift, however, is anxious to make clear that refusing to accept Wood's copper coin is in full accordance with the law, since only gold and silver are properly money with legal tender. His monetary theory, like much Irish thinking on the subject in the early eighteenth century, is deeply influenced by the pamphlets which John Locke had written in the debates which preceded the great English silver recoinage of 1696–98.[21] Unlike Bindon, Swift does not allude to Locke's work in the Wood's Halfpence controversy, though he does mention the recoinage in *The Seventh Drapier's Letter* and had the relevant pamphlets in his library.[22] Taking his stand on Locke's guiding principle of intrinsic value, Swift argues that while English copper pieces "pass for very little more than they are worth ... Mr. Wood made his H A L F - P E N C E of such *Base Metal* ... that the Brazier would hardly give you above a *Penny* of good Money for a *Shilling* of his" (*PW* x: 4).[23] But as long as the Revenue Commissioners continue to refuse to accept the new money at face value, the project cannot hope to prevail. If Wood succeeds, however, the result will be impoverishment for all classes from landowners to beggars, as Ireland is drained of its remaining gold and silver.

The *Second Letter*[24] deals with Wood's responses at a hearing before the English Privy Council to the charges made by the Irish parliament, especially his undertaking to limit the amount coined to £40,000, in return for a restricted right of legal tender. Assuming a need for two shillings in change per family, Swift calculates Ireland's total requirement for copper money to be £25,000, that is, under a quarter of the amount authorized in the original patent, and still considerably less than Wood's new proposal. Despite the latter's threats of procuring a proclamation to force his money on the Irish people, the Drapier urges his readers to take heart from the fact that the king cannot issue proclamations other than within the terms of the existing law. The *Third Letter* considers the shortcomings of the assay of Wood's coin conducted by the London Mint under the aegis of Sir Isaac Newton, in permitting Wood himself to select the coins submitted for trial.[25] It also highlights defects in the patent, particularly the absence of the obligation imposed on earlier patentees to redeem their coin for silver. This last point leads Swift to assert the need for an Irish Mint, though his arguments are based more on political considerations than appreciation of the economic advantages. The latter are effectively brought out, however, in David Bindon's *Essay on the Gold and Silver Coin Current in Ireland* (1729), which shows how a local mint will enable a favorable proportion to be kept between the large and small denominations of coin, and overcome the difficulties occasioned by the lack of coins adapted to prices expressed in the Irish money of account.[26]

The fourth (and best known) of the series, *A Letter to the Whole People of Ireland* (1724), presented an overt challenge to British authority that forced the new viceroy, Lord Carteret, to offer a reward for the discovery of the author. However, neither it nor the two ensuing letters, addressed respectively to Lords Molesworth and Midleton, contain much by way of direct economic argument. More interesting in this respect is the *Seventh Letter, An Humble Address to Both Houses of Parliament* (which remained unpublished until 1735), in which Swift proposes that copper money should be coined in Ireland under the supervision of the Irish parliament. He goes on to call for maintaining the integrity of the monetary standard, which is "the *tenderest* Point of Government, affecting every Individual, in the highest Degree" through safeguarding the value of property. Moreover, England should treat Ireland in a more equitable fashion "on Account of that *immense Profit* they receive from us; without which, that Kingdom would make a very *different* Figure in *Europe*, from what it doth at present' (*PW* X: 128). As evidence Swift specifies the rents paid to absentees, together with pensions and the salaries of civil and military officials, imports of coal, corn, and Indian textiles, and the losses arising from the woollens export prohibition, the total value of which he puts at nearly £700,000. The *Humble Address* concludes with various proposals for improving the economy, including reducing textile imports, steps to "civilize the poorer Sort of our Natives," and the encouragement of agriculture and forestry, all measures intended to compensate for the impossibility of either reducing the absentee burden or persuading the British to end their commercial restrictions (*PW* X: 139).

Similar views would emerge as constant themes in the third period of Swift's economic pamphleteering, which saw the production of his most sophisticated tracts with the publication of *A Short View of the State of Ireland* in March 1728 and *A Modest Proposal*, some eighteen months later. Swift's concerns over Ireland's problems did not, however, evaporate in the interval.

On his visit to London in 1726 he sought to intervene directly with Walpole himself and obtained an interview in which he attempted to persuade the minister of the urgency of Ireland's predicament. Walpole, however, proved unreceptive, though Swift made one final attempt to influence the minister by setting down his arguments on paper for presentation through their mutual friend, Lord Peterborough (C III: 131–35). Shorn of rhetorical exaggeration, this brief analysis of Ireland's problems and Swift's perceived solutions is a valuable synopsis of his thinking on Ireland's economic problems, which bears a remarkably close resemblance to his subsequent sermon, "Causes of the Wretched Conditions of Ireland."[27]

A Short View of the State of Ireland (1727/8) was probably prompted by a pamphlet by Sir John Browne entitled *Seasonable Remarks on Trade* (1727–28), which Swift saw as a clumsy attempt to convince Englishmen that conditions in Ireland were by no means as bad as generally represented (*PW* v: 256–57). His response was a vigorous presentation of the reality of Ireland's predicament in the form of an argument showing that the country was a living contradiction of all the principles of economic theory as to what made for prosperity elsewhere.[28] Fueling the indignation with which Swift repudiated the claim that things were not so bad in Ireland was his concern at the rapidly worsening manifestations of famine brought about by the series of bad harvests and severe climatic conditions which had started in 1725 (and would continue to the summer of 1729). The discussion of the fourteen natural conditions or economic factors which make for prosperity elsewhere is intended to point the contrast between England, where such factors are allowed to operate unrestrained, and Ireland, where they are thwarted by a combination of British jealousy and malevolence and Irish greed and stupidity. Most important are the natural factors, namely the fertility of the soil, the industry and number of the people, and abundance of suitable ports and havens. The other circumstances considered are institutional, moral, or political factors, such as freedom of trade, being governed by laws to which the people have consented, the encouragement of agriculture and population growth, restricting public employment to natives, spending rents and state revenue within the country, effective currency management through a local mint, and finally a disposition to consume domestic manufactures rather than imported luxuries. Swift then goes through each of the fourteen topics in turn, showing how contrary circumstances prevail in Ireland, and concludes ironically: "I would be glad to know by what secret Method, it is, that we grow a rich and flourishing People, without *Liberty, Trade, Manufactures, Inhabitants, Money,* or the *Privilege of Coining;* without *Industry, Labour,* or *Improvement of Lands.*" Rather than the picture of prosperity "with the

Improvement of the Land...the Abundance and Vicinity of Country-Seats; the commodious Farmers Houses and Barns...the Shops full of Goods... [and] the comfortable Diet and Dress, and Dwellings of the People" which English visitors would expect to find in Ireland, reality would make the stranger think he was "in *Lapland*...rather than in a Country so favoured by Nature as ours"(*PW* XII: 9–10).

Irish economic problems also featured in the periodical *The Intelligencer*, which Swift launched with his friend, Thomas Sheridan, in mid-1728.[29] In late November, No. 15 of the paper reprinted *A Short View* with an introductory note by Sheridan explaining why it was being reissued. In No.19, in the following month, Swift broke fresh ground in examining the lamentable state of the currency under the guise of a letter from an Ulster MP and landowner. This opens with an account of the inconveniences suffered by the squire as a result of shortage of coin, going on to point out how much more acute the difficulties were for day-laborers and rural artisans. The latter's problems are shown particularly to hamper the linen industry, once regarded as the only sector of the Irish economy capable of prospering. The piece also confronts the question central to Ireland's ill-functioning currency system of the government's failure to maintain a correct ratio between gold and silver, particularly since the British reduction of the guinea from 21s. and 6d. to 21 shillings in 1717.[30] Towards the end, Swift engages with the for-him-new phenomenon of emigration from Ulster to North America, an issue to which his reactions are somewhat ambivalent. While loss of one of the few industrious sectors in the population is a serious threat, and also represents a further drain of money in the form of the capital which emigrants take with them, Swift questions whether they will really be better off in the New World as the accounts of earlier Ulster emigrants have led them to believe. At another level, since many of the emigrants are dissenters, who blame the tithe burden imposed by the Anglican church for their misery, Swift is not altogether sorry to see their departure.[31]

The elapse of nearly three centuries has not dimmed the impact of the central theme of *A Modest Proposal for Preventing the Children of Poor People in Ireland, from being a Burden to their Parents or Country: and for making them beneficial to the Publick* of 1729, namely the horrific proposal of selling poor children for food. The pamphlet is intended to shock contemporaries into realization of the enormity of the current crisis through the contrast between its horrifying subject matter and the objective-sounding economic language employed to present the projector's research into potential markets, methods of cooking the flesh, and profitable side-products such as fine leather for ladies' gloves and gentlemen's boots. In its dismissal of the pamphlet literature, parliamentary debates, and popular discussion of the past ten years as altogether without effect, *A Modest Proposal* seems to reflect Swift's overwhelming despair at the failure of contemporary economic wisdom to offer any solution to Ireland's problems: "as to myself; having been wearied out for many Years with offering vain, idle, visionary Thoughts; and at length despairing of Success," he sees the sale of Irish children as the only project that will not excite English jealousy. So impossible of achievement is Ireland's need "to find Food and Raiment, for a Hundred Thousand useless Mouths and Backs," that the constantly urged remedies of

> *taxing our Absentees... Of using neither Cloaths, nor Household Furniture except what is of our own Growth and Manufacture... Of curing the Expensiveness of Pride, Vanity, Idleness, and Gaming in our Women; Of introducing a Vein of Parsimony, Prudence and Temperance; Of learning to love our Country... Of teaching Landlords to have, at least, one Degree of Mercy towards their Tenants... Of putting a Spirit of Honesty, Industry and Skill into our Shop-keepers*   (*PW* xii: 116–17)

will all prove ineffective.

However rhetorically powerful, Swift's contribution to the debate of 1727–29 is in economic terms rather disappointing. Not only does he have no new remedies to offer beyond import substitution and the promotion of agriculture, but his emphasis on England's overwhelming responsibility for Ireland's predicament – "The Causes of this... are Clear... [namely] the Hatred, and Contempt, borne us by our Neighbours, and Brethren, without the least grounds of Provocation, which keeps us from enjoying the common Benefits of Mankind" – runs counter to an emerging consensus that Ireland can still hope to prosper within the British mercantile system.[32] This call for co-operation within an imperial commercial system was advocated by, amongst others, Thomas Prior, David Bindon, and above all Arthur Dobbs, who also called for political union as well. Even Archbishop King, long an exponent of the view that Irish prosperity would ever fall victim to British commercial jealousy, had confided to Edward Southwell in the later stages of the Wood's Halfpence controversy that England's efforts to restrain competition from Irish exports of both cattle and woollen cloth had unexpectedly turned to the country's long-term benefit rather than loss.[33] For all his prestige as the Drapier and the champion of the Irish poor, Swift at the end of the 1720s can be seen therefore to represent not only a profoundly disenchanted but more significantly an increasingly outdated view of Ireland's economic prospects. More specifically his views, together with the warnings of his long-term adversaries the bankers, were probably responsible for the Dublin administration's decision in 1729 not to lay before parliament the proposals for devaluing gold and issuing an adequate supply of copper money which Archbishop Boulter had sought to persuade Walpole were the solution to the problems of the Irish currency system.[34] When finally adopted in 1737, these remedies – though even then desperately resisted by rearguard action from Swift – proved sufficient to restore stability to monetary conditions and bring to an end nearly two decades of acute disruption.

Although Swift was to continue to publish on economic issues till 1737, thereby belying the apparent finality of his position in A Modest Proposal, his later works take him little further in terms of economic understanding. The fact that many of these writings were abandoned unfinished, or left unpublished, suggests that continuing despair of improving conditions in Ireland outweighed Swift's occasional moments of hope, a state of affairs reflected in his letters of the 1730s (C IV: 41–52, 249). Of all that he had called for, only the adoption of English legislation requiring burying in wool had been implemented (in 1734), and then only through the agency of others than himself (PW IX: 16). However, though no major development marked the evolution of Swift's economic ideas over the nearly two decades from the Proposal for the Universal Use of Irish Manufacture (1720) to the Scheme for giving Badges to Beggars (1737), there are indications that as the range of his concerns expanded his views in some respects grew more sophisticated and better informed. This greater awareness of the nature of economic problems reflects both reading and practical experience. The sale catalogue of Swift's library includes a somewhat conventional range of mercantilist writers, such as Petty, Child, Locke, and a number of works of Charles Davenant, another author widely read in Ireland. Other works, such as Molesworth's 1723 pamphlet on agriculture and poor relief in Ireland, and Sir William Fownes' 1725 scheme for dealing with the poor, are referred to (sometimes indirectly) in Swift's own writings (PW IX: 58–59; PW XIII: 134–36). Yet there is little indication that he was familiar with the more sophisticated Irish writings of the later 1720s and 1730s, such as those of Prior, Bindon, and Dobbs. While the question of who was reading the vast volume of Irish economic tracts that appeared in these years is hard to determine, it is interesting to find Swift's name figuring in the only item in this literature to have a subscription list, along with those of Arthur Dobbs and Samuel Madden.[35]

Central to understanding what motivated Swift's writing on economic matters is his deep ambivalence towards Ireland and her problems. This ambivalence is very apparent in An Answer to a Paper called a Memorial of the Poor Inhabitants, Tradesmen, and Labourers (1728), which deals with a proposal to relieve unemployment amongst Dublin weavers by importing corn

on a substantial scale. Swift's reply, attributing the weavers' problems largely
to their own insufficiency and dishonesty, makes clear his reluctance to have
forced on him the role of spokesman for threatened groups. Elsewhere, especially in letters to friends in England, he alternates between disgust at being
forced to remain in exile amidst such hopeless misery, and anger at English
indifference and Irish fecklessness (*PW* xii: 15–25; *C* iii: 341; *C* iv: 349).
The indignation which drove him – almost against his better judgement –
to enter the public debate over Ireland's predicament frequently precluded
dispassionate analysis of the factors responsible. Despite the maxim which
he recommended to Bolingbroke and Pope in 1726, even intellectually Swift
could not be the wise man who kept money in his head but not in his heart.[36]
His goal remained the practical welfare of his countrymen, and it is perhaps
more appropriate to judge him in terms of the sincerity of his aspirations to
benefit the public than on the basis of his capacity for technical economic
analysis. As the title of his sermon during the Wood's halfpence affair –
"Doing Good" – indicates, his ultimate objective in his economic writings
is the practical manifestation of love of country through doing good to the
public:

> I shall think my time not ill spent, if I can persuade most or all of you...to
> shew the love you have for your country, by endeavouring, in your several
> stations, to do all the public good you are able. For I am certainly persuaded,
> that all our misfortunes arise from no other original cause than that general
> disregard among us to the public welfare. (*PW* ix: 234)

NOTES

1. For these developments, see P. G. M. Dickson, *The Financial Revolution* (London:
   Macmillan, 1967); John Carswell, *South Sea Bubble* (London: Cresset, 1960),
   chapter 1; Geoffrey Holmes, *The Making of a Great Power: Late Stuart and
   Early Georgian Britain, 1660–1722* (London: Longman, 1993), chapters 3, 17,
   and 18.
2. For Swift's reflections on these developments, see *The Examiner*, Nos. 1, 24, 35,
   and 44 (1710–11) in *PW* iii: 5–7, 67–68, 124–25, 169–70. Also see his comments
   in *The Conduct of the Allies* (1711) in *PW* vi: 10; his letter to Pope, January 10,
   1720/1, printed in *PW* ix: 32.
3. *PW* vi: 20, 41–43, 133. Also see *The History of the Last Four Years of the Queen*
   (1758) in *PW* vii: 65–69.
4. *Reasons Why we should not lower the Coins now current in this Kingdom*
   (1736) and *A Proposal for Giving Badges to Beggars* (1737) in *PW* xiii: 119–20;
   129–40. For a checklist of Swift's Irish writings see Joseph McMinn (ed.) *Swift's
   Irish Pamphlets: an Introductory Selection* (Gerrards Cross: Colin Smythe, 1991),
   pp. 179–86.

5. See L. M. Cullen, "The Value of Contemporary Printed Sources for Irish Economic History in the Eighteenth Century," *Irish Historical Studies*, 14 (1964), 142–55; S. J. Connolly, "Swift and Protestant Ireland: Images and Reality," in Aileen Douglas, Patrick Kelly, and Ian Campbell Ross (eds.) *Locating Swift: Essays from Dublin on the 250th Anniversary of the Death of Jonathan Swift, 1667–1745* (Dublin: Four Courts Press, 1998), pp. 35–45. For a more favorable assessment, see James Kelly, "Jonathan Swift and the Irish Economy of the 1720s," *Eighteenth-Century Ireland: Iris an dá chultúr* 6 (1991), 7–36.

6. See especially the analysis of the secular decline in the purchasing power of money in *PW* IX: 47–51, which draws on William Fleetwood's *Chronicon Preciosum* (1707), a work Swift had in his library. For the latter, see Item 417 in Sir Harold Williams (ed.) *Dean Swift's Library, with a Facsimile of the Original Sale Catalogue* (Cambridge: Cambridge University Press, 1932), hereafter *Swift's Library Catalogue*.

7. For the early eighteenth-century Irish economy, see L. M. Cullen, *An Economic History of Ireland*, 2nd edn. (London: Batsford, 1987), pp. 39–49; L. M. Cullen, "Economic Development, 1691–1750," in T. W. Moody and W. E. Vaughan (eds.) *A New History of Ireland*, vol. IV: *Eighteenth-Century Ireland, 1691–1800* (Oxford: Clarendon Press, 1986), pp. 123–58; S. J. Connolly, *Religion, Law and Power: The Making of Protestant Ireland, 1660–1760* (Oxford: Clarendon Press, 1992), pp. 41–59; and James Kelly, "Harvests and Hardship: Famine and Scarcity in Ireland in the Later 1720s," *Studia Hibernica* 26 (1992), 65–105.

8. See David Bindon, *An Essay on the Gold and Silver Coin Current in Ireland* (Dublin, 1729), p. 7.

9. Joseph Johnson, "The Irish Currency in the Eighteenth Century," in *Berkeley's Querist in Historical Perspective* (Dundalk: Dundalgan Press, 1970), chapter 6; L. M. Cullen, *Anglo-Irish Trade in the Eighteenth Century* (Manchester: Manchester University Press, 1968), pp. 155–58; and Albert Feavearyear, *The Pound Sterling: a History of English Money*, 2nd edn. (Oxford: Clarendon Press, 1963), p. 158.

10. For details see *A Defence of the Conduct of the People of Ireland in their Unanimous Refusal of Mr. Wood's Copper-Money* (Dublin, 1724), pp. 21–23.

11. Michael Ryder, "The Bank of Ireland, 1721: Land, Credit and Dependency," *Historical Journal* 25 (1982), 557–82.

12. For general background, see *E* III: 187–317.

13. [Henry R. Wagner], *Irish Economics, 1700–1783: A Bibliography with Notes* (1907; reprinted New York: Kelley, 1969). Also see L. W. Hanson, *Contemporary Printed Sources for British and Irish Economic History, 1701–1750* (Cambridge: Cambridge University Press, 1963), and vol. I of M. Canney and David Knott (eds.) *Catalogue of the Goldsmith's Library of Economic Literature, Printed Books to 1800* (Cambridge: Cambridge University Press, 1970).

14. See *PW* X: 82, 89; *The Intelligencer*, ed. James Woolley (Oxford: Clarendon Press, 1992), pp. 173–74; and *PW* XIII: 129.

15. See for example the *First Drapier's Letter* (1724) in *PW* X: 3; *A Letter to the Archbishop of Dublin concerning Weavers* (1729) in *PW* XII: 65–71, and *Observations Occasion'd by Reading a Paper, Entitled 'The Case of the Woollen Manufactures'* (1733) in *PW* XII: 89–92.

16. Swift emphasized this point several times in 1729: "there is no topic so fallacious ...as to argue...how we ought to act in Ireland from the example of England, France, Holland, or any other country." See *PW* xii: 124; also *PW* xii: 79, 131.

17. The *Answer to the Craftsman* (1731) exploited economic reasoning to demonstrate that Irish recruitment into French and other Catholic European armies benefitted rather than harmed the Protestant interest: *PW* xiii: 173–5.

18. See further J. M. Treadwell, "Swift, William Wood, and the Factual Basis of Satire," *Journal of British Studies* 15 (1976), 76–91; and Patrick McNally, "Wood's Halfpence, Carteret, and the Government of Ireland,1723–6," *Irish Historical Studies* 30 (1997), 354–76.

19. Philip Perceval to Lord Perceval, January 12, 1725/6 (British Library, Add. MS 47030). See further, Marmaduke Coghill's comment on *A Short View of the State of Ireland* (1727/8): *PW* xii: xiii.

20. Oliver W. Ferguson, *Jonathan Swift and Ireland* (Urbana: University of Illinois Press, 1962), p. 96.

21. John Locke, *Some Considerations of the Consequences of the Lowering of Interest, and Raising the Value of Money* (London, 1692), *Short Observations on a Printed Paper* (London, 1695), and *Further Considerations concerning Raising the Value of Money* (London, 1695).

22. *PW* x: 128. Swift owned Locke's pieces in the collected volume, *Several Papers Relating to Money, Interest and Trade, &c.* (London, 1696): *Swift's Library Catalogue*, Item 300. Also see David Bindon, *Some Reasons Shewing the Necessity the People of Ireland are under, for Continuing to refuse Mr. Wood's Coinage* (Dublin, 1724), pp. 13–14.

23. However, the assay undertaken for the Irish parliament in October 1723 showed the bullion content to be approximately 40 percent of the face value: Bindon, *Some Reasons Shewing*, pp. 14–5, 19–20.

24. *A Letter to Mr Harding the Printer, Upon Occasion of a Paragraph in his News-Paper of Aug. 1st. Relating to Mr. Wood's Half-Pence* (Dublin, 1724).

25. Despite the misgivings of the Treasury, it was Newton himself who had insisted on Wood's pieces being brought to London rather than sending Mint personnel to carry out the assay in Bristol: P. R. O., London; Mint 19/ii/471.

26. Bindon, *An Essay on the Gold and Silver Coin*, pp. 18–21.

27. *PW* ix: 199–209. For revised dating, see Kelly, "Jonathan Swift and the Irish Economy of the 1720s" (note 5 above), p. 23.

28. See Swift's 1729 *Maxims controlled in Ireland* in *PW* xii: 131–7.

29. The introduction and notes to James Woolley's exemplary edition of *The Intelligencer* (Oxford: Clarendon Press, 1992) are a mine of information on Swift's economics and the Irish background.

30. The point had already been made in the anonymous *Observations on the Raising of Money* (Dublin, 1718), p. 11, and by David Bindon in *Some Reasons Shewing*, p. 4.

31. In the unpublished *Answer to... Unknown Persons* of 1729, Swift also identifies the oppression of landlords and barring dissenters from state employment as causes of emigration: *PW* xii: 78.

32. *The Intelligencer*, ed. Woolley, No. 19, p. 208.

33. Thomas Prior, *List of the Absentees of Ireland... With Observations on the Present State and Condition of That Kingdom* (Dublin, 1729), p. 18; [David

Bindon], *A Scheme for Supplying Industrious Men with Money to carry on their Trades* (Dublin, 1729), p. 21; Arthur Dobbs, *Essay on the Trade of Ireland* (Dublin, 1729), pp. 1–2. William King to Edward Southwell, June 9, 1724: Trinity College, Dublin, MS 2537/110–3.

34. *Letters Written by his Excellency, Hugh Boulter, D.D., Lord Primate of all Ireland*, 2 vols. (Dublin, 1770), vol. I, pp. 197, 198–99.

35. Namely, David Bindon's translation of Melon's *Essai Politique sur le Commerce* (Dublin, 1738).

36. "That a wise man ought to have Money in his head, but not in his heart": see C III: 328.

8

IAN HIGGINS

Language and style

Jonathan Swift had a lifelong interest in the English language. The extent of this interest is extraordinary. It includes language history and theories; dialect, jargon, and slang; vocabulary, orthography, and punctuation; etymology; rhetoric and dialectic; code and private languages; puns and language games; the social and political function of language and its abuse in propaganda. A received view in the extensive modern scholarship on Swift and the English language is that Swift is a linguistic conservative. He deplores the impurity, instability, and impermanence of English and aspires to arrest its obsolescence and purge it of corrupt words. He prescribes standardization in spelling and punctuation. He insists on simplicity and stylistic propriety, which he polices in his satiric invective against offending authors. Yet, paradoxically, Swift's stylistic practice is characterized by unconstrained linguistic freedom. Swift was certainly called to account by contemporary critics for his impropriety. In the "Apology" for his brilliant early satire *A Tale of a Tub* the "Author" acknowledges that *"he gave a Liberty to his Pen, which might not suit with maturer Years, or graver Characters"* (PW I: 1–2).

Swift's discursive works on language and style include an essay in *The Tatler* No. 230 (September 28, 1710); *Hints towards an Essay on Conversation* (written *c.* 1710–12); *A Proposal for Correcting, Improving and Ascertaining the English Tongue In a Letter to the Most Honourable Robert Earl of Oxford and Mortimer, Lord High Treasurer of Great Britain* (1712); and *A Letter to a Young Gentleman, Lately enter'd into Holy Orders* (1721). This chapter will examine what Swift writes about language and style in these works and will consider aspects of his actual practice in his writings. The focus in this chapter will be on Swift's politics of language. Importantly, Swift's discursive writings on language were part of a larger political project: an aspect of his activism against post-1688 Whig regimes. His account of linguistic and literary history and proposals for correcting and settling the English language drew contemporary attention precisely because they were a political confrontation to cultural views being propounded by Whig writers.

Swift's linguistic challenge was also delivered, with extra menaces, in his great prose satires *A Tale of a Tub* and *Gulliver's Travels*, in several poems, in his punning treatises and practice, and in his copious satiric compilation *A Complete Collection of Genteel and Ingenious Conversation, According to the Most Polite Mode and Method Now Used at Court, and in the Best Companies of England* (1738).

The exhortations on language and style in the didactic *A Letter to a Young Gentleman, Lately enter'd into Holy Orders* (*PW* IX: 61–81) express Swift's characteristic general linguistic positions. Swift recommends to the gentleman entering the Church of Ireland "the Study of the *English* Language" and the avoidance of "barbarous Terms and Expressions, peculiar to" Ireland (*PW* IX: 65). Swift's stark comments elsewhere in his work on English linguistic imperialism in Ireland testify to his understanding of language as an index of cultural identity and instrument of hegemony (see *PW* IV: 280–84; IX: 202; 12: 89). The surviving traces of Swift's contact with the bardic culture of Catholic Jacobite Gaelic Ireland (*C* II: 440–41) and of an interest in Irish poetry as reflected in his poem "The Description of an Irish Feast" (*Poems* 221–23) might suggest counter-hegemonic sympathies in Swift. In *A Letter to a Young Gentleman*, Swift declares that "Proper Words in proper Places, makes the true Definition of a Stile" and he proscribes the use of "obscure Terms" (*PW* IX: 65). The prescription of plain language, expressed in *A Letter to a Young Gentleman*, is the positive behind the parody of obscure and esoteric authors in *A Tale of a Tub* and of specialist language as obscurantist jargon in *Gulliver's Travels*. Swift admonishes the young gentleman to avoid the affectation of politeness and to use "that Simplicity, without which no human Performance can arrive to any great Perfection" (*PW* IX: 68; see also *PW* II: 177; IV: 15). He counsels against "that Part of Oratory, which relates to the moving of the Passions." For such oratory is the stylistic symptom of "*Enthusiastick*" preachers, whose belief in personal spiritual revelation and inspiration Swift satirizes in *A Discourse Concerning the Mechanical Operation of the Spirit* as a subversive sexual pathology (*PW* IX: 68; *PW* I: 171–90).

Swift's prescriptivist model of linguistic simplicity and propriety seems exemplified in the conversation of those equine Ancients the Houyhnhnms in Book IV of *Gulliver's Travels*. Gulliver reports that in Houyhnhnm "Conversations," "nothing passed but what was useful, expressed in the fewest and most significant Words: Where (as I have already said) the greatest *Decency* was observed, without the least Degree of Ceremony; where no Person spoke without being pleased himself, and pleasing his Companions: Where there was no Interruption, Tediousness, Heat, or Difference of Sentiments"

(*PW* xi: 277). Amusingly, Gulliver is unable to emulate the perfection he reports, straying into an unnecessary parenthesis. The Houyhnhnms illustrate what Swift said in *Hints towards an Essay on Conversation* were the "two chief Ends of Conversation ... to entertain and improve those we are among, or to receive those Benefits ourselves." In the *Hints* Swift condemned as unfit for conversation those who possess "the Itch of Dispute and Contradiction." Human nature "is most debased, by the Abuse of that Faculty which is held the great Distinction between Men and Brutes" (*PW* iv: 92, 94). In *Gulliver's Travels* the Swiftian ideal of conversation is practiced by a mythic animal species, not by humankind. The subjects of Houyhnhnm discourse are ethically serious (*PW* xi: 277–78). Swift's principal exhibit of contemporary language abuse and conversational anility was the polite conversation "at Court, and in the Best Companies of England." Swift was its satiric anthologist. *A Complete Collection of Genteel and Ingenious Conversation* (*PW* iv: 97–201) is a compendium of clichés, platitudes, proverbial commonplaces, and a numbing display of systemic word abuse.

Swift's advocacy of a plain style in his didactic and satiric writings reflects a dominant cultural attitude to language and literary style. Swift's exhortations can be paralleled in works from the mid-seventeenth century onward recommending a simple, straightforward plain style. In a famous passage of one such work, Thomas Sprat's *History of the Royal Society* (1667), Sprat reports that the Royal Society has made "a constant Resolution, to reject all the amplifications, digressions, and swellings of style: to return back to the primitive purity, and shortness, when men deliver'd so many *things*, almost in an equal number of *words*."[1] Although the Houyhnhnms might be seen to exemplify this "primitive purity, and shortness," the Royal Society's prescription of a plain style, and particularly the materialism in its emphasis on "words" giving a grasp of "things," does not escape Swift's satiric ridicule. In Book iii of *Gulliver's Travels* the plain communication of things has become a project "to shorten Discourse" and "a Scheme for entirely abolishing all Words whatsoever." The professors of language in the Academy of Lagado propose "that since Words are only Names for *Things*, it would be more convenient for all Men to carry about them, such *Things* as were necessary to express the particular Business they are to discourse on" (*PW* xi: 185). In this burlesque of the theory that words and things are in one-to-one connection, the "word" has become the "thing" itself. In a characteristic Swiftian satiric literalization, the Lagadian sages sink under the weight of the bundle of things that they carry on their backs for conversation.

The lumbering linguists in Lagado are also a *reductio ad absurdum* of universal language schemes associated with the Royal Society. According to John Wilkins (1614–72), one of the founders of the Royal Society and a universal language theorist, the great advantage of a universal language scheme was that it would "mightily conduce to the spreading of all arts and sciences: because that great part of our time which is now required to the learning of words, might then be employed in the study of things."[2] For the absurd linguists in Lagado dispensing with words in favor of carrying *"Things"* would "serve as an universal Language to be understood in all civilized Nations... And thus, Embassadors would be qualified to treat with foreign Princes or Ministers of State, to whose Tongues they were utter Strangers" (*PW* XI: 186). Yet the idea of a universal language returns with a satiric charge in *Gulliver's Travels*. The Houyhnhnms may "have no more Existence than the Inhabitants of *Utopia*"(*PW* XI: 8), but their plain-style simplicity and propriety in conversation represent a Swiftian ideal and are offered as a contrast to European corruption. Their language, which is oral not written, and so presumed to have escaped the corruption of textuality, is wryly implied at one point to be an appropriate model for a universal language. Gulliver observes of the Houyhnhnm language that "the Words might with little Pains be resolved into an Alphabet more easily than the *Chinese*" (*PW* XI: 226). Chinese was thought suitable as a universal language model.[3] It is admired for its permanence in Swift's *Proposal for Correcting the English Tongue* (*PW* IV: 9). The Houyhnhnm language is ideal in Swift's satire because of its simplicity and brevity and because it is free from the fate of human language, which is to degenerate. Swift's linguistic didacticism coexists with a love of verbal play. The invented names and language given to the peoples Gulliver meets on his voyages display Swift's love of word games and mock languages, a playfulness evidenced also in the "little language" employed in his correspondence with Esther Johnson ("Stella") and Rebecca Dingley and in the punning language games he enjoyed in his correspondence and collaborations with his friend Thomas Sheridan.

An advocate of a plain style, Swift rejected stylistic amplification in his verse and prose. He typically eschewed what he called the "lofty style" (*Poems* 518, 520). But although he preferred a plain style, he hardly practiced plain statement. Beneath the seeming simplicity of his concise plain style is a challenging complexity. Swift is not reader-friendly. He deploys putative speakers and prefers impersonation to speaking *in propria persona*. Readers have to negotiate writing that is radically parodic, ironic, and oblique. When Gulliver says he chose "to relate plain Matter of Fact in the simplest Manner and Style" the passage in fact parodies the claims made by contemporary voyagers and the linguistic prescriptions of the Royal Society (*PW* XI: 291). Gulliver's plain style is the vehicle for a bewildering array of ironies, parodies, and attacking purposes. The ubiquity of parody in Swift's writings has been explained in psychological terms as a personal defensiveness. Claude Rawson comments that it "springs from a certain temperamental reluctance to expose himself too openly in his own person, just as his frequent resort to the obliquities of irony protected him from the vulnerabilities and the simplifying commitments of plain statement."[4] Certainly, much of Swift's political work is guarded, as Murray Pittock says, "into irretrievable ambivalence."[5] In Swift's Opposition political writing, particularly on the dangerous dynastic issue of the time (that is, whether to support the Hanoverian succession to the throne or to restore the exiled Stuarts in the person of James II's son, "James III" or the "Pretender"), the use of putative speakers, parody, ironic indirection, and ambiguity afforded considerable advantages. In a culture where there were "two communities of allegiance,"[6] Jacobite and Hanoverian, and conditions of censorship in which a Whig government was willing and able to prosecute disaffection that favored the exiled House of Stuart, such figurative resources enabled Swift to say politically unspeakable things. Expressions of his anti-Hanoverianism are often punctuated as an aside, delivered indirectly or in undertone. The pun and the parenthesis (disliked by Whig cultural ideologues such as Joseph Addison, Richard Steele, John Dennis, and Daniel Defoe because of their indirection and dubiety) are favorite Swiftian figures. A few simple examples of Swift's stylistic strategy on the most dangerous political topic of the day must suffice here.

In "On Poetry: a Rhapsody" virulent anti-Hanoverianism pretends not to be:

> But now go search all Europe round,
> Among the savage monsters crowned,
> With vice polluting every throne
> (I mean all kings except our own).
>
> (*Poems* 533)

In this case the self-protective parenthesis also functions as ironic intensification of the satire. The inhumanity of the Hanoverian monarch is imputed in Swift's most famous satire, but indirectly, through fictional characters. In Book I of *Gulliver's Travels* Gulliver in Lilliput is arbitrarily convicted of high treason. The Emperor of Lilliput's "great *Lenity*" to Gulliver manifests itself in commuting immediate capital punishment to blinding and starvation. Gulliver reports the propagandist abuse of language which is the Lilliputian court style:

> It was a Custom introduced by this Prince and his Ministry, (very different, as I have been assured, from the Practices of former Times) that after the Court had decreed any cruel Execution, either to gratify the Monarch's Resentment, or the Malice of a Favourite; the Emperor always made a Speech to his whole Council, expressing his *great Lenity and Tenderness, as Qualities known and*

confessed by all the World. This Speech was immediately published through the Kingdom; nor did any thing terrify the People so much as those Encomiums on his Majesty's Mercy; because it was observed, that the more these Praises were enlarged and insisted on, the more *inhuman* was the Punishment, and the *Sufferer more innocent.* (*PW* xi: 72)

After the Jacobite rising of 1715 and the execution of the Jacobite leaders and transportation of many others, King George in speeches to his parliament in 1716 and 1717 referred to "the numerous instances of mercy which I have shown" and his "clemency" in the treatment of the Jacobite rebels.[7] Swift's satire of the Emperor of Lilliput's mercy (and the parenthesis indicating that such abuses did not happen in former reigns) is an attack on the Hanoverian regime in fictional disguise. The Jacobite Matthias Earbery was outlawed in 1717 for an outspoken attack on King George called *The History of the Clemency of Our English Monarchs.* The elaborate eulogy of the Emperor of Lilliput's mercy juxtaposed with the articles of impeachment by which Gulliver "shall be liable to the Pains and Penalties of High Treason" (*PW* xi: 68–72) satirizes Whig propaganda. Thomas Burnet's *The British Bulwark* (1715), for example, eulogized King George as "exemplary for the Mildness of his Government" then listed all the clauses in the draconian treason statutes by which supporters of the exiled Stuarts could incur imprisonment, forfeitures, torture, and death.[8] In a brilliant passage in Book III of the *Travels*, the King of Luggnagg's "great Clemency, and the Care he hath of his Subjects Lives, (wherein it were much to be wished that the Monarchs of *Europe* would imitate him)" is so elaborated as to accentuate his actual arbitrary homicide of his subjects (*PW* xi: 205).

As Dean of St. Patrick's Cathedral in Dublin and an Opposition figure often accused of Jacobitism, Swift felt constrained to make public declarations of his allegiance to the Hanoverian monarchy. Whatever secret irony might be lurking in his sometimes hyperbolic public professions of loyalty – apparently at odds with the violent hostility toward the Hanoverian kings expressed in his satire and correspondence – they are nevertheless plain declarative statements. When Swift, exceptionally, does seem to express solidarity with the Jacobite community of allegiance, it is marked as in strictest confidence, delivered as an oblique hint with a punning proverbial phrase and a parenthesis. The following couplet appears in his "Epilogue" to a performance of *Hamlet* for the benefit of the poor Irish weavers. It expresses cross-class sympathy and perhaps something else:

> Under the rose, since here are none but friends
> (To own the truth) we have some private ends.
>
> (*Poems* 228)

In popular Jacobite verse the white rose was the symbol of the House of Stuart (King George was symbolized as a turnip) and the proverbial "under the rose" (meaning in strictest confidence) was used in this period as a Jacobite motto.[9] Swift's allusive political writing artfully operates in danger zones and depends on context for full effect. The scabrous contemporary Jacobite slander of King George as the "Turnip" is ingenuously insinuated in Swift's punning pamphlet of 1732, *An Examination of Certain Abuses, Corruptions, and Enormities in the City of Dublin*. Jacobites are said to use "a Cant-way of talking in their Clubs, after this Manner: *We hope to see the Cards shuffled once more, and another King* TURNUP *Trump*" (*PW* XII: 231). Swift's obituary for himself, *Verses on the Death of Dr. Swift* (written *c*. 1731–32), registers the ambiguity about Swift's allegiance in the Hanoverian period, by a pun within a parenthesis, as an aside about cards, during a ladies' card game: "*(I wish I knew which king to call)*" (*Poems* 491).

Writing on the English language and English literary history in Swift's lifetime was a profoundly politicized activity. For Stuart loyalists and Tories such as John Dryden and Francis Atterbury, the English language approached perfection and literary culture its greatest politeness after the restoration of the Stuart monarchy in 1660. For Whig writers on language and literature such as Joseph Addison, Daniel Defoe, John Dennis, John Oldmixon, Richard Steele, and Leonard Welsted, the Revolution of 1688 and William III's reign were foundational for liberty and the perfection of the language and the polite arts.[10] Whig cultural ideologists such as Anthony Ashley Cooper, the third Earl of Shaftesbury, envision the Revolution of 1688 as inaugurating a "culture of politeness."[11] Swift's contribution to the *Tatler* No. 230 (September 28, 1710) is a hostile linguistic critique of the new "Affectation of Politeness" (*PW* II: 173). The Revolution and beginning of William III's reign are identified with the decline of the English language; the Stuart era with its improvement. Swift complains of "*the continual Corruption of our* English *Tongue; which, without some timely Remedy, will suffer more by the false Refinements of Twenty Years past, than it hath been improved in the foregoing Hundred*." He recommends "an annual *Index Expurgatorious*" to expunge corrupt words and sentences by authority (*PW* II: 174, 176). The Stuart loyalist, Tory version of the literary past is presented in epitome in Swift's punning work *A History of Poetry* (1726). The reigns of Charles I and Charles II are the apogee of poetic achievement. Under Cromwell and the Commonwealth 'we fell into Burlesque' and upon the Revolution of 1688 "Poetry seem'd to decline" (*PW* IV: 273–75).

As the author of *The Examiner* and such celebrated works of propaganda as *The Conduct of the Allies*, Swift was a high-profile Tory writer.

By the end of Queen Anne's reign he was being placed by contemporaries "in the first list of Rank Tories" (*CW* I: 605). A public indication of his Tory party-political alignment was the publication of his major pamphlet on the English language, *A Proposal for Correcting, Improving and Ascertaining the English Tongue*, to which he affixed his name, something which he very rarely did. Swift's proposal for a society or academy to fix the language is emphatically Tory and ambiguously Jacobite in character. Contemporary Whig critics were quick to recognize its political character, even though Swift adduces in support of his proposal the authority of his Whig friend Joseph Addison who had advocated, in *The Spectator*, "something like an Academy" to settle language controversies.[12] Proposals for a language academy were not new and had been advanced several times since the Restoration. The political provenance of such proposals was various: royalist and Church of England Tory as well as Presbyterian Whig. The politics of Swift's language academy becomes apparent when it is compared with these earlier proposals. The loyalist Tory Thomas Sprat, for example, had proposed an academy for perfecting the English language based on the model of the French Academy founded by "the *Great Cardinal de Richelieu*" and Royal Charter in 1635. Sprat complained of the "many fantastical terms, which were introduc'd by our *Religious Sects*" during the English Civil Wars. An English academy would correct words and emend accent and grammar so that the language would achieve "the greatest smoothness, which its derivation from the rough *German* will allow it."[13] Daniel Defoe's more recent proposal for an academy was consonant with his Presbyterian Whig conception of the role of the Godly Protestant prince. The foundation of the academy is proper only for King William III, who will thereby eclipse the French monarchy. For Defoe the English language is "capable of a much greater Perfection" than the French. Its "Comprehensiveness of Expression" excels that of its neighbors. Defoe's academy would exclude the clergy and other impolite professions. For Defoe "*Custom*" is "now our best Authority for Words." King William III's academy would be an original source of customary usage and a judicature.[14]

Significantly, Swift's "Society" is to look to the "Example of the *French*" academy (*PW* IV: 14, 20). For Swift the English language is "less refined than those of *Italy, Spain*, or *France*" (*PW* IV: 6), but it "received most Improvement" during the reigns of Queen Elizabeth I and King Charles I. The apogee of English politeness is the period of King Charles I's personal rule. The language was corrupted during the Civil Wars and Commonwealth period (*PW* IV: 9–10). Contemporary Whigs such as Defoe and Oldmixon accept the authority of custom and admit that language inevitably changes. They follow John Locke in understanding language as a human creation. In contrast, Swift does not accept customary authority. He wants to correct, improve, and fix the language for ever. He implicitly appeals to the idea of a universal grammar and divine authority. English "offends against every Part of Grammar" (*PW* IV: 6). A defective language made familiar and customary by usage over time is still to be corrected. The standard for the language is God's Word as mediated by the Church of England. The King James Authorized Version of the Bible, the Common Prayer Book, and Liturgy, perpetually read in English churches, are the proven standard for language and stylistic eloquence and simplicity (*PW* IV: 15). Swift says elsewhere that it is the Divines of the Church of England who have brought the language to its highest standard (*PW* II: 97). Obviously, the clergy have a central role in Swift's project for the language.

Swift wishes to resist language change, which he equates with violent conquest and revolution, and approves of languages supposed to have resisted change (*PW* IV: 9). Swift's satire reflects ideas on language expressed in the *Proposal*. In Book III of *Gulliver's Travels*, the language of the kingdom of Luggnagg is "always upon the Flux" and the immortal "*Struldbruggs* of one Age do not understand those of another" (*PW* XI: 213). However, the utopian Houyhnhnm culture in Book IV seems immemorial. Their poetry is Homeric in character. The speech of these horses "approaches nearest to the *High Dutch* or *German*," one of the languages Swift listed in the *Proposal* as admitting little change, "but is much more graceful and significant" (*PW* XI: 234; *PW* IV: 9).

Swift's *Proposal* expresses intense animus against the Saxon language. Swift objects to the number of monosyllables in English, which is due to the fact "that the *Latin* Tongue in its Purity was never in this Island" and that Britain was occupied by the Saxons, who imposed their imperfect language (*PW* IV: 6–7). Swift laments that "we are naturally not very polite" and seems to conceive his linguistic task as fencing against the "Barbarity" of Saxon influence (*PW* IV: 12). The Whig press decoded Jacobitism in Swift's hostility to the Saxon language and approval of the romance languages. Excluding the Hanoverian dynasty and restoring the exiled Stuart Pretender would ensure "no new Addition of *Saxon* Words."[15] In this context, Swift's later virulently anti-Hanoverian poem "Directions for a Birthday Song" shows that Swift's Whig critics were not too far off the mark. The poem's putative Whig panegyric poet must confront the offence to British patriotism and the English language which the German royal family represents:

> A skilful critic justly blames
> Hard, tough, cramp, guttural, harsh, stiff names.
> The sense can never be too jejune,

But smooth your words to fit the tune,
Hanover may do well enough,
But George, and Brunswick are too rough.
Hesse Darmstadt makes too rough a sound,
And Guelph the strongest ear will wound.
In vain are all attempts from Germany
To find out proper words for harmony.

(*Poems* 393)

John Oldmixon's Whig *Reflections* on the *Proposal* delights in discrediting Swift's authoritarian prescriptiveness by quoting Swift's transgressions of propriety in works such as *A Tale of a Tub*, and even in this very *Proposal* (Swift's fulsome panegyric of Robert Harley, the Lord Treasurer, contradicts his own strictures about stylistic propriety). Swift's *Proposal* was considered to be an impolite and Jacobite project by his Whig critics. But it was answered also by a Jacobite Anglo-Saxon scholar, Elizabeth Elstob. She exposed Swift's ignorance about Saxon and defended antiquarian Anglo-Saxon scholars from Swift's casual belle-lettrist scorn (see *PW* IV: 18). Unlike Whig answerers, Elstob expresses no objection to the political implications of Swift's *Proposal* but counters his censure of monosyllables, for example, by quoting from Swift's monosyllabic verse.[16]

The view of language and style in the *Proposal* and elsewhere in Swift's writings raises the question of his response to John Locke's influential philosophical work on language in Book Three of *An Essay Concerning Human Understanding* (1690). For Locke words are signs of ideas in the mind rather than things in the world and the relation between those signs and ideas is arbitrary rather than natural. Tacit consent and social convention about the ideas signified by words enable communication. Locke is concerned about the "Abuse of Words" where the word is made to signify different ideas, thereby frustrating serious intention and destabilizing consensual meaning. Swift parodied "the refined Way of Speaking...introduced by Mr. *Locke*" and believed there were "some dangerous Tenets" in Locke's "*Human Understanding*" (*PW* II: 80, 97). Nevertheless, Swift shared Locke's concern about the abuse of words. A memorable passage from Locke's *Essay*, about scholastic learning destroying the instruments of communication, is refunctioned in the moral satire of Book IV of *Gulliver's Travels* when Gulliver explains the legal profession's systemic language abuse in the service of injustice. Locke had written: "But though unlearned Men well enough understood the Words *White* and *Black*, etc. and had constant Notions of the *Ideas* signified by those Words; yet there were Philosophers found, who had learning and *subtlety* enough to prove... that *White* was *Black*".[17] Gulliver reports that "there was a Society of Men among us, bred up from their Youth in the Art of proving by Words multiplied for the Purpose, that *White* is *Black*, and *Black* is *White*, according as they are paid" (*PW* xi: 248). Like Locke here, Swift typically trusts in the common sense of ordinary unlearned people in linguistic matters rather than in learned professionals (see *PW* iv: 13; *PW* ix: 65–66; *PW* xi: 185).

However, Locke is hostile to rhetorical tropes and ambiguous word-play which disrupt the plain communication of human understanding. Lockean theory in this area was appropriated by Addison and others in what amounted to a Whig cultural proscription of figures such as the pun and the parenthesis as crimes against common discourse. The pun introduced an unsettling homonymic ambiguity disrupting the serious connection between word and intended idea. It represented a threat to the linguistic order of plain communication. For Whigs, the pun was associated with impoliteness; the corruption identified with the Stuart dynasty.[18] The parenthesis was a licentious abuse associated with dubiety and disruptive indirection.[19] However, the pun and the parenthesis are very much part of Swift's satiric arsenal against individual and group targets. Swift mocked the Whig cultural project against the pun (*PW* ii: 92; *PW* 12: 231). One of Swift's first explicitly Tory party-political works is a punning ballad entitled *A Dialogue between Captain Tom and Sir Henry Dutton Colt* (1710; *Poems* 112–13). One of his first works in the Hanoverian period is *A Modest Defence of Punning* (1716; *PW* iv: 205–10). His intervention on the side of Bishop Atterbury in the paper war concerning the Bishop's arrest and conviction for Jacobite conspiracy is a venomously adroit display of punning, titled *Upon the Horrid Plot Discovered by Harlequin the Bishop of Rochester's French Dog* (*Poems* 247–49).

Swift exploited the opprobrium with which the parenthesis was held in the Whig culture of politeness. In "Verses wrote in a Lady's Ivory Table-Book," as published in Swift's *Miscellanies in Prose and Verse* of 1711, the fashionable clichés, corrupt orthography, and grammar of the lady and her beau – the linguistic signs of their inanity – are placed within the despised marks of parenthesis, as if quarantined within the poem. As John Lennard observes in a delightful study of parentheses, a "Table-Book" appears to mean in Swift's poem a memoranda book composed of tablets rather than paper pages. Pencilled entries on the tablets could be wiped away by, as the poem puts it, the "power of Spittle" and a cloth. The "Table-Book" thus images the fate of ephemeral and defective modern writing. In Swift's printed poem the offensive linguistic abuses fated to be erased are put in parentheses.[20] In Swift's satiric pamphlet *A Letter of Thanks from My Lord Wharton To the Lord Bishop of S. Asaph, In the Name of the Kit-Cat-Club*

(1712), a reference to language change is wittily arrested in a parenthesis. Swift is attacking the oratorical style of the Whig Bishop, William Fleetwood: "whatever Changes our Language may undergo (and every thing that is *English* is given to change) this happy Word ['SUCH'] is sure to live in your immortal Preface" (*PW* VI: 153). Swift mocks the Bishop's use of a "moving *Parenthesis*," but his own parentheses in this pamphlet are explosive devices of satiric exposure (*PW* VI: 154).

A signature of Swift's style for his contemporaries was its extremism. His polemic and satire direct considerable and often literal violence against its targets. For all the uncertainty of its indeterminate irony and indirection, Swift's polemic and satire implied off-the-page menaces for his contemporaries. There are oblique and explicit calls to massacre throughout Swift's writings. A short way with dissenting preachers is imagined in Section I of *A Tale of a Tub* (*PW* I: 34–36). The wish is expressed in his Irish tracts for an annual hanging of half a dozen bankers, or indeed the hanging of all bankers, as a way of delaying the ruin of the Irish economy (*PW* XII: 11, 177). The majority of Irish beggars, like the Yahoos, deserve "to be rooted out off the Face of the Earth" (*PW* XIII: 139; *PW* XI: 271). As Claude Rawson has said of this exterminatory rhetorical extremism in Swift, it "is assumed not to be quite literal but flirts actively with its literal potential." There is a radical uncertainty about the ironic status of such utterances, "Swift doesn't 'mean it,' though he doesn't *not* mean it either."[21] In *To a Lady*, Swift describes his Opposition political poetry. He says he just laughs at Walpolean politicians:

> Like the ever-laughing sage,
> In a jest I spend my rage.
> (Though it must be understood,
> I would hang them if I could:)
> (*Poems* 519)

The parenthesis is disturbing because it cannot be discounted as irony. The simulated joking is over and the aside registers an undertone of menace. In "The Revolution at Market Hill," Swift imagines himself and his Jacobite friend Henry Leslie plotting a revolution, after which they would act as Whig politicians have done and dispossess and "hang" the "rogues" (*Poems* 396–98). Certainly we know that when Swift did have access to state power during the Tory administration of 1710–14 he did not just rely on the lash of satire to castigate his political enemies. For instance, he instigated the arrest of the Whig journalist Abel Boyer for attacking him in print: "One Boyer, a French dog, has abused me in a pamphlet, and I have got him up in a messenger's hands: the secretary [of state] promises me to swinge him...I must make that rogue an example for warning to others" (*PW* XVI: 384–85). (The "rogue" was arrested but escaped punishment.) Swift went on to pursue other Whig writers such as Richard Steele and Gilbert Burnet in his polemical satire. Swift pillories them for what "the Poverty of our Language forceth me to call their Stile" (*PW* IV: 57).

Swift's project to fix the English language sought plainness and permanence. Yet his polemic and satire characteristically exploit the ambiguity and instability of language, but for precise effects in specific historical situations. Swift's use of language is at its most unstable when his political satire enters the discursive space covered by the English statute defining High Treason. That statute (25 Edward III, Stat. 5, Cap. 2) declares in part that it is High Treason to "compass or imagine the Death of our Lord the King" or to "levy War against our Lord the King in his Realm, or be adherent to the Kings Enemies."[22] In private letters to his friends in the political Opposition in 1735 Swift reveals an extremist political imaginary. He wishes "princes had capacity to read the history of the *Roman* emperors; how many of them were murdered by their own army, and the same may be said of the *Ottomans* by their janissaries" (*C* IV: 337). The intention of such rhetoric is ambiguous, but that the target is the Hanoverian king is unmistakable, if not explicitly stated. As Swift said in another letter: "if I were younger, I should probably outlive the Liberty of England, which, without some unexpected assistance from Heaven, many thousand now alive will see governed by an absolute Monarch" (*C* IV: 381). Swift's manuscripts also reveal the extremism of his political imaginary. In the manuscript of *An Enquiry into the Behaviour of the Queen's Last Ministry* (1715–19) there is a passage imagining a civil war against King George and the Whig regime. It is crossed out (*PW* VIII: 218). Also left in manuscript and not printed in Swift's lifetime is a passage in Book III of *Gulliver's Travels* that encodes a threat of successful Irish resistance to King George's government. Gulliver is assured that "the Citizens were determined . . . to kill the King and all his Servants, and entirely change the Government" (*PW* XI: 310). Aspects of Swift's rhetorical violence were unspeakable and could not be safely printed even within parentheses.

NOTES

1. Thomas Sprat, in Jackson I. Cope and Harold Whitmore Jones (eds.) *The History of the Royal Society* (London: Routledge, 1959), Part 2, Section XX, p. 113.
2. *The Mathematical and Philosophical Works of John Wilkins*, 2 vols. (London, 1802), vol. II, p. 54, quoted in Clive T. Probyn, "Swift and Linguistics: The Context behind Lagado and around the Fourth Voyage," *Neophilologus* 58 (1974), 425–39, especially 428.
3. Probyn, "Swift and Linguistics," 437, 439 n. 35.

4. C. J. Rawson, " 'I the Lofty Stile Decline': Self-apology and the 'Heroick Strain' in Some of Swift's Poems," in Robert Folkenflik (ed.) *The English Hero, 1660–1800* (Newark: University of Delaware Press; London and Toronto: Associated University Presses, 1982), pp. 79–115, especially p. 94.

5. Murray G. H. Pittock, *Poetry and Jacobite Politics in Eighteenth-Century Britain and Ireland* (Cambridge: Cambridge University Press, 1994), p. 127.

6. Howard Erskine-Hill, "Twofold Vision in Eighteenth-Century Writing," *English Literary History* 64 (1997), 903–24, especially 910.

7. William Cobbett (ed.) *The Parliamentary History of England*, 36 vols. (London, 1806–20), vol. VII, cols. 386, 448.

8. Thomas Burnet, *The British Bulwark* (London, 1715), p. 12; Joan Pittock, "Thomas Hearne and the Narratives of Englishness," *British Journal for Eighteenth-Century Studies* 22 (1999), 1–14, especially 7–9.

9. Paul Monod, *Jacobitism and the English People, 1688–1788* (Cambridge: Cambridge University Press, 1989), pp. 57–58 (turnip), pp. 64–66, 210–20 (rose), p. 289 ("under the rose"); Pittock, *Poetry and Jacobite Politics*, pp. 119–28.

10. David Womersley (ed.) *Augustan Critical Writing* (Harmondsworth: Penguin, 1997), pp. xii, xiv–xix.

11. Lawrence E. Klein, *Shaftesbury and the Culture of Politeness: Moral Discourse and Cultural Politics in Early Eighteenth-Century England* (Cambridge: Cambridge University Press, 1994).

12. PW IV: 16; No. 135, in *The Spectator*, ed. Donald F. Bond (Oxford: Clarendon Press, 1965), 5 vols., vol. II, p. 35; John Oldmixon, *Reflections on Dr. Swift's Letter to the Earl of Oxford, about the English Tongue* (London, 1712) and Arthur Mainwaring, in Louis A. Landa (ed.) *The British Academy* (London, 1712), *The Augustan Reprint Society*, No. 15 (Los Angeles: William Andrews Clark Memorial Library, 1948).

13. Sprat, *The History of the Royal Society*, Part I, Sections XIX–XX, pp. 39, 42.

14. Daniel Defoe, *An Essay upon Projects* (London, 1697; reprinted Menston: Scolar Press, 1969), "Of Academies," pp. 227–51.

15. *The Medley* May 23–26, 1712, quoted by Louis A. Landa in *PW* IV: xiii.

16. Elizabeth Elstob, *An Apology for the Study of Northern Antiquities* (1715), ed. Charles Peake, *The Augustan Reprint Society*, No. 61 (Los Angeles: William Andrews Clark Memorial Library, 1956).

17. John Locke, *An Essay Concerning Human Understanding*, ed. Peter H. Nidditch (Oxford: Clarendon Press, 1975), Book III, chapter X, section 10, p. 495.

18. The Whig campaign against the pun can be followed in *The Tatler* No. 32 (June 23, 1709 by Steele), *The Spectator* No. 61 (May 10, 1711 by Addison) and *The Guardian* No. 36 (April 22, 1713 by Steele). See Klein, *Shaftesbury*, pp. 209–10; Simon J. Alderson, "The Augustan Attack on the Pun," *Eighteenth-Century Life* 20 (1996), 1–19 and his "Swift and the Pun," *Swift Studies* 11 (1996), 47–57.

19. Defoe, *An Essay upon Projects*, p. 245; John Lennard, *But I Digress: The Exploitation of Parentheses in English Printed Verse* (Oxford: Clarendon Press, 1991), p. 90.

20. *P* I: 60–61; Lennard, *But I Digress*, p. 109.

21. Claude Rawson, "Killing the Poor: An Anglo-Irish Theme?" *Essays in Criticism* 49 (1999), 101–31, especially 102, 124; and his *Order from Confusion Sprung: Studies in Eighteenth-Century Literature from Swift to Cowper* (London: George Allen & Unwin, 1985), p. 195.

22. *Collection of the several Statutes, and Parts of Statutes, Now in Force, relating to High Treason, and Misprision of High Treason* (London, 1709), p. 5.

9

MARCUS WALSH

Swift and religion

It can be no surprise that Jonathan Swift wrote throughout his life on matters relating to the Anglican church, religion, worship, and discipline. He lived in a kingdom the overwhelming majority of whose inhabitants were believing, observing Christians. In England, much the greater part were baptized and practicing members of the Anglican church, the church established by law (the case in Ireland, as we shall see, was both demographically and politically rather different). Works of theology, divinity, and biblical commentary constituted, in the seventeenth century and through most of the eighteenth century, the most numerous of any class of writings published in Britain. And Swift of course, for virtually all his adult life, was an ordained member of the Anglican priesthood, engaged in its daily duties and its high political interests, and for three decades Dean of St. Patrick's Cathedral in Dublin.

It is not easy for us now, however, to think of Swift as primarily a Christian writer. The works we most regularly read, and which have the firmest place in university syllabi, are not his most obviously Christian: *Gulliver's Travels*, the *Modest Proposal*, such poems as "A Beautiful Young Nymph Going to Bed" or "Cassinus and Peter," or "A Description of a City Shower." Our favorites among Swift's religious works include *A Tale of a Tub*, or the *Argument against Abolishing Christianity*, or the *Discourse Concerning the Mechanical Operation of the Spirit*; writings, in fact which particularly satisfy our modern preference for uncertainty and reflexivity of voice, for the parodic and indeterminate. Many of Swift's most significant and exemplary religious statements, however, including his eleven surviving sermons, the *Letter to a Young Gentleman, Lately enter'd into Holy Orders*, or the *Sentiments of a Church-of-England Man*, use a simpler, more direct, and altogether less playful voice.

Further, Swift must appear in his religious writings, to modern readers, an awkwardly conservative and conventional thinker. Of course we cherish our image of Swift the servant of human liberty, the defender of the lower clergy, the advocate of the Irish common people, the spokesman for Irish economic, political, and ecclesiastical interests.[1] Many of his attitudes fit badly or not at all, however, with a modern democratic or ecumenist or pluralist view: his impassioned resistance to the "comprehension" of dissenters or non-conformists (their admission to worship and employment within the established church); his insistence that, while thought is free, religious and political expression must be restricted, even censored; his acceptance, and indeed advocacy, of subordination in society and of episcopacy (government by the bishops) in the church; his arguments for the role of mystery in belief; his apparently almost total disinterest in matters of personal faith, and in the individual's relationship to God. These positions need to be delineated and explained in the light of Swift's own life and career, and of the historical circumstances and political and religious debates of his times.

Having begun his career as a protégé of the English statesman and diplomat Sir William Temple, Swift was ordained as a deacon in the Anglican church in 1694, at the age of twenty-six, and as a priest in January 1695. In 1695 he was appointed to Kilroot, in the diocese of Down and Connor in County Antrim, in the capacity of prebendary (the holder of an ecclesiastical living derived from land and property in and around the village itself). As a clergyman in the Church of Ireland – that is, the Anglican church in Ireland – he joined an embattled institution, under severe economic strain, politically dominated by England and the English church hierarchy, struggling to maintain its devotional and pastoral position as a minority group of believers amongst indigenous Roman Catholics and immigrant Presbyterians. He found at Kilroot a parish without a useable church building, almost without parishioners, much of its land alienated from the church, many of its tithes taken from the clergyman's benefice and appropriated to lay use. Of equal concern from his own point of view, Swift found himself surrounded by a flourishing population of Presbyterians, Scottish small farmers and their descendants, who had flooded into northern Ireland in the reigns of James I and Charles I, hostile to episcopacy and the Church of England liturgy, and vigorously favored by King William and his ministers.[2] These years, and this experience, no doubt strengthened if they did not originate Swift's outspoken antipathy to dissent in all its forms, and his lifelong resistance to the repeal of the Test Act, or Sacramental Test, which excluded from public offices all but those who were prepared to take communion under Anglican forms.

Swift was resident in his Antrim parishes no more than a year before going back to the household of Sir William Temple at Moor Park in Surrey. He returned to Ireland however as chaplain to Charles Berkeley, Lord Justice of Ireland, and was appointed to a prebend (a post entitling him to a share in the cathedral's revenues) at St. Patrick's in Dublin in 1700, his church livings including Laracor (of which he was vicar) and Meath. The diocese of Meath differed from Down and Connor in that here Swift and his small Church of Ireland congregation found themselves outnumbered not by Presbyterians but by native Catholics. It resembled Down and Connor however, and all too many other dioceses, in the dilapidation of its churches, the lack of lands and residences for the lower clergy, and the alienation of church tithes into lay hands. Swift's years at Kilroot and Laracor made him all too aware of the weakened temporal condition of the Irish church, and more especially of the impoverished state of the lower clergy, who subsisted on inadequate stipends, had to spread their ministry over scattered pluralities, and struggled to secure payment of tithes from resentful Anglican landlords. More than two decades later he would complain that "the Maintenance of the *Clergy*, throughout the Kingdom, is precarious and uncertain" (*PW* xii: 191). In these first positions he personally felt the effects of the alienation (or "impropriation") of tithes into the hands of the local Anglican gentry, and in writings even two and three decades later he continued to inveigh against clerical poverty and its causes, and especially the difficulties raised by the Anglican gentry, as well as by Catholics and dissenters, in the payment of tithes.[3]

In 1707 he was deputed by the Irish bishops to undertake in London a major political enterprise, the solicitation of the remission of two taxes which bore especially heavily on the impoverished lower clergy, the "First Fruits," payable to the crown by every incumbent as he assumed his benefice, and the "Twentieth Parts," a sum amounting to one-twentieth of the annual value of a benefice. Swift found the Whig ministry uncooperative, however, the Lord Treasurer Godolphin effectively refusing to agree unless the Irish bishops would accept the removal of the Test in Ireland. This was a concession which Swift, opposed throughout his life to the comprehension of dissenters, of course could not make. It was not until the Whig ministry fell, and Godolphin was succeeded by Harley as Lord Treasurer, that Swift, returning to London once more in 1711, was able to bring his mission to a successful conclusion. His political skills and prominence did not result in the English bishopric for which he had hoped, but in his appointment in 1713 as Dean of St. Patrick's in Dublin.

In this position, until the onset of incapacity in 1742, Swift exercised his most conspicuous influence as a preacher, Christian apologist, and active member of the church as an institution. The Dean of St. Patrick's had almost a bishop's dignities and privileges, and Swift exerted his authority in the cathedral with determination; "it is an infallible maxim," he declared, in a letter of 1721, "that not one thing is done here without the dean's consent" (*C* ii: 377). Swift's assertion of his decanal prerogatives not infrequently brought him into conflict with William King, Archbishop of Dublin, whose jurisdictions overlapped with those of the Dean.[4] Beyond St. Patrick's itself,

Swift as Dean had jurisdiction over the "liberties," an urban area of a few acres around the cathedral building. Indeed, over the years he would claim not merely a legal writ but a kind of popular leadership, describing himself as "absolute monarch in the *Liberties*, and King of the Mob."[5] Swift did not confine himself however to the exercise of his rule. He made every effort to secure the finances, repair and improve the building, maintain the worship, and oversee the music of the cathedral. He was particularly concerned to improve the cathedral choir, critically listening to the performance of the anthem each Sunday evening, and appointing choristers to vacant places on the basis of their musical abilities rather than their connections (C II: 339). He devoted particular attention to the writing and delivery of his sermons; though only eleven survive, they are more than enough to demonstrate the care he took over their composition, and the stress he placed on the preacher's clear, intelligible delivery of the central beliefs and morals of Christianity (or, to put it more particularly, of Anglican Christianity).[6]

Throughout his years as Dean, Swift was heavily involved in both the theory and the practice of Christian charity. Like most of his contemporaries, Swift accepted at the same time that all are created equal in the sight of God, and that society is inevitably built on a system of subordination which distributes wealth and power unequally. In his two sermons on the subject, "On Mutual Subjection" and "On the Poor Man's Contentment," Swift warns the poor to accept their subjection, but equally insists on the rich man's duty of charity to those less fortunate, expounding the familiar and conventional notion that a Christian may possess wealth only as a steward of God's bounty. Swift was not, however, merely a theorist of charity. His personal charitable giving amounted to a third of his (not inconsiderable) decanal income.[7] He was concerned especially with the often precarious condition of the small weavers and tradesmen, and their families, who lived in the vicinity of St. Patrick's. In 1716 he helped to found a charity school for the poor children of the St. Patrick's "liberties." Nine years later he was appointed to the board of the Blue Coats charity school. But his greatest charitable act was the bequeathing of his fortune towards the founding of St. Patrick's Hospital in Dublin, famously and ironically referred to, in the concluding lines of the *Verses on the Death of Dr. Swift*, as "a house for fools and mad"(E III: 817–19).

Swift defended the political and temporal interests of the Anglican church, and of the Church of Ireland, throughout his career. He maintained that, though episcopacy could not be shown to be of divine right, "the Scheme established among us of Ecclesiastical Government ... is most agreeable to primitive Institution; fittest ... for preserving Order and Purity, and ... best calculated for our Civil State" (*PW* II: 5). In Swift's view the church had endured a long history of depredation and despoliation, initiated by Henry VIII. Going far beyond a necessary and justifiable reformation, King Henry had seized the lands of the great abbeys, and had applied them to profane uses, rather than to the enrichment of poor bishoprics, or the augmentation of the benefices of parish clergy with cultivable land. Income from tithes and other ecclesiastical dues had been taken from the monasteries, and put into lay hands, leaving parishes stripped of income, and their pastors destitute. The poverty of the lower clergy remained a scandal in the eighteenth century, made most familiar in Swift's writing in his jibe, in the *Argument Against Abolishing Christianity*, that "there are ... in this Kingdom, above Ten Thousand Parsons; whose Revenues added to those of my Lords the Bishops, would suffice to maintain, at least, two Hundred young Gentlemen of Wit and Pleasure."[8] Swift wrote especially energetically on behalf of the Irish church, whose condition had been the same and worse as a consequence of Ireland's tumultuous and violent history: churches destroyed by the "fanatick zeal" of the Puritans, houses in disrepair, church lands constantly vulnerable to successive conquerors, parishes appropriated to the crown, impoverishment so severe that in many cases up to five or six parishes might be forced into amalgamation to provide a bare support for a single overworked incumbent.[9] Swift's most significant and practical contribution to the cause of the church and clergy was his embassy to England to gain for the Irish establishment the remission of the First Fruits and Twentieth Parts. He argued effectively for the building of new churches to serve the expanding population of the English cities, and especially of London (*PW* ii: 61). Amongst other significant causes, Swift was especially vocal on the subject of the Irish "interest" in the church, that is, in the cause of filling senior Irish church positions with those educated (as he had been) in Ireland, rather than with clergy sent from England. In this he had a political motive, opposing the Whig government's attempt to gain interest on the Irish episcopal bench. Swift's was a constant voice too for the public reputation as well as the material conditions of the lower clergy. Churchmen long before the end of the seventeenth century had deplored the "contempt of the clergy" (the phrase had been made familiar in John Eachard's tract, *The Grounds and Occasions of the Contempt of the Clergy and Religion Enquired into* [1670]), and the topic was a regular theme with Swift. His Church-of-England Man wonders "how that mighty Passion for the Church, which some Men pretend, can well consist with those Indignities, and that Contempt they bestow on the Persons of the Clergy." He alleges that free-thinkers in general are characterized by the contempt of priests, and, more particularly, he charges Bishop Burnet with indulging the high church habit of "of railing at the *Clergy*, in the Number of which he disdains to be reckoned, because he is a *Bishop*."[10]

None of Swift's views on Christian belief, worship, and behavior are significantly at variance with orthodox thinking amongst late seventeenth-century Anglican writers. Nor do they differ in substance from the public and accepted formulations of belief of the Church of England comprised in the *Book of Common Prayer* (as compiled in 1549 and 1552, and revised in 1662), and particularly the Thirty-Nine Articles of Religion (drafted in 1571), and the three Creeds (Apostles', Athanasian, and Nicene) which Anglicanism inherited from the early church. Throughout his life, despite his gloomy and embattled sense of the increasing wildness of the project, he stood up in defense of "*real* Christianity," as opposed to the nominal Christianity endorsed by the persona through whose voice is spoken his *Argument Against Abolishing Christianity* (*PW* II: 27). His position as a Christian priest is most fully and most straightforwardly set out in Swift's sermons, where we may find him using (in Louis Landa's words) "the heritage of ideas – the traditional counsel, the fixed doctrinal notions, the homiletic wisdom of the ages – that any clergyman had at hand for the edification of his flock" (*PW* IX: 101). Swift states more briefly some of the grounding assumptions of "real" Christian belief in his *Sentiments of a Church-of-England Man*: "whoever professes himself a Member of the Church of *England*, ought to believe a God, and his Providence, together with revealed Religion, and the Divinity of *Christ*" (*PW* II: 4). Swift believed that man is fallen, and may aspire to (though he may never finally achieve) virtue only through the Christian moral law, and the promise of future rewards and punishments.[11] Equally conventionally, and fundamentally, Swift believed that Christian truth was revealed to man by God, and that the Holy Scriptures were the source of that revelation, adequate and comprehensible for the communication of things necessary to belief; "uncorrupt, sufficient, clear, intire," in John Dryden's famous formulation, "in *all* things which our needfull *Faith* require."[12] Some of those truths are simple, and readily accessible to the exercise of any man's reason. Some, however, are mysteries which pass understanding, and for that very reason must not be exposed to prying enquiry, or to the grubby particularities of doctrinal polemics.

One of Swift's consequently very rare statements on doctrinal matters, his sermon "On the Trinity," provides us with the fullest and clearest statement of his beliefs regarding the revelation afforded by Scripture, the nature of divine mystery, and the role and limits of human reason in understanding and accepting God's revealed truth. "On the Trinity" is a sermon on a text, in this case the scriptural verse which states and communicates, as Swift would insist, this essential doctrine: "For there are three that bear record in heaven, the Father, the Word, and the Holy Ghost: and these three are one" (1 John 5: 7). This verse, the celebrated and notorious "*Comma Johanneum*," had been for centuries the subject of anxious and often abstruse interpretative debate amongst Christian theologians and controversialists. In the later years of the seventeenth century and the opening decades of the eighteenth century it had involved Anglican divines in argument with opponents of a variety of persuasions, Socinians (who claimed that Christ was human), Arians (followers of a more ancient heresy, who claimed that Christ was not truly divine, but was created by God), and deists (who, in different ways, argued for a natural and rational religion, monotheistic and non-sectarian). A particular focus of argument was Samuel Clarke's *Scripture Doctrine of the Trinity*, published in 1712, and accused by some of Clarke's many opponents of Arianism. Like many other divines of his time, however, Swift thought such public indulgence in scholastic enquiry and disagreement, on such an issue and such a text, both unnecessary and dangerous, multiplying controversies "to such a Degree, as to beget Scruples that have perplexed the Minds of many sober Christians, who otherwise could never have maintained them" (*PW* IX: 160). Scripture is the only revelation that God has afforded us, and the Trinity must be understood, Swift insists, in the plain sense of the words of Scripture, even though we cannot conceptualize and rationalize what those words mean. Hence, from Scripture, "it is plain, that God commandeth us to believe that there is a Union and there is a Distinction; but what that Union, and what that Distinction is, all Mankind are equally ignorant, and must continue so, at least until the Day of Judgment, without some new Revelation." The Trinity, in fact, is a mystery which God has commanded us to believe, but which man's reason cannot reach. In this respect it resembles other mysteries, such as the incarnation of Christ, which Swift elsewhere characterizes as "an astonishing Mystery, impossible to be conceived by Mans Reason."[13] Swift did not discount the role of individual human reason in religion. In the Trinity sermon he allows that "every Man is bound to follow the Rules and Directions of that Measure of Reason which God hath given him," and indeed, to follow the rules of reason is to understand that the scriptural expression must be intended as a mystery. Similarly, in his *Thoughts on Religion*, he insists that "I am in all opinions to believe according to my own impartial reason, which I am bound to inform and improve, as far as my capacities and opportunities will permit" (*PW* IX: 161, 261). Individuals, however, cannot depend entirely on their own reason. Reason itself is "true and just," but "the *Reason* of every particular Man is weak and wavering." Man after all is not a rational animal, *animal rationale*, but only capable of reason, *rationis capax*, as Swift famously wrote, with reference to *Gulliver's Travels*, in a letter to Alexander Pope (*C* III: 103). (The Houyhnhnms, who had no mysteries, could never have understood this point.) We are driven by our interests, our passions, and our vices. Our limited reason must work together with revelation. Using a distinction which had been for decades the stock in trade of such mainstream Anglican divines as Archbishop Tillotson, Swift insists that "Things may be above our Reason, without being contrary to it," and such things include "the Power, the Nature, and the universal Presence of God." Those who apply mere human reason to the mystery of the Trinity "shew how impossible it is that *Three* can be One, and *One* can be Three," but the Scripture "saith no such Thing... but only, that there is some kind of Unity and Distinction in the Divine Nature, which man cannot possibly comprehend: Thus the whole Doctrine is short and plain, and in itself uncapable of any Controversy; since God hath pronounced the Fact, but wholly concealed the Manner." So the Trinity sermon, exemplifying the business of the Christian preacher, concludes by resisting the exercise of reasoning pride, and places the doctrine of the Trinity "upon a short and sure Foot, levelled to the meanest Understanding" (*PW* IX: 167–68).

Issues of authority as well as of reason are involved here. Swift argues in this sermon, as elsewhere, for what his age called "implicit faith." Doctrines expressed as mysteries in Scripture are to be accepted on the authority of God himself (and, by the congregation, on the authority of the preacher, who delivers the doctrine "as the Church holds it").[14] Nothing can be more reasonable than to believe what God reveals, even if what is communicated is beyond our grasp. In making this confident assertion Swift took arms, with other orthodox believers, against the extreme rationalism of deists such as Matthew Tindal (1657–1733) and John Toland (1670–1722), who insisted rather on "explicit faith." For the deists, all things were subject to the strict interrogation of human reason, including our understanding of Scripture, and matters of faith. Toland for instance asserted that "to be confident of any thing without conceiving it is no real *Faith* or Perswasion, but a rash Presumption and an obstinate Prejudice.... *REASON* is the only Foundation of all Certitude; and ... nothing reveal'd, whether as to its *Manner* or *Existence*, is more exempted from its Disquisitions, than the ordinary Phenomena of Nature."[15]

For Swift, however, unlike the deists, human reason on its own can never be an adequate authority. Ultimately all human claims to knowledge are self-obsessed pride: the pride of the projectors of Laputa, who imagine that all knowledge is attainable through the chance operations of a word-frame, or the pride of the hack-narrator in Swift's *Tale of a Tub*, who puts himself forward as apologist for all modern projects, and whose tale itself claims to be no less than "a faithful Abstract drawn from the Universal Body of all Arts and Sciences" (*PW* I: 23). So far from understanding God, we cannot even understand the familiar phenomena of nature.[16] Man on his own can never know the truth of belief, and must rely on God's guidance. This conservative skepticism has very deep roots, in Greek philosophy and, more pertinently, in St. Paul, who warned the contentious Corinthians against "the wisdom of this world," and insisted that "we speak the wisdom of God in a mystery, even the hidden wisdom, which God ordained before the world unto our glory" (I Corinthians 2: 6, 7). For Swift, and for such later writers as Sterne, this kind of Christian skepticism, which sought refuge from human uncertainty in the rock of faith, was mediated and transmitted by such key figures as Erasmus, Rabelais, and Montaigne.[17]

Swift shared this distrust of mortal reason, and grounding of knowledge in faith or revelation, with many contemporaries. The consequence of their belief might seem to us paradoxical. The unreliability of human knowledge is taken by Swift to point not (as a more modern radical skepticism might conclude) to an absolute relativity, an epistemological sea of shifting sands, but to the overriding need for all in society to accept existing institutions, political as well as religious. What an individual knows cannot be a basis for civil quiet or religious agreement. One man's opinions differ from another's, and even one man, over the course of his life, presents no more than "a Bundle of inconsistencies and Contradictions" (*PW* I: 244). Such variousness within a man's own head, and from man to man, must create a dangerous confusion within the state. Dissent and its leaders, such as Swift attacked in *A Tale of a Tub* (particularly in the chapter on the "Aeolists"), in claiming a truer and newer, and more individual alternative to the established system of governance and belief, can only be a threat to public safety:

> *Schism* lies on that Side which opposeth it self to the Religion of the State . . . I think it clear, that any great Separation from the established Worship, although to a new one that is more pure and perfect, may be an Occasion of endangering the publick Peace . . . For this Reason, *Plato* lays it down as a Maxim, that *Men ought to worship the Gods, according to the Laws of the Country.*
>
> (*PW* II: 11–12)

Political dissent and religious schism of every kind, from this point of view, are dangerous. The ordinary man must accept government as it is, and the ordinary believer must accept the church by law established, submitting to be guided in matters of behavior and profession (though not in matters of internal belief) by the church and the preacher.

Swift's strongly held and enduring views on these matters were the result not merely of philosophical persuasion, but of his reading of national history, and his personal experience. Swift grew up in the aftermath of the Civil War, when memories of the overthrow of monarchy and the established church, the death of a king and years of bloodshed and violence, were fresh. His first years of pastoral responsibility were passed in Presbyterian Antrim, where he had ample opportunity to develop negative views of the religious and political character of dissent. Though his first publications belong to the opening years of the eighteenth century, Swift may properly be seen as a writer whose mind was deeply and permanently influenced by the events and ideas of the seventeenth century (in all likelihood the religious allegory of *A Tale of a Tub* was written in the Kilroot years, and bears the fresh stamp of his Kilroot experiences).

Swift left copious written evidence of his own understanding of the bearing of dissent on English church and state history, particularly in his numerous writings against the repeal of the Test Act, and the comprehension of dissenters. The Sacramental Test originated in England in the post-Restoration politico-religious struggle between king and Commons, between Tories and Whigs. The first Test Act of 1673 (extending provisions of the Corporation Act of 1661) provided that any person holding any civil or military office must take the oaths of supremacy and allegiance, subscribe to a declaration against transubstantiation, and receive the sacrament according to the rites of the Church of England. The Sacramental Test was extended to Ireland in 1704. By orthodox Anglicans, such as Swift, the Test was welcomed and energetically endorsed as a support of the church, guaranteeing that the holding of public posts and the making of policy could belong only to Anglican believers (and to "occasional conformists," dissenters who were prepared to go so far as to take Anglican communion as the Test Act required). To other dissenters, and to Whig ministers, the Test was anathema, excluding large sections of the population from public responsibility and power. To Swift the Test seemed especially essential to the very survival of the church in Ireland, given how numerous the Presbyterians had become in that country. Swift and other Irish clerics had before their eyes the dreadful example (as it seemed to them) of Scotland, where Presbyterians were sufficiently numerous and powerful to persecute the adherents of the church.

The Sacramental Test and the comprehension of dissenters are major topics or central themes of several important writings written as a response to the agitation of the first decade of the eighteenth century, including the *Argument against Abolishing Christianity* (1708) and *A Letter from a Member of the House of Commons in Ireland to a Member of the House of Commons in England concerning the Sacramental Test* (1708). Provoked by a further attempt by non-conformists to move parliament to repeal the Test Act, Swift returned energetically and angrily to the subject in 1732 and 1733, in a series of pamphlets including *Queries Relating to the Sacramental Test, The Advantages Propos'd by Repealing the Sacramental Test,* and (an ironic text, written in the persona of a Roman Catholic) *Reasons Humbly Offered to the Parliament of Ireland, for Repealing the Sacramental Test*. Swift offers an extended and highly partial historical narrative in *The Presbyterians Plea of Merit, In Order to take off the Test, Impartially Examined*, published in Dublin in 1733. He traces Presbyterianism back to the exiles who left England in Queen Mary's reign and "went to *Geneva*; which City had established the Doctrine of *Calvin*, and rejected the Government of Bishops." Returning to England on Queen Mary's death (1558), they preached their new political and theological views, and attacked the episcopal system and the rites and ceremonies of the church. Despite the discouragement of Elizabeth, "this Faction, under the Name of *Puritan*, became very turbulent," and in the reign of James I and Charles I "their Numbers, as well as their Insolence and Perverseness, so far increased, that...many Instances of their Petulance and Scurrility, are to be seen in their Pamphlets." At first, Puritans had written and preached as ordained members of the church, but after the beginning of the Rebellion, Swift explains, "the Term *Puritan* gradually dropt, and that of *Presbyterian* succeeded; which Sect was, in two or three Years, established in all its Forms." The guilt and dishonesty of the Presbyterians did not end with the Civil War. Their claim to have assisted in the Restoration, in 1660, is fallacious. They colluded with the Catholic James II on his accession in 1685, petitioning for the repeal of the Sacramental Test, "with bitter Insinuations of what they had suffered" (*PW* XII: 264–69). Swift's characterization in these pamphlets of the history of Puritan and Presbyterian dissent is remorselessly negative, insisting on its enduring turbulence, perversity, insolence, petulance, and scurrility. The deepest sin of the Presbyterians, however, was of course their involvement in rebellion against church and state in the years of the Civil War and Protectorate (1642–58), culminating in "the three most infernal Actions, that could possibly enter into the hearts of Men, forsaken by God; which were, the Murder of a most pious King, the Destruction of the Monarchy, and the Extirpation of the Church; and succeeded in them all" (*PW* XII: 255).

For Swift dissent was associated with "enthusiasm," the reference of Christian truth to the inner voice and individual opinion, and more especially the claim by individuals to the private inspiration of the Holy Ghost. Such fanaticism, as he judged it, and its consequences are amongst the earliest targets of Swift's satire. In Section VIII of *A Tale of a Tub* the Puritan preacher is transformed into a "Sacred *Aeolist*," and his inner voice is transformed from spiritual afflatus to material wind, as he "delivers his oracular *Belches* to his panting *Disciples*." The "Digression on Madness," one of the most brilliant and characteristic parts of the *Tale*, satirizes self-obsessed system builders and innovators of all kinds. No sane man would attempt to "reduce the Notions of all Mankind, exactly to the same Length...of his own," yet this is precisely the aim, and the danger, of projectors in philosophy, or politics, or religion. The result of the sleep of reason is the eviction of common sense, of communal understanding, in the individual, and then in his sectarian followers: "when a Man's Fancy gets *astride* on his Reason... and common Understanding, as well as common Sense, is kickt out of Doors; the first Proselyte he makes is Himself, and when that is once compass'd, the Difficulty is not so great in bringing over others" (*PW* I: 108). The "*Fanatick Strain*, or Tincture of *Enthusiasm*" hence leads to revolution and conflict.[18] Public safety and quiet depends upon common sense, which must be, as far as religious matters are concerned, the shared and communal bedrock of the key tenets and agreed forms of worship of the Anglican church. Against the demonstrated destructive effects of enthusiastic schism there is, all nations agree and Swift repeatedly asserted, a necessary remedy: that of making "one established form of doctrine and discipline" (*PW* XII: 243–44). The chaos of unbrotherly disagreement, of individual opinion and multiplying dissent, must be opposed and resolved by the authority of a legally established church. It is no accident that in his sermon "On Brotherly Love" Swift makes no approach to the wider issue of charity, but provides rather his main statement of the need for a publicly accepted national church. All varieties of genuine Christian belief are entitled, Swift insisted, to the furthest extent of toleration, but they must nonetheless be categorically excluded from comprehension, and power, within the national church and state. A genuine Church-of-England Man, Swift assures us, "is for tolerating such different Forms in religious Worship as are already admitted," and has "a due Christian Charity to all who dissent from it out of a Principle of Conscience; the Freedom of which, he thinketh, ought to be fully allowed, as long as it is not abused." Dissenting consciences, however, as English history all too dreadfully shows, must not be admitted to office in either church or state. Where sects are tolerated, "it is fit they should enjoy a full Liberty of Conscience, and every other Privilege of free-born Subjects, *to which no Power is annexed. And to preserve their Obedience upon all Emergencies, a Government cannot give them too much ease, or too little power.*"[19] Hence Swift's strenuous defense of the Sacramental Test, in his political courses and in his writings over a period of three decades, as the necessary means by which dissenters should be excluded from the rewards of a church and state whose principles they did not in his view support, and as the ultimate bulwark against dire political and ecclesiastic revolutions.

For Swift, in the most absolute sense, all men are free-thinkers. All have liberty of conscience, which, "properly speaking, is no more than the liberty of possessing our own thoughts and opinions, which every man enjoys without fear of the magistrate" (*PW* IX: 263). The expression of one's thoughts, however, has consequences in the polity and in the church, and carries responsibilities. If people publish their thoughts to the world, "they ought to be answerable for the effects their thoughts produce upon others" (*PW* IV: 49). Freedom of expression stops short of the right to shout "fire!" in a crowded theater, and for Swift, as for so many of his contemporaries, post-Civil-War and post-Revolution Britain was just such a theater. Swift regularly represented those whom he thought to be the enemies of state and established church, more particularly the deists and rationalists, as claiming the right not only to think freely, but to publish their thoughts, at the peril of public concord and safety.[20] The "friend" of Anthony Collins, who is the authorial persona of Swift's *Mr. C—ns's Discourse of Free-Thinking, Put into plain English, by way of Abstract, for the Use of the Poor* (1713), is made to insist on the right and duty of every free-thinker to disseminate his opinions, and is made too to acknowledge the probable, and historical, result: "if Ten Thousand Free thinkers thought differently from the received Doctrine, and from each other, they would all be in Duty bound to publish their Thoughts (provided they were all sure of being in the right), though it broke the Peace of the Church and State, Ten thousand times."[21] Worse, Swift repeatedly alleges, all kinds of dissenting opinion are characterized not only by an overwhelming urge to publish themselves, but by "a furious zeal for making proselytes," a deliberate attempt "to propagate the Belief as much as they can, and to overthrow the faith which the Laws have already established."[22] Neither the state nor the church can allow such freedom, and such danger, and in a number of places Swift frankly proposes the censorship of books written in contradiction to the essential shared tenets of public Christian belief. The Church-of-England Man "thinks it a Scandal to Government, that such an unlimited Liberty should be allowed of publishing Books against those Doctrines in Religion, wherein all Christians have agreed." In his *Project for the Advancement of Religion* he asks "why a Law is not made for limiting the Press; at least so far as to prevent the publishing of such pernicious Books, as under Pretence of *Free-Thinking*, endeavour to overthrow those Tenets in Religion, which have been held inviolable almost in all Ages by every sect that pretends to be Christian."[23] In his *Remarks* on Tindal's *Rights of the Christian Church*, he wonders "whether the Clergy have not too little Power, since a Book like his, that unsettleth Foundations, and would destroy all, goes unpunished" (*PW* II: 95). Swift was not alone in desiring restraint of such works, and certainly had grounds for thinking there was no adequate control. The English church had no effectual scheme for licensing publication. Legislation of 1698 "for the suppressing all pernicious books and pamphlets, which contain in them impious doctrines against the Holy Trinity" was not effective.

In an established church founded upon shared and accepted truths it is naturally the business of preaching to communicate those truths plainly to an audience of real men and women. Swift makes his views on pulpit oratory explicit in two key texts, the sermon "Upon Sleeping in Church," and *A Letter to a Young Gentleman, Lately Enter'd into Holy Orders*. For Swift, "the two principal Branches of Preaching, are first to tell the People what is their Duty; and then to convince them that it is so," with topics drawn from Scripture and from reason. He insists that "the Doctrine delivered by all Preachers is the same." It is precisely by repeatedly covering "old beaten Subject[s]" that a pastor inculcates the church's doctrine. The congregation should not expect "a constant Supply of Wit and Eloquence on a Subject handled so many Times"; a sermon is concerned with truth, not entertainment. The language of the preacher should be plain and comprehensible; "Proper words in proper Places, makes the true Definition of a Style." He warns his newly ordained gentleman against hard and obscure words, in particular the jargon of the higher theological debate, for "a Divine hath nothing to say to the wisest Congregation of any Parish in this Kingdom, which he may not express in a Manner to be understood by the meanest among them." Swift warns too against what he calls the "moving manner of preaching," which has been in fashion not only amongst preachers of "the *Fanatick* or *Enthusiastick* Strain," but also amongst divines of the Church of England itself. The purpose of the preacher must be to inform and persuade his flock, and in Swift's mind "A Plain convincing Reason may possibly operate upon the Mind both of a learned and ignorant Hearer, as long as they live; and will edify a Thousand Times more than the Art of wetting the Handkerchiefs of a whole Congregation."[24]

Like so much else in his writings on Christianity, these views demonstrate Swift's profound sense of the public functions and responsibilities of the church, combining a powerful and committed populism with an impassioned defense of shared and lasting truths. At the outset of this chapter I suggested that Swift might seem to a modern sensibility an awkwardly conventional thinker. Certainly he must be viewed as a profoundly skeptical conservative, who placed his trust more in institutions and stability than in individuals and change. Swift's passionate endorsements of public Christianity and orthodox doctrine, and his equally forceful attacks on the individualistic, the charismatic, and the innovative, are neither reactionary nor extreme, but consistent with common positions in his own time, common and widely accepted positions which were in many ways apparently under threat, and apparently worth fighting for.[25] It is not appropriate to judge him by modern standards of pluralism, ecumenism, and egalitarianism. Nor is it appropriate to judge him by modern assumptions about individual Christian spirituality and behavior. Though he says so little about his personal belief, and though he famously described himself as "not the gravest of divines" (*P* II: 764), the seriousness of his Christian faith, as well as his commitment to his church, are not in doubt. If Swift preferred the middle road of orthodox Anglicanism, it is clear he did so with careful consideration of where that route led, and of the enemies which had to be fought on either side. Swift's religious writings, combative, partial, engaged with political as well as theological particularities, are the characteristic products of a warfaring as well as a wayfaring Christian.

NOTES

1. These issues have been widely discussed, but see especially Louis A. Landa, "Jonathan Swift and Charity," *Journal of English and Germanic Philology* 44 (1945), 337–50; Carole Fabricant, "The Voice of God and the Actions of Men: Swift among the Evangelicals," in Hermann J. Real and Helgard Stöver-Leidig (eds.) *Reading Swift: Papers from the Third Münster Symposium on Jonathan Swift* (Munich: Wilhelm Fink, 1998), pp. 141–54.
2. The fullest narratives of Swift's church career are given in Louis A. Landa, *Swift and the Church of Ireland* (Oxford: Clarendon Press, 1954) and in Irvin Ehrenpreis, *Swift: the Man, His Works, and the Age*, 3 vols. (Cambridge, MA: Harvard University Press, 1962–83).
3. See Landa, *Swift and the Church of Ireland*, pp. 16–18, 151–2; *E* II: 158.
4. See especially on this subject *ibid.*, pp. 77–84, 87–91.
5. See Carole Fabricant, *Swift's Landscape* (Notre Dame and London: University of Notre Dame Press, 1995), pp. 234, 244–45.
6. For a fuller account, see *E* III: 74–81.
7. *The Correspondence of Alexander Pope*, ed. George Sherburn, 5 vols. (Oxford: Clarendon Press, 1956), vol. v, p. 13. Swift's attitudes to charity are discussed at length in Landa's "Jonathan Swift and Charity" (note 1 above).
8. *A Preface to the B—p of S-r-m's Introduction to the Third Volume of the History of the Reformation of the Church of England*, *PW* IV: 64–65; *Concerning that Universal Hatred, which Prevails against the Clergy*, *PW* XIII: 123–25; *An Argument against Abolishing Christianity*, *PW* II: 30.
9. *On the Bill for the Clergy's Residing on their Livings*, *PW* XII: 183–84; *Memorial to Robert Harley Concerning the First-Fruits*, *PW* XVI: 677, 678.
10. *Sentiments of a Church-of-England Man*, *PW* II: 8; *Mr. C—ns's Discourse of Free-Thinking, Put into plain English*, *PW* IV: 43; *Preface to the B—p of S-r-m's Introduction*, *PW* IV: 70.
11. See, for instance, *Mr. C—ns's Discourse of Free-Thinking, Put into plain English*, *PW* IV: 40.
12. John Dryden, *Religio Laici*, lines 299–300.
13. *Mr. C—ns's Discourse of Free-Thinking, Put into plain English*, *PW* IV: 35. The words are a quotation from Dr. South, and here put by Swift into the mouth of his persona, a friend of Collins.
14. *A Letter to a Young Gentleman, Lately Enter'd into Holy Orders*, *PW* IX: 77.

15. Quoted by Louis Landa in the course of his extended discussion of this issue in "Swift, the Mysteries, and Deism," in his *Essays in Eighteenth-Century English Literature* (Princeton: Princeton University Press, 1980), 89–106, especially pp. 104–05. See also J. A. Richardson, "Swift's *Argument*: Laughing us into Religion," *Eighteenth-Century Life* 13: 2 (1989), 35–45, especially pp. 37, 39.
16. Landa compares Swift's position here with John Locke's discussion of the limits of human understanding in the *Essay Concerning Human Understanding* (4. 6. 12); "Swift, the Mysteries, and Deism," pp. 100–1.
17. The nature and provenance of late seventeenth-century skepticism has been richly described: see, notably, Richard H. Popkin, *The History of Scepticism from Erasmus to Spinoza* (Berkeley: University of California Press, 1979), and Louis I. Bredvold, *The Intellectual Milieu of John Dryden* (Ann Arbor: University of Michigan Press, 1956). A cogent account of Swift's relation to the tradition is given in Tim Parnell, "Swift, Sterne, and the Skeptical Tradition," *Studies in Eighteenth-Century Culture* 23 (1994), 221–42. Also see Claude Rawson's extensive treatment of the connection between Swift and Montaigne, in particular, in *God, Gulliver, and Genocide: Barbarism and the European Imagination, 1492–1945* (Oxford: Oxford University Press, 2001), especially pp. 5–9, 17–91.
18. *A Discourse Concerning the Mechanical Operation of the Spirit, PW* I: 174.
19. *The Sentiments of a Church-of-England Man, PW* II: 6–7, 12; "On Brotherly Love," *PW* IX: 178.
20. For an important discussion of Swift's understanding of the liberty of conscience, and its relation to familiar thinking on the subject amongst orthodox contemporaries, see Roger Lund, "Swift's Sermons, 'Public Conscience,'and the Privatization of Religion," *Prose Studies* 18 (1995), 150–74, especially pp. 166–70.
21. *PW* IV: 36. Compare the *Argument against Abolishing Christianity, PW* II: 29.
22. "On the Testimony of Conscience," *PW* IX: 151; "A Sermon upon the Martyrdom of K. Charles I," *PW* IX: 227.
23. *A Project for the Advancement of Religion, and the Reformation of Manners, PW* II: 60–61. Compare *The Sentiments of a Church-of-England Man, PW* II: 10.
24. *A Letter to a Young Gentleman, PW* IX: 65–66, 68–70; "On Sleeping in Church,"*PW* IX: 213, 214.
25. As has been shown, from a variety of different positions, by such recent commentators as Donald Greene, "The Via Media in an Age of Revolution: Anglicanism in the Eighteenth Century," in Peter Hughes and David Williams (eds.) *The Varied Pattern: Studies in the Eighteenth Century* (Toronto: A.M. Hakkert, 1971), pp. 297–320; Lund, "Swift's Sermons, 'Public Conscience,' and the Privatization of Religion;" and Parnell, "Swift, Sterne, and the Skeptical Tradition."

10

PAT ROGERS

Swift the poet

Like the rest of his writing, Swift's poetry is often disturbing and uproariously funny at the same time. It can be excessive, ungenteel and informal: equally it can be surprisingly conventional in form and dry in tone. Its language may be robust or, on occasions, almost prim. One of the things that makes the poems so appealing and accessible is their gusto, which comes in part from a scorn for false solemnity, self-pity, and existential complaints. The famous *Verses on the Death of Dr. Swift* provide a case in point.

The *Verses* explore some uncomfortable issues surrounding our response to the fact of dying, but they face the truth with a sense of courage and humanity, so that the final effect is more consolatory than depressing. Franz Kafka might have given this theme a sense of tragic helplessness, while Swift's countryman Samuel Beckett would probably have introduced a bleak comedy of the absurd. Instead, Swift makes us recognize that our own death will not ripple the surface of most other people's lives, and that our hopes of immortality are likely to be doomed to failure. Yet the energy, wit, and invention of the poem contradict this message in the very act of its assertion. According to the publisher, Bernard Lintot, Swift's books will soon become waste paper – this is what he tells the would-be buyer, an old-fashioned rustic bumpkin:

> Some country squire to Lintot goes.
> Inquires for Swift in verse and prose:
> Says Lintot, "I have heard the name:
> He died a year ago." "The same."
> He searcheth all his shop in vain;
> "Sir, you may find them in Duck Lane:
> I sent them with a load of books,
> Last Monday to the pastry-cook's.
> To fancy they could live a year!
> I find you're but a stranger here.

The Dean was famous in his time;
And had a kind of knack at rhyme:
His way of writing now is past;
The town has got a better taste:
I keep no antiquated stuff..."
(*Poems* 492)

The text subverts itself, since today we are still reading this "antiquated stuff," and Lintot's confident prediction about the short date of Swift's fame has been totally disproved by later history. The joke is partly directed against complacent metropolitan taste, which despises what it sees as provincial and lacking in trendiness. There is something joyous in the way that the poetic life of this passage – the vigor of its language, the sharpness with which speech rhythms are caught, and the deft simplicity of the rhymes – *deny* the power of death. Negatives are converted into positives. Such an effect is characteristic of Swift's poetry, both major and minor.

Writing with the left hand

Tucked away in the raggletaggle group of poems designated by Swift's editor as "Trifles," we come on an item called "Dr. Swift's Answer to Dr. Sheridan." It is headed "December 15th" and starts in this way:

The verses you sent on the bottling your wine
Were in every one's judgement exceedingly fine,
And I must confess as a dean and divine,
I think you inspired by the muses all nine.
I nicely examined them every line,
And the worst of them all like a barn-door did shine.
Oh, that Jove would give me such a talent as thine!
With Delany or Dan I would scorn to combine;
I know they have many a wicked design,
And give Satan his due, Dan begins to refine.
(*Poems* 199)[1]

And so on for another twenty-four lines, all using the same rhyme sound – a trifle indeed. Can this possibly come from the hand of that scabrous author of biting satire, who savagely criticized our most ingrained flaws and exposed our deepest self-deceptions as he set out to vex the world? The answer is yes, for the common notion of Swift is derived primarily from prose works, such as *Gulliver's Travels*, *A Tale of a Tub*, and *A Modest Proposal*. These combine moral intensity with skillful and often virtuosic use of language: they exhibit great rhetorical sophistication, and they require to be read (as they seem to have been written) with fierce concentration, in case the author should ambush us into accepting some enormous or absurd position which he has slipped into the text.

It is all very different with Swift's reply to Sheridan. The title proclaims its casual origin among a series of exchanges between close friends. The dateline at the head of the manuscript certifies its immediacy, but also its likely limitations for a modern reader (temporal particularity, narrowness of focus, absence of a general theme or occasion). Plainly, the year – 1719, as it happens – does not need to be given, and this must increase our sense that we are dealing with a mere jotting, or a piece of diurnal flotsam. It turns out that this item actually forms a direct response to a poem written by Sheridan: this in turn came in reply to a letter, partly in verse, which Swift had addressed to his friend, as recently as one o'clock on the previous evening.[2] Such exchanges may remind us of a rapid-fire volley of e-mails, or perhaps a madly accelerated version of the correspondence in Richardson's *Pamela* as the heroine's suitor Mr. B closes in for the kill – a joke already anticipated by Henry Fielding in his parody *Shamela*. However, the form of the poem would not automatically convey to us the presence of a serious literary intent. The multiple rhymes, known as a "crambo," belong to the area we assign to puzzles and word games.

In addition to that, Swift's poetic technique looks crude: the trimeter skips off in a jaunty enough fashion, once we hear "every" in line 5 as a comically strained trisyllable, but the start of each verse seems to shift pointlessly between amphibrachs and anapests – that is, metrical feet of three syllables with the stress on the first or third syllable respectively. Moreover, the expletive "did shine" occurs in a metrically exposed position, and it is followed by a poeticizing gesture, "Oh, that," which may seem false to the informality of manner which comes across elsewhere. Modern readers are apt to feel uncomfortable with the introduction of first names and especially short forms – it may recall to us of the way Wystan and his buddies crop up in poetry produced by W. H. Auden and his circle in the 1930s, when names like "Wilfred" and "Kathy" could be casually dropped, and it produces an effect less of intimacy than of undue familiarity. The homely proverb "give Satan his due" adds little by way of dignity or point, as poetry has mostly been conceived for the last two hundred years. Then there is the comparison with a barn-door, which is actually quite gross: it draws on an expression too coarse to appear in many collections of proverbs. In his robust way, Swift was happy enough to use it in *Polite Conversation*, albeit in a bowdlerized form: "Why, Miss. You shine this morning like a sh–barn door" (*PW* IV: 149). Finally, the presentation appears rough and ready, with its minimal punctuation, as well as oddities in matters like the use of capitals. It all looks like a piece of crass masculine bonding, both trivial (that is, slight but inoffensive) and trifling (irresponsible and nasty, perhaps).

In fact, the "Answer" is fully representative of a large portion of Swift's practice as a poet. It does not rank, of course, among his most important or striking works, even in the lighter category. However, it exemplifies some of the most prominent attributes of his poetry at large, and it does illustrate some of his characteristic effects in tone and cadence. The group of "Trifles" includes a "Left-Handed Letter to Dr. Sheridan," written a year earlier than the last item: "I beg your pardon for using my left hand," runs a note at the end of this poem, "but I was in great haste, and the other hand was employed at the same time in writing some letters of business" (*Poems* 676). An early printing of the item indicates that the manuscript was actually written out "Backwards or with the left hand": again, this involves literalizing Swift's claim that he has more important business to be going on with. Famously, Swift liked to refer in a disparaging way to his own productions in verse: he would acknowledge grudgingly that he sometimes dealt in rhyme, but that is about as far as it goes. The assertion is less disingenuous than it is usually taken to be: Swift very likely did write many of his poems in the intervals of more pressing concerns, and may well have considered much of what he produced as a kind of hobby. Unlike his sustained works of political, historical, or moral commentary, which were almost entirely reserved for prose, his poetic output seldom reaches out beyond its initial impulse, whether this is an event, a conceit, or a bit of social gallantry. His "Trifles" include items such as "Mary the Cook-Maid's Letter to Dr. Sheridan," a vigorous, witty, and linguistically rich portrayal of a member of Swift's own circle. It hardly suffers by comparison with the much better-known poem, "Mrs. Harris's Petition," which appears in a different context of Swift's career and has never been labeled a trifle. We can indeed trace a continuum which runs from riddles and rebuses, or experiments in macaronics (poems in two languages) like the half-dotty lines in Latino-Anglicus he essayed from time to time,[3] through rough lampoons such as "An Elegy on Mr. Partridge" or "A Serious Poem upon William Wood," all the way to the best-known poems such as *Verses on the Death of Dr. Swift* and "On Poetry: A Rhapsody." The trifles, it emerges, can deal with serious matters, and the serious poems can be trifling when it suits them. This means that a reader who enjoys none of the effects in "Dr. Swift's Answer to Dr. Sheridan" is likely to miss some of the sources of the imaginative power in the latter items.

Criticism and the canon

We should now be in a better position to understand a singular fact about the reception of Swift's work. Ever since his own day, the tendency has been to relegate the poetry to a separate and almost always inferior branch of his writing. In the nineteenth century, this was in part for the obvious reason that the genres he chiefly practiced were regarded as sub-poetic. Many pages in the collected *Poems* are taken up with items the Victorians would have placed very little above the category of outright trifles. These include acknowledged "libels," lampoons, and other modes of personal satire which even today scarcely figure in our main anatomy of criticism. For two reasons, it is still hard to assimilate such works to our overall sense of Swift's achievement, even when they take such impressive form as "The Virtues of Sid Hamet the Magician's Rod," with its series of damning analogies. The first reason is that such works often made an appearance, known or unknown to their author, in the collection of *Poems on Affairs of State* which year by year dished out the filthiest dirt on public life of the time. We think that we have moved beyond the Victorians' moral distaste for such things, but we have hardly begun to work out a satisfactory poetic for describing the elaborate mix of burlesque, travesty, and parody which complicates their invective, and feeds into Swift's own style.

Second, we no longer have an active partner to oppose satire in the traditional opposition of praise and blame which underlay all Augustan practice in this mode. That is, we do not understand the satire/panegyric coupling, where the slash represents opposition but also a kind of involuntary identity. All Swift's satirical rhetoric depends on the fact that he *could* have written in the alternative vein: thus, his crushing onslaught on Lord Wharton in *The Examiner* No. 18 (which appeared at almost the same time as "The Virtues of Sid Hamet" in November 1710) does little more than invert the standard commonplaces of an encomium. As it happens, writers were still producing encomia, that is formal eulogies of prominent persons, often attributing godlike status to leaders of the state; and Swift in another mood could write of his patron Harley as a man gifted with "transcendent Genius for Publick Affairs" (*Examiner* No. 45). We can see what happens if we look at passages of mock-panegyric which occur regularly in the poems, such as a burst of self-praise at the end of the *Verses on the Death* or some preposterously laudatory lines in the savage work "On Poetry: A Rhapsody":

> Your panegyrics here provide,
> You cannot err on flattery's side.
> Above the stars exalt your style,
> You still are low ten thousand mile.
> (*Poems* 535)

And the rhapsodist has already proved the point with his apostrophe to "Fair Britain in thy monarch blessed," and his invocation of "Our eldest hope, divine Iulus"(*Poems* 533–34): this last is an absurd linkage of the unpromising Prince of Wales to an ancestor of the Emperor Augustus. The difficulty for us is that all panegyric is now unavailable for serious use, and therefore gradations of better and worse are impossible to calculate in this area. This has meant the blunting of an entire range of weapons in satire and parody. You can scarcely have a mock-form where the primary mode has utterly decayed.

Even in recent years, Swift's poetry has proved recalcitrant. Twenty years ago a burst of monographs in this field promised much: half a dozen timely readings of the oeuvre came out in as many years. Some were perhaps unambitious in the narrowness of their focus, and none attempted to construct a grand narrative of Swift's poetic career. As it turned out, it was a book not confined to the verse, *Swift's Landscape* (1982; 1995) by Carole Fabricant, which provided the most coherent overview of the subject. This was partly because Fabricant surveyed a wider range of poems, doing full justice to the occasional items and "trifles"; but it was also because she offered a clear reading of the entire oeuvre from a single political standpoint, to which we shall return in due course. This work, along with the other more specialized monographs, gave hope that the poems would at last enter the mainstream of critical discussion. The reverse has been the case: even the most challenging accounts of Swift in the past decade have needed for their own purposes to show the poetry out of the main critical space where his works are debated. This is especially true in the case of those enterprises which have borrowed from modern linguistic theory to illuminate Swift's praxis. More remarkably still, Robert Phiddian has managed to write a searching book on Swift's parody without devoting anything beyond a few lines to the poems: this, despite the fact that parody is one of the staple elements in the verse, more pervasively so indeed than in the bulk of the prose works. The curious fact is inescapable. Postmodernist studies pay even less attention to this branch of Swift's writing than did the old-fashioned commentaries which relied on a basically Romantic approach to literature.

Again, the reasons for this state of affairs seem to be broadly susceptible of explanation. First, Swift the verse man continues to suffer because he worked on a smaller scale than that of the major prose works. Obviously he has no *Faerie Queene* or *Paradise Lost* – for that matter, no *Prelude*. Beyond that, he attempted no large-scale series of linked poems such as the fables of Dryden or Gay, or the *Imitations of Horace* undertaken by Pope. Swift himself wrote some effective variations on odes and satires by Horace, but he failed to produce the organized and schematic group which Pope made out of materials scarcely more coherent in themselves. The advantage of an item like *Gulliver* or the *Tale* is that, just as it can be appreciated at leisure in a belletrist vein or explored in detail, so it can be deconstructed with comparative ease. In each book the form is substantial enough to expose cracks in the design; while its rhetorical trajectory is pronounced enough to make swerves and backtracking plainly visible. By contrast, hardly any of Swift's poems have much *cumulative* effect: those addressed to Stella are tied to the particular birthday and the local occasion, rather than to any ongoing rhetorical plan, so that (except for the last, anticipating Stella's death) they could be printed in almost any order. The so-called progress poems came to a halt after three or four items, of which the best is perhaps "The Progress of Beauty": the term then implied step-by-step movement, usually deterioration, as in William Hogarth's series *The Rake's Progress* (1733–35). Then there are the urban eclogues, poems which replicate the themes and language of classical pastoral, but transfer the action to a modern city: these also peter out after two or three. Apart from the early imitations of the grand Pindaric ode in Cowley's manner, which went on maybe longer than Swift's ability to believe in his talent for such things, the standard groupings into which his poems are divided show a markedly ramshackle quality. The "excremental" group include one poem, "A Beautiful Young Nymph Going to Bed," which has very little to do with excrement. The "Market Hill" group, relating to the home in County Armagh of Swift's friend Lady Acheson, make up about twelve poems, but they are primarily linked by mere location, while the poems on Wood's Halfpence in 1724–25 constitute a brief efflorescence of writings on a topical issue, couched in differing modes. Some of the most striking individual items such as "A Pastoral Dialogue between Richmond Lodge and Marble Hill," "The Place of the Damned" or "On the Day of Judgment" differ widely in theme and tone, but each is a one-off *tour de force*, which Swift never tried to repeat.

A second factor is that the poems almost all operate in a comic mode, and provoke laughter of a more or less discomforting kind. The slighter pieces display Swift parading as the jocular Dean, enlisting verse as one of the social skills which enabled him to make his friends love him – at the same time that he took good care to ensure that the wider world regard him with fear and awe. Some of the more considerable items utilize a blacker kind of humor: for example, "The Legion Club" (1736), a biting satire on the Irish parliament, comes close to the territory of curses, imprecations, and black magic spells as it envisages the destruction by the devil of the new assembly building in Dublin. But it also plays grisly games with the nursery rhyme, "Oranges and Lemons":

> There sit Clements, Dilkes, and Harrison,
> How they swagger from their garrison.
> Such a triplet could you tell
> Where to find on this side hell?
> Harrison, Dilkes, and Clements,
> Souse them in their own excrements.
>
> (*Poems* 555)

The trouble is that Swift's burlesques and travesties conduct their own acts of self-demolition, and recent critics have found difficulty in boldly going where Swift had not gone before. Deconstruction works best where the text retains its opacities: but with these poems the workings are seldom occluded. For a critic bent on ludic rearrangement of parts, there is little that is quite so disconcerting as a piece of writing which disowns its potential seriousness of purpose and which (sincerely or not) brandishes its own flippant disregard of high ambitions. Constantly Swift's poems subvert grandiose expectations, and they often resist the efforts of a well-intended critic to carry out further subversion of their workings.

A third differential factor lies in the question of identity. The major prose satires complicate the relations of author and reader by using the role of an assumed speaker. By contrast, few of the poems beyond *Verses on the Death of Dr. Swift* employ this device. There are first-person monologues, notably the "Humble Petition" of Mrs. Frances Harris or the "Lamentation and Complaint against the Dean" by Lady Acheson; but it is unhelpful to think of these as using personae, since they establish no conscious or ironic distance between Swift and the speaker – they are rather dramatic utterances by a character as different from the author as Laertes is from Shakespeare. Similarly, poems in which Swift offers an apologia for his career cannot strictly be said to employ an unreliable narrator. This term should be reserved for cases where the putative speaker deliberately misleads the reader or falls into self-contradiction: it fits Gulliver well enough, or Kinbote in Vladimir Nabokov's *Pale Fire*. But Swift's poems resemble more closely stories such as *Great Expectations*. In that novel, we may think that Pip gets things wrong, but the narration reveals this very fact to us: it does not matter whether we agree with his judgments, or whether Dickens does, because the rendition authentically reproduces Pip's version of events. Similarly, Swift delivers in

"The Author upon Himself" a version of his past which he wants us to accept at face value: it may involve rewriting history, but it requires no deceits concerning authorial viewpoint. In short, the poem may be *biographically* unreliable, but that is quite another thing from saying that it is unreliable in *narratological* terms. The poems in fact display a remarkable stability of self, with the author regularly presented as sensible but bossy, good-humored but mistreated, driven by noble ideals but fated to encounter ingratitude and neglect.

Admittedly, the situation is not the same with the famous *Verses on the Death*. Readers have notoriously differed widely in assessing the intent of a panegyric on Swift, which is delivered by an admirer at the Rose Tavern, and occupies the last 180 lines of the poem. The passage, claiming to draw Swift's "character impartial" begins in a studiously noncommittal fashion:

> The Dean, if we believe report,
> Was never ill received at court:
> As for his works in verse and prose,
> I own myself no judge of those.
>
> *(Poems 493)*

Clearly we are still far from reaching a consensus on the drift of the *Verses*.[4] Swift would probably have been happy enough if readers were able to take all the claims made here more or less as they stand. He knew that this was unlikely, since some contradictory elements can be discerned by internal scrutiny: thus, the claim that Swift "never courted men in station / *Nor persons had in admiration*" (*Poems* 564) sits uneasily with the subsequent reference to his lengthy attempts "To reconcile his friends in power" – especially as this is soon followed by a list of these same men as they strove to "save their sinking country" in the last years of Anne's reign (*Poems* 567–68). But the utterance as a whole seems too close to Swift's own deepest feelings about the betrayal of his cause to be altogether convincing as a statement by a detached third person. In this instance, we *do* need to wonder if the teller is telling the tale Swift thinks he is.

An even more pervasive strand in recent criticism isolates matters relating to gender. Among the total of about 280 poems in English, which can with confidence be laid at his door, no more than fifteen or twenty clearly qualify under this aspect, as confronting gender per se. This neglect of fashionable topics has limited the choice of poems for general critical debate in recent years, and thus the full spectrum of Swift's work as a poet has been largely overlooked. This is a pity, for the poems are marked by energy, drama, and subversive wit. As soon as we open our minds, and ears, to these works, we shall find them engaging and often startling in their originality. If we are to come to terms with Swift's achievement in this area, we must look at a broad range of his verse, and take account of its diversity in mood and style.

Parerga

Let us recall the terms in which Swift described his "left-handed" letter: his right hand was employed in writing simultaneously "letters of business." The lesser poems could technically be thought of *parerga*, that is literally works on the side, or "subsidiary business," as Greek lexicons have it. One way of defining Swift's achievement might be to say that he makes neglected and slighted modes into vehicles of his deepest feelings: in other words, he makes the side-business central.

It may be no accident that so many key terms which find concrete embodiment in Swift's poetic practice all derive from the same particle *para*, that is ultimately from the Greek preposition παρά, meaning "beside, alongside." There are several obvious examples, starting with *parody*, going back to a Greek word which refers to a singing or utterance on the side, hence an imitation or burlesque. Another clear case is *parallel*, designating some entity lying "beside another thing." Swift's verse uses a number of forms of parallelism, but we might think initially of the corresponding text of Horace which accompanies his own versions, though strictly at the foot of the page. A term he actually employs in a related context is *paraphrased*, found at the head of two such Horatian items (the ode addressed to Steele in 1714, and the one inscribed to Ireland around 1724). Educated readers of the day well understood the difference between a "paraphrase," which stands alongside the original, and a "metaphrase," which gives the literal sense and in a way replaces the original. We shall encounter this difference again in a moment. A further case is *paradox*, a rhetorical device employed by almost all Augustan poets, but one that is utilized with particular brilliance in a poem like "Vanbrugh's House," where the small and derivative attainments of the Moderns are exactly the things on which they pride themselves most, scorning the grandeur of the Ancients. A further term from rhetoric is *paronomasia*, a naming beside, that is, a pun. Swift excels even Byron or Thomas Hood in making the use of punning a constructive element in poetry.[5] Entire poems rest on the device: thus, "The Place of the Damned" came out as a broadside (a work treating contemporary politics in rough populist idiom) in 1731, and it is built around the repetition of "damned" eighteen times in as many lines. Each usage straddles the meaning of "condemned" (to hell) with the profane sense of "bloody."

Another device, *parataxis*, is seen in Swift's fondness for lists and catalogues placed in apposition without any syntactical connective. It is notable that Pope insinuates some ordering principle into such lists, for example through the insertion of an obvious give-away element ("Puffs, powders, patches, *bibles*, billet-doux"). As critics such as Claude Rawson, W. K. Wimsatt, and A. B. England have observed, Swift's catalogues generally avoid discrimination and hierarchy among the component parts; thus, the "inventory" of the contents found in the lady's dressing room uncovers a composite paste made up of "Sweat, dandruff, powder, lead and hair" (*Poems* 449). The whole point about this series is that nothing is better or worse to the horrified gaze of the observer: the items could come in any order. Such refusal to set up any ranking may be seen as consciously un-Augustan, but this is to say that it depends on the breach of a habitual decorum. Another apposite term is *parenthesis*, that is, laying alongside: Swift is famous for the brilliant juxtaposition of alternating voices, as in the layered presentation of card-game and banal chat about the Dean in *Verses on the Death of Dr. Swift*. But he is also adept at the insertion of apparent digressions, such as the miniature fables he incorporates into such narratives as the lines "Upon the South Sea Project," his fantasy based around the great financial scandal of 1720, a debacle which implicated some of the major figures in national life. These fables make up small confirmations of the running argument, but they stand by themselves as rhetorical equivalents of the main narrative. Such devices shade into *parable*, a short didactic tale. In Swift this is most commonly an episode within a larger design, employed much as the preacher in this period might enlist biblical stories to enforce a moral message: see for example one of the poems on Wood's coinage, "A Simile" (*Poems* 290).

The common feature of these mechanisms is that they place one thing against another: they align differing entities or orders of significance next to each other. Swift's imitations of Horace require the existence, indeed the presence, of the original: they are very directly *parasites* on the host text. Such allusive forms in Swift's time perform the opposite of modern intertextual references, where the new text absorbs its predecessor. Such is the case with Joyce's parody of classic writers in the "Oxen of the Sun" episode of *Ulysses*, based on random extracts from anthology of English prose: Pepys, Gibbon, and the rest are there to be made over *as* Joyce, that is to become part of the continuous, fluid medium of the narrative. Significantly, modernist and postmodernist discourse alike tend to rely heavily on terms derived from the Greek preposition *meta*, meaning "among, in the midst of, after." The derivatives include words like that ubiquitous coupling *metaphor* and *metonymy*, not to add *metamorphosis* or *metaphysical*. The key element here is an idea of transference or transformation: as with the use of *metastasis* in disease, where the spreading growth envelops and destroys almost everything in its path. In addition, there is the burgeoning group of expressions using the same particle to express a reflexive or critical approach to a given practice, as in *metafiction*. Joyce or Thomas Pynchon can be said to write metanovels, whereas Swift writes parapoetry: the early odes keep his seventeenth-century model Abraham Cowley at a safe distance, borrowing the idiom of his predecessor without supplanting it. With his interest in word-play, Swift might have enjoyed such a thought, given his professed scorn for metaphysics.

All this helps to explain why Swift has an ambiguous place in the long history of transforming genres. He established a new form, technically, with the urban pastorals "A Description of the Morning" and "A Description of a City Shower." Shortly afterwards his friend William Harrison, almost certainly in collaboration with Swift, produced "A Town Eclogue" (see *Poems* 115–17), further developing the conceit; and his close ally John Gay, along with Lady Mary Wortley Montagu, gave the town eclogue a brief currency. But these poems rest on the authority and primacy of the serious pastoral, and never escape its clutches. Whereas prose fiction quickly transcends its models, so that the "comic epic in prose," as Fielding called *Joseph Andrews*, is immediately setting up its own decorum and its own rhetorical properties, Swift carefully confines the scope of his innovation. We can see this in his culminating series of urban pollutants in the "Description of a City Shower":

> They, as each torrent drives, with rapid force
> From Smithfield, or St. Pulchre's shape their course;
> And in huge confluent join at Snow Hill ridge,
> Fall from the conduit prone to Holborn Bridge.
> Sweepings from butchers' stalls, dung, guts, and blood
> Drowned puppies, stinking sprats, all drenched in mud,
> Dead cats and turnip tops come tumbling down the flood.
>
> (*Poems* 114)

The mere locations are unsuitable to bucolic, whereas the setting in Fielding's *Tom Jones* is perfectly apt to its novelistic purpose, and their names convey not just a modern or urban site, but a kind of debased ancestry ("St. Pulchre's" is itself a malformed derivation) and a gesture towards origins in the world of nature which their present condition belies ("field," "hill," "bourne" = stream). Moreover, the language of the concluding lines expresses in its plosive force a peculiar distaste which might seem to go beyond a normal reaction. City-dwellers of this period were familiar enough with such stench and ordure (and of course most of the detritus of the poem would pass completely unobserved in a real farmyard, as opposed to a bucolic landscape): but Swift, with his almost allergic sensitivity to such things, gives them specially concrete presence. What enables this from a literary standpoint is the remoteness of the diction from the prettified vocabulary of pastoral convention. In other words, the jolt which the reader experiences is *directly* tied to the felt absence of norms which retain their authority. This is totally different from the creation of an autonomous form, which exists by the act of transgressing the rules of its predecessors so comprehensively that it makes them obsolete.

Swift's parody, then, requires a parity of host and invader. To be sure, the poet echoes, replays, transposes, and updates the models he has inherited; but he generally does so in order to launch an attack on some *tertium quid*, an external target, rather than to devalue this model. An example is the sudden incursion of a biblical paraphrase in the poem "Upon the South Sea Project": here, Swift interjects a perfectly respectable shot at a verse such as one would find in the metrical psalms which were then commonly used in church services (lines 157–60, in *Poems* 212). Far from guying the original, the effect is to deepen the tone of this prophetic work as we hear the voice of a psalmist crying in the wilderness which is England. Later in the same poem (lines 217–20), Swift presents a kind of abbreviated Litany, this time drawing chiefly on New Testament sources and the Magnificat. Once again the context fails to debase the borrowing, and this is crucial to Swift's purposes. His poetry lives alongside its sources, which continue to resonate behind the text, like receding overtones of the fundamental note.

Politics and the poet

We should find it hard to know from Swift's verse just where he stood on the large political issues of his day. He avoided Britain's involvement in the wider world and its historic role within the community of nations. Such matters were confronted directly by Pope in *Windsor-Forest*, culminating in a triumphant vision of a world made free and safe by trade, where slavery will be "no more." Some readers find this vision unconvincing or inauthentic, but it genuinely addresses major concerns – something that could be said of Swift only if we detect in *Gulliver's Travels* an adumbration of this theme at a disguised level. The politics of Swift's poetry is always local and usually topical.

The most obvious place to look for engaged commentary is the group of poems relating to Ireland: many of these seem remote from serious political affairs, but this leaves a number which deal directly with matters of state. Elsewhere, Swift shifts his focus rather disconcertingly from Dublin to London, a process which may be related to his dependence on Pope for an intimate hold on social, cultural, and political doings. As already indicated, the most provocative account of Swift's politics has been given by Carole Fabricant in her book *Swift's Landscape*. The argument presented there is that Swift's work testifies to the need for "morally informed passion and political struggle," and for a commitment to "perpetual revolution," not just within the human heart but also "on the larger stage of human history."[6] This resonant conclusion seems to many scholars hard to defend in its entirety, whichever portion of Swift's work and/or biography we examine: as a comment on the poetry, it surely goes quite a lot too far. Nevertheless, much of Fabricant's discussion provides a valuable lead, and her willingness to look for evidence to bolster her case in the smaller occasional poems, usually so neglected, does lend weight to her views. It may also be that she is forced to this position because she gets a nil return when scanning the more obviously substantial items such as *Cadenus and Vanessa*, which is left totally out of account, along with many items such as "The Virtues of Sid Hamet's Rod," composed in support of the Tory cause between 1710 and 1714. The justification for this emphasis is that Swift, according to Fabricant, achieved little during the years of the Harley administration, felt increasingly remote from his former friends, and was compelled by a *force majeure* to turn to Irish affairs as the staple of his verse. This will appear to some a skewed version of events, but it has the merit of supplying a rationale for looking closely at the Irish poems.

Undeniably, the pace of Swift's verse production increased sharply in his later years: over two-fifths of his surviving poems were written in his sixties. The jump did not occur straight away on his return to Dublin in 1714: rather, the take-off can be dated around the 1720s, with a gradual acceleration throughout that decade. The most barren period occurs immediately after the Hanoverian accession, when Swift was forced to come to terms with his own removal from the center of political and ecclesiastical influence: for some years, he had been consorting on a daily basis with the chief ministers, and had enjoyed a conspicuous role at court. It is natural that some of his most nakedly autobiographic pieces, including the imitation of Horace which he addressed to Harley (now Lord Oxford), as well as "The Author upon Himself" and "In Sickness," emerged around this time, while the Tory ministry broke apart and the Stuart dynasty wobbled into oblivion. Condemned to what was by comparison an extremely provincial and limited world, Swift fell into almost total silence for the next few years. His friends and patrons were scattered once they fell from power: after the failure of the Jacobite rising in 1715–16, some of its leaders like Viscount Bolingbroke and the Duke of Ormonde had fled into exile, while the Earl of Oxford (formerly Robert Harley) and the poet Matthew Prior were incarcerated in the Tower of London. All of these individuals had been on familiar terms with Swift while the Tories held power between 1710 and 1714. Swift managed to compose lines in imitation of an ode by Horace, which he adapted to fit the situation of Lord Oxford, the former Lord Treasurer, who was lying in prison awaiting trial for treason. Highminded and orotund, the poem gives off an impression of strain as though Swift felt a degree of guilt about his own modest but secure station. It may be significant that he deliberately mistranslated the most famous verse of the original: where Horace writes, *"Dulce et decorum est pro patria mori"* – it is sweet and honorable to die for one's country – Swift gives us "How *blessed* is he, who for his country dies" (*Poems* 170, italics added). The threat of a public beheading was close and real enough for Swift to see Oxford as a martyr in the nation's cause.

In the event, Swift seems to have eased himself back into poetry around 1715–20 by writing trifles, indeed precisely the kind of lighthearted exchanges with men like Sheridan from which we began. Gradually he gained confidence to write on public themes again, although his poems on affairs of state after this date sometimes interact with private concerns and often share a common stylistic register with the personal items. The South Sea Bubble had its repercussions for Ireland in 1720, although it was in essence an English phenomenon. Then in 1722–23 came the Jacobite scare known in shorthand terms as the Atterbury affair, when the treasonable correspondence of the Bishop of Rochester was decoded to give authorities warning of a planned invasion by Stuart supporters. During his time in London, Swift had been well acquainted with Francis Atterbury, a High Churchman who stood at the center of this controversy, although by this date the bishop was much closer to Pope. Each episode provoked a characteristic and powerful poem: the poem on the Bubble (1720–21) launches a series of witty parallels serving to literalize the fate of investors in the South Sea:

> Thus the deluded bankrupt raves,
> Puts all upon a desperate bet;
> Then plunges in the Southern waves,
> Dipped over head and ears – in debt.
> *(Poems* 208)

We might notice first the assured handling of the alternately rhymed quatrains: far more of Swift's best poems are in such patterned stanzaic forms than is generally realized. (The poet to whom he owes most technically may well be not Samuel Butler, the author of the rambunctious satire *Hudibras*, but rather Matthew Prior: look at "Hans Carvel" or "The Ladle"as models for fables and fabliaux.) A second relevant point is that the poem on the Bubble was reprinted more often than almost any other in Swift's lifetime. It came out in a variety of guises, including one appearance as the caption to a satirical print. This shows that the populist Swift started to emerge within his poetic output long before the Drapier stood forth as a tribune of the Irish nation. Then, in the lines he wrote "Upon the Horrid Plot" (1722–23), the poet manages to suggest by an ingenious chain of proverbs that the blame for the whole Atterbury affair lay squarely on the government, even though it is the informers and corrupt witnesses who are mentioned by name.

Ironically, the hated Robert Walpole got Swift fully into his stride, when the prime minister embarked on his long period of power stretching through the 1720s and 1730s: for Walpole came to stand as a symbol for the triumph of Whiggism and commercial values, and represented a mighty opposite to the humanism of Swift, Pope, and their friends. However, it was the episode of "Wood's halfpence" which launched the author into a new role within the community. Without doubt, the letters Swift composed as the Drapier did most to arouse public opinion against the coinage scheme, but he also wrote about ten poems on matters relating to the controversy. The earliest may well be "A Serious Poem upon William Wood" (1724), and it is among his most effective political verses. Unquestionably serious in its implications, its manner is dismissive, derisory, and profane. A single couplet points to Walpole as "Brass," a dragon who "had gotten two sows in its belly"; while another mentions "two hags in commission," which indicates the Hanoverian duchesses whom Wood had bribed to obtain his patent (*Poems* 274–75). Otherwise the attack is concentrated wholly on Wood, as a villain and a suitable tool for unholy purposes. A succession of wounding comparisons is made by application to stock expressions involving the common noun "wood": again, proverbs are much in evidence, as when Swift writes,

> And England has put this crab to hard use,
> To cudgel our bones, and for drink give verjuice.
>
> (*Poems* 274)

This goes back to an old saying, "Hang a dog on a crab tree and he'll never love verjuice" (that is, the sour juice of unripe fruit). Of course, the poem is intimating that Wood deserves to be hanged; he is like one of the dirty dogs who contrived Atterbury's arrest in the earlier poem. At the conclusion, Swift picks up another stock expression and does it over for his own ends:

> But soft, says the herald, I cannot agree;
> For metal on metal is false heraldry:
> Why that may be true, yet Wood upon wood,
> I'll maintain with my life, is heraldry good.
>
> (*Poems* 276)

Wittily, the resources of homespun language are made to settle the point regarding Wood's guilt and suitable punishment.

We are touching here on a central aspect of Swift's poetic mode. The implicit argument of the poem is that someone called Wood will live up to his name, and that his personal attributes will be deducible from folk wisdom concerning that material. Even those most skeptical of Locke's theories concerning language would have accepted that names are peculiarly arbitrary with regard to the people who bear them. But Swift pretends, here and elsewhere, that name and owner are mysteriously connected, so that the stock of everyday expressions which relate to a common noun can be applied to the proper noun. In a similar way, Swift's method in his poem on the Atterbury affair is to treat the little dog Harlequin (who was used by the authorities to clinch their case against the Jacobite conspirators) as a fount of proverbial morality: "And 'twas but just; for, wise men say, / That, 'every dog must have his day.'" Such maxims are tested and sometime found wanting: the fact that one of the main prosecution witnesses, Philip Neyno, was drowned when trying to escape from custody prompts the Tory speaker in Swift's dialogue to comment, "Why then the proverb is not right, / Since you can teach dead dogs to bite"(*Poems* 248). The last line alludes to the old saying, "Dead dogs don't bite," but also neatly recalls the cadence of an equally venerable expression, "You can't teach old dogs new tricks." By implication, Neyno was saved from a deserved hanging by his watery death: this goes back to the proverbial idea, drawn on by Gonzalo in *The Tempest*, to the effect that "He that is born to be hanged, will never be drowned." We can be sure that Swift was familiar with this, because he quotes the saying in *Polite Conversation* (PW IV 4: 147), and plays with it in "The South Sea Project." As the Atterbury poem comes to an end, the Tory interlocutor scornfully remarks to the Whig, "Your bishops all are dogs indeed" (*Poems* 249). Underlying all this may be the expression, "Give a dog a bad name and hang him": the subliminal idea works to suggest (1) that this is the way in which the government has trapped Atterbury and his co-conspirators; (2) that in a just world it is ministers like Walpole who would face condign punishment.

The effect is to produce an equivalence of signifier and signified. Far from being random, the connection between things or persons and the name they bear is precise and reliable. A broadly parallel technique can be discerned in the political poems which Swift wrote during his sojourn in England. In "A Dialogue between Captain Tom and Sir Henry Dutton Colt" (1710), Swift attacks a busybody Whig politician: while in "An Excellent New Song" (1711), he assaults his enemy the Earl of Nottingham. Each depends on a barrage of puns. For Swift, homology in sound slides into a homology in sense: the Earl is made to say that he will "quit my best friends, while I'm not in game" (*Poems* 118). So the popular mind often works: during the Second World War British people cruelly and rather unjustly observed when Noel Coward appeared to keep himself safely remote from hostilities, "Coward by name and Coward by nature." There is a pervasive sense that the facts of ordinary usage in speech will come to the aid of the satirist, as his words float on the breath of the people. A favorite expression runs along the lines, "As wise men say," which we have just encountered in the Atterbury poem.

Another characteristic technique which first appeared in the poetry dealing with English politics takes the form of a chain of linked analogies. Swift's methods have been seen as subversive of logic, but in fact analogy is not antilogical, simply alogical. What these poems do is to suggest that a man's attributes may be known by the linguistic company they keep. In "The Virtues of Sid Hamet the Magician's Rod" (*Poems* 110–12), the basic conceit resides in finding parallels to the Lord Treasurer's white staff. ("Sid" comes from Godolphin's first name Sidney, while "Magician" conveys not just, ironically, wonder-worker, but also charlatan.) Of course, such an emblem should bespeak the honor of high office, and should express the holder's commitment to the nation as well as his loyalty to the crown. As soon as Oxford rises to this dignity, a year or so later, we hear nothing but good of such trappings. But Godolphin's staff suggests to Swift other rods which resemble it to varying degrees and set up damaging comparisons. Running through each similitude is the idea that the Lord Treasurer is a stage magician or conjuror, who plays tricks instead of attending to the real business of his high calling. Unlike the rod of Moses in Exodus, Godolphin's staff, though made of "honest English wood," begins to hiss and sting like a serpent when the Treasurer assumes its care. In this way it resembles a broomstick, available for nefarious magic when ridden at night by the witch, but otherwise an inoffensive domestic object. The "wand of Sid" proves to be closely similar to a divining rod, since Godolphin uses his power to find out hidden gold mines, that is sources of graft which he can tap into. Like the caduceus of Mercury, the white staff enables its bearer to induce sleep – in this case, the Lord Treasurer's bored auditors in parliament. Further parallels allude to a conjuror's wand, the scepter of Achilles, the golden bough, Aaron's rod, and finally a jockey's whip (scornfully recalling Godolphin's obsessive interest in horse racing). The concluding paragraph is built around Godolphin's removal from office in August 1710, when he was required by the queen to break his staff as a gesture of resignation. By his petulant manner of smashing the staff, it is insinuated, Godolphin has made "a rod for [his] own breech," a saying interpreted by the contemporary lexicographer Nathan Bailey as meaning "to prepare one's own punishment." He can now look forward to "a rod in piss": Bailey glossed the phrase, "reward you according to your deserts."[7]

Swift himself called this poem "a lampoon": this accurately describes its merits, which proceed from a vivid exaggeration of loosely connected attributes. Where metaphysical wit asks us to admire the ingenious discovery of a far-fetched likeness, Swift's verses ask the reader to discern a deep congruity in apparently disparate elements: an authentic, rather than a momentary or contingent, similitude. There is something in effect *essential* which links the different forms of staff, and that is the word "rod" which applies to all of them: there is no appeal against linguistic fiat, since common usage determines the way they exist in the world. Like Humpty Dumpty, the modern author or reader makes words mean whatever he or she chooses, since their signification is arbitrary and capricious: for Swift, words have an inviolable existence out there which cannot be gainsaid at will. And, once again in this poem, the proverbs blurt out the truth in defiance of anything Godolphin can say.

Much of Swift's political poetry takes the form of a more or less sophisticated version of name-calling. In some of the later Irish poems, the verbal habits display brutal simplicity: "From his father's scoundrel race, / Who could give the looby such airs?" ("Traulus"). Here, "looby" is an old word for an awkward, shambling individual. A few lines later: "Hence the greasy clumsy mien, / In his dress and figure seen" (*Poems* 426). Sometimes there is an incantatory air, as with the refrain of "The Yahoo's Overthrow," one of several vicious onslaughts on the lawyer and politician Richard Bettesworth: "*Knock him down, down, down, knock him down*" (*Poems* 539–41). The verse engages in huffing and puffing to bring the giant to his knees: nursery rhymes become a mode of political rhetoric. Just as "The Legion Club" invites two of the poet's enemies, "Dear companions hug and kiss, / Toast old Glorious [William of Orange] in your piss," so it characterizes the relatives of the hated Lord Allen as "Son and brother to a queer, / Brainsick brute, they call a peer"(*Poems* 554–55). More naked anger appears in these later items, perhaps because Swift had despaired of more civilized modes of response: he has more regular recourse to obscenity and personal calumny, as though his rhetorical technique can no longer cope in an equable manner with the enormity of Irish reality.

Carole Fabricant is certainly right to point out that Swift drew on the vigor and directness of the common people, though some think it an exaggeration to claim that Swift achieved "a bond of imaginative identification between himself and the servant class," and that this "makes him a figure who seems far more at ease in the cramped stench-filled alleys of the Liberties than in the fashionable, expansive landscape of a typical Augustan estate."[8] It is true that Swift showed great charity in his treatment of the poor, especially in the Liberties, slums surrounding his deanery at St. Patrick's Cathedral.

Nevertheless, his portrayal of servants in poetry goes little beyond vivid mimicry (remarkable though that is); his depiction of members of this class depicts them unsentimentally, with sympathy but no false idealization. We need not appeal to the harsh satire of the *Directions to Servants* to see that Swift had a strong sense of hierarchy in domestic affairs as elsewhere. In real life we know that Swift showed no tendency to quit his comfortable deanery, or to fraternize with the mob more than it suited his immediate purposes. Ever-conscious of his dignity as a Dean, he confined his closest relations to people of substance and usually breeding.

Equally, while Swift wrote a number of disparaging poems about his friends' country houses (Delany's at Delville, Sheridan's at Quilca), these hardly seem to represent a thoroughgoing subversion of the country house ideal. The joke in the Quilca poems is that Dr. Swift, the great Dean, should be forced to slum it in a rotten cabin, amid "Sloth, Dirt, and Theft" (*Poems* 300). This is clear from verses by Swift's friend Thomas Sheridan, describing a visit to the country retreat in 1724:

> To see him now a Mountaineer!
> O what a mighty fall is here!
> From set'ling Governments & Thrones
> To splitting Rocks & piling Stones
> Instead of Bolinbroke & Anna,
> Shane Tunelly & Bryan Granna,
> Oxford & Ormond he supplies
> In ev'ry Irish Teague he spies;
> So far forgetting his old Station
> He seems to like their Conversation.
> Conforming to the tatter'd Rabble
> He learns their Irish Tongue to gabble,
> And what our Anger more provokes
> He's pleas'd with their insipid jokes.
> (*P* III: 1040, slightly normalized).

Swift enjoyed mixing with this "tattered rabble," instead of the queen and her ministers, but he never forgot the company he had once kept. Repeated references in his correspondence show how proud he was of the intimacies he had enjoyed during the years of the Harley ministry (and the *Journal to Stella* displays some of his authoritarian side). What the poems about simple country living exhibit is a way of coping with a great comedown: the *locus amoenus* is negated not by a great cultural shift but by human incompetence, laziness, and poor workmanship.

What remains true is that Swift felt a strong attachment, almost Joycean in its fervor, to the small affairs of life. He was able to enter into the voice of Dublin tradesmen less because he shared their outlook, political or otherwise, than because he listened so carefully to the accents of everyday speech, and relished the tang of local idiom. While there is no evidence that he ever really mastered the Gaelic language, he certainly was alert to the ring of Dublin *craic* (fun, joking), and drew on traditions of vernacular writing. This contributes to the powerful quality of *earthiness* which his poetry so obviously exudes. Swift starts from the physical and material. One of the most suggestive comments ever made about him was that of Denis Donoghue, to the effect that "Swift was uneasy with anything that did not occupy space; so he treated words as if they were things."[9] Disregarding any implications this may have for wider philosophic issues, it is surely clear that this need to register thingness imparts a striking quality to his poetic lexicon: it makes for the concise accuracy of his descriptions. This applies equally to the contents of a prostitute's bedroom, or to the starving Scottish cows with whom Stella is shamelessly compared in "A Receipt to Restore Stella's Youth" (*Poems* 298–99). Almost any poem will display this feature, but a not-quite-random choice might fix on a passage such as this:

> Next day, to be sure, the Captain will come,
> At the head of his troop, with trumpet and drum:
> Now, madam, observe, how he marches in state:
> The man with the kettle-drum enters the gate;
> *Dub, dub, a-dub, dub.* The trumpeters follow,
> *Tantara, tantara*, while all the Boys holler.
> See, now comes the Captain all daubed with gold lace:
> O lor'! The sweet gentleman! look in his face;
> And see how he rides like a lord of the land,
> With the fine flaming sword that he holds in his hand,
> And his horse, the dear *creter*, it prances and rears,
> With ribbons in knots, at its tail and its ears...
>
> (*Poems* 383)

The choice was not arbitrary, since this comes from one of the so-called Market Hill poems, entitled "The Grand Question Debated," and it involves an impersonation of Lady Acheson's servant Hannah. There is consequently a particular effect deriving from the use of slang, dialect, and a certain gushing garrulity ("like a lord of the land"), all apt to the speaker. But for the most part the qualities we find here are likely to be present in any sustained passage of verse which Swift wrote after he abandoned his Pindaric attempts.

A poetry of concrete objects, certainly then. But Swift is no commodity fetishist: he seldom dilates on the sensuous or consumerist attributes of these objects, as Pope does in *The Rape of the Lock*. Rather he presents the reader with things which do occupy space, which have mass rather than exchange value, or which at the most have an assigned political value. Thus he lists the imported silks foisted on the people as "Brocado's, and damasks, and tabbies, and gauzes" in "An Excellent New Song" of 1720 (*Poems* 217), where the fancy names make these stuffs appear somehow flimsy and vulgar in comparison with plain Irish wool.

The poems on Irish politics often gain in force and point from these features of Swift's language. Their appeal is limited by a quality of repetition: the same targets reappear in the shape of Swift's personal enemies, such as Richard Tighe, Richard Bettesworth, Joshua Allen, Thomas Prendergast, and their kin. Nor were these men caught up in any great crisis such as the coinage episode which had brought together large segments of the Irish nation (more strictly the Dublin people, since even Wood's halfpence caused much less uproar among the great bulk of the population who lived outside the capital). The result was that Swift found it hard to dramatize Irish affairs with the immediacy he had achieved in his poems at the time of *The Drapier's Letters*. The people he hated most of all were probably fellow members of the Anglo-Irish establishment, born and based in the island, who had been able to accommodate their opinions to serve the Westminster administration: men like William Connolly and Lord Chief Justice Whitshed. They were upstarts like himself, but more successful. It is hard to avoid the conclusion that Swift's resentment was based partly on envy and rancor, occasioned by his own disappointed hopes of preferment. He is comparatively mild on the subject of the true importees, such as Lord Carteret, a Lord-Lieutenant who, like most of his kind, had no permanent links with Ireland; or even Thomas Rundle, a bishop thought by some to hold heretical beliefs. The trouble is that Swift did not have any alternative to offer to Walpole's way of doing things. His friends across the Irish Channel, whether proscribed Tories or disaffected Whigs, lacked a policy which would have bettered the political and economic situation of Ireland: there was no alternative government in waiting among the native Irish, and an absence of any feasible plan which would not involve replacing Walpole's ministry with another set of remote functionaries and a different parcel of Anglo-Irish agents in Dublin. It is perhaps unhelpful to bundle the Irish situation into a broader framework given the label of colonization, since the differences between this and the experience of (say) Spanish America were immense, owing to the tiny distances involved, as well as the functioning in Ireland of a parliament and a system of courts which were not in every way less meaningful than their English equivalents. (A dissident like Atterbury would probably rather have faced trial in Dublin than go before his peers in the House of Lords; and a member of the proscribed Tory party had scarcely more access to the summit of power in the Westminster assembly than he had across the water.) All the same, the discontents of the Irish nation were manifest, and even if Swift's loyalties were divided at the level of ideological commitment he assuredly came to feel a good deal of sympathy at first hand with the men and women around him.[10] The poetry reflects the strength of this feeling, but also testifies to the lack of any real answers to the political problem in its bursts of impotent fury.

Conclusion

Swift produced a poetic oeuvre which is too extensive and too diverse to be adequately explored in a brief survey like this. An effective reading strategy must take account of this range of achievement: we should pay attention to the acknowledged "major" poems, but we should also seek to incorporate apparently slighter items such as the exchanges with Sheridan and the group centering on Lady Acheson. We need to include private poems, including those in which Swift fashions, or massages, his own literary identity, but also those on public themes. In this latter group, we ought to allow full weight to works concerned with English politics as well as those of Ireland. As the discussion here should reveal, there is a great deal of continuity between the two: when Swift discovered a new cache of material in Dublin, initially with the affair of Wood's coinage, he was able to cling on to the values and poetic ambitions he had first displayed during his involvement with the Tory ministry in 1710–14. In this respect, he was aided by his continuing friendship with men like Bolingbroke, Lord Bathurst, Gay, and above all Pope: one of the strangest features of poems like "On Poetry: a Rhapsody" is its reliance on a cast of villains drawn from the English realm – minor writers like Leonard Welsted and James Moore-Smythe who owed their inclusion to their battles with Pope, while the reprobate Colonel Charteris was a Scot tainted by his association with Walpole. Similarly, the London publisher Bernard Lintot is allotted a significant role in the *Verses on the Death* despite the fact that he had given Swift little cause to like or dislike him. It was Pope whose career had always been closely tied in with Lintot's business, just as it was Pope who had tangled with Lewis Theobald, a rival editor of Shakespeare as well as a dramatist. Beyond this, we can detect a deeper link between the poetry of the English and Irish phases by noting a congruence in poetic idiom: all the main techniques utilized in Swift's "Serious Poem" on Wood had been pioneered years earlier in his attacks on Godolphin, Vanbrugh, Partridge, and others.

Among all the features of his poetry, the most striking effect comes from Swift's ability to harness the resources of familiar speech to sustain argument, allegory, or narrative. The stock of household words Swift would assemble to create his anthology of commonplace ideas known as *Polite Conversation* adds zest to his works right across the board: cliché, catch-phrase, and proverb energize the language, as well as dialect, slang, and rough colloquialism. That much is true of the fierce "libels," with their brutal assault on the person of corrupt politicians, and it also applies to the lighthearted *vers d'occasion*, right down to the riddles and quibbling messages which lie unmolested among the "Trifles." An inquiring reader will find the same wit in the gentle raillery of the birthday poems to Stella as in strenuous display-pieces like the verses "Upon the Horrid Plot." The left-handed letters make heavy use of puns, but then we turn to the verses on Swift's death, and encounter this:

> Now Curll his shop from rubbish drains
> Three genuine tomes of Swift's remains.
>
> (*Poems* 490)

The primary meaning here refers to the literary flotsam and jetsam which the publisher Edmund Curll – again a leader of the *London* trade – was in the habit of dredging up after an author died. In the context of the ongoing argument, we are unavoidably reminded of the Dean's corpse stretched out, ready for burial. Like Mercutio's line about "finding me a grave man," it wonderfully suggests two things at once: how comic devices can make serious points, and how the great solemnities of life can be viewed as heartbreakingly funny.

NOTES

1. The rough-hewn quality of this poem is seen more clearly in the original manuscript, reprinted in *P* iii: 1017. The "Trifles" occupy *P* iii: 965–1052 in this edition, along with a group of riddles at *P* iii: 911–43.
2. Another time Swift even got back to Sheridan his poetic response "written, sign'd, and seal'd," so he claimed, "five minutes and eleven seconds after the receipt of yours, allowing seven seconds for sealing and subscribing" (*P* iii: 980). The physical process of writing and transmitting the message seems almost to override its content: this is truly to textualize the act of composition.
3. See *P* iii: 1038–39; and for the background, see George P. Mayhew, *Rage or Raillery* (San Marino, CA: Huntington Library, 1967).
4. Some of the most influential readings of this passage are collected in David M. Vieth (ed.) *Essential Articles for the Study of Jonathan Swift's Poetry* (Hamden, CT: Archon Books, 1984). See also James D. Woolley, "Autobiography in Swift's Verses on his Death," in John I. Fischer, Donald Mell, Jr, and David Vieth (eds.) *Contemporary Studies of Swift's Poetry* (Newark: University of Delaware Press, 1981), pp. 112–22.

5. There are other more technical terms, such as *paronym*, meaning a word taken from a foreign language. Like Pope, Swift uses the verse paragraph as the principal mode of organization above that of the couplet: one possible effect has been defined as the "radiantly disjunct concentrations" found in *Verses on the Death of Dr. Swift*: see W. K. Wimsatt, "Rhetoric and Poems: The Example of Swift," in Vieth (ed.) *Essential Articles*, pp. 87–104. On Swift's practice of parody in poetry, see Michael Suarez's chapter in this volume and also Michael J. Conlon, "Singing 'Beside-Against': Parody and the Example of Swift's 'A Description of a City Shower,'" *Genre* 16 (1983), 219–32.

6. Carole Fabricant, *Swift's Landscape* (Baltimore: Johns Hopkins University Press, 1982), p. 271.

7. *Old English Proverbs Collected by Nathan Bailey*, ed. John Ettlinger and Ruby Day (Metuchen, NJ: Scarecrow Press, 1992), p. 98.

8. Fabricant, *Swift's Landscape*, p. 42.

9. Denis Donoghue, *Jonathan Swift: A Critical Introduction* (Cambridge: Cambridge University Press, 1969), p. 131.

10. Fabricant, in *Swift's Landscape*, pp. 214–18, ingeniously argues that Swift's repeatedly expressed sense of exile in Ireland serves to confirm his affinities with the Irish, since they too were "strangers in a strange land" (as Swift himself expressed his dilemma). This involves eliding much of the evidence concerning Swift's continuing ties to England and loyalty to his friends there, but it might explain some of the desperation we can detect in the later poems.

11

JUDITH C. MUELLER

A Tale of a Tub and early prose

Right from the gate, Swift emerged as an original. He shocked, amused, perplexed, and outraged his first readers just as he has three centuries of readers
since. Swift desired the lasting fame that even his earliest writings secured,
but he originally addressed these works to specific people in specific historical circumstances that they might change. Although Swift often despaired
of satire's efficacy, no satirist more forcefully provokes in his audience an
embarrassed discomfort with the world as it is. The sharp aggression in
Swift's writing speaks of the writer's deeply held beliefs about the true and
the good and his outrage at their violation. And yet even in this conviction
Swift betrays an equally deep vein of skepticism. From this volatile mixture
of faith and distrust, Swift's early writing usually confronts us not with clear
affirmation but with irony and unsettling contradiction – a particularly dangerous tack for a reformer to take. Swift's perilous strategy effectively puts
his readers off balance, and that is precisely where the satirist wants us.

Swift's earliest prose works were not of course all satires. His first foray
into the world of publishing was the opportunity between 1700 and 1709 to
edit the memoirs and essays of the English statesman and man of letters, Sir
William Temple. In 1701, Swift made his solo entry into published prose with
A *Discourse of the Contests and Dissentions Between the Nobles and the
Commons in Athens and Rome*. This work contributed to an ongoing propaganda war over the impeachment of several Whig Lords. Though Swift's
Discourse won the admiration of Whig leaders, it is finally less a defense
of the impeached Whigs than an argument for balance of power in govern-
ment – between king, lords, and commons. Swift's *Discourse* here echoes
his mentor, Temple's, views of politics and government. In the wake of the
seventeenth-century English revolutions, Swift most fears what he terms the
"Tyranny of the Many," the commons' seizing excessive power (*PW* I: 209).
This recalls Temple's warnings that popular dissension naturally contracts
itself "till it ends in a point or single person" – a tyrant.[1] Swift blames the
"Tyranny of the Many" for the Puritans' "bloody revolution" of the previous

century which had placed too much power in the hands of one man, Oliver Cromwell. Dark assumptions about human nature, deepened by the shadow of that violent recent past, underlie both Swift's and Temple's political views and lead them to conclude that the body politic requires careful vigilance to avoid the same slide into brutality and despotism. Like Temple, Swift also condemns the new party politics for producing social discord.

Though the *Discourse* owes much to Temple, Swift's inventive use of historical authority sets him apart. Some commentators call the *Discourse* a "parallel history" which shows Swift's genius in linking the classical past with present events. But the parallels often prove to be far from historical. In the work, Swift appeals to the moral authority of a presumably knowable, classical past. When necessary, however, he alters both classical examples and contemporary events to suit satiric purposes.[2] Even if Swift's *Discourse* does not always accurately portray the ancient past, it relies for its rhetorical force upon a profound respect for that past. Swift like Temple often attaches great moral consequence to the superiority of former ways. From his earliest writings, Swift rails against a world in decline. Although he is skeptical about our ability to get in touch with that past, Swift holds it up as a model for present emulation.

Such faith in ancient models of taste and morality is a feature that defined the Ancients' camp in what was known as the "Ancients and Moderns" controversy of the day. Swift's *Battle of the Books* and *A Tale of A Tub*, published together in 1704, take the side of Sir William Temple and the Ancients, though not unequivocally. Temple's 1690 essay, *Upon Ancient and Modern Learning*, had inflamed a controversy brewing for some time. To the twenty-first century reader, the Ancients and Moderns debate might look like petty squabbling between privileged men with nothing better to do; but for the participants, the course of civilization was at stake. The argument raged on in Swift's time with the same intensity of feeling as the so-called culture wars of our day; indeed, our wars and theirs have much in common.

By "Ancients" and "Moderns" we do not refer simply to old authors and new, nor to those who prefer one or the other, but most importantly to two groups advancing two different concepts of knowledge. Swift's free treatment of history in the *Contests and Dissentions* might reflect the Ancients' sensibility, since for them the purpose of history was not so much to recover the facts of the past as it was to improve the reader through eloquence and moral example. "Ancients" were generalists who stressed the relationship between learning and the welfare of the people. Statesmen, they argued, should be schooled in letters to enable them to govern justly. The proper end of learning is a good, moral life, and the study of ancient authors best achieved that end.

"Moderns," by contrast, saw knowledge as part of a progress toward ever greater degrees of understanding about experience. Impressed by the remarkable recent achievements of the new science, most Moderns assumed humanity could progress in other areas of learning as well. Often equally as learned in the classical world as the so-called Ancients, Moderns like Richard Bentley tended to look at the past as scientists rather than moralists. They assumed that they could know more than their predecessors simply because they had the advantage of building upon previous work. The French writer, Fontenelle, went beyond touting the excellencies of the new science and modern philosophy to suggest that Moderns even may surpass the Ancients in arts and letters, the most important areas of learning to Temple's mind. In his 1690 response to Fontenelle, Temple had argued that modern learning had added nothing significant to the accomplishments of the ancient Greeks and Romans. He believed that in the works of classical Greece and Rome humankind had already achieved the highest possible understanding of morality and governance, the most worthy ends of learning.

Responding to Temple's essay, William Wotton published his *Reflections upon Ancient and Modern Learning* (1694). Wotton was an enormously gifted classical scholar, famous for facility in languages. Temple's and Wotton's differences may seem small to us now; in fact, Wotton agreed with Temple that modern orators and poets fell short of the Ancients, but reasoned that in time they could equal and perhaps even surpass them. Further, Wotton held that the tools of modern scholarship yielded more accurate knowledge of the whole of the ancient world than any particular writer of ancient Greece or Rome could have achieved. Thus a modern scholar might know the ancient world in its entirety better than any single Ancient could have. The controversy reached its height in 1697 when Wotton appended to the second edition of his *Reflections* an essay by his friend Richard Bentley, the greatest philologist of the age. Bentley used modern scholarly tools to expose embarrassing mistakes in Temple's essay on *Ancient and Modern Learning*. Temple had extolled the fables of Æsop and the *Epistles of Phalaris* as examples of ancient eloquence, assuming they had come down from ancient Greek. In his *Dissertation on the Epistles of Phalaris*, Bentley proved that both the fables and the *Epistles* had been written much more recently than Temple realized. Neither work turned out to be ancient. After these assertions, attacks and counter-attacks followed from both sides. The Ancients' defense of Temple relied often more on defamation than on careful scholarship, since Wotton and Bentley were largely right. To Temple's allies, Wotton and Bentley appeared unmannerly, even barbarous, in attacking a respected nobleman.

In Swift's contribution to the fray, *The Battle of the Books*, the books themselves do the fighting. Although Swift's attitude toward the controversy remains ambiguous, he apparently defends Temple and sides with the Ancients. Swift never questions the accuracy of Bentley's analysis. Instead, throughout the *Battle*, Swift emphasizes aesthetics and morality, placing the weight of both on the Ancients' side. Indeed, for Swift's Ancients, beauty and virtue – sweetness and light – are what the fight is all about. From the Ancients' perspective, the Moderns threaten to empty the world of both.

Just as the battle begins, the combatants are interrupted by an argument between a spider and a bee. Observing the quarrel, Æsop shows why he belongs to the Ancients, regardless of when his fables were written. He argues that like the bee who ranges abroad, gathering nectar from distant flowers to produce honey and wax, honorary Ancients such as Temple realize their dependence on the flowers of ancient learning and nature itself for their work – work that endures. The Moderns, by contrast, resemble the spider who, proudly convinced of his self-sufficiency, spins filth from his own entrails – a web that soon disintegrates. Pride, in both Christian and classical traditions, is a moral menace that threatens to unravel social and spiritual order. Destructive, divisive pride marks the Moderns in the *Battle*, who quarrel from the start over who will lead them. Despite the dangers the Moderns pose, they finally appear impotent in the *Battle's* allegory. Swift suggests the insignificance of Bentley's analysis when the portly Modern can only run around Æsop and Phalaris "trampling and kicking and dunging in their Faces." Even after he steals their armor, they remain unscathed (*PW* 1: 162). Similarly, Temple does not even feel the strike from Wotton's lance. Though the battle is left incomplete, the heroic Ancients seem destined to prevail.

The very incompleteness of the *Battle*, however, with its missing passages, like those found in old damaged manuscripts, tends to undermine the Ancients' position. Swift's asterisks indicate missing passages in seven places in the text, including its end. So we do not actually have, as Swift's longer title advertises, *A Full and True Account of the Battle Fought last Friday in England*. Swift leaves us wondering how we can trust in the completeness of ancient learning and its transmission over far greater reaches of time and geography. Swift's work seems to subvert the Ancient position in other ways, as well. The narrator suggests that both sides – Ancients and Moderns – have their share of ugly rancor when he insists before the battle that "the Champions of each side should be coupled together" so that "like the blending of contrary Poysons, their Malignity might be employ'd among themselves"(*PW* 1: 140). The unruly mix of genres in the *Battle* – epic, animal fable, philosophic and political treatise, history – has been read as an imitation of bad modern writing that only affirms the Ancients' superiority because of its very confusion. But perhaps in all this fuss about spiders, bees and warring books in a dusty library on a Friday afternoon, Swift would suggest the absurdity of the controversy. Although the Ancients fare better than the Moderns in the *Battle of the Books*, Swift's precise position remains unclear. Even greater uncertainties mark the reader's experience of *A Tale of a Tub*, Swift's most dazzling satiric achievement, so wild and ingenious that it surprised Swift himself as an older man. Probably written over a seven- or eight-year period, the *Tale* was published anonymously in 1704 with the *Battle of the Books* and *The Mechanical Operation of the Spirit*, and created a stir, provoking commentaries, keys, imitations, and spurious attributions. Though the author was also accused of blasphemy and plagiarism, the work was admired by many. The *Tale* may have contributed to Swift's never receiving the bishopric he desired; but it also established his fame.

In 1710, he added an "Apology" to defend his work. Ironically, Swift's seemingly straightforward "Apology" for a text that examines corruptions in writing, reading, and knowing is itself riddled with ambiguities. The apologist assumes a posture of innocent shock that the *Tale* has offended anyone, but his misdirections actually let Swift's reader in on a secret – he is not sorry or shocked at all that he has offended. Furthermore, the "Apology" highlights a few of the *Tale's* best structural jokes: he claims no knowledge of the footnotes added to the 1710 edition, but since the bulk of them are lifted verbatim from an unsympathetic commentary on the *Tale* written by his and Temple's adversary, Wotton, Swift's hand in the jest seems unmistakable. He blames gaps in the text on his having lost control of the manuscript before its publication, but the gaps appear located by design, often when the work's mad narrator has written himself into a corner.

Like the *Battle of the Books*, the *Tale* parodies bad modern writing. It begins with an absurdly bloated train of prefatory matter, including a list of fictitious "Treatises wrote by the Same Author," two letters of dedication (one to Prince Posterity), a letter from "The Bookseller to the Reader," a Preface and an Introduction. The "Apology" only lengthens this list. The tale proper – a story about three brothers and the coats their father wills them – begins in section II, but not for long. The remainder of the text alternates between sections devoted to this story and digressions with such titles as "A Digression in the Modern Kind" and "A Digression in Praise of Digressions." Finally the tale proper disappears altogether and the text ends with a conclusion in which the narrator resolves to *"write upon nothing"* (*PW* I: 133).

The structure of *A Tale of a Tub* – its copious prefatory matter and its digressiveness – seems determined to keep the reader from the heart of the matter. In fact, the *Tale's* egomaniacal narrator, not to be confused with Swift, claims in the Preface that the purpose of his work is not so much to say something as to divert the attention of those who would attack religion and government: just as "Sea-men have a Custom when they meet a *Whale*, to fling him out an empty *Tub*, by way of Amusement, to divert him from laying violent Hands upon the Ship" (*PW* 1: 24). The monstrous whale threatening the ship of state, according to the narrator, is Thomas Hobbes' influential *Leviathan* (1651) and the imitations it inspired; the empty tub is the *Tale* itself (*PW* 1: 1). We should not trust the purpose implied in this metaphor, however; the tub is hardly empty, and the *Tale's* narrator proves no great champion of his stated cause.

Despite its complications, the "Apology" offers a more reliable account of the purpose and structure of the *Tale*. Swift explains that he had intended to satirize "the numerous and gross Corruptions in Religion and Learning." He would expose "abuses in Religion" in the tale of the three brothers. "Those in Learning he chose to introduce by way of Digressions" (*PW* 1: 1). His satire on abuses in religion targets both Catholicism and Puritanism. Satire on the latter focuses particularly on enthusiastic sects who emphasized the gifts of the spirit: miraculous phenomena such as speaking in tongues, healing, and prophecy. Believing that a nation without a state religion risks chaos and disintegration, Swift viewed non-Anglican religious belief (at least belief publicly stated) as a serious threat to the established government. He consistently defended the Test Act, a controversial law that made taking communion in the Anglican church a requirement for government service. The isolation and poor working conditions Swift endured in 1695 during his first ecclesiastical appointment as prebend in the largely Presbyterian parish of Kilroot in the north of Ireland only confirmed his hostility toward non-conformists and his belief in the dangers of dissent.

Swift's satire on abuses in learning in the *Tale* has multiple targets, all of which he considered dangerous to the nation. He blasts everything modern, including modern writing and modern philosophy. Swift parodies modern book titles and provides a list of "Treatises wrote by the... Author" of the *Tale*, including "A General History of Ears" and "A Panegyrick upon the World," titles that reflect the banal and reductive thinking Swift derides throughout the *Tale*. The two targets of Swift's satire, abuses in religion and learning, converge on key issues, including the power of print. Swift writes the *Tale* after the lapse of the Licensing Act, at a time when printed materials had begun to proliferate as never before and literacy rates were rising among all social classes. As print culture accelerated, Swift and his contemporaries experienced a marked tension between two perceptions of the book: as a source of authority on the one hand, and of subversion, on the other.[3] The appearance of words in print somehow invested them with authority, and this worried Swift. He feared the subversive effects of bad books on undiscerning readers. A *Tale of a Tub* is a mock-book that seeks to awaken its readers' discernment. In its extravagant textual apparatus, its lengthy prefatory matter, and ample footnotes, Swift's mock-book works to deflate the mystique of the book, demanding we question its authority and recognize its dangers. Swift does not reject textual authority altogether but insists that it be vested in the proper places and that subversive texts be condemned or, better, censored. Throughout his career, Swift advocated censorship of writing he considered harmful to the public peace, including works that questioned the existence of God or that challenged the established church. If Swift lacked the power to control what was printed, he could write a mock-book to make readers less comfortable in their consumption of bad books.

Swift's satire against bad books, however, always threatens to backfire. He fears modern writing because of its subversive content as well as its stylistic flaws. Like other Ancients, Swift believed that bad ideas and bad writing weaken a civilization. The *Tale* parodies the bad writing he fears. But parody itself is intrinsically unstable and subversive. In imitating the sort of writing Swift finds objectionable, A *Tale of a Tub* risked being objectionable itself, as its initial reception showed. Though Swift often mistrusts readers' abilities, his writing requires much of them. In the *Tale* proper – the story of the three brothers – Swift's reader must identify the terms of the religious allegory. More demandingly, in the digressions, the reader must shift reading styles and tease out Swift's position in the mad, multi-layered irony. Swift's irony is not the simple sort that means the opposite of what it says, although it sometimes does. Like many speakers in Swift's satires, the *Tale's* narrator is not a consistent persona but rather the shifting expression of a *mélange* of perspectives, some of them Swift's, some of them targets of derision. His readers face the daunting task of distinguishing between them.

If the *Tale* requires great interpretative acumen, it also expresses a fundamental mistrust of interpretation itself. In the *Tale* proper, an allegory of the reading of the scriptures throughout Christian history, interpretation usually results in corruption. A father (God) leaves his three sons coats (the Christian faith) and directions for the proper care of their coats in a will (the scriptures). If the sons abide by the will, their coats will last and fit them properly through all changes. The will "consisted wholly of certain plain, easy Directions about the management and wearing of their Coats" (*PW* 1: 121). Swift found the notion of a "plain text," whose meaning is perfectly clear, deeply appealing, as did many of his contemporaries.[4] He affirmed this in suggesting that the father's will really requires no interpretation. Its meaning and incontestable authority lie on its surface, self-evident, plain. Swift derided readers like the three brothers who disregarded the authority of their father's will. Their rebellion takes the form, first and foremost, of interpretation.

Swift suggests then that the interpretation of sacred texts is typically motivated by something other than the desire to know God's will. In order to pursue their pleasures and to follow the latest fashions, the brothers twist and wring unintended meanings from the will. Brother Peter (Catholicism) distinguishes himself early as a shrewd interpreter. The father's will, we are told, "was very precise." The sons were "not to add to, or diminish from their Coats, one Thread, without a positive Command in the Will" (*PW* I: 49). Through perverse interpretations of the will itself, nonetheless, Peter justifies adding forbidden adornments (*PW* I: 49). The ultimate motive for scriptural interpretation becomes evident as Peter uses it for power, first over his brothers and then over the world. Peter's attempts to force the text shows a pride that knows no bounds. By his final appearance in the *Tale*, he is calling himself "*God Almighty* and sometimes *Monarch of the Universe*" (*PW* I: 71). The father's authoritative, plain text finally proves a troublesome obstacle to Peter's desire; with fitting irony, Peter, the consummate interpreter, eventually stops reading altogether and locks up the will in a strong-box. Within the religious allegory, this represents the Catholic church's early history of denying the laity access to the scriptures. The locked box also represents the practical fate of any text subject to a corrupt reader's will. Captive to a self-serving interpretation, the written word finally has no say.

In the allegory's depiction of the Protestant Reformation, Peter's two brothers – Martin and Jack – eventually break from him and retrieve the will. Although they resolve to "reduce all their future Measures to the strictest Obedience prescribed therein" (*PW* I: 83), corrupt interpretation soon returns. The figure of Jack represents Protestant dissenters and various fundamentalist sects who were subject to what was then negatively called religious "enthusiasm." For Swift's first readers, Jack would have brought to mind not only John Calvin but an array of figures Swift would dub "Fanaticks": Puritans and Presbyterians, Methodists and Quakers, Baptists and Independents. Though Jack's style of interpreting differs greatly, he abuses the will as shamelessly as Peter. While Peter hunts for arcane signs and allegorizes, Jack literalizes in ways that prove equally distorting. If the will expressly forbids additions to their coats, then Jack will tear and rend frantically until all additions are removed, heedless of the damage he does to the fabric of the coat itself. Jack's behavior here reflects the actions of violent Protestant sects; not only does his tearing recall their vandalizing of Catholic churches and monuments during the Reformation, it also suggests the damage Swift believes their divisiveness has done to the Christian faith itself. In his interpretative passion, Jack rips his coat to shreds. Again, Swift stresses the motives for interpretation, in this case, malice toward the Catholic Church: "the memory of *Lord Peter's* Injuries, produced a Degree of Hatred and Spight which had a much greater share of inciting [Jack] than any Regards after his Father's Commands" (*PW* I: 86). Like Peter, Jack is deluded. Unconscious of his own base motives, he believes his fanaticism to be righteousness. Passion and pride propel both brothers' styles of interpretation, and Jack finally resembles Peter.

The third brother, Martin, probably named after Martin Luther but generally thought to represent the Anglican Church, offers an altogether different style of reading. Martin resolves to keep some additions to his coat when their removal would damage the fabric of the coat itself, "which he thought the best Method for serving the true Intent and Meaning of his Father's *Will*" (*PW* I: 85). Swift stresses the plainness of the will, but even Martin must interpret beyond its simple terms; in order to honor its spirit, he compromises and thus violates its strict precepts. As much as Swift would like to suggest otherwise, interpretation seems inevitable. Of course, most texts, including the actual scriptures, are not as plain and simple as the father's will. Texts are typically read in complex circumstances like Martin's, in which he must determine how to obey laws that have already been violated.

Some readers have doubted whether Martin offers an attractive alternative to Peter and Jack. On one hand, Swift stresses Martin's radical differences from his crazed brothers. When Jack tells Martin, "Tear, Pull, Rent, Flay off all, that we may appear as unlike the Rogue Peter, as it is possible," Martin responds calmly, "Peter was still their Brother ... [I]t was true, the Testament of their good Father was very exact in what related to the wearing of their Coats; yet was it no less penal and strict in prescribing Agreement, and Friendship and Affection between them" (*PW* I: 87). Love for his brothers and respect for his father seems to enable Martin to know his father's will. Nonetheless, many readers have wondered at Swift's flat portrayal of Martin, whom the narrator describes as "extremely flegmatic [that is, passionless] and sedate" (*PW* I: 87). The narrator claims that Martin's "gravely" delivered "Lecture on Morality," from which Jack flies, would contribute to the "Reader's *Repose, both of Body and Mind*" (*PW* I: 87). Many find Martin ponderous and dull, not to mention largely absent. Perhaps his supposed dullness reflects badly on the moralizing spirit. Some readers even think that in Martin we see a more subtle form of pride. But Swift's treatment of Martin might actually incriminate the narrator, Jack, and the sort of readers who find morality boring. In the end, it remains unclear whether Swift finally offers a satisfying model for honest reading. With two clearly bad models in Peter and Jack, and one ambiguous one in Martin, Swift does not seem to offer a genuinely clear guide for avoiding the corruptions of interpretation or for knowing the father's will. Similarly, in the digressions in the *Tale* that satirize abuses in learning, Swift is more apt to present corruptions and raise questions than to offer clear, positive models for knowing. The narrator himself often serves to illustrate intellectual and moral corruption. In Swift's day, writing and printing frequently served as metaphors for human thinking, and the chaotic text before us surely reflects a mind in disarray. Swift's narrator boasts that he once belonged to "that honourable Society" of Bedlam, the London mental hospital (*PW* I: 111). Like Peter and Jack, the narrator often betrays a pride that has lost hold on reality. In his delusion, he expects universal approbation for this "Divine Treatise," which he assumes will be translated into languages across the globe "for the universal Benefit of Mankind" (*PW* I: 66, 117). Corruptions throughout the *Tale* often prove inseparable from the sort of mental and moral degeneracy portrayed in the narrator's pride.

The narrator complains that "a superficial Vein among Readers of the present age" has hindered the reception of fine modern writing such as his. He laments that readers "will by no means be persuaded to inspect beyond the Surface and the Rind of things" (*PW* I: 40). Here as elsewhere in *A Tale of a Tub*, Swift raises important questions about knowledge and interpretation in the opposition between surface and depth. The sorts of "Wisdom" that the narrator claims the superficial reader misses confirm the impression that Swift attacks self-styled "deep" writers and readers. The narrator implies that readers must "dig out" the modern text's "Wisdom," which he compares to "a *Cheese*, which by how much the richer, has the thicker, the homelier and the coarser Coat; and whereof to a judicious Palate, the *Maggots* are the best" (*PW* I: 40). Claims to deep wisdom seek only to justify thick, ugly, and coarse writing whose buried treasures finally prove to be as repugnant as maggots. The good text – the plain text – requires no digging. *A Tale of a Tub* would appear, therefore, to be a very bad text indeed. As a parody of bad writing, the *Tale*'s badness of course makes good satiric sense. Much that makes the *Tale* truly great depends paradoxically on having the very qualities Swift ridicules. The narrator, for example, explains that modern writers "have always chosen to convey their Precepts and their Arts, shut up within Vehicles of Types and Fables" (*PW* I: 40). The *Tale*'s ingenious allegories, types, and fables have kept readers busy digging deeply for centuries, forcing them to interpret in ways it seems to condemn.

Swift's treatment of interpretation appears inconsistent in the *Tale*, and it remains unclear precisely what he would approve and what condemn. When he gives the opposition between depth and surface a more distinctly moral turn in the *Tale's* "Digression on Madness," the narrator seems to contradict earlier claims. Elsewhere, the narrator praises modern writing for its depth and darkness; here, he extols "that Wisdom which converses about the Surface" (*PW* I: 109). To illustrate, he offers two examples: "Last week I saw a Woman *flay'd*, and you will hardly believe how much it altered her Person for the worse. Yesterday I ordered the Carcass of a *Beau* to be stript in my Presence; when we were all amazed to find so many unsuspected Faults under one Suit of Clothes" (*PW* I: 109). Rather than making a compelling case for surface wisdom, these examples expose the moral vacuity of our narrator whose concern with appearances blinds him to the far more significant realities of suffering and death. Neither surface wisdom nor depth proves to be a completely acceptable means of knowing. Surface wisdom, nonetheless, says the narrator, affords us "the sublime and refined point of felicity, called, *the Possession of being well deceived*; The Serene Peaceful State of being a Fool among Knaves" (*PW* I: 110). He leaves us with an untenable choice between being happy fools, whose minds dwell upon "the Superficies of Things" or knaves with a more penetrating understanding. If there is a third alternative, Swift never makes it clear.

Along with satirizing deep reading, Swift also ridicules a kind of surface wisdom in his attack on materialism and Hobbes' philosophy, in particular. Although Swift shares Hobbes' dark vision of human nature and his healthy mistrust of interpretation, Swift considers the materialism underlying *Leviathan* a serious threat to religion and the state. In satirizing the Taylor worship in section II of the *Tale*, Swift attacks reductive "Systems" that deny spiritual reality. Like the materialist who reduces all to physical matter, the Taylor worshipers believe "the Universe to be a large *Suit of Clothes*" and "man ... a *Micro-Coat*" (*PW* I: 46–7). In a striking inversion, the Taylor worshipers believe that "the outward Dress must needs be the Soul" (*PW* I: 48). Swift's satire here has multiple targets, including materialism in the more ordinary sense of the term: in a society where citizens are more preoccupied with surface appearances than with matters of the spirit or mind, philosophies that deny the spirit easily take hold.

Various materialisms pervade the *Tale* and a work published with it, *A Discourse Concerning the Mechanical Operation of the Spirit*. Both satirize the unwitting materialism underpinning Christian sects that emphasize outward signs of things spiritual. For the enthusiastic fundamentalist, the scriptures themselves are mired in the material. Jack debases the father's word in using pieces of the will to wrap a sore toe. In the *Mechanical Operation*, if the fundamentalist steps safely over an open sewer, "some Angel, unseen, descended on purpose to help him by the Hand" (*PW* I: 180). Although the enthusiast thinks his religious rapture signals the presence of the Holy Spirit, both the *Tale* and the *Mechanical Operation* suggest a much less exalted origin, the body. Here, the "fanatick" fit can be induced "by frequently moving your Body up and down ... till you are perfectly dosed and flustred like one who drinks too much in a Morning" (*PW* I: 178). Inducing such fits is a "trade" practiced by "workmen," or dissenting preachers.

Swift brings together various targets in the *Tale* – including religious enthusiasm and secular, philosophical system building – in the extraordinary "Digression on Madness," which develops his own materialist theory and possibly undermines much of what he claims the work defends. The narrator hails madness as the source of "the greatest Actions that have been performed in the World, under the influence of Single Men; which are, *The Establishment of New Empires by Conquest: The Advance and Progress of New Schemes in Philosophy; and the ... propagating of New Religions*" (*PW* I: 102). Only madness, the prideful delusion of the sort we see in Peter and Jack, the narrator concludes, can explain such conquests and systems. Such delusion has a bodily, usually sexual, source: "Vapours," which ascend "from the lower Faculties to over-shadow the Brain" (*PW* I: 105). Of the military offensive launched by a "Great Prince," he asks "what hidden Spring could put into Motion so wonderful an Engine?" The answer: "an absent Female, whose Eyes had raised a Protuberancy, and before Emission, she was removed into an Enemy's Country" (*PW* I: 103). A painful case of flatulence motivates another king's invasion of a neighboring country. The raptures of religious fanaticism have similar origins. Swift uses unmistakably sexual language to describe the ecstasy of both the "fanatick" preacher and his congregation in the *Mechanical Operation* and the *Tale*.

Swift's materialist reading of such "madnesses" may have an unintended consequence; for, as many readers have observed, nothing prevents us from extending the same analysis of madmen involved in "the propagating of New Religions" to Christ himself. Could Swift have failed to recognize this? Although he declared in the "Apology" that he intended to celebrate the Church of England, the *Tale's* most powerful and ingenious section leaves its reader wondering about the author's opinion of any and all religious belief. If "Things Invisible" remain among things "impossible to be known" with any certainty (*PW* I: 105), Swift's readers remain unsure of how he imagines we can sanely embrace any faith at all.

Perhaps the only avenue Swift offers out of this uncertainty can be found in his frequent insistence on deference to the authority of established church, moral convention, ancient learning, and social hierarchy. Unlike some of his contemporaries – particularly those he would dub "free-thinkers" – Swift sees in uncertainty no reason to reject or rebel against established authority; indeed, established authority may be the only safeguard against social, moral, and intellectual chaos. Swift's skepticism only confirms him in his conservatism.

A defense of established authority motivates Swift's attack on the astrologer John Partridge in the so-called *Bickerstaff Papers* (1708). Partridge, shoe-maker and quack, wrote popular almanacs full of astrological predictions and also criticized the established church. That a tradesman could find a wide audience provoked Swift and fed his contempt for a print culture that produced, and a reading public that consumed, what he considered rubbish. In *Predictions for the Year 1708*, Swift posed as one Isaac Bickerstaff, astrologer and apologist for astrology. Bickerstaff criticizes the vagueness of astrological predictions peddled by current practitioners who had given his "Art" a bad name. He insists that authentic astrologers can offer precise predictions. To show the truth of this, he makes a prediction himself, the death of John Partridge "upon the 29th of *March* next, about eleven at Night, of a raging Fever" (*PW* II: 145). Soon after, Swift published an anonymous letter by a witness to Partridge's death. In an ingenious play of identity, Swift uses a fictional author to kill off a real one. When Partridge published a letter insisting he was still alive, Bickerstaff wrote another to refute it.

Although *The Bickerstaff Papers* jeer at astrology's unfounded claims to knowledge, Swift's reasons for singling out Partridge have more to do with poems in his almanac critical of the established church and sympathetic to dissenting sects. Swift wrote *The Bickerstaff Papers* around the same time he drafted a series of pamphlets and satires defending the Anglican church. In *The Bickerstaff Papers*, he wished to discredit a dissenting voice that was reaching a wide audience. Though not as pointed as Swift's religious satire in the *Tale of a Tub* and the *Mechanical Operation of the Spirit*, scattered throughout *The Bickerstaff Papers* are jabs at religious enthusiasts whom Swift blames for the bloody revolution of the previous century.

Despite Swift's frequent defense of authority, however, his own relationship to it is vexed and contradictory. He criticizes men like Partridge for "meddling in public concerns" (*PW* II: 149); but from the moment Swift embarked on his career as a writer, he meddled in public concerns, continually questioning the actions and policies of those he dubbed "*the* weightiest Men in the weightiest Stations" (*PW* I: 5). Although deference to authority might answer the problems of skepticism that so concerned Swift, authority itself – whether in persons, texts, or institutions – often proved to be riddled with maddening imperfection. And so Swift wrote and railed, risking damage to the very things he would protect.

NOTES

1. Sir William Temple, *Miscellanea* (London, 1680), p. 75.
2. See J. A. Downie, "Swift's *Discourse*: Allegorical Satire or Parallel History?" *Swift Studies* 2 (1987), 25–32.
3. For a discussion of the early modern book, see Adrian Johns, *The Nature of the Book: Print and Knowledge in the Making* (Chicago: University of Chicago Press, 1998).
4. On this notion, see Hans Frei, *The Eclipse of Biblical Narrative: A Study of Eighteenth and Nineteenth Century Hermeneutics* (New Haven: Yale University Press, 1974), pp. 55–56; and Marcus Walsh, "Text, 'Text,' and Swift's *A Tale of a Tub*," in Claude Rawson (ed.) *Jonathan Swift: A Collection of Critical Essays* (Englewood Cliffs, NJ: Prentice Hall, 1995), pp. 82–98. For a helpful discussion of the various materialisms in the *Tale*, see Roger D. Lund, "Strange Complicities: Atheism and Conspiracy in *A Tale of a Tub*," in Robert DeMaria, Jr. (ed.) *British Literature 1640–1789: A Critical Reader* (Oxford: Blackwell, 1999), pp. 142–68.

12

J. PAUL HUNTER

Gulliver's Travels and the later writings

Swift's most ambitious, most accessible, and most enduring literary work –
Gulliver's Travels – first appeared on October 28, 1726, just over a month
before his fifty-ninth birthday. Its actual title was *Travels into Several Remote
Nations of the World*, and it appeared anonymously, or rather pseudonymously, as by "Lemuel Gulliver, first a Surgeon, and then a Captain of several
Ships." Swift had gone to elaborate lengths to disguise his authorship and
create a sense of mystery about the book's origins,[1] but "Gulliver" quickly
became the talk of the town and Swift's authorship soon was an open secret.
The first printing sold out in a matter of days, and within five weeks two more
printings were issued. We do not know the size of the print runs, but it is a
safe guess that more than 20,000 copies of *Gulliver's Travels* were circulating
among London's half-million people by the end of December – almost seven
times the number of copies of *The Spectator* that Addison claimed would
reach 60,000 readers – and the book's fame spread quickly throughout both
England and Ireland.[2]

Swift was already famous, of course – for both literary and political reasons – but *Gulliver's Travels* extended that fame considerably, and readers
spent hours puzzling out references, allusions, and possible coded meanings
in the text.[3] Swift and his friends amused themselves in their letters by imagining readers coming to terms with the book's slippery relationship of fact
to fiction; Swift himself, for example, pretended that readers got out maps
to try to trace Gulliver's voyages; he claimed that an "Irish bishop" believed
that the "Book was full of improbable lies, and for his part, he hardly believed a word of it" (*C* III: 189). And his friend John Gay suggested that
Swift return to London (he had gone to Dublin immediately after arrang-
ing surreptitiously for the publication) so that trendy readers could explain
contemporary political meanings to him. *Gulliver's Travels* quickly became
a conversation piece, and soon it was a classic, rivaling *Pilgrim's Progress*
and *Robinson Crusoe* as the best-selling text written in English for almost
three centuries.

But from the beginning, *Gulliver's Travels* did have detractors, mostly on political grounds, for Swift's views stirred powerful reactions, resentments, and suspicions. Literary doubts surfaced early as well. Even Swift's best friends confessed to reservations about parts of Book III[4] (Book III has also fared less well with modern critics), and there have always been complaints about both the simplistic metaphorics of Books I and II and (contrariwise) the asymmetries of Books III and IV. Too, religious, philosophical, and moral objections arose early and often: charges of misanthropy and misogyny have repeatedly swirled around the text, especially calling into dispute the definitions of humanity in Book IV and Gulliver's revulsion with (and ultimate retreat from) family and human society more generally. Even Pope, although more gently than most contemporaries, pointedly teased Swift in a poetic complaint lodged in the name of Gulliver's neglected wife, Mary:

> Welcome, thrice welcome to thy native Place!
> – What, touch me not? what, shun a Wife's Embrace?
> Have I for this thy tedious Absence born,
> And wak'd and wish'd whole Nights for thy Return?
> In five long years I took no second Spouse;
> What *Redriff* Wife so long hath kept her Vows?
> Your Eyes, your Nose, Inconstancy betray;
> Your Nose you stop, your Eyes you turn away.
> . . .
> My Bed, (the Scene of all our former Joys,
> Witness two lovely Girls, two lovely Boys)
> Alone I press; in Dreams I call my Dear,
> I stretch my Hand, no *Gulliver* is there!
> I wake, I rise, and shiv'ring with the Frost,
> Search all the House; my *Gulliver* is lost!
> Forth in the Street I rush with frantic Cries:
> The Windows open; all the Neighbours rise:
> *Where sleeps my* Gulliver? *O tell me where?*
> The Neighbours answer, *With the Sorrel Mare.*[5]

This substantial and incisive poem (110 lines long) is usually thought a mere bauble, but it represents serious literary, philosophical, and psychological criticism and stands as a summary of some of the most thoughtful and lingering objections to Swift's outlook.

Most famously, perhaps, Samuel Johnson openly disparaged the creative imagination behind *Gulliver's Travels*: "When once you have thought of big men and little men, it is very easy to do all the rest."[6] Voltaire, too, was unimpressed: "Nothing unnatural may please long," he wrote in a 1727 letter.[7] Some later famous commentators also went against the popular grain.

Macaulay thought that Swift had "a heart burning with hatred against the whole human race, a mind richly stored with images from the dunghill and the lazar house," and Thackeray charged that Swift "enters the nursery with the tread and gaiety of an ogre . . . as for the moral, I think it horrible, shameful, unmanly, blasphemous." He reserved his strongest venom for Book IV, which he described as "gibbering shrieks and gnashing imprecations against mankind – tearing down all shreds of modesty, past all sense of manliness and shame; filthy in word, filthy in thought, furious, raging, obscene."[8]

The extraordinary popularity, then, from the beginning existed within a context of lively controversy and disagreement, and, ever since, a series of issues – literary, political, philosophical, social, and moral – have generated continuous debate. *Gulliver's Travels* has been read many different ways – in support of, and against, a host of ideologies and opinions on such issues as human nature, the ethics of social practices, scientific method, and the process of reading itself. Its critical heritage illustrates nearly every direction in criticism and critical theory over the past three centuries, and here we can only sample the rich, contested interpretive directions. My first aim is to situate *Gulliver's Travels* in its cultural, intellectual, and literary moment, and then I will discuss briefly issues of genre, rhetoric, authority and perspective, structure, and philosophical assumptions, before turning at the end to Swift's gloomy, frustrated, and dark final years.

The literary and cultural context

The 1726 appearance of *Gulliver's Travels* inaugurated an unprecedented thirty-month burst of important London print activity in which literary issues and political ones were almost impossible to separate. These were the golden days for the "Augustan" writers Swift associated with; besides Swift, both Pope and Gay produced their single most powerful and ambitious achievement – *The Dunciad* and *The Beggar's Opera* – in this glittering literary moment, and London writers of the late 1720s arguably assembled the most reaching, most cogent, and most articulate cultural critique ever articulated. But the accomplishment was not without personal, cultural, and even literary cost.[9]

The public prominence of literature in debates about cultural values and social direction – fed by the powerful coffee-house and periodicals phenomena and the more general rise of urban and cosmopolitan consciousness and conversation – had been escalating for more than two decades. In one sense, this perceived importance of literature in everyday public life was a triumph for the republic of letters, for important new works were virtually guaranteed public attention and prominence in conversation. But in another sense – perhaps the more important one, practically speaking – it was a cultural disaster with long-term literary fallout: nearly any published text of any significance was immediately identified with some party or ideology and quickly both praised and denounced for whatever its loyalties and implications were perceived to be. Veiled hints and secret meanings were everywhere suspected, and just about any major publication was followed by a parody, a "key" (connecting and coding the text to current public, usually political events), an "answer" (which in turn often spurred a "rejoinder," which might lead to a long chain of interactive pamphlets), or some other parodic, inverting, explanatory, or argumentative response. Among writers, both individually and in groups, there was virtual war, and among rivals much personal unpleasantness. The now much-discussed development of a "public sphere,"[10] however admirable its long-term consequences, was thus achieved at the expense of often ugly public debate and through downright personal nastiness in the political and writing communities, and public attacks on individuals – usually in print but sometimes in violent and debasing physical confrontation as well – were often conducted with little dignity or personal respect.[11]

To the modern reader, the fact that public figures (such as the first minister, Sir Robert Walpole, or even the king and queen) were treated roughly in the press is not very surprising, but the deep embroilment of men (and a few women) of letters is. Politics is, by definition, oppositional, and the give-and-take of everyday politics in the early years of what was becoming a deeply imbedded party system made for rugged and repeated struggles for power, or even survival. Power, then as now, meant influence, prestige, and often wealth. Loss of place could easily mean ostracism, legal prosecution, or even banishment – as it did in the 1710s and early 1720s for several members or close friends of the Swift–Pope group. What is distinctive, however, about the early eighteenth century in England is the way the leading writers became caught up in – and sucked into the center of – the public fray. Just about every major literary figure of the first third of the century – Swift, Pope, Daniel Defoe, Joseph Addison, Delariviere Manley, Sir Richard Steele, John Dennis, Eliza Haywood, Colley Cibber, and Henry Fielding – and a host of lesser lights became deeply enough involved (or implicated) politically that simply to name them called up strong positions and associations in the public mind. No matter how they struggled to free themselves of party taint, writers found that their values and opinions (or *presumed* values and opinions) preceded them.

One reason was that literature then was so aggressively devoted to present events and issues. Despite traditional labels for the literary period that associate its values mainly with the past ("neoclassical period," "Augustan age") and despite constant attempts by the writers themselves to evoke honored moments in the classical or Christian past, the texts regularly and aggressively addressed themselves to present events, ideas, and crises of some public kind. The writers saw themselves as performing a crucial cultural, social, and political role. By interpreting current events in some coherent way (often with direct comparison to past values and patterns), they could influence the now enlarged reading public significantly, according to their own individual (or group) lights. Their loyalties might be to party, class, religion, gender, or a host of other identity groups, but whatever their convictions and prejudices, each saw him- or herself as helping to define a new national tradition of identity, ideas, values, and literature. And beyond the large, popular audience that nearly everyone sought (although some pretended to address only the elite, the powerful, the educated, and the informed), writers felt themselves to be near the actual seats of power and personally influential with policy-makers and trendsetters. Most of the writers I have mentioned (and many others) were on personal terms with major figures in government, leading members of the aristocracy, and even members of the royal family, and (although they often complained that their societal role was diminished from that of writers past) they regarded themselves not only as arbiters of taste and morals, but as cultural and political watchdogs and as philosophical and political guides. And so they found themselves increasingly embroiled in quarrels both mighty and petty – and increasingly tarred by the brushes of opponents who (however inaccurate or inept they might be) often succeeded in their broad strokes that grouped people, events, and ideas into very simplistic categories and divided the world neatly into the sheep and the goats, the chosen and the rejected, the readable and the unread: good and evil.

By 1726 the vehemence and cruelty of public rhetoric had reached brutal proportions, and although just about every writer of note claimed to rise above politics and petty personal quarrels (and some actually tried), the truth is that no one, no matter how high-minded, could long remain aloof from what was genuinely a battle for cultural respect, supremacy, and survival. One indicator of how widespread and vicious the battles became was the colorful array of nicknames, caricatures, and slanderous anecdotes that individual writers attracted. Pope, for example, repeatedly drew enemy fire directed more at his person and personality than his poetry; he was regularly described as a devil, monster, or animal of some kind – a toad, a serpent, a wasp, and especially an ape – and he was standardly referred to in pamphlet prose as "A. P-E." Such "code" was ostensibly an abbreviation of his name but pointedly a reference to his gnarled body (he had been a hunchback since his teenage years when tuberculosis of the spine permanently disfigured him) and to the way he was bestially represented in pictorial caricatures. Swift was treated similarly: one published response to *Gulliver's Travels* offered this biographical "account" of its author:

[T]he first Instance he gave of his Genius and Spirit, was sh—g in his School-Master's Slippers...[H]e proceeded to other Exploits; stole the Neighbours Hens; poison'd their House-Dogs, and was at last whipp'd, and turn'd out of School, for pinning the Cook-Maid's Petticoats about her Ears, as she lay sleeping by the Kitchen-Fire...[He] grew intolerably insolent and vain on account of his Writings; insomuch that he turned light-headed, and in his mad Fits, abused Every Body that came in his Way, sometimes spit, and sometimes piss'd in their Faces, and kick'd all the Dogs that he met.[12]

Such battles of "wit" continued to deteriorate through the 1720s, and if *Gulliver's Travels* itself is relatively free of pointed references to literary – political feuds and public representations of them, its appearance had the effect of letting loose the fury and venom that turned the late 1720s into the most explosive and most vicious period of literary vilification in modern history, though it was also one of the most concentrated periods of literary brilliance.

Only a few scattered parts of *Gulliver's Travels* need to be glossed directly in the light of the literary quarrels of the time. The most significant passages, perhaps, are the prefatory "Letter from...Gulliver to...Cousin Sympson" – with its disclaimers (and anxieties) about the impotence of satiric art,[13] and the pointed account in Book IV of the lack of a textual, written tradition among the Houyhynhnms.[14] But the whole thrust of *Gulliver's Travels* (and its direct relationship to other writings of the time, a topic to which I turn next) needs to be seen in terms of the established literary – political contexts of suspicion and attack and the calculated decision of the Pope–Swift group to launch a major counter-offensive, thus escalating the gratuitous personal attacks on them as individuals and a group into a full-scale culture war with personalities cum politics as the central thrust. If Swift's basic literary program as engaged in *Gulliver's Travels* means to "vex" the world where it then stood, an important aspect of his challenge involves the way that readers presume to know the political underpinnings of texts, and the process of reading that *Gulliver's Travels* proposes (and perhaps dictates) involves negotiating the assumptions of his time in a direct and demanding way. Whether the textual details allegorize history or only allude more generally to contemporary cultural practice, every reader of the late 1720s would inevitably have been drawn into a swirl of political interpretation and debate. Even later readers who are thoroughly disengaged from those issues often wonder about possible local and historical referents and look for resonant applications. Who *is* Flimnap, we wonder, and what cultural models lie behind Laputa? The central issues have worn well historically and still seem to have considerable relevance, but they also seem very particular to Europe in 1726.

Comparative reading: Gulliver and other writers

Gulliver's Travels is a very bookish book, highly self-conscious of its relationship to other texts both new and old. Its contemporary readers would have recognized more fully than we do its dependence on classical and Christian myth and tradition, its invocation of conventions characteristic of contemporary genres and modes, its spare (but distinctive) references to individual texts and authors, and also its several more sweeping allusions.[15] Beyond its important but somewhat reluctant place in contemporary debate about the place of writing in English culture, the relationship of *Gulliver's Travels* to other books can be usefully approached in at least two other ways: (1) generically, as a kind of demonstration of what can be done with varieties of contemporary writing which provide signposts and expectations for readers familiar with their habits; and (2) as echoes of specific contemporary authors and books. The fabric of literary reference and allusion implicitly recommends a "comparative" reading strategy, so that reading the book responsively with other texts is an active, work-intensive process for a reader who has to remain alert to rapidly changing textual signals. In the opening pages of the book, Swift invites us to think both generically and allusively and sometimes to mix the two procedures creatively for ourselves.

The title page places the text firmly in the wake of more than a century of popular travel writings. Here is a promise of knowledge of "Remote Nations" and a recital of the author's informational authority: Gulliver the author has been both a ship's surgeon and a captain of ships, and here is his reliable eyewitness account. Swift's text, of course, provides anything but factual geographical and anthropological data in the usual sense, and the cartographical claims are ludicrous. If readers were for an instant taken in by the claims of authenticity, neither the maps nor Gulliver's detailed "facts" remain useful to anyone for long. Quite beyond setting up its own plot or fable (which it does at the same time), the highly circumstantial narrative has the effect of raising questions about the authority of the genre – as well it might, since a high percentage of the books of exploration and discovery written in London by authors who had never left home and whose facts were often wildly inaccurate.[16] Readerly curiosity about faraway places and exotic people had been building for more than a century: travel books, unreliable as they often were, addressed an important cultural hunger, implicitly challenging English notions of normativity and offering a glittering array of possibilities about otherness in all its forms. Swift's formal choice to cast his satire as a travel book had a lot to do with the popularity of travel and adventure narratives – and with the difficulty of discriminating factual narratives from their fictional counterparts – but travel is not just a convenience. Travel – movement through space in a way that involves accumulation of facts towards a coherent narrative about place, culture, and humanity – recapitulates a mode of education characteristic of Swift's time and replicates the rhetorical and epistemological mode of many characteristic contemporary genres, including conduct books, autobiographies, memoirs, and novels.

What travel and travel writing stands for is a particular kind of intellectual curiosity. Having spent most of his life in a land whose people, customs, and thinking habits were foreign to him, Swift was himself fascinated by cultural difference and became something of a student of it. But he knew that curiosity's satisfaction involved more than lists of flora and fauna and a description of local manners, habits, and rites. Some famous travel writers he invokes directly – the famous voyager William Dampier, for example, whom he refers to as "Cousin Dampier" – and he adopts the extreme detail and circumstantiality of the form, in one case (Book ii, chapter 1) copying virtually word for word a jargon-laden passage from Samuel Sturmy's *Mariner's Magazine*:

> Finding it was like to overblow, we took in our Sprit-sail, and stood by to hand the Fore-sail; but making foul Weather, we looked the Guns were all fast, and handed the Missen. The Ship lay very broad off, so we thought it better spooning before the Sea, than trying or hulling. We reeft the Foresail and set him, we hawled aft the Fore-sheet. (*PW* xi: 84)

Such burlesque plagiarism continues for nearly a page, and every Book contains, suggestively, maritime or anthropological details just as space-wasting and irrelevant, long after readers have given up any hope of gathering factual information. Swift does not say that all travel books are lies and cheats, but his book illustrates, by absurd parody, how it is done. And in the process of destroying authoritative confidence in the mode of presentation he both undermines belief in that mode's assumptions and creates (almost in spite of himself) a persuasive, comparative account of what characterizes the cultural life of Gulliver's (and Swift's – and the reader's) homeland. Travel turns out, in this fictional inversion, not to produce knowledge of alterity but of home. Imagining foreignness returns one to native, English issues and ultimately to the self.

Sometimes *Gulliver's Travels* is infuriating in its insistence on detail, especially when Gulliver is between countries and the circumstances of his movement are not very interesting in themselves. Once we *know* that the voyage framework is just a convenience rather than a geographical guide – and once we no longer care about Gulliver's authenticity and veracity – why does each succeeding voyage go through the same motions and keep reminding us of the travel genre framework? One reason, I think, is that each voyage needs to stand by itself for individual or successive readings. We can, as readers have often done, refuse the book-dictated order and read each voyage as an independent text, and the repeated frames not only permit but almost encourage us to do so, providing a "sufficient" relationship between readers and text in every individual voyage or book.[17] Another reason is that the repetition of structure drums home the fact that the voyages do not involve learning or improvement or progress in the teleological way implied by travel narratives and the travel motif itself. Gulliver does not learn from his previous mistakes, or indeed from anything he experiences. Only at the end of Book IV (and then disastrously) does he try to take any lessons home. Otherwise, the voyages just accumulate, without adding up. Even Gulliver's in-book observers do not learn; Gulliver's record at sea is not exactly inspiring for its evidence of either navigational or leadership skills, but by the beginning of Book IV he has risen despite his seafaring failures from surgeon to captain. Earlier, at the beginning of Book III, he had been unaccountably recruited by a captain who was evidently even less observant than Gulliver himself: William Robinson offers twice "the usual Pay," and "having experienced my Knowledge in Sea-Affairs" offers to "enter into any Engagement to follow my Advice" (*PW* XI: 153). The human refusal or inability to learn anything from past experience is a central issue for Swift, and the repetition of frame narratives (with all their details about ships and directions and how many children he produced on his latest visit home) are an important device in driving home the point.

There are also good reasons, though somewhat contrary ones, for thinking about *Gulliver's Travels* in relation to the novel[18] and perhaps especially to one book that took the market by storm at about the time Swift began working on what in his letters he called "my Travels." That book is *The Life and Strange Surprizing Adventures of Robinson Crusoe, of York. Mariner*, by Daniel Defoe. Swift found Defoe unspeakable in many religious and political and perhaps artistic ways: even though he for some years worked alongside him in the Harley administration, he once referred to him as "the Fellow that was *pilloryed*, I have forgot his Name" (*PW* II: 113). The introductory paragraphs of *Gulliver's Travels* seem almost a parody of (or answer to) Defoe and his hero Crusoe.[19] Whether or not Swift had Defoe (and Crusoe) consciously in mind when he constructed Gulliver's background, character, and career – and there is persuasive textual evidence that he did[20] – much of what Swift does generically amounts to a revisionary corrective to the developing novelistic mode that was then beginning to codify modern urban patterns of subjectivity and quotidian particularity. Quite a few features of *Gulliver's Travels*, including the conception of Gulliver himself as a narrator (see below, p. 226), make emphatic anti-novelistic statements, usually via parody: the episodic structure and lack of narrative development, the gross exaggeration of subjectivity and character inconsistency, the excessive re-counting of irrelevant "realistic" details (including Gulliver's obsessive re-tailing of maritime locations and business arrangements and his insistence on telling us about his various bodily evacuations), the sour and bathetic ending in which Gulliver, unlike the buoyant Crusoe, finds it impossible to rejoin humanity after his alienating experiences abroad. I am on record as believing that Defoe's narrative is a brilliant, original, and satisfying early example of the novel form, but it does depend on a series of artistic and philo-sophical assumptions – about subjectivity and human nature, for example – that Swift (and the whole Augustan circle) found laughable, repugnant, and even dangerous.[21]

Swift undercuts novelistic practices and assumptions repeatedly and sys-tematically, but nowhere so fully as in the outcome of Book IV when Gulliver comes home to his family and his stable. Here the disillu-sioned hero resembles some of the real-life prototypes of Robinson Crusoe (Alexander Selkirk, for instance) more than Defoe's adaptable Crusoe, who after twenty-eight years of isolation – most of it without speech or human companionship – readjusts quickly and easily to human society. Selkirk, on the other hand, who had spent only four years on a similar solitary island, never did return to ordinary life, spending (according to contemporary accounts) his final years gloomily in solitude in Scotland, some said in a cave. Swift clearly thinks that the pretended ordinariness and "realism" in the new novelistic narratives is not merely a misleading literary convention but a life ruse as well. His engagement with genre is not merely a convenience but a searching critique of contemporary books and habits that represents an extension of the Augustan critique of publishing and reading practices more generally.

So what kind of book, then, is *Gulliver's Travels* itself? Its broad invoca-tion of many traditional or contemporary kinds and modes (philosophical voyages, utopias, memoirs, and autobiographies, for example, in addition to travel books and novels) – and its occasional imitative and comparative uses of them for purposes of its own clarification – implies that it is many things at once. This multiplicity seems appropriate to its satiric aims, for satire is more of a literary mode than a kind or genre in itself, and often it finds its form by invading and inhabiting one or more existing genres and thus making encroachment, infiltration, possession, and subversion its central way of life. The very promiscuity of the text's allegiances suggests its complex, protean nature and makes it not so surprising that readers have turned to it for so many different uses, and critics for so many kinds of argument.

The hazards of interpretation: Gulliver as observer and narrator

Lemuel Gulliver's exact role in the *Travels* is not easy to describe. On the one hand he is *everything* – participant, observer, narrator, commentator, at once hero and interpreter – and without him the book does not exist. We as readers know nothing that does not come filtered through him; his eyes and voice are all we have. Yet he is a pathetic thing, not nearly the keen observer and judicious analyst he believes himself to be, and he has trouble keeping his opinions consistent and his facts straight. Proud of his navigational skills, he never gets to where he wants to go and always ends up lost, shipwrecked, captured, or deluded. Arrogant about his knowledge of languages and his rhetorical abilities, he does not fathom what "Laputa" means (in Spanish, "the whore") and makes up instead an absurd etymology. And he loses almost every debate in every place he visits. Boastful about his judgment and ability to make careful distinctions, he cannot tell a Houyhnhnm from an ordinary horse, abroad or at home. He is very much an enigma if we try to take him seriously as a person – even a fictional person – for he does not operate in a lifelike, "realistic," or probable way. It is not just that he is mercurial, contradictory, and inconsistent, but that he seems to function in different ways at different moments in the book. Trying to sort out what ontological state Gulliver occupies – and exactly how he functions in the book to clarify things he himself is not clear about – is central to coming to terms with Swift's satire. "Unreliable" is a good word to describe the kind of narrator Gulliver is – for his naive gullibility along with his blustering self-confidence make us leery of his reportage from the first – but it is not an adequate word. Lots of narrators in fiction are limited, biased, or confused, but in the kinds of representational narratives that comprise most modern reading, narrators usually have a certain human credibility and are at least consistently inconsistent. Gulliver, on the other hand, is all over the place – sometimes a trustworthy reporter and commentator, sometimes a sophisticated ironist, sometimes an innocent or a fool or just a stick figure.

How we respond to the role of Lemuel Gulliver as narrative voice pretty well determines – even more than in most narratives – how we read the text. Gulliver is not a character, or even a narrator, in the usual sense – certainly not in the way a character operates in a typical novel. He does not grow, develop, change, or "learn" from his experiences (except for his at-home response to his last voyage), and he displays no consistency of attitude or, despite his protests, integrity of character. He is pretty much whatever Swift wants or needs him to be at any given point in the narration; he is more of a rhetorical figure than a human one. Sometimes he says sensible things and operates more or less as a spokesman for Swift, but often he is obtuse, misleading, or just wrong. Sometimes he vociferously defends empire and chauvinistic ideas about his native land; sometimes he is ashamed of home habits and sees virtue only in otherness of some kind. He is, in Swift's own terms, a "personation" (*PW* I: 3) – someone who can put on different acts and faces at various moments when a particular stance or effect is needed – but he does not himself add up to anything coherent, cogent, or plausible. He is given a family background and a series of characteristics *as if* he were a representational or realistic character, but once he is set in motion he operates in a completely different mode, seemingly a denizen of a textual world that makes up its own laws as it goes.

Nearly all readers from the beginning experience Gulliver as unreliable and, if usually comic, almost always infuriating, whether he is pompously interpreting the obvious, totally missing the point of an experience, or staunchly defending English stereotypical positions that we (to our embarrassment) may discover that we too hold. He is the kind of gull who can only exist as an extreme stereotype, and that is why he can move blithely through such a variety of places, and customs, and experiences without having anything permanently rub off on him. But the fact that, in Book IV, he finally does respond to something and modify his behavior – that is, become a fictional character whose responses seem humanly representational (even if extreme and bizarre) – means that we have to confront his early role or roles more fully in order to comprehend the nature of his narration and his contribution to the satire.

Much of the undercutting of Gulliver is subtle, almost buried in a text that seems to be striving to do something else than keep track of its facts. Gulliver's early account of himself when he comes ashore in Lilliput suggests how he – and the narrative – are going to work. Early in Book I, for example, he offers a bizarre account of his passage to shore (after a shipwreck) carrying virtually a shipload of goods on his person. Here is what Gulliver – presumably desperate against overpowering seas – lugs with him as he struggles against the waves: a large sword, a set of pistols, a snuffbox, a diary, a comb, a razor, a set of eating utensils, a watch, a handkerchief, a pouch of gunpowder and another of bullets, silver and copper money and several pieces of gold, a pair of spectacles, a pocket perspective, a full set of clothes including a hat, and "several other little Conveniences" (*PW* XI: 37). These items become, one by one, useful to the narrative as Gulliver tries to account for European customs and history, and it is easy to ignore their presence (as Gulliver apparently does) when he first strives for the gently sloped and finely nuanced shores of Lilliput (which he also notices only dimly). But once the items are enumerated, the picture of Gulliver that emerges is ludicrous.[22] Does he not know that – hat, sword, pistols, and all – his excess baggage impedes his progress and threatens his survival? Is the narrative inconsistent, are facts being forgotten, or is the narrative out of his control? Gulliver the traveler and Gulliver the narrator are not one here, and we either have to conclude that Swift is forgetful or that the absent-minded and absurd Gulliver is a function of Swift's calculated art.

The point is repeated time and time again. When, for example, later in Lilliput, he is accused of having an inappropriate relationship with Flimnap's wife, Gulliver offers a deadpan defense with a mixture of obtuseness, arrogance, and absurdity, as if the charge that he – 1,728 times as large – could have a sexual relationship with a Lilliputian woman was plausible. Swift milks Gulliver's lengthy defense for all it is worth here, playing naiveté against sexual braggadocio. Implicitly Gulliver once more celebrates his sexual gigantism (as he had done earlier, in Book I, chapter three when he had assumed the spread-legs posture of a Colossus and reported the "Laughter and Admiration" of the uplooking soldiers who marched under his torn breeches [*PW* XI: 42]), but Swift also has him underscore his popularity with all the ladies:

> I am here obliged to vindicate the Reputation of an excellent Lady, who was an Innocent Sufferer on my Account. The Treasurer took a Fancy to be jealous of his Wife, from the Malice of some evil Tongues, who informed him that her Grace had taken a violent Affection for my Person; and the Court-Scandal ran for some Time that she once came privately to my Lodging. This I solemnly swear to be a most infamous Falshood, without any Grounds, farther than that her Grace was pleased to treat me with all innocent Marks of Freedom and Friendship. I own she came often to my House, but always publickly, nor ever without three more in the Coach, who were usually her Sister, and young Daughter, and some particular Acquaintance; but this was common to many other Ladies of the Court ... And I have often had four Coaches and Horses at once on my Table full of Company, while I sat in my Chair leaning my Face towards them; and when I was engaged with one Sett, the Coachmen would gently drive the others round my Table. I have passed many an Afternoon very agreeably in these Conversations ... I should not have dwelt so long upon this Particular, if it had not been a Point wherein the Reputation of a great Lady is so nearly concerned; to say nothing of my own; although I had the Honour to be a *Nardac*, which the Treasurer himself is not; for all the World knows he is only a *Clumglum*, a Title inferior by one Degree.   (*PW* XI: 65–66)

There is so much twisting and turning and intertwining of satirical objects here that a reader hardly knows where to begin in sorting out the effects; here is satire on (among other things) Gulliver's own pretensions and pride, on male fantasy and credulity more generally, on female lechery that exceeds the physics of the possible, on political and marital intrigue, on the trivial bases of human ceremony and custom, and on the pettiness of ambition, jealousy, envy, lust, and pride. One of the most appealing things about Gulliver is that we can repeatedly feel superior to him even as we too are allowed fantasies of size, recognition, relationship, and control.

Perspective and shape: formal issues

It is not hard to "get" the central issues of perspective in Books I and II, as the reputation of the book as a children's classic readily suggests. Gulliver's experience of himself relative to others is almost exactly inverted in these books, and a major effect of reading them – especially in the order in which Swift arranges them – involves the radical shift in perspective that they embody. Children (and most adults reading *Gulliver's Travels* for the first time) seem almost instinctively to understand what it is like to be larger than life and to have the feeling that huge possibilities of power and effectiveness are open for them. Perhaps the desire suddenly to dwarf everyone else – and all human limitations and predicaments – is a common human tendency. Certainly the naval heroics of Gulliver in saving his host nation (and his wondrous Herculean feats in building things and in transforming national space, not to mention in consuming and defecating) resonated for Swift's contemporaries. They would readily have recognized the little allegory involving the incessant wars with France and persistent references to common cultural, religious, and social practices. Here is a calculation (on several different levels at once) to elevate physical exploit to the highest imaginable level; no wonder children, longing to be bigger, love it, along with adults conditioned to confront every day their humiliating limitations. And then, in Book II, the abrupt reversal undoes the reader as well as Gulliver, so that our humiliating smallness seems smaller still. His (and our) experiences in Books I and II are almost perfect mirror images of one another, and there is a sense in which Dr. Johnson's famous remark about big and little people is almost adequate to describe how perception works in Books I and II.

Science was hardly an idol for Swift (as the several satirized nations in Book III quickly show); he knew very little about scientific procedure and even less about theory, and his yearning for clear authority (combined with his persistent distrust of human knowledge and judgment) meant that he had little respect for intellectual ambition. Even more strongly, he distrusted the hubristic desire to understand the physical nature of a universe in both its small details and its huge cosmic dimensions (which he interpreted in orthodox Christian terms as a legacy of the Fall, caused by intellectual over-reaching). And he did not believe in the doctrine of progress that under-lay such organizations as the Royal Society and scientific exploration more generally. But he was aware of modern scientific developments (and re-searched some details for Book III carefully), and he was not above using the findings as well as the manners and habits of contemporary science when they were of use to him – as they were in the issue of proportion and perspec-tive. The microscopic and telescopic views (based on the recent invention, development, and increasingly common use of those instruments) provided Swift with extremes of seeing and being seen, virtually all of his conceptual frame for the first two books. It was a device especially useful for elevating the observer and observed into satiric prominence, for it gave the narrative point-of-view device a built-in sense of justified – because constantly used – exaggeration.

Seeing and perceiving are crucial issues throughout *Gulliver's Travels*, es-pecially when sight and insight fail its hero-reporter, the safety of whose eyes and spectacles obsess him wherever he goes.[23] Because he has at his dis-posal both long and short views, Swift can readily offer a "perspective" on the magnitude of England's national ambitions and international relations as well as the gross physical details calculated to disgust us out of lust and the satisfaction of human desire more generally. Here deformity, defecation, and sexuality become repugnant reminders of our absurd and grimly limited physical selves, and (whatever they tell us about Swift's psychological fears, prejudices, and personal hang-ups) the exaggerated physical features of the narrative's human population ground our tendencies to elevate our belief in ourselves as above it all.[24] Exaggeration is the coin of satire, of course, but the physical (and especially scatological) heightening Swift adored was especially effective as olfactory suggestion in a time when travelers toward London consistently reported that they could smell it before they could see it – not because of the industrialization which historically lay just ahead but because of the primitive plumbing and open sewers that could only inade-quately serve the physical needs of the teeming city.

The order of the voyages to Lilliput and Brobdingnag is crucial. Because we experience the proportions of things through Gulliver, we can in the be-ginning imagine ourselves very large and grand in our relation to common places and things (not to mention other people), and, when the proportions are reversed, the shock of our smallness, ineptitude, and helplessness is all the greater, just like Gulliver's. Swift tells us that the Lilliputians are one-twelfth as tall as humans and otherwise proportionate, which means that (because we are three-dimensional) ordinary humans are 1,728 times as large – and which means that Gulliver's adjustment (and ours) from Book I to Book II involves a proportional reduction factor of 152,064. And so it is with our powers – and thus the effect on our accustomed pride. There are many thematic concerns in the book, but one of the most insistent involves human pride,[25] and the size metaphor (and all it represents) makes the point powerfully. When, for example, Gulliver in a giddy mood in Brobdingnag decides he has to leap over a pile of cow dung to prove his physical prowess, his falling short demonstrates his limits rather dramatically and humbles his pride filthily. Such reminders follow easily from the aggrandizement and then diminution of Gulliver's status in his world, and the order of things in the world (as Swift asks us to see it) is rhetorically produced by the order of Gulliver's visits to little and then big societies. The humiliation of pride (both Gulliver's and ours) goes hand in hand with the dashing of our hopes for heroism, greatness, and grandeur. Lands that seem at first wildly foreign in their smallness if not their pettiness – and then just as alien in their magnitude and sometime magnanimity – rhetorically reduce our inflated sense of ourselves in a spectacular way. The shape of Books I and II is both rhetorically effective for Swift's purposes and aesthetically satisfying in its strategies of parallelism, symmetry, mirroring, and reflection.

The shape of the rest of *Gulliver's Travels* is more problematic, and critical tradition has never entirely come to terms with the formal issues the text raises, perhaps because traditional aesthetic theory has been uncomfortable with variant principles in the same work. The second half of the book clearly works very differently from the first half. Nothing like simple inversion or an easy contrast of perceptions holds Books III and IV together, and in fact the movement from I and II to III and IV is neither logical nor symmetrical: Gulliver simply continues to go to new places, and the kinds of places he goes to vary considerably in their analogous relation to any known lands and cultures: we are no longer dependent on the single differentiation of size. There is a powerful *internal* coherence in Book IV – with its sharp contrast between Houyhnhnms and Yahoos and its careful revision of originary myths and the sorting processes of history – and as an individual voyage it seems almost complete in itself, more like a modern novel (even if controlled by allegory), for here Gulliver (like a novelistic character) takes away a lesson (however misunderstood or misapplied) and tries to live it out once he returns home. But Book IV does not parallel or match up with Book III in any direct or obvious way, and Book III itself is primarily additive, with visits to many kinds of lands (including, in fact, one actual land, Japan) all crammed into a single continuous narrative.

What Swift's formal plan (if any) may have been we do not know: he said very little, beyond reporting his desire to "vex" the world, about his intentions in *Gulliver's Travels* (C III: 102). And we know little about the composition process itself, for in his letters as they have come down to us he mentions his work on the book only occasionally and sparingly. It does seem probable that Swift wrote Book III last, and its episodic structure – with new cultures, visits, and people simply accumulating one after another – seems almost to suggest that Swift was dropping all his fugitive targets and leftovers into the text at that point, without much thought for form or aesthetics or even for the rhetorical and psychological effects that seemed to govern the *Travels* in its first half. But *Gulliver's Travels* obviously "works" for most readers; the history of satisfaction and popularity is an impressive one, and if we are not too rigid and doctrinaire about a single "governing" plan – or insistent on some single standard of form – it is possible to construct a plausible account of *how* it works within Swift's intention to challenge and unnerve us. For it is precisely in giving us a firm sense of direction and shape, and then startling us with different directions and probabilities, that the book proceeds from beginning to end – first giving us one principle of relationship (diminution) in Book I, then reversing it (magnification) in Book II, then wildly shifting principles one after another in Book III (where the particular grotesqueries involve mental as well as physical distortions), then returning to a single distinction which embodies an otherness that replicates shape distinctions back home but here transforms them into mental (and perhaps spiritual) ones. It is the book's final aesthetic irony that Gulliver here comes to believe in the last distinction as the only true one and – believing in its stability – tries to take it home and literalize it as a governing principle.[26] The ultimate vexation of our sense of our expectation and discovery – and I think of Swift's sense of balance – comes in Book IV, chapter 11 when our hero, now at home in his stable, finds it impossible to reestablish communion with his family:

> During the first Year I could not endure my Wife or Children in my Presence, the very Smell of them was intolerable; much less could I suffer them to eat in the same Room. To this Hour they dare not presume to touch my Bread, or drink out of the same Cup. (*PW* XI: 289–90)

Many readers, most extensively Howard Erskine-Hill in his fine analysis of the subject, have noted how little direct theology and religion there is in *Gulliver's Travels*,[27] but for a moment the Anglican priest does here triumph in the text as Gulliver is held to a standard of human communion he does not comprehend. Gulliver does not know the humanity he is missing, but the allusion, expectation, and pacing of the text allows readers one final time to read the body of the narrator better than he himself can.

The nature of humankind: Swift and misanthropy/misogyny

The critical history of *Gulliver's Travels* is fraught with battles of interpretation over many other issues that I have mentioned only briefly or not touched on at all. Central to most of them – including the most pressing issues at the moment, issues of gender on the one hand and of nationalism, empire, and colonialism on the other – is the pervasive and enduring question of Swift's attitude toward human nature and human perfectability. At one time, for almost an entire academic generation, debate about this issue focused intensely on the viability of the Houyhnhnms as a human ideal and . on Gulliver's reverence for them. Do we as readers admire the Houyhnhnms, · find them funny or disgusting, or regard them as some kind of inhuman, and humanly unattainable, ideal? That debate now seems rather dated (as do all critical and theoretical disagreements sooner or later), and it is now chiefly interesting for its various special pleadings and selective readings of portions of the text, but once it threatened to divide the whole of scholarly interpretation about eighteenth-century literature and intellectual history. Was Swift – and perhaps the eighteenth century more generally – utopian in desires, or pragmatic, suspicious, and dystopian about ideals beyond human reach? The debate developed its own specialist vocabulary – the "hard" school read the Houyhnhmns as human paradigms and the "soft" interpreters saw them as false ideals[28] – and interpreters were seldom allowed compromise or deviation from the established party lines. The energy of the debate has considerably subsided, and historical reinterpretation of the eighteenth century more generally has made it easier to "place" Swift more subtly and accurately within complex intellectual currents of his time. But the "modeling" issue is · still a crucial one for this text as it is for the procedures of satire more generally. Does satire always have to incorporate some viable ideal, as earlier, twentieth-century formalists insisted, or can it accomplish its purposes by a succession of graded distortions and possibilities?[29]

And so it goes. Or rather went. In post-World War II debate, utopian issues and questions of perfectability were crucial issues, and frets about scatology and satiric decorum and outreach were frequent. Every age, in rethinking old books, takes its own most pressing concerns to their interpretation. Today, the most vigorous debates involve gender (see especially Ruth Salvaggio and Felicity Nussbaum), nationalism (Carole Fabricant and Howard Weinbrot), imperialism (Laura Brown), and (once again) politics more generally.[30] It is one kind of tribute to Swift that he continues to vex us philosophically and ideologically now in quite a different world, and it is another to notice how his clear style and tough prose continue to please and perplex our sense of art.

After *Gulliver's Travels*: age and decline

Like Swift, Gulliver was not a young man when he embarked on his "Travels." By conservative calculation from the early years chronicled in the opening paragraphs, he is at least thirty-nine when he embarks on his voyage to Lilliput, and so – after a lifetime of experience and many years at sea – he is nearly Swift's age when he takes to reflecting, reminiscing, pronouncing, reforming, and writing his memoirs. Swift has a great deal of fun with Gulliver's experience and maturity – his half-learned truths and pretensions to wisdom – and it would be pointless to make much of the precise biographical parallels between the author and his narrator: Gulliver is like a parody of Swift, or an emblem of late middle age going wrong, much as Defoe's life and writings were for Swift a grotesque version of his own career and values (Defoe too had produced his epic narrative voyage at almost exactly the same age).[31] But Swift was highly cognizant of his age and frailty, anxious in his fears about mental (as well as physical) deterioration when he abandoned the orphanlike manuscript of *Travels* to booksellers and printers in 1726. Three years earlier – citing the ancients for authority – he had speculated, perhaps facetiously, that mental powers deteriorated at a certain age, and that writers produced no major work beyond that point. The age he chose as pivotal was forty-nine, and although Swift when he finished Gulliver was nearly a decade older – and plainly not yet diminished – he was highly conscious of the miseries of physical and mental loss.

The painfully long story of the Struldbruggs in Book III, chapter 10 – they seem to be the only reason for a sojourn in Luggnugg – poignantly suggests Swift's fear of old age and the dire outcomes of physical and mental decay. Into this account Swift piles virtually every mortal anxiety except the fear of mortality itself; rather than being freed of mortal limits when death is no threat, the Struldbruggs continue haunted (and devastated) by the ravages of time. Their memory disappears (they remember only the events and responses of their youth), and they combine nostalgia with rigidity and intolerance. Gulliver, as usual, tries to admire and defend them but ultimately has to admit "the dreadful Prospect of never dying" and summarizes them devastatingly: they are "opinionative, peevish, covetous, morose, vain, talkative ... uncapable of Friendship, and dead to all natural Affection ... Envy and impotent Desires, are their prevailing Passions" (*PW* XI: 212). These feelings were hardly abstract to Swift at this point in his life, and he details the implications ruthlessly. His fears would prove all too realistic and personal.

Swift lived almost twenty years after fathering Gulliver – and he produced several other significant writings, most notably *A Modest Proposal* (at age sixty-two), *Verses on the Death of Dr. Swift* (a "prophecy" written fourteen years before the actual event), the lively *Directions to Servants* and *Complete Collection of Genteel and Ingenious Conversation*, and quite a few of his best poems, most notably many of the "lady" poems (including "The Lady's Dressing Room," "A Beautiful Young Nymph Going to Bed," and "Cassinus and Peter") that once contributed to his misogynous reputation but that now have become crucial to his rehabilitation among feminist critics because of their shrewd analysis of what social custom and traditional gender roles do to women's identity and self-conception. The poems written by Swift in his early sixties are especially worth reading to see the older Swift, more angry than bemused, contemplating absurdities legislated by habitual English and European practice. For all of his authoritarian habits and traditional prejudices, the older, more reflective Swift found much of human absurdity to be more dependent on custom, habit, and construction than on human nature per se. His human definition of *rationale capax* and its consequences (meaning that human beings are capable of reason rather than reasonable creatures) suggested that postlapsarian history was largely a record of failure, a matter of custom rejecting and dragging down divine plan.

Even though Swift had begun worrying about the decay of his imaginative powers much earlier, the evidence of *A Modest Proposal* suggests that Swift was still at the top of his form, both intellectually and rhetorically, into his early sixties. There the force of his irony is at its most powerful – issues of Ireland always seemed to focus or even heighten his considerable linguistic and imaginative skills – and the poems written at about the same time show him near the peak of his stylistic and tonal control. His irony and comic sense are clearly undiminished in the *Verses on the Death of Dr. Swift* where he imagines the responses of his contemporaries, including his best friends, to his own death:

> Poor Pope will grieve a month; and Gay
> A week, and Arbuthnot a day.
> (*Poems* 491)

There are moments of nostalgia and stifled ambition in the poem, but hardly a hint of self-pity or even sadness about the world's failures. The high spirits that allowed Swift's imagination to soar at the very thought of human frailties and stupidities is very much on display throughout the poem.

But as the 1720s dwindled into the 1730s – and with the thirty-month Augustan moment of 1726–29 having ended with the thud of Colley Cibber's new appointment to the laureateship – the celebratory consciousness that the Pope–Swift circle developed to combat their depression waned notably. Here was a new era that Swift – unlike his friend Pope who characteristically continued to turn his bitter fruit into a commercial palliative – would never be comfortable in. His health was deteriorating and his creative, intellectual, and mnemonic powers beginning to slip, or at least wobble. The Ménière's Syndrome which had begun to affect his balance (and which produced a disconcerting hum in his ears that became virtually constant) began to take larger tolls, and Swift's later life was one of increasing discomfort, discontent, disillusion, and (ultimately) madness or something close to it. If he never became Gulliver, naysaying inappropriately in his isolation, he did become a sad old man, increasingly friendless and alone in a land that was always alien to him, even though the land of his birth. The winter years confirmed and extended Swift's characteristic crustiness, eccentricity, crotchetiness, and pessimism, and gradually he slipped more and more into solitude and emotional isolation. He could hear and understand less and less, and the voices of those he communed with must have more and more become, in his ears, the kind of blunted bestial sounds that only distantly reminded him of rational discourse and sustaining friendships. By 1738 his correspondence with Pope ceased, and by 1740 his memory was gone. The later Dublin years – while perhaps sustained somewhat by his clerical duties and the rage he continued to feel for Ireland's plight – deteriorated into increasing vertigo, anger, acrimony, frustration, dementia, and (ultimately) textual silence. He had, in a manner of speaking, become the old Lemuel Gulliver after all.

Swift's powerful textual accomplishments, impressive as they still are after three centuries, never quite obscured for him the pain and disappointments of mortality and an emotional consciousness that, whatever male and female friendships it enjoyed, never realized the hungry desire for community, belonging, satisfaction, and love. His love affair with print – whose vulgar manifestations he hated with all his being – long kept him sane but ultimately failed him too. It was only, perhaps, his human affection for Ireland (a failed land with human problems that could not be wished, reasoned, or negotiated away), his passion for justice and truth (and especially the refusals of self-delusion), and his love of the wonders and betrayals of language that kept him sane as long as it did. Besides his own writings, the most telling memorials of him are the words of Pope when he dedicated *The Dunciad* to him, and the Latin inscription (which he wrote for himself) on his tomb at St. Patrick's elucidating his love of liberty and savage indignation (*saeva indignatio*) with the world. In Yeats' memorable translation,

> SWIFT has sailed into his rest;
> Savage indignation there
> Cannot lacerate his breast.
> Imitate him if you dare,
> World-besotted traveller; he
> Served human liberty.[32]

NOTES

1. Swift's negotiation with the bookseller Benjamin Motte was a cloak-and-dagger affair, conducted under the name of a fictional cousin of the fictional Gulliver, and when the published book appeared – with the type set by four different printers so as to meet Swift's demands of speedy publication – Swift complained loudly about printing errors and editorial modification. It is hard to know where jesting leaves off here and anxiety begins; Swift may genuinely have feared prosecution or retribution for his contemporary satiric jabs, or he may have believed that the bookseller failed him out of his own fears of legal prosecution or physical harm, but Swift can hardly have imagined that his authorship would remain unknown indefinitely (and likely would have been disappointed had it been so). Swift actually arranged to have the manuscript dropped off in Motte's garden under cover of night, and quite possibly Motte had no idea.

2. *Gulliver's Travels* did not, of course, circulate as easily among readers as did *The Spectator*, which consisted of a single broadsheet easily passed from hand to hand in company. But volumes circulated much more readily and informally in those years of high-priced books, few libraries, and common lending and sharing practices among readers.

3. Alexander Pope himself had published *A Key to the Lock* shortly after *The Rape of the Lock* in order to preempt a "decoding" by others, and scores of such "keys" to eighteenth-century works were published.

4. For other contemporary criticisms, see C: III: 189.

5. *The Poems Of Alexander Pope*, ed. John Butt (London: Methuen, 1963), pp. 486–87.

6. Boswell, *Life of Johnson*, ed. George Birkbeck Hill, revised L. F. Powell, 6 vols. (Oxford: Clarendon Press, 1934), vol. II, p. 319.

7. From a March 1727 letter, in English, to Thieriot. See Letter 34, *Correspondance de Voltaire*, ed. Lucien Foulet (Paris: Librairie Hachette, 1913), p. 90.

8. Macaulay, as cited in Michael Foote's introduction to *Gulliver's Travels* (Harmondsworth: Penguin, 1967), pp. 12–13; W. M. Thackeray, *English Humorists of the Eighteenth Century* (London, 1853), p. 40.

9. The reception of *Gulliver's Travels* – a combination of exhilarating celebrity and rancorous puzzlement about hermeneutic and cultural issues – in many ways stands for the Augustan moment of both triumph and frustration. The most important and most lasting work of each member of the Pope–Swift "Augustan" group was published in the two and a half year period between late 1726 and 1729; John Gay's sensationally successful play, *The Beggar's Opera* was produced in 1728, and Pope's *Dunciad* was published in 1728, with the Variorum to follow in 1729; the four volumes of Pope–Swift *Miscellanies* also reprinted, starting in 1727, much of the earlier work the group wished to be remembered for, including John Arbuthnot's *History of John Bull*. Shortly thereafter Henry Fielding's theatrical career began with early Augustan-like plays such as *The Tragedy of Tragedies*. The run of so many similar artistic triumphs in so short a space of time was perhaps unprecedented in literary history.

10. On this, see especially Jürgen Habermas, *The Structural Transformation of the Public Sphere*: *An Inquiry into a Category of Bourgeois Society*, trans. Thomas Burger and Frederick Lawrence (Cambridge, MA: MIT Press, 1991).

11. John Dryden, an older contemporary of Swift and poet laureate in the late seventeenth century, was at the height of his writing career actually beaten up in an alley, presumably by political enemies. For Pope's fanciful account of a wished-for attack on a piratical publisher, see *A Full and True Account of a Horrid and Barbarous Revenge By Poison On the Body of Mr. Edmund Curll* (1716). Pope's enemies repeatedly fantasized attacks on his deformed and vulnerable body.

12. Jonathan Smedley, *Gulliveriana* (London, for J. Roberts, 1728), pp. 4–8.

13. The letter was not in the first edition; it was apparently written about the time it claims to have been, in 1727, and first appeared in the 1735 edition which most modern editions use as copy text. An exception is Albert Rivero's new *Norton Critical* edition (New York and London: Norton, 2001) which boldly returns to the first edition.

14. See Terry Castle, "Why the Houyhynhyms Don't Write: Swift, Satire, and the Fear of the Text," *Essays in Literature* 7 (1980), 31–44, reprinted in Christopher Fox's edition of *Gulliver's Travels* (Boston and New York, Bedford; London, Macmillan,1995), pp. 379–95.

15. See the chapter on title pages in Janine Barchas' *Graphic Design, Print Culture, and the Eighteenth-Century Novel* (Cambridge: Cambridge University Press, 2002), chapter 3.

16. Percy G. Adams, *Travellers and Travel Liars: 1660–1800* (Berkeley and Los Angeles: University of California Press, 1962).

17. There are of course major structural and aesthetic losses in such procedure, a matter I take up later (p. 229).

18. What I am here calling "the novel" is a distinctive (and then quite innovative) kind of prose fiction – featuring a concern with subjectivity and the consciousness of ordinary people, ordinary language, and everyday contemporary events – that emerged in Europe at various points in the sixteenth and seventeenth centuries and that began to dominate the popular market in England in the early eighteenth century, shortly before Swift wrote *Gulliver's Travels*; it then governed taste in continental Europe for the next two centuries. Sometimes the term "novel" is used more broadly (and I think confusingly) to describe all prose fiction dating back to the Greeks (or perhaps the mind of God) and even to include longer narratives in verse. But whatever we label this new, popular kind of new subject-centered narrative, it included a number of formal features – the exploration of individual consciousness, for example, usually through a first-person, more-or-less autobiographical narrator – that were extremely repugnant to Swift. Accounts differentiating *Gulliver's Travels* from the novelistic tradition are legion; see, for example, my "*Gulliver's Travels* and the Novel," in Frederik N. Smith (ed.) *The Genres of Gulliver's Travels* (Newark: University of Delaware Press, 1990), pp. 56–74.

19. Swift criticism traditionally has been reluctant to pursue the parallels seriously. Nigel Dennis, for example in *Jonathan Swift: A Short Character* (New York: Macmillan, and London: Collier-Macmillan, 1964) offers a wonderful detailed account of textual parallels and philosophical differences but thinks it unwarranted to think of *Gulliver* as a deliberate response to Defoe (pp. 123–33). More recent criticism has, usually implicitly but sometimes directly, assumed a more conscious rebuttal.

20. It is quite possible that the verbal pun on Master Bates – withheld three times in the first three paragraphs and then finally sprung – is a jab at Defoe and a reference to contemporary jokes about Defoe's refusal to raise the issue of sexuality during Robinson Crusoe's solitary twenty-eight-year exile on a desert island. See especially the textual analysis of Christopher Fox, "The Myth of Narcissus in Swift's *Travels*," *Eighteenth-Century Studies*, 20 (1986–87), 17–33. It may be, too, that Gulliver's compulsive descriptions of his excremental habits owe something to Crusoe's total omission of such issues in his otherwise insistently circumstantial account (although, of course, Swift elsewhere needed no prompt to dwell on similar details). It is also possible to think of Gulliver's final refusal of human company as a similar objection to *Robinson Crusoe*'s happy ending – with no "realistic" indication that all those years of non-human association might take a non-reversible psychological toll.

21. See J. Paul Hunter, *The Reluctant Pilgrim: Defoe's Emblematic Method and Quest for Form in Robinson Crusoe* (Baltimore: Johns Hopkins University Press, 1966) and, more generally, *Before Novels: The Cultural Contexts of Eighteenth-Century English Fiction* (New York and London: W. W. Norton and Co., 1990).

22. The primary butt of the joke here may again be Defoe and the "circumstantial realism" of *Robinson Crusoe*. Charles Gildon had made elaborate fun of Defoe's sea knowledge in *The Life and Strange Surprizing Adventures of Daniel Defoe, Hosier* (London, 1719), noting that when Crusoe stuffs his seaman's pockets with biscuits during his rescue of cargo from a shipwreck, Defoe seems not to know that seamen's britches have no pockets. *The London Journal* in 1724 reiterates the joke as a common topic of London conversation. See my *"Gulliver's Travels* and the Novel," pp. 67–68.

23. See Pat Rogers, "Gulliver's Glasses," in Clive T. Probyn (ed.) *The Art of Jonathan Swift* (London: Vision Press, 1978), pp. 179–88.

24. Norman O. Brown's powerful essay, "The Excremental Vision," (reprinted in Ernest Lee Tuveson [ed.], *Swift: A Collection of Critical Essays* [Englewood Cliffs, NJ: Prentice-Hall, 1964], pp. 31–54), offers a famous corrective to the rather speculative psychoanalytic tradition of mid-century.

25. Samuel Holt Monk, "The Pride of Lemuel Gulliver," reprinted in Robert A. Greenberg and William B. Piper (eds.) *The Writings of Jonathan Swift* (New York: Norton, 1973), pp. 631–47; originally published in *Sewanee Review* in 1955.

26. Swift is especially fond of literalizing metaphors and turning them into narrative events; he has, for example, courtiers walk tightropes, dance before the king, etc.; he has Gulliver urinate on the royal palace and land in excrement when he tries too ambitious a leap; and the government of Laputa oppresses its subjects by hovering over them or physically crushing their rebellion. The stable society at the end of *Gulliver* seems to me to have a similar status.

27. See Howard Erskine-Hill, *Jonathan Swift: Gulliver's Travels* (Cambridge: Cambridge University Press, 1993), especially pp. 19–21.

28. For a good example of the "hard" school, see Edward W. Rosenheim, Jr., *Swift and the Satirist's Art*, Chicago: University of Chicago Press, 1963; for the "soft," see Monk, "The Pride of Lemuel Gulliver" (note 24 above). C. J. Rawson, *Gulliver and the Gentle Reader* (London and Boston: Routledge & Kegan Paul, 1973), pp. 1–32, offers an especially sensible account of the issues.

29. On the basis of this formal assumption, see Alvin Kernan, *The Plot of Satire* (New Haven and London: Yale University Press, 1965). For a different sense of satire's norms, see Robert C. Elliot, *The Power of Satire* (Princeton: Princeton University Press, 1960), and Dustin Griffin, *Satire: A Critical Reintroduction* (Lexington: University Press of Kentucky, 1994).

30. See for example Ellen Pollak, *The Poetics of Sexual Myth: Gender and Ideology in the Verse of Swift and Pope* (Chicago and London: University of Chicago Press, 1985); Ruth Salvaggio, *Enlightened Absence: Neoclassical Configurations of the Feminine* (Urbana and Chicago: University of Illinois Press, 1988); Felicity Nussbaum, *Torrid Zones* (Baltimore: Johns Hopkins University Press, 1995); Carole Fabricant, *Swift's Landscape* (Baltimore: Johns Hopkins University Press, 1982; 2nd rev. edn. Notre Dame, IN and London: University of Notre Dame Press, 1995); Howard D. Weinbrot, *Britannia's Issue: The Rise of British Literature from Dryden to Ossian* (Cambridge: Cambridge University Press, 1993); and Laura Brown, *Ends of Empire: Women and Ideology in Early Eighteenth-Century English Literature* (Ithaca and London: Cornell University Press, 1993).

31. The date of Defoe's birth is unknown, but if he was born in 1660 (as most scholarship now assumes) he was fifty-nine when *Robinson Crusoe* came into the world. It too is a late-in-life, retrospective narrative or memoir (that is, Crusoe supposedly writes it after he returns to England in old age). In sending Gulliver on several futile voyages Swift may be glancing at Defoe's insistence on providing *Farther Adventures*.

32. See "Swift's Epitaph" in *The Collected Poems of W. B. Yeats* (London: Macmillan, 1971), p. 277. The original Latin epitaph can be found in Denis Johnston's *In Search of Swift* (Dublin: Hodges, Figgis and Company, 1959), opposite p. 188.

13

SEAMUS DEANE

Classic Swift

In all my Writings, I have had constant Regard to this great End, not to suit and apply them to particular Occasions and Circumstances of Time, of Place, or of Person; but to calculate them for universal Nature, and Mankind in general.

(*PW* 1: 174)

Madness

In the Preface to *A Tale of a Tub* (1704), Swift finds a classic way to define the kind of writing that is not classic and the kind of reading that should properly accompany it. Shadowing this passage is Cicero's declaration in *De Re Publica* (*The Republic*) of the unchanging and everlasting law of right reason. In place of law, Swift gives us modern wit which, we are told, does not travel well. Even "the smallest Transposal or Misapplication" can annihilate it (*PW* 1: 26). Some jests are only comprehensible at Covent-Garden, some at Hyde-Park Corner. All the universal truths about modernity are sourced in its provinciality. Similarly, the intellectual position of a modern is open to parody, when it is rendered as a physical position:

> Too intense a Contemplation is not the Business of Flesh and Blood; it must by the necessary Course of Things, in a little Time, let go its Hold, and fall into *Matter*. Lovers, for the sake of Celestial Converse, are but another sort of *Platonicks*, who pretend to see Stars and Heaven in Ladies Eyes, and to look or think no lower; but the same *Pit* is provided for both; and they seem a perfect Moral to the Story of that Philosopher, who, while his Thoughts and his Eyes were fixed upon the *Constellations*, found himself seduced by his *lower Parts* into a Ditch. (*PW* 1: 189–90)

Here the transposition of the sexually candid phrase "seduced by his lower parts" from the lovers to the philosopher, and from the idea of intercourse to the idea of falling into a ditch and from that to the reference to the human fall into the pit of Hell makes the declaration of the writer's faith in matter more emphatic, and yet also ridicules it. Swift is indeed saying that the most extreme religious enthusiasts have a gross conception of the spiritual which is explicable in psychological and physiological terms; they are ultimately materialists. But the reader's attention is taken not only by the object of the attack but also by the position of the person or persona who conducts the assault. He may himself be an embodiment of the very thing he assaults; thus his tone of svelte disengagement is deceitful. To establish the voice of the norm and then to make it the voice of deviancy, while attributing to it every form of awareness except self-awareness, has at the very least a confusing effect. Swift produces a similar confusion at the level of form when he makes digressions central to his undertaking, thus making a nonsense of the standard opposition between digression and main text upon which his humor depends.

Swift's suppleness of phrasing and of figuration has the dual effect of intensifying and of vaporizing the detail of his more vertiginously satiric passages. The world he creates is packed tight and it is also empty. He dislocates the reader by revealing that the momentum of the logic of an argument or of a figure, or of both, can lead or can seem to lead the author into unexpected trouble. For the whole notion of authority and control is questioned when the language seems to take on a life of its own, independent of any authorial restraint. And yet to represent that very condition is itself an ingenious exercise in authorial mastery.

One of Swift's great gifts is to find a way of telling stories in the voice and accent of monomaniacs, obsessives, and ideologues who are entirely unaware of their fixated condition. Sometimes he plays the role of mimic; sometimes, more subtly and dismayingly, that of ventriloquist. In general, the mimicry creates ironic effects, the ventriloquial efforts, sustained for longer and with stonier dedication (*Gulliver's Travels, A Modest Proposal*), create parody. Fanaticism has great allure for Swift. His scorn for it is the more effective because of his relish for it; he has an eye for the behavior of the crazed who believe themselves to be rational and who can persuade others of this too. The fanatic begins by surrendering his intelligence and is thereafter no longer exercised by the labor of using it. His energy is instead devoted to consuming it, energy converting mass, the adrenalin of madness masking its hyperactivity as the operation of reason. Sometimes we listen to juvenile opinions repeated endlessly with stentorian force, the loudness of voice indicating both the strength of the convictions and their echoing vacuity. At other times, the madness is quieter in tone. Rather than the crazed blusterings of a religious enthusiast, we have the assured expositions of an expert, delivered with a smiling sibilance.

And, it is exactly at one Year old, that I propose to provide for them in such a Manner, as, instead of being a Charge upon their *Parents*, or the *Parish*, or *wanting Food and Raiment* for the rest of their Lives; they shall, on the contrary, contribute to the Feeding, and partly to the Cloathing, of many Thousands.

(*PW* xii: 110)

The frenzy of religious enthusiasm that had, in Swift's view, caused so much political and social strife in the seventeenth century was still a force to be reckoned with; his sojourn at Kilroot outside Belfast among the northern Presbyterians made that painfully clear to him. But in the new era of the Moderns, such frenzy had migrated into more secular forms; the good of mankind had taken over from redemption as the ostensible motive for virtuous action. Swift repeatedly assumes the persona of the "most devoted Servant of all *Modern* Forms" (*PW* i: 27) seeking to accomplish "the general Good of Mankind" (*PW* i: 77). Such a "Modern" could be a politician, a hack writer, a religious bigot, an economist, a believer in the radical goodness or benevolence of humankind; whatever the role or profession, the Modern, by the abuse of "feeling" or "reason" – now beginning to separate into opposites – had become dangerously insane. Against the insanity of ideologues and sentimentalists, Swift responded in the classically satiric manner – by caricaturing them in stories that were parables or allegories or sermons although these were often written in the well-named "realistic" mode of the Moderns – that of the "history" or novel.

The constitutional historian Hallam, writing in 1827, argued that Swift's writings in *The Examiner* and elsewhere are the first in which a government, rather than seeking a solution in the law of libel, decided to "retaliate with unsparing invective and calumny" against its vociferous enemies in the press.[1] Swift was indeed a remarkably effective political journalist. Yet Hallam, like many others, locates Swift in his historical circumstances and still implies that there is in his writings something fierce and repellent the explanation for which must be sought beyond history. This alternative source is Swift's psyche, to which many commentators have claimed special access.

Thus, enseamed within the long history of commentary on Swift the writer is the commentary on Swift's psychology and pathology. Madness, illness, sexual disturbance, revulsion at the human body and its functions, and a whole fleet of other guesses or claims are cited to explain what is remarkable about his work. This, we have been told for two and a half centuries, is what ultimately gives to Swift's work that intensity which distinguishes it from that of the other great satirists with whom he is often compared or

associated – Juvenal, Rabelais, Pope, Dryden, Voltaire. The diseased subjectivity of the author is paraded as the cause of or simply described as
misanthropy. Swift's eccentricity then becomes the basis for a dark view of
human nature that has to be disavowed (on the grounds that it is a slur
on humankind) or admitted (on the grounds that it is a penetrating truth
discoverable only by the disturbed). The very brilliance of Swift's rhetoric
is taken to be an index of a deep-seated disturbance that finds the corruptions and vices (radical or contingent) of his contemporaries so offensive.
So his "madness" restricts the range but deepens the reach of his access to
certain aspects of human experience denied to the unafflicted. It is ironic
indeed that Swift, who so often used madness as an emblem of the Modern's self-involvement, should himself be subject to this kind of interpretation. It is as though he had become for his readers one of his own adopted
personae.

It is Swift's impersonation of the forms of modernity's assault on traditional moralities that makes him so anomalously and yet decisively a modern
writer. The loss of secure authority is disturbing because it is so often exposed by the serene confidence of the first-person narrator who embodies the
modern spirit by showing that its investment in personal, authentic experience is foolhardy and yet securely insecure. Swift does indeed record some
of the ways in which a traditional moral discourse mutates into a modern
commercial discourse and how, in the process, the claims to Christian or
moral behavior are the more aggressive as the grounds for such behavior
are abandoned. Yet his intensities are still disproportionate to such expla-
nations. The question recurrently is, in what does this difference, or this
radically disturbing element, consist?

In this form, the question is never satisfactorily answered. But it has been
countered by the contradictory claim that Swift displays the fundamental
sanity that is always to be found in classic writers.[2] Yet the accounts of his
sanity inevitably segue into assertions of the intensity with which he defended
traditional commonplace beliefs; the trouble is that the descriptions of the
intensity return the commentator to the issue of Swift's uniqueness and the
problem of distinguishing this from extremism or imbalance. Revulsion and
disgust at physical and sexual functions are the most alarming elements in this
intensity, even though these are traditional features in satiric writing. F. R.
Leavis finds Swift shares "a peculiar emotional intensity" with "the shallow-
est complacencies of Augustan common sense."[3] In an essay more noticed
than distinguished, George Orwell sees Swift as a commonplace and reactionary thinker, obsessed with dirt and disease, and yet redeemed by a Leavis-
like "terrible intensity of vision"; this vagueness aids Orwell towards his
well-known declaration "that, if the force of belief is behind it, a world-view

which only passes the test of sanity is sufficient to produce a great work of art."[4] Edward Said takes issue with Orwell and, by implication, with Leavis, of whose essay Orwell's is a rewriting, arguing that Swift is, above all things, a self-conscious intellectual, a writer in a world of power.[5] Even with Said, there seems to be a relation, more sensed than articulated, between Swift's intensity and his sanity. The sanity is always under threat from the intensity; an ordinary and an extraordinary universe are combined within one vision that can thus appear either commonplace or uniquely uncompromising. As with the various arguments about Swift's "style," there is little agreement on what constitutes it. He writes in various registers, but no one of them seems to predominate sufficiently to be called his "style," even though again a conflict between the homely and the commonplace on the one hand and something remarkably and intensely fierce is widely remarked.[6]

Swift can thus combine contraries of the most compelling kind. John Wesley cites from Book IV of *Gulliver's Travels* in his "Doctrine of Original Sin" (1757) to demonstrate the ineluctable depravity of human nature while in *The Enquirer* (1797), the anarchist/utilitarian William Godwin sees the Houyhnhnms as emblems of human perfectibility. An Anglican priest and traditional Christian who could not tolerate any threat to the supremacy of the national church, in England or in Ireland,[7] he was, in Sir James Mackintosh's words, "an ecclesiastical Tory, even while he was a political Whig."[8] The need to defend his church in the circumstances of England and Ireland in the long crisis that stretched from the 1640s to the 1730s may explain the venomous ingenuity that he deployed to secure a position that varied from the threatened to the indefensible.[9] His Anglicanism or his "Toryism," even if wholly traditional, make him seem like an ideological curiosity, especially when combined with a coarseness of invective that threatens all established values.

Swift's coarseness and "misanthropy" were often linked to one another and to his final state of madness. Sir Walter Scott claimed the grossness of Swift's writing could be explained by the author's mental "peculiarities" and the conditions of the time; it was the combination that was "nearly allied to the misanthropy" which preceded his final madness. Scott's attempts to understand Swift scarcely soften his ultimate condemnation of Book IV of *Gulliver's Travels*, "this libel on human nature,"[10] but they certainly form a telling contrast with the disturbed rant of Thackeray in his *English Humorists*, an essay that steeply intensified the tone of outrage that had been a recurrent feature of reaction to Swift and specifically to Book IV, at least since the comments of Lord Orrery and Patrick Delany in 1752 and 1754 respectively.

Politeness and civic virtue

One other way of discounting Swift as an exceptionally misanthropic author is to see him as a writer in the "selfish" or cynical tradition of those authors from La Rochefoucauld to Hobbes, from Mandeville to Helvétius, who have been routinely accused of having a narrow and gloomy view of human nature, because they give primacy to the passion of self-love. Mandeville was especially notorious during Swift's lifetime for his great work, *The Fable of the Bees: or, Private Vices, Publick Benefits* (1714 and 1729). It is not that Swift is in any sense like Mandeville, although they are sometimes paired together. Mandeville is renowned for his attack, not on virtue as such, but on the ways in which it had been traditionally understood, especially if it depended upon a denial of self-love or selfishness as a motor principle in human behavior or on the overly sanguine and demonstrably foolish view of the benevolists like Shaftesbury who "seems to require and expect Goodness in his Species, as we do a sweet Taste in Grapes and China Oranges, of which, if any of them are sour, we boldly pronounce that they are not come to that Perfection their Nature is capable of."[11]

Swift is not at all given to any revision or reconsideration of the traditional Christian concepts of virtue, none of which would have denied the power of self-love, although Shaftesbury's malleability on the topic was anathema to him. The best-known Anglican synthesis of traditional and modern ethical systems is Bishop Joseph Butler's *Fifteen Sermons*, published in the same year as *Gulliver's Travels* (1726). It is milder in tone and more accommodating than Swift, but not fundamentally different in its doctrinal basis. However, Swift is extraordinary to the degree that he is both repelled and fascinated by humankind's resourcefulness in disguising viciousness and corruption as virtue. Pride is a fundamental sin, hypocrisy the age-old disguise that it wears. Mandeville shocked his readers because he claimed that what had been taken to be the antithesis of virtue was that in which virtue consisted. His argument was the more upsetting because it further claimed that now, in a polite age, some of the old barbaric distinctions – like that between sin and virtue – could be abandoned and replaced by something more rational and enlightened, more in conformity with human nature and the human capacity to master and order a secular world – especially the world of material goods and luxury.[12] When the hunger for luxury and consumption has become a virtue, then a key Swiftian inversion has truly been realized.

Swift may not have mastered the economic discourse that was developing to describe the emergent systems of the colonial and Atlantic worlds of which Ireland formed a part.[13] But he understood enough to recognize that a form of rational analysis based on quantification was beginning to dominate in social and moral thinking; and its linkage with the new forms of civility and politeness that were so assiduously promoted in contemporary writing. Mandeville had given terms like "luxury" and "consumption" a bad name by showing their intimate connection with dirt and selfishness and the welfare of society in general.[14] These associations were redescribed by Hutcheson in a more muted, less scandalous manner; yet he retained the declaration that goodness (interpreted as the happiness or welfare of the many) was something that could be quantified and that the impulse to produce it was something that could be, indeed could not but be, strongly felt; and that to act in accord with such a feeling was to be in accord with our God-given nature. Thus an affective morality that could be quantified in its effects was now available for the polite world of commerce, where markets expanded to meet the demands of appetite and appetite had lost many of its traditional and pejorative connotations. Appetite provided the dynamic for an economy of gratification for the self and for others. This was the world of the modern economist and of the modern moralist; in short, of utilitarianism. In Swift's view it was no more than a glossy version of the self-involved fanaticisms of religious sectaries who had, just as much as the Moderns, believed in a version of the "inner light" of personal conviction and its harmony with God's wish. Like the Moderns, these old-generation bigots believed that the authority of an opinion lay in the strength with which it was held. To Swift, this was a dangerous and ludicrous conviction; it sought and found authority within itself and demanded universal consent to this discovery. On the other hand, the emphasis upon consequence and the weakened role of intention or motive allowed for so much computational casuistry that moral judgment seemed to depend upon the ingenuity of the apologist rather than on any antecedent and traditional body of truth.

Yet it is also true that Swift used the conversational mode of address so favored by those who wished to establish a standard of politeness in social and literary forms that would allow England to compete with France and with an idea of ancient Rome. The dissonance between civility and savagery in Swift is a studied satiric effect, but it also implies a repudiation of the belief in the "progress" of politeness and the triumph of prudence and moderation over factional enthusiasm celebrated by Hume in particular.[15] Hume's version of the development of English literary style from the mid-seventeenth to the early eighteenth century is a case in point; it was only in Swift's era that English letters emulated the French, the "judicious imitators" of the Ancients.[16] With Swift, however, the civil mode is often sustained in circumstances so grotesque that its imperturbability becomes a symptom of disturbance. The heroic and the tragic dimensions of human existence do not fit within this reduced and mundane world; yet their inversion into various extreme forms of debauchery is perfectly in accord with its appalling and dead carnality. Swift dissects the "Carcass of *Humane Nature*" (*PW* 1: 77) to divert rather than instruct. The analytic and instructive exposure becomes pornographic and shocking. It is a disturbingly modern mode of defending the Ancients. In satirizing the modern world of innovation and inversion Swift also demonstrates its displacement of the traditional world it sometimes imitates and at other times derides.

The aspiration to classic status in literature (and in other arts) was central to the long disputes between Ancients and Moderns in France and England in the seventeenth and eighteenth centuries. It seemed obvious to the "Ancients" in this dispute that if any modern work were to prove as durable as the Greek and Latin classics, it must in some sense be an imitation of those features in the originals that had given them such lasting appeal. This was a much-contested feature of the theory of imitation. Against that, it was argued that the modern was specific to itself, and that imitation of the classics was rarely creative and almost always slavish or routine. Swift entered into this dispute with the famous defense of his mentor Sir William Temple against the redoubtable and much-superior scholar Richard Bentley in *The Battle of the Books* (1704). But he especially emphasized how absurd and dangerous it was to replace the inherited traditions of the classics with work of recent vintage. Thus he dramatizes in his satires the distinction between the local and the universal, almost always tying the local not only to a particular time and place but also to the psychic freakishness of a disturbed or deranged subjectivity or to the sociological novelty of the professional writer dependent upon patronage and/or the market to an unprecedented degree. A swarm of Grub Street hacks could scarcely be expected to produce a literature that would rival the serenity and wisdom of the ancient classics. They were doomed to a momentary notoriety rather than elected to a long-lasting fame unless, that is, their notoriety were to be so commemorated in the satire they provoked, that it would there be permanently preserved as an emblem of foolishness and pride. These hack writers, Swift (and Pope) would argue, were hopelessly marooned in the present moment precisely because they affected to ignore or dispense with the past.

Ireland

Swift witnessed two revolutions. One was the Glorious Revolution of 1688–89 which initiated a profound reordering of the internal world of the British isles. This was an intricate process. Among its most notable events were the end of the Jacobite war in Ireland and the establishment of Protestant power after 1691; the Penal Laws passed from 1695 against the Irish

Catholics to destroy them as a political, economic, and cultural force; the Union of England and Scotland to form Great Britain in 1707; the abortive attempts by Irish Protestants to assert a meaningful independence, especially in economic matters, against Great Britain; the defeats of the Jacobite cause in 1715 and in 1745, the year of Swift's death; the destruction of Scottish Gaelic culture. The other revolution was European. It was completed by the Treaty of Utrecht which brought an end to the War of the Spanish Succession and Louis XIV's ambitions for a universal monarchy that would dominate the continent. It created the system of nation-states and inaugurated the *Ancien Régime*, a system that was to endure for no more than seventy-five years and was to be replaced, after another titanic struggle between Britain and France, in 1815.

Swift's work certainly belongs in this modern European world, partly because of its oblique relationship to the European Enlightenment, partly because its mixed English and Irish origins enabled him to question the new alliances between power and civility that were so fundamental to Britain's and Europe's self-images. A common feature of the commentary on Ireland and on Irish writing, then and since, has been its preoccupation with the issues of Irish peripherality and its troubled relationship to a metropolitan center, usually London, occasionally Paris.

In 1922, T. S. Eliot, continuing the Arnoldian search for the universal element in literature that would supervene over provinciality, claimed that Joyce's *Ulysses* was "the first Irish work since that of Swift to possess absolute *European significance*."[17] The remark indicates Swift's importance, as well as Eliot's ignorance of other Irish authors, including many of Swift's contemporaries. Swift was one of a gifted generation of writers whose political conception of Ireland was integral to their work or to the commentary it provoked or to both. Outrage at Ireland's ill-treatment at English hands, hatred of its provinciality and squalor, and the encouragement within it of a species of economic and political autonomy are evident in the more than sixty Irish pamphlets he wrote, particularly in the decades of the 1720s and 1730s. Of these, *The Drapier's Letters* and *A Modest Proposal* are the most widely advertised as works that have a universal moral and political appeal.

Nevertheless, it is somewhat remarkable that Swift's reputation in this regard should exceed that of contemporaries like John Toland or Francis Hutcheson, both of whom were much less confined and orthodox than he in their opinions. Toland's *Christianity Not Mysterious* (1696) had several targets, among them the exercise of political control through the creation by a priestly elite of mystery about religious matters.[18] The confessional basis of the British state, most especially as it applied to Ireland, could be said to be challenged by Toland's argument; no sect, no church had a claim as such to total political control. But it is clear that Toland, although born an Irish-speaking Catholic, came to detest "Popery, Prelacy, and arbitrary power,"[19] and that his attack on "priestcraft" was more truly directed at Roman Catholicism than at Anglicanism. Nevertheless, the book was a rational dissenter's credo; no churchman in particular could accept the deistic implications of its arguments. Toland's politics were, however, solidly Protestant and chauvinist. He had, as he said in a pamphlet of 1701, two chief aims – "the stopping of the progress of the *French* Greatness" and keeping "*England* the head of the Protestant Interest all over the World,"[20] even if this meant finding a way to accept the monarchy of William III by regarding it as a "commonwealth." Yet his criticisms of Anglican sectarianism and of monarchy were sufficient to make him appear radical in comparison with Swift and he signally lacked diplomacy and seemed almost to fear tact. "There was not in his whole composition, one single grain of that useful quality which *Swift* calls *modern discretion.*"[21]

Hutcheson, who appears much less threatening politically than Toland, perhaps struck more deeply at the moral basis of Swift's and of Anglican political thought when he argued, in his *Inquiry* (1725), against the spirit of sectarianism and its link with exclusivity and despotism; the consequences were the destruction of "national love," social harmony, and civil society itself.[22] Although the question of toleration for Catholics is thereby raised, it forms no central part of Hutcheson's project, since the search for the "basis of moral knowledge independent of church authority and available to the ordinary reasonable and conscientious person"[23] was a specifically Protestant search. In Ireland especially, the universalist claims for such a basis were always threatened by the charge of sectarianism and would in the end succumb to it. But before that could happen, a particular conception of civil society as an instrument of moral improvement was formulated not in Ireland, but in Scotland, where Hutcheson became a famous teacher and earned the title of the father of Scottish philosophy. Thus, on the rare occasions when they were not wholly absorbed into accounts of English political and moral philosophy, Toland was assigned to Europe and Hutcheson to Scotland. Swift, while a classic of English writing, was nevertheless also and always associated with Ireland.

Or, more exactly, with two Irelands. One is the Ireland of the Protestant patriots, the other is the country of Irish nationalism, predominantly Catholic. The latter was to have its first signal success with the Catholic Emancipation Act of 1829, the act which finally brought an end to the confessional Protestant British state that emerged in 1688; the former was to end in 1800–01 with the Act of Union that created the United Kingdom of Great Britain and Ireland, and began with the publication of William Molyneux's

The Case of Ireland ... Stated (1698).[24] It is with this latter group that Swift has been most frequently and persuasively associated. Certainly his *Drapier's Letters* and Molyneux's pamphlet have been widely regarded as the source books for the eighteenth century's Protestant nationalism, that culminated in 1782 when Henry Grattan reportedly welcomed legislative independence with the words, "Spirit of Swift! Spirit of Molyneux! Your genius has prevailed. Ireland is now a nation." By the end of the century, despite the 1798 Rebellion and the Union that extinguished the experiment in independence, Molyneux and Swift had been elevated from spokesmen for an exclusively Protestant patriotism to a nobler, more inclusive role: Irish minds had been opened by this pair and had been taught to "nurture the seeds of freedom, and to vindicate those rights, which heaven has bestowed upon the human race."[25]

This was the benign "national" view of Swift as the first author who had been driven beyond the limits of his initial view of Ireland and the Irish to embrace a more generous, if paternalistic, vision of the moral and economic duties and imperatives involved in the Protestant interest in Ireland. It was not uncontested. In his famous *Memoirs of Captain Rock* (1824), Thomas Moore presents an alternative view of an intolerant Swift who "for the misery and degradation of his Roman Catholic countrymen ... seems to have cared little more than his own Gulliver would for the suffering of so many disfranchised Yahoos."[26]

The spirit of party certainly heightened Swift's view of the Irish–English relationship, especially after his career in English politics came to an end with the accession of Queen Anne. In the next five years, that relationship degenerated into a bitter and humiliating dispute. Molyneux had argued that Ireland was a separate kingdom, not a colony. Yet Swift, like many others, was sorely struck by the melancholy consequences for Ireland of the English connection – the conditions of poverty and famine, the punitive commercial relationship, the formation of the patriot "persona" as a surrogate identity for a minority group that was parasitically dependent on the polity it attempted to resist.[27]

This was intensified by Swift's awareness of the very different relationship established in 1707 by the union between England and Scotland. A community of dissenters, with a marked commercial tendency, had been given preferential treatment over a community of Anglicans with a record of political loyalty and much more need of every form of political, economic, religious, and cultural support. The Wood's halfpence affair led from small beginnings to a significant victory that had wide implications, some of them exaggerated in retrospect, although the exaggerations themselves became important.

The political conflict generated by the Irish–English relationship has deep connections with Swift's obsessive rhetorical figurings of the autonomous body and the body that has neither identity nor control and that can, as a consequence, issue only in excrement, vapors, or be represented merely as an object of consumption or derision.[28] From Swift's early allegorization of political and sexual union in *The Story of the Injured Lady* (1707), his determination to expose the actuality of a maimed condition and the cosmetic pretense of a "normal" one had been intermittently expressed. This has often been said to provide the evidence for his misanthropy and, more specifically, his misogyny.[29]

But in the 1720s, its expression became both more intense and more consistent. In fact, as Emer Nolan argues, by 1729, the year of *A Modest Proposal*, the "debate between civic virtue and *homo economicus*" has been transmogrified:

> The Drapier represented an ambivalent but useful blend of the language of economics and the language of civic virtue, but now the Proposer represents their divergence . . . there is no solution: this is a satire of both colonialism and of the resistance to colonialism, in the form in which it could then be articulated by protestant Ireland.[30]

The political impasse, finally exposed in and by the English–Irish colonial relationship, is figured finally as a murderous action in which the atrocity of nurturing children to be eaten is redescribed in the modern way as the production of a crop or commodity that satisfies a theory of economic behavior. Swift's writing seems classically colonial to many precisely because of this internal disturbance; it is "a rhetoric characterized by constant crisis, just as colonial rule itself continually creates its own crisis of authority."[31]

Some earlier modern readings see Swift's work in general, and *Gulliver's Travels* in particular, as characteristic examples of the Enlightenment's assault on the assumptions of traditional authority. The unreliability or instability of the narrator is thus taken to be an index of the writer's awareness of a new form of sensory and intellectual relativism. That itself had a peculiarly Irish origin in the new epistemological questions raised by William Molyneux's work on optics, *Dioptrica nova* (1692) and Bishop Berkeley's *Essay towards a New Theory of Vision* (1709).[32]

This at least has the merit of establishing a philosophical rather than a political connection between Swift and his compatriots that might account for or supplement the anxiety about authority and about the concession of trust to the government either of the senses or of the British state. But it is not often that Swift has been seen as a witting or unwitting contributor to the Enlightenment and its subversion of authority. It is the collapse of traditional authority, not the absurdity of its claims, that enraged him. He has left many after-images – the defender of Liberty, the creator of Irish national consciousness, the writer torn by his "*saeva indignatio*" at the spectacle of injustice and corruption, the party hack, the greatest satirist of early modernity. These versions of him influenced the form of his commemoration by two of his country's greatest writers, Joyce and Yeats. In *Ulysses* (1922), he is the misanthropic dean: "A hater of his kind ran from them to the wood of madness, his mane foaming in the moon, his eyeballs stars. Houyhnhnm, horsenostrilled."[33]

In Yeats' play, *Word Upon the Window-pane* (1934), and in the Preface to it, which is a sustained, if shrill, meditation on Swift and on his notion, expressed as early as 1701 in *A Discourse of the Contests and Dissentions Between the Nobles and the Commons in Athens and Rome* of "the universal bent and current of a people," Swift becomes a tragic figure whose dread of "the historic process became... a dread of parentage." He was of the traditional world that Rousseau and the French Revolution destroyed, profoundly opposed to democracy and yet that "created the political nationality of Ireland."[34]

Irish democracy's celebration of Swift has had many unintended ironies – one of which is that any democracy should celebrate one who so much dreaded its arrival. Eliot's strange pairing of Swift and Joyce helped to emphasize another. In 1978, Swift appeared on the Irish Republic's currency, on the ten-punt note; in 1994 he was replaced by Joyce. Now, perhaps sometime in the future of the Euro-currency, the Drapier might yet make another appearance on coin or paper. Even the shade of William Wood might smile at that Euro-Hibernian prospect.

NOTES

1. Henry Hallam, *The Constitutional History of England from the Accession of Henry VII to the Death of George II*, 4 vols. (Paris: Baudry, 1827), vol. III, pp. 446–67.
2. See Ricardo Quintana, *The Mind and Art of Jonathan Swift* (London and New York: Oxford University Press, 1936), p. 37.
3. F. R. Leavis, "The Irony of Swift," in *Determinations* (London: Chatto and Windus, 1934), pp. 72–87.
4. George Orwell, "Politics *vs.* Literature: An Examination of *Gulliver's Travels*" (1950), in Sonia Orwell and Ian Angus (eds.) *The Collected Essays, Journalism and Letters* (London: Secker and Warburg, 1968), vol. IV, pp. 205–23, especially 222–23.
5. Edward Said, "Swift as Intellectual," in *The World, the Text, and the Critic* (Cambridge, MA: Harvard University Press, 1983), pp. 72–89, especially 87; see also the preceding essay, "Swift's Tory Anarchy," pp. 54–71.

6. See William Wotton and Frances Jeffrey, quoted in Kathleen Williams (ed.) *Swift: The Critical Heritage* (London: Routledge & Kegan Paul, 1970), pp. 316, 324, 45. Also see Thomas De Quincey, *Works*, 15 vols. (Edinburgh: Black, 1862–63), vol. VII, pp. 47–50.

7. *E* I: 220; Louis A. Landa, *Swift and the Church of Ireland* (Oxford: Clarendon Press, 1954); Phillip Harth, *Swift and Anglican Rationalism: The Religious Background of A Tale of a Tub* (Chicago and London: Chicago University Press, 1961); Michael DePorte, "Swift, God, and Power," in Christopher Fox and Brenda Tooley (eds.) *Walking Naboth's Vineyard: New Studies of Swift*, (Notre Dame, IN: University of Notre Dame Press, 1995), pp. 73–97; Robert Eccleshall, "Anglican Political Thought in the Century after the Revolution of 1688," in D. George Boyce, Robert Eccleshall, and Vincent Geoghegan (eds.) *Political Thought in Ireland Since the Seventeenth Century* (London and New York: Routledge, 1993), pp. 36–72.

8. *Memoirs of the Life of the Right Honourable Sir James Mackintosh*, 2 vols. (London: Moxon, 1835), vol. I, p. 178.

9. See Warren Montag, *The Unthinkable Swift: The Spontaneous Philosophy of a Church of England Man* (London and New York: Verso, 1994).

10. Williams (ed.), *Swift: The Critical Heritage*, pp. 296, 313.

11. Bernard Mandeville, *The Fable of the Bees: or, Private Vices, Publick Benefits*, ed. F. B. Kaye, 2 vols. (Oxford: Oxford University Press, 1924), vol. I, p. 323. Mandeville's work was published in two Parts, I in 1714 and II in 1729.

12. See Albert O. Hirschmann, *The Passions and the Interests; Political Arguments for Capitalism before its Triumph* (Princeton: Princeton University Press, 1977), p. 19.

13. See Nicholas Canny, "Identity Formation in Ireland: The Emergence of the Anglo-Irish," in Nicholas Canny and Anthony Pagden (eds.) *Colonial Identity in the Atlantic World* (Princeton: Princeton University Press, 1987), pp. 159–212; Brendan Bradshaw and John Morrill (eds.) *The British Problem, c. 1534–1707: State Formation in the Atlantic Archipelago* (New York: St. Martin's Press, 1996).

14. M. M. Goldsmith, "Liberty, Luxury and the Pursuit of Happiness," in Anthony Pagden (ed.) *The Languages of Political Theory in Early-Modern Europe* (Cambridge: Cambridge University Press, 1987), pp. 225–51.

15. Nicholas Phillipson, "Politeness and Politics in the Reigns of Anne and the Early Hanoverians," in J. G. A. Pocock, *et al.* (eds.) *The Varieties of British Political Thought 1500–1800* (Cambridge: Cambridge University Press, 1993), pp. 211–45.

16. David Hume, *The History of England from the Invasion of Julius Caesar to The Revolution in 1688*, 6 vols. (London: T. Cadell, 1778), vol. VI, pp. 543–45.

17. T. S. Eliot, "The Three Provincialities," *Tyro* 2 (1922), 11.

18. Philip McGuinness, Alan Harrison and Richard Kearney (eds.) *John Toland's Christianity not Mysterious* (Dublin: The Lilliput Press, 1997).

19. See the account of his life that prefaces John Toland's *A Critical History of the Celtic Religion and Learning* (1722; rpt. London: Lackington, 1810), p. 40.

20. *The Art of Governing by Partys* (London: Lintott, 1701), p. 145.

21. Toland, *A Critical History*, p. 41.

22. Francis Hutcheson, *An Inquiry into the Original of our Ideas of Beauty and Truth* (London: 1725) Treatise II, Section IV, pp. 9–22.

23. John Rawls, *Lectures on the History of Moral Philosophy* (Cambridge, MA: Harvard University Press, 2000), p. 8.

24. William Molyneux, *The case of Ireland's being bound by acts of parliament in England, stated*, ed. J. G. Simms, afterword by Denis Donoghue (Dublin: The Cadenus Press, 1977).

25. Francis Plowden, *An Historical Review of the State of Ireland from the Invasion of that Country under Henry II to its Union with Great Britain on the 1st of January, 1801*, 3 vols. (London: Egerton, 1803), vol. 1, p. 390; see also Thomas Campbell, *An Historical Sketch of the Constitution and Government of Ireland* (Dublin: Luke White, 1789), p. 362. For Grattan, see *The Speeches of Henry Grattan* 2 vols. (London: Lackington, 1822), vol. 1, p. 123.

26. *Memoirs of Captain Rock, the celebrated Irish Chieftain, with some account of his ancestors* (London: Longmans, 1824), pp. 123–24. For a general account of Swift's reception among Irish Protestants and Catholics, see Robert Mahony, "Swift and Catholic Ireland" in Fox and Tooley (eds.) *Walking Naboth's Vineyard*, pp. 178–99.

27. See Carole Fabricant, *Swift's Landscape* (1982; 2nd rev. edn. Notre Dame, IN: University of Notre Dame Press, 1995); and her "Jonathan Swift as Irish Historian," in Fox and Tooley (eds.) *Walking Naboth's Vineyard*, pp. 40–72; Joseph McMinn, "A Weary Patriot: Swift and the Formation of an Anglo-Irish Identity," *Eighteenth-Century Ireland: Iris an dá chultúr* 2 (1987), 103–13; Robert Mahony, *Jonathan Swift: The Irish Identity* (New Haven and London: Yale University Press, 1995); Thomas McLoughlin, *Contesting Ireland: Irish Voices against England in the Eighteenth Century* (Dublin: Four Courts Press, 1999), pp. 41–87; S. J. Connolly (ed.) *Political Ideas in Eighteenth-Century Ireland* (Dublin: Four Courts Press, 2000).

28. See Emer Nolan, "Swift: The Patriot Game," *British Journal for Eighteenth-Century Studies* 21 (1998), 39–53; and Robert Mahony, "Protestant Dependance and Consumption in Swift's Irish Writings," in S. J. Connolly (ed.) *Political Ideas In Eighteenth-Century Ireland*, pp. 83–104.

29. See Ellen Pollak, *The Poetics of Sexual Myth: Gender and Ideology in the Verse of Swift and Pope* (Chicago and London: University of Chicago Press, 1985), pp. 13–21, 163–72.

30. Nolan, "Swift: The Patriot Game," pp. 45, 49.

31. David Spurr, *The Rhetoric of Empire: Colonial Discourse in Journalism, Travel Writing, and Imperial Administration* (Durham, NC and London: Duke University Press, 1993), p. 11.

32. Ernst Cassirer, *The Philosophy of the Enlightenment*, trans. F. C. A. Koelln and J. C. Pettegrove (1932; Boston: Beacon Press, 1951), pp. 108–17; David Berman, "The Irish Counter-Enlightenment," in Richard Kearney (ed.) *The Irish Mind* (Dublin: Wolfhound Press, 1985), pp. 119–40.

33. James Joyce, *Ulysses*, ed. Hans Walter Gabler, *et al.* (London: Bodley Head and Penguin, 1986), 33, pp. 109–11.

34. *Explorations* (New York, Macmillan, 1962), pp. 343–369. Among other Irish literary treatments of Swift are Shane Leslie, *The Skull of Swift* (1928), Paul Vincent Carroll's BBC television program, *Farewell to Greatness* (1956), and Denis Johnston's play, *The Dreaming Dust* (1940) and biography *In Search of Swift* (1959) and Tom McIntyre's play *The Bearded Lady* (1984).

BIBLIOGRAPHY

The number of books and articles about Swift is extensive. The works listed below only begin to suggest the sheer range of writing on Swift. This list can be updated and supplemented by consulting the works listed in the bibliographical section below and by browsing such online search engines as *MLAIB, The MLA International Bibliography of Books and Articles on the Modern Languages and Literatures* and *ABELL*, the *Annual Bibliography of English Language and Literature*. Printed journals such as *The Scriblerian* and *Swift Studies* also contain helpful listings of recent work.

Modern editions

Correspondence. Ed. Harold Williams. Oxford: Clarendon Press, 1963–65. 5 vols. Standard edition, but see David Woolley below.

Correspondence. Ed. David Woolley. Frankfurt-am-Main: Peter Lang, 1999–. In progress, with four volumes projected, two published at this time.

Poems. Ed. Harold Williams. 2nd edn. Oxford: Clarendon Press, 1958. 3 vols.

Complete Poems. Ed. Pat Rogers. Harmondsworth: Penguin and New Haven: Yale University Press, 1983. Excellent annotations.

Prose Works. Ed. Herbert Davis *et al.* Oxford: Blackwell, 1939–74, 14 vols. Standard edition. Volume XIV contains an index.

Swift's Irish Pamphlets: An Introductory Selection. Ed. Joseph McMinn. Gerrards Cross: Colin Smythe, 1991.

Jonathan Swift. Ed. Angus Ross and David Woolley. Oxford and New York: Oxford University Press, 1984. Helpful annotations.

Individual works

A Discourse of the Contests and Dissentions Between the Nobles and the Commons in Athens and Rome. Ed. Frank H. Ellis. Oxford: Clarendon Press, 1967. Excellent edition of Swift's first major published work.

The Drapier's Letters. Ed. Herbert Davis. Oxford: Clarendon Press, 1935. Annotations.

Gulliver's Travels. Ed. Paul Turner. London: Oxford University Press, 1971; 2nd rev. edn. 1986. Excellent annotations.

Gulliver's Travels: Case Studies in Contemporary Criticism. Ed. Christopher Fox. Boston and New York: Bedford Books and St. Martin's Press; London:

Macmillan, 1995. Contains a brief critical history and essays from five different theoretical stances.

Gulliver's Travels. Ed. Albert J. Rivero. New York and London: Norton, 2002. Based on the first edition of 1726; contains sections devoted to contexts and criticism.

The Intelligencer. Ed. James Woolley. Oxford: Clarendon Press, 1992. Splendid annotations and information on Swift's collaboration with Thomas Sheridan.

Journal to Stella. Ed. Harold Williams. Oxford: Clarendon Press, 1948. 2 vols. Sometimes also listed by scholars as volumes xv and xvi of the Davis *Prose Works.*

Memoirs of Martinus Scriblerus. Ed. Charles Kerby-Miller. New Haven: Yale University Press, 1950; reprinted New York: Russell and Russell, 1966. Splendid edition of Swift's collaboration with Arbuthnot, Pope, and the Scriblerians.

Polite Conversation. Ed. Eric Partridge. London: Deutsch, 1963.

Swift vs. Mainwaring: The Examiner and the Medley. Ed. Frank H. Ellis. Oxford: Clarendon Press, 1985.

A Tale of a Tub. Eds. A. C. Guthkelch and D. Nichol Smith. 2nd edn. Oxford: Clarendon Press, 1958.

A Tale of a Tub and Other Works. Eds. Angus Ross and David Woolley. Oxford: Oxford University Press, 1984. Helpful annotations.

Bibliographical

Berwick, Donald M. *The Reputation of Jonathan Swift, 1782–1882.* 1941; reprinted New York: Haskell, 1965.

Landa, Louis and James Edward Tobin. *Jonathan Swift: A List of Critical Studies Published from 1895 to 1945.* New York: Octagon Books, 1975.

Stathis, James J. *A Bibliography of Swift Studies 1945–1965.* Nashville, TN: Vanderbilt University Press, 1967.

Rodino, Richard H. *Swift Studies, 1965–1980: An Annotated Bibliography.* New York: Garland, 1984.

Teerink, H. and Arthur H. Scouten. *A Bibliography of the Writings of Jonathan Swift.* 2nd edn. Philadelphia: University of Pennsylvania Press, 1963. The standard listing of all Swift's writings.

Vieth, David M. *Swift's Poetry 1900–1980: An Annotated Bibliography of Studies.* New York: Garland, 1982.

Voigt, Milton. *Swift and the Twentieth Century.* Detroit: Wayne State University Press, 1964.

Williams, Kathleen, ed. *Swift: The Critical Heritage.* London: Routledge & Kegan Paul, 1970. Helpful selection of the earliest responses to Swift from the eighteenth-century to 1819.

Biographical

Ehrenpreis, Irvin. *Swift: The Man, His Works, and the Age.* London and Cambridge, MA: Harvard University Press, 1962–83. 3 vols. The standard biography.

Elias, Jr., A. C. *Swift at Moor Park: Problems in Biography and Criticism.* Philadelphia: University of Pennsylvania Press, 1982. Studies Swift's years with Sir William Temple.

Harrison, Alan. *The Dean's Friend: Anthony Raymond 1675–1726, Jonathan Swift And the Irish Language*. Dublin: Éamonn dc Búrca, 1999. Swift and Irish speakers.

Johnson, Samuel. *Swift*. In George Birkbeck Hill (ed.) *Lives of the English Poets*. 3 vols. Oxford: Clarendon Press, 1905. Vol. III, pp. 1–74. Influential.

McMinn, Joseph. *Jonathan Swift: A Literary Life*. New York: St. Martin's Press, 1991. Concise and lucid.

Nokes, David. *Jonathan Swift, A Hypocrite Reversed: A Critical Biography*. Oxford: Oxford University Press, 1985. Fine one-volume study.

Orrery, John Boyle, Fifth Earl, *Remarks On The Life And Writings of Dr. Jonathan Swift*. Ed. João Fróes. Newark: University of Delaware Press, 2000. Annotated edition of influential 1751 work.

Pilkington, Laetitia. *Memoirs*. Ed. A. C. Elias, Jr. Athens and London: The University of Georgia Press, 1997. 2 vols. Contemporary view of Swift by one who knew him well.

General critical studies

Brown, Laura. "Reading Race and Gender: Jonathan Swift." *Eighteenth-Century Studies* 23 (1990), 425–43.

Brown, Norman O. "The Excremental Vision." In *Life Against Death: The Psychoanalytical Meaning of History*. London: Routledge and Kegan Paul, 1959, pp. 179–201.

Brückmann, Patricia Carr. *A Manner of Correspondence: A Study of the Scriblerus Club*. Montreal: McGill-Queen's University Press, 1997.

Connery, Brian "Self-Representation, Authority, and the Fear of Madness in the Works of Swift." In Leslie Ellen Brown and Patricia B. Craddock (eds.) *Studies in Eighteenth-Century Culture*, vol. XX. East Lansing, MI: Colleagues Press, 1990, pp. 165–82.

Crook, Keith. *A Preface to Swift*. London and New York: Longman, 1998.

Deane, Seamus. "Swift and the Anglo-Irish Intellect." *Eighteenth-Century Ireland: Iris an dá chultúr* 1 (1986) 9–22.

Donoghue, Denis. *Jonathan Swift: A Critical Introduction*. Cambridge: Cambridge University Press, 1969.

Doody, Margaret Anne. "Swift Among the Women." *Yearbook of English Studies* 18 (1988), 68–92.

Downie, J. A. *Jonathan Swift: Political Writer*. London: Routledge and Kegan Paul, 1984. Advances view of Swift as an "Old" Whig.

Robert Harley and the Press: Propaganda and Public Opinion in the Age of Swift and Defoe. Cambridge: Cambridge University Press, 1979.

Elliott, Robert C. *The Power of Satire: Satire, Ritual, Myth*. Princeton: Princeton University Press, 1960. A classic study.

The Literary Persona. Chicago: University of Chicago Press, 1982.

Fabricant, Carole. *Swift's Landscape*. Baltimore: Johns Hopkins University Press, 1982; 2nd rev. edn. Notre Dame, IN and London: University of Notre Dame Press, 1995. One of the best general studies.

"The Battle of the Ancients and (Post) Moderns: Rethinking Swift Through

Contemporary Perspectives." *The Eighteenth Century: Theory and Interpretation* 32 (1991), 256–73.

Ferguson, Oliver. *Jonathan Swift and Ireland.* Urbana: University of Illinois Press, 1962. Excellent on Irish contexts.

Flynn, Carol Houlihan. *The Body in Swift and Defoe.* Cambridge: Cambridge University Press, 1990.

Francus, Marilyn. *The Converting Imagination: Linguistic Theory and Swift's Satiric Prose.* Carbondale and Edwardsville: Southern Illinois University Press, 1991.

Goldgar, Bertrand A. *Walpole and the Wits: The Relation of Politics to Literature, 1722–1742.* Lincoln: University of Nebraska Press, 1976.

The Curse of Party: Swift's Relations With Addison and Steele. Lincoln: University of Nebraska Press, 1961.

Harth, Phillip. "Swift's Self-Image as a Satirist." *Proceedings of the First Münster Symposium on Jonathan Swift.* Eds. Hermann J. Real and Heinz J. Vienken. Munich: Wilhelm Fink, 1985, pp. 113–21.

Higgins, Ian. *Swift's Politics: A Study in Disaffection.* Cambridge: Cambridge University Press, 1994. Views Swift as Jacobite.

Kelly, Ann Cline. *Jonathan Swift and Popular Culture: Myth, Media, and the Man.* New York and London: Palgrave, 2002.

Swift and the English Language. Philadelphia: University of Pennsylvania Press, 1988.

Landa, Louis A. *Swift and the Church of Ireland.* Oxford: Clarendon Press, 1954.

Leavis, F. R. "The Irony of Swift." In *Determinations.* Chatto and Windus, 1934, pp. 79–108. Highly influential.

Levine, Joseph M. *Dr. Woodward's Shield: History, Science, and Satire in Augustan England.* Berkeley: University of California Press, 1977.

Lock, F. P. *Swift's Tory Politics.* London: Duckworth, 1983.

McMinn, Joseph. *Jonathan's Travels: Swift and Ireland.* Belfast and New York: Appletree Press and St. Martin's Press, 1994. Swift's travels in his native land.

Mahony, Robert. *Jonathan Swift: The Irish Identity.* New Haven and London: Yale University Press, 1995. Helpful on Swift's reputation in Ireland.

Mullan, John. "Swift, Defoe, and Narrative Forms." In Steven N. Zwicker (ed.) *The Cambridge Companion To English Literature 1650–1740.* (Cambridge: Cambridge University Press, 1998), pp. 250–75. Splendid comparison that illuminates both writers.

Paulson, Ronald. *The Fictions of Satire.* Baltimore: Johns Hopkins Press, 1967.

Phiddian, Robert. *Swift's Parody.* Cambridge: Cambridge University Press. 1995.

Pollak, Ellen. *The Poetics of Sexual Myth: Gender and Ideology in the Verse of Swift and Pope.* Chicago and London: University of Chicago Press, 1985.

Quintana, Ricardo. *Swift: An Introduction.* London: Oxford University Press, 1955. Still one of the best introductions.

The Mind and Art of Jonathan Swift. Oxford, 1936; reprinted Gloucester, MA: Peter Smith, 1965. Classic study.

Rogers, Pat. *Hacks and Dunces: Pope, Swift, and Grub Street.* London: Methuen, 1980.

Rawson, Claude. *God, Gulliver, and Genocide: Barbarism and the European Imagination, 1492–1945.* Oxford: Oxford University Press, 2001.

Satire and Sentiment 1660–1830. Cambridge: Cambridge University Press, 1994.

Order from Confusion Sprung: Studies in English Literature from Swift to Cowper. London: Allen and Unwin, 1985.

"The Character of Swift's Satire: Reflections on Swift, Johnson, and Human Restlessness." In *The Character of Swift's Satire: A Revised Focus*. Newark: University of Delaware Press; London and Toronto: Associated University Presses, 1983, pp. 21–82. Insightful comparison of Swift and Samuel Johnson.

Real, Hermann J. and Heinz J. Vienken. "Psychoanalytic Criticism and Swift: The History of a Failure." *Eighteenth-Century Ireland: Iris an dá chultúr* 1 (1986), 127–41.

Reilly, Patrick. *Jonathan Swift: The Brave Desponder*. Carbondale and Edwardsville: Southern Illinois University Press, 1982.

Said, Edward W. "Swift's Tory Anarchy" and "Swift As Intellectual." In *The World, The Text, and The Critic*. Cambridge, MA: Harvard University Press, 1983, pp. 54–89. A starting point for most contemporary discussions.

Steele, Peter. *Jonathan Swift: Preacher and Jester*. Oxford: Clarendon Press, 1978.

Wyrick, Deborah Baker. *Jonathan Swift and the Vested Word*. Chapel Hill: University of North Carolina Press, 1988.

Collections of essays

Donoghue, Denis, ed. *Jonathan Swift: A Critical Anthology*. Harmondsworth: Penguin, 1971. Helpful selection of early responses and of twentieth-century criticism.

Douglas, Aileen, Patrick Kelly, and Ian Campbell Ross, eds. *Locating Swift*. Dublin: Four Courts Press, 1998.

Fox, Christopher and Brenda Tooley, eds. *Walking Naboth's Vineyard: New Studies of Swift*. Notre Dame, IN: University of Notre Dame Press, 1995.

Fischer, John Irwin, Hermann J. Real, and James Woolley, eds. *Swift and His Contexts*. New York: AMS Press, 1989.

Jeffares, A. Norman, ed. *Fair Liberty Was All His Cry*. London: Macmillan, 1967.

Palmeri, Frank, ed. *Critical Essays on Jonathan Swift*. New York: G. K. Hall, 1993.

Probyn, Clive, ed. *The Art of Jonathan Swift*. London: Vision Press, 1978.

Rawson, Claude, ed. *The Character of Swift's Satire: A Revised Focus*. Newark: University of Delaware Press; London and Toronto: Associated University Presses, 1983.

Jonathan Swift: A Collection of Critical Essays. Englewood Cliffs, NJ: Prentice Hall, 1995. Helpful selection of twentieth-century criticism.

Real, Hermann J. and Helgard Stöver-Leidig, eds. *Reading Swift: Papers from The Third Münster Symposium on Jonathan Swift*. Munich: Wilhelm Fink, 1998. Excellent papers by leading scholars. Also see the 1985 and 1993 volumes, eds. Hermann J. Real, *et al.*

Schakel, Peter J., ed. *Critical Approaches to Teaching Swift*. New York: AMS Press, 1992. Helpful introductory material.

Tuveson, Ernest, ed. *Swift: A Collection of Critical Essays*. Englewood Cliffs, NJ: Prentice Hall, 1964.

Vickers, Brian, ed. *The World of Jonathan Swift*. Cambridge, MA: Harvard University Press, 1968.

Wood, Nigel, ed. *Jonathan Swift*. London: Longman, 1999.

Poetry

Barnett, Louise K. *Swift's Poetic Worlds*. Newark: Associated University Presses, 1981.

Bogel, Fredric V. "Swift's Poems: Satire, Contamination, Authority." In *The Difference Satire Makes*. Ithaca: Cornell University Press, 2001, pp. 106–31.

Conlon, Michael J. "Anonymity and Authority in the Poetry of Jonathan Swift." In Howard D. Weinbrot, Peter J. Schakel and Stephen Karian (eds.) *Eighteenth-Century Contexts: Historical Inquiries in Honor of Phillip Harth*. Madison: University of Wisconsin Press, 2001, pp. 133–46.

"Singing Beside-Against: Parody and the Example of Swift's 'A Description of a City Shower.'" *Genre* 16 (1983), 219–32.

England, A. B. *Energy and Order in the Poetry of Swift*. Lewisburg, PA: Bucknell University Press, 1990.

Feingold, Richard. "Swift in His Poems: The Range of His Positive Rhetoric." In Claude Rawson (ed.) *The Character of Swift's Satire: A Revised Focus*. Newark: University of Delaware Press, 1983, pp. 166–202.

Fischer, John Irwin. *On Swift's Poetry*. Gainesville: University Press of Florida, 1979.

Fischer, John Irwin, Donald Mell, Jr., and David Vieth, eds. *Contemporary Studies of Swift's Poetry*. Newark: University of Delaware Press, 1981.

Greene, Donald. "On Swift's 'Scatological' Poems." *Sewanee Review* 75 (1976), 33–43.

Jaffe, Nora Crowe. *The Poet Swift*. Hanover, NH: University Press of New England, 1977.

Johnson, Maurice. *The Sin of Wit: Jonathan Swift as a Poet*. Syracuse, NY: Syracuse University Press, 1950.

Karian, Stephen. "Reading the Material Text of Swift's *Verses on the Death*." *SEL: Studies in English Literature 1500–1900* (2001), 515–44.

Kulisheck, Clarence L. "Swift's Octosyllabics and the Hudibrastic Tradition." *Journal of English and Germanic Philology* 53 (1954), 361–68.

Mueller, Judith C. "Imperfect Enjoyment at Market Hill: Impotence, Desire, and Reform in Swift's Poems to Lady Acheson." *English Literary History* 66 (1999), 51–70.

Nussbaum, Felicity. "The 'Sex's Flight': Women and Time in Swift's Poetry." In *The Brink of All We Hate: English Satires, 1660–1750*. Lexington: University Press of Kentucky, 1984, pp. 94–116.

Pollak, Ellen. "'Things which must not be exprest': Teaching Swift's Scatological Poems about Women." In Christopher Fox (ed.) *Teaching Eighteenth-Century Poetry*. New York: AMS Press, 1990, pp. 177–86.

Rawson, Claude. "'I the Lofty Stile Decline': Self-apology and the 'Heroick Strain' in Some of Swift's Poems." In Robert Folkenflik (ed.) *The English Hero 1660–1800*. Newark: University of Delaware Press; London and Toronto: Associated University Presses, 1982, pp. 79–115.

"The Nightmares of Strephon: Nymphs of the City in the Poems of Swift, Baude-laire, Eliot." In Maximillian E. Novak (ed.) *English Literature in the Age of Disguise*. Berkeley and Los Angeles: University of California Press, 1977, pp. 57–99.

Rees, Christine. "Gay, Swift, and the Nymphs of Drury-Lane." *Essays in Criticism* 23 (1973), 1–21.

Schakel, Peter J. *The Poetry of Jonathan Swift: Allusion and the Development of a Poetic Style*. Madison: University of Wisconsin Press, 1978.

A Tale of a Tub

Adams, Robert M. "The Mood of the Church and *A Tale of a Tub*." In H. T. Sweden-berg, Jr. (ed.) *England in the Restoration and Early Eighteenth Century*. Berkeley and Los Angeles: University of California Press, 1972, pp. 71–99.

Clark, John R. *Form and Frenzy in Swift's Tale of a Tub*. Ithaca: Cornell University Press, 1970.

Connery, Brian. "The Persona as Pretender and the Reader as Constitutional Subject in Swift's *Tale*." In James A. Gill (ed.) *Cutting Edges: Postmodern Critical Essays on Eighteenth-Century Satire*. Knoxville: University of Tennessee Press, 1995, pp. 159–80.

DePorte, Michael. *Nightmares and Hobbyhorses: Swift, Sterne, and Augustan Ideas of Madness*. San Marino, CA: Huntington Library, 1974.

"Vehicles of Delusion: Swift, Locke and the Madhouse Poems of James Carkesse." In Christopher Fox (ed.) *Psychology and Literature in the Eighteenth Century*. New York: AMS Press, 1987, pp. 69–86.

Levine, Jay Arnold. "The Design of *A Tale of a Tub* (with a Digression on the Mad Modern Critic)." *English Literary History* 33 (1966), 198–227.

Harth, Phillip. *Swift and Anglican Rationalism: The Religious Background of A Tale of a Tub*. Chicago: University of Chicago Press, 1961.

Hawes, Clement. "Return to Madness: Mania As Plebeian Vapors in Swift." In *Mania and Literary Style: The Rhetoric of Enthusiasm From the Ranters to Christopher Smart*. Cambridge: Cambridge University Press, 1996, pp. 101–125.

Lund, Roger D. "Strange Complicities: Atheism and Conspiracy in *A Tale of a Tub*." *Eighteenth-Century Life* 13 (1989), 34–58.

Mueller, Judith C. "Writing Under Constraint: Swift's 'Apology' for *A Tale of A Tub*." *English Literary History* 60 (1993), 101–15.

Nash, Richard. "Entrapment and Ironic Modes in *A Tale of A Tub*." *Eighteenth-Century Studies* 24 (1991), 415–31.

Paulson, Ronald. *Theme and Structure in Swift's Tale of a Tub*. New Haven: Yale University Press, 1960.

Saccamano, Neil. "Authority and Publication: The Works of 'Swift.'" *The Eighteenth Century: Theory and Interpretation* 25 (1984), 241–62.

Seidel, Michael. *Satiric Inheritance: Rabelais to Sterne*. Princeton: Princeton University Press, 1979.

Smith, Frederik N. *Language and Reality in Swift's "A Tale of a Tub."* Columbus: Ohio State University Press, 1979.

Starkman, Miriam K. *Swift's Satire on Learning in A Tale of a Tub*. Princeton: Princeton University Press, 1950.

Walsh, Marcus. "Text, 'Text,' and Swift's *Tale of a Tub*." *The Modern Language Review* 85 (1990), 290–303.

Zimmerman, Everett. *Swift's Narrative Satires: Author and Authority*. Ithaca: Cornell University Press, 1983.

Gulliver's Travels

Barchas, Janine. "Prefiguring Genre: Frontispiece Portraits from *Gulliver's Travels* to *Millenium Hall*." *Studies in the Novel* 30 (1998), 260–86.

Brady, Frank, ed. *Twentieth-Century Interpretations of Gulliver's Travels*. Englewood Cliffs, NJ: Prentice-Hall, 1968.

Bruce, Susan. "The Flying Island and Female Anatomy: Gynecology and Power in *Gulliver's Travels*." *Genders* 2 (1988), 60–76.

Carnochan, W. B. *Lemuel Gulliver's Mirror for Man*. Berkeley and Los Angeles: University of California Press, 1968.

Castle, Terry. "Why the Houyhnhnms Don't Write: Swift, Satire and the Fear of the Text." *Essays in Literature* 7 (1980), 31–44.

Clifford, James L. "Gulliver's Fourth Voyage: 'Hard' and 'Soft' Schools of Interpretation." In Larry Champion (ed.) *Quick Springs of Sense: Studies in the Eighteenth Century*. Athens: University of Georgia Press, 1974, pp. 33–49. Classic look at different ways of interpreting Book IV.

Crane, R. S. "The Houyhnhnms, the Yahoos, and the History of Ideas." In J. A. Mazzeo (ed.) *Reason and Imagination: Studies in the History of Ideas, 1600–1800*. New York: Columbia University Press, 1962. Excellent and influential.

Doody, Margaret Anne. "Insects, Vermin, and Horses: *Gulliver's Travels* and Virgil's *Georgics*." In Douglas Lane Patey and Timothy Keegan (eds.) *Augustan Studies: Essays in Honor of Irvin Ehrenpreis*. Newark: University of Delaware Press, 1985, pp. 147–74.

Downie, J. A. "Political Characterization in *Gulliver's Travels*." *Yearbook of English Studies* 7 (1977), 108–20.

"The Political Significance of *Gulliver's Travels*." In John Irwin Fischer, Hermann J. Real, and James Woolley (eds.) *Swift and His Contexts*. New York: AMS Press, 1989, pp. 1–19.

Erskine-Hill, Howard. *Gulliver's Travels*. Cambridge: Cambridge University Press, 1993. Excellent introduction to the work.

Fox, Christopher. "The Myth of Narcissus in Swift's *Travels*." *Eighteenth-Century Studies* 20 (1986–87), 17–33.

"Of Logic and Lycanthropy: Gulliver and the Faculties of the Mind." In Roy Porter and Marie Mulvey Roberts (eds.) *Literature and Medicine during the Eighteenth Century*. London: Routledge, 1993, pp. 101–17.

Hammond, Brean. *Gulliver's Travels*. Philadelphia: Open University Press, 1988.

Harth, Phillip. "The Problem of Political Allegory in *Gulliver's Travels*." *Modern Philology* 73 (1976), 540–47.

Hawes, Clement. "Three Times Round the Globe: Gulliver and Colonial Discourse." *Cultural Critique* 18 (1991), 187–214.

Higgins, Ian. "Swift and Sparta: The Nostalgia of *Gulliver's Travels*." *Modern Language Review* 78 (1983), 513–31.

Keener, Fredrick M. *The Chain of Becoming*. New York: Columbia University Press, 1983. Excellent on *Gulliver*.

Lock, F. P. *The Politics of Gulliver's Travels*. Oxford: Clarendon Press, 1980.

McKeon, Michael. "Parables of the Younger Son (II): Swift and the Containment of Desire." In *The Origins of the English Novel 1600–1740*. Baltimore: Johns Hopkins University Press, 1987, pp. 338–56.

Mezciems, Jenny. "'Tis not to divert the Reader': Moral and Literary Determinants in Some Early Travel Narratives." *Prose Studies* 5 (1982), 1–21. Helpful on connections to travel literature.

"Utopia and 'the Thing which is not': More, Swift, and Other Lying Idealists." *University of Toronto Quarterly* 52 (1982), 40–62.

Monk, Samuel Holt. "The Pride of Lemuel Gulliver." *Sewanee Review* 63 (1955), 48–71. Influential account of the moral significance of Swift's work.

Nicholson, Marjorie Hope and Nora M. Mohler. "The Scientific Background of Swift's *Voyage to Laputa*." In Marjorie Nicholson, *Science and Imagination*. Ithaca, NY: Great Seal Books, 1956, pp. 110–154.

Nussbaum, Felicity. "Gulliver's Malice: Gender and Satiric Stance." In Christopher Fox (ed.) *Gulliver's Travels: Case Studies in Contemporary Criticism*. Boston and New York: Bedford Books and St. Martin's Press, 1995, pp. 318–34.

Nuttall, A. D. "Gulliver Among the Horses." *Yearbook of English Studies* 18 (1988), 51–67.

Oakleaf, David. "*Trompe l'oeil*: Gulliver and the Distortions of the Observing Eye." *University of Toronto Quarterly* 53 (1982), 48–59.

Patey, Douglas Lane. "Swift's Satire on 'Science' and the Structure of *Gulliver's Travels*." *English Literary History* 58 (1991), 809–39.

Probyn, Clive T. "Haranguing upon Texts: Swift and the Idea of the Book." In *Proceedings of the First Münster Symposium on Jonathan Swift*. Eds. Hermann J. Real and Heinz J. Vienken. Munich: Wilhelm Fink, 1985, pp. 187–97.

Rawson, C. J. *Gulliver and the Gentle Reader: Studies in Swift and Our Time*. London and Boston: Routledge and Kegan Paul, 1973. Excellent and influential.

Real, Hermann J. "Voyages to Nowhere: More's *Utopia* and Swift's *Gulliver's Travels*." In Stephen E. Karian, Peter J. Schakel, and Howard Weinbrot (eds.) *Eighteenth-Century Contexts: Historical Inquiries in Honor of Phillip Harth*. Madison, Wisconsin: University of Wisconsin Press, 2001, pp. 96–113.

Rodino, Richard. "'Splendide Mendax': Authors, Characters and Readers in *Gulliver's Travels*." *Publications of the Modern Language Association of America* 106 (1991), 1054–70.

Rogers, Pat. "Gulliver's Glasses." In Clive T. Probyn (ed.) *The Art of Jonathan Swift*. London: Vision Press, 1978, pp. 179–88.

Rosenblum, Joseph. "Gulliver's Dutch Uncle: Another Look at Swift and the Dutch." *British Journal for Eighteenth-Century Studies* 24 (2001), 63–75. Dutch as symbol of modernism.

Seidel, Michael. "*Gulliver's Travels* and the Contracts of Fiction." In John Richetti (ed.) *The Cambridge Companion to the Eighteenth-Century Novel*. Cambridge: Cambridge University Press, 1996, pp. 72–89.

Smith, Frederik N., ed. *The Genres of Gulliver's Travels*. Newark: University of Delaware Press; London: Associated University Presses, 1990. Splendid essays.

Tippet, Brian. *Gulliver's Travels: An Introduction to the Variety of Criticism.* Basingstoke and London: Macmillan, 1989.

Todd, Dennis. "The Hairy Maid at the Harpsichord: Some Speculations on the Meaning of *Gulliver's Travels*." *Texas Studies in Language and Literature* 34 (1992), 239–83.

Traugott, John. "The Yahoo in the Doll's House: *Gulliver's Travels* the Children's Classic." In Claude Rawson (ed.) *English Satire and the Satiric Tradition.* Oxford: Basil Blackwell, 1984, pp. 127–50.

The Drapier's Letters, A Modest Proposal and shorter prose

Canning, Rick G. "'Ignorant, Illiterate Creatures': Gender and Colonial Justification in Swift's *Injured Lady* and *Answer to the Injured Lady*." *English Literary History* 64 (1997), 77–98.

Carey, Daniel. "Swift Among The Freethinkers." *Eighteenth-Century Ireland: Iris an dá chultúr* 12 (1997), 89–99.

Fabricant, Carole. "Speaking For the Irish Nation: The Drapier, The Bishop, and The Problems of Colonial Representation." *English Literary History* 66 (1999), 337–72.

Kelly, James. "Jonathan Swift and the Irish Economy of the 1720s." *Eighteenth-Century Ireland: Iris an dá chultúr* 6 (1991), 7–36.

Levine, Joseph M. *The Battle of the Books: History and Literature in the Augustan Age.* Ithaca: Cornell University Press, 1991. Excellent on historical contexts of Swift's *Battel of the Books.*

Lowe, N. F. "Why Swift Killed Partridge." *Swift Studies* 6 (1991), 70–82.

Lund, Roger D. "Swift's Sermons, 'Public Conscience,' and the Privatization of Religion." *Prose Studies* 18 (1995), 150–74.

McLoughlin, T. O. "Jonathan Swift and the 'Proud Oppressor's Hand.'" In T. O. McLoughlin, *Contesting Ireland: Irish Voices against England in the Eighteenth Century.* Dublin: Four Courts Press, 1999, pp. 65–87.

Mahony, Robert. "The Irish Colonial Experience and Swift's Rhetorics of Perception in the 1720s." *Eighteenth-Century Life* 22 (1998), 63–75.

"Protestant Dependence and Consumption in Swift's Irish Writings." In S. J. Connolly (ed.) *Political Ideas In Eighteenth-Century Ireland.* Dublin: Four Courts Press, 2000, pp. 83–104.

Mayhew, George P. "Swift's Bickerstaff Hoax as an April Fools' Joke." *Modern Philology* 61 (1964), 270–80.

Nolan, Emer. "Swift: The Patriot Game." *British Journal for Eighteenth-Century Studies* 21 (1998), 39–53. Excellent on the political languages of Swift's Irish tracts.

Rawson, Claude. "A Reading of *A Modest Proposal*." In J. C. Hilson *et al.* (eds.) *Augustan Worlds.* Leicester: Leicester University Press, 1978, pp. 29–50.

"The Injured Lady and the Drapier: A Reading of Swift's Irish Tracts." *Prose Studies* 3 (1980), 15–43.

Treadwell, J. M. "Swift, William Wood, and the Factual Basis of Satire." *Journal of British Studies* 15 (1976), 76–91. Excellent context for the Drapier affair.

Wittkowsky, George. "Swift's *Modest Proposal*: The Biography of an Early Georgian Pamphlet." *Journal of the History of Ideas* 4 (1943), 75–104.

SUBJECT INDEX

Addison, Joseph: *Cato*, 42; friend to Swift, 32, 39–40; language academy proposal, 153; literature, power union, 44; stylistic differences from Swift, 42–43
Aeneid (Virgil), 82
ancients/moderns controversy: in *The Battel of the Books*, 80; Swift on, 41–43, 118, 203–6, 248; in *A Tale of a Tub*, 80
Anglo-Irish elite, 57–58
Anne, Queen of England, 23, 33, 35, 44
Antrim County, Kilroot parish, 18, 93–94, 162, 170, 207, 243
Arbuthnot, John, 32, 41
Atterbury, Francis, 156, 191
authority of the Church, 172, 208; established forms of, 213–14; free-thinkers vs., 214; in government, 37; Swift and, 61, 164, 168–69, 213–14, 252; subversion vs., in print materials, 208
autobiography, in works of Swift (*see also entries under Gulliver's Travels; Verses on the Death of Dr. Swift*): "The Author Upon Himself," 23, 185, 190; *Family of Swift*, 15, 16, 27, 68; "In Sickness," 190; Market Hill group, 52; *Polite Conversation*, 125–26; Pope, letter to (1722), 25, 26

Bailey, Nathan, 194
Ball, Elrington, 104
Barber, Mary, 106, 108
Behn, Aphra, 41
Bentley, Richard, 204–5, 248
Berkeley, Earl of (Charles), 19, 162, 252
Bettesworth, Richard ("Booby"), 63, 195
Bindon, David, 136, 137
Bolingbroke, Viscount (Henry St. John), 32, 36, 40, 43

Borges, Jorge Luis, 60
Boulter, Archbishop Hugh, 62
Boyle, John (Earl of Orrery), 15, 106, 108
The British Bulwark (Burnet), 151
Brown, Norman O., 28
Browne, John, 138
Burnet, Bishop Gilbert, 77–78, 165
Burnet, Thomas, 151
Burney, Frances, 108
Butler, Joseph, 246
Butler, Samuel, 76, 191
Butterfield, Herbert, 2

career, early years: overview, 49–50; Temple's executor, 18; Temple's secretary, 17, 18
career, literary: ambition in: disappointments, 70, of legacy, 59, 81, 202, religious principles vs., 18, 19, 20, 126; background, 17, 50; censorship advocated, 208; old age, 27, 234; sedition accusations, 24, 25; success in, 58–59
career, political: ambition in, 21–22, 23, 31, 40; disappointment in, 50, 198–99; First Fruits negotiation, 20–21, 33, 163, 165; friendships from, 32; literature, power union in, 44–45; Pope, letter to (1722), 25, 26; retirement from, 23; as Tory party supporter, 21–22, 23, 34–35, 38–39; as Whig party supporter, 33, 37; Whig vs. Tory allegiance, 2, 19–20, 35–36, 38–39, 40
career, political-writer: overview, 31; ambition in;, 40 *The Examiner* editor, 21–22, 34–35, 40; Irish perspective, 32; personal loyalties in, 32–33; religious orientation in, 32–33
career, religious (*see also entries under* St. Patricks' Cathedral; religion, Swift's

vocation): ambition in, 44, 49, 50, 163, 198; chaplain to Earl of Berkeley, 19, 162; defender of the church, 8–9, 18, 33, 164–65, 172, 214, 245; dissent/dissenters, position on, 9, 18, 20, 33, 35, 139, 162, 207; First Fruits negotiation, 20–21, 33, 163, 165; Kilroot parish, County Antrim, 18, 93–94, 162, 170, 207, 243; Laracor parish, County Meath, 19, 21, 50, 162–63; ordination, 17; Sacramental Test Act position, 162, 170–71, 172, 207; Stella as hazard to, 99; *A Tale of a Tub* and, 35, 206
Carolan, Turlough, 63
The Case of Ireland . . . Stated (Molyneux), 251
Castle, Terry, 84
Cato (Addison), 42
Cato's Letters (Gordon and Trenchard), 42
Christianity Not Mysterious (Toland), 249–50
Church of Ireland (*see* Ireland, Church of)
Cibber, Colley, 235
Clarke, Samuel, 167
The Closing Years of Dean Swift's Life (Wilde), 15
comic sense in Swift's work: comic hero of love, 109; in poetry, 183–84, 196, 200, 235; in prose, 67, 119, 125, 188
Congreve, William, 39, 48
copper-coinage controversy (*see* Wood's Halfpence project)
Cotton, Charles, 81, 83
Cowley, Abraham, 188
Cromwell, Oliver, 203
Curll, Edmund, 200

Dampier, William, 80, 223
Davys, Mary, 108
Defoe, Daniel: imprisonment, 44; Swift's dislike of, 85, 224, 234; language academy proposal, 153; *The Life . . . of Robinson Crusoe . . . Mariner*, 224–25; literature, power union, 44; the novel in works of, 41; *The Shortest-Way with the Dissenters*, 44; as Whig, 37
Delany, Rev. Patrick, 3, 24, 52, 106
Denham, John, 118–19
Dingley, Rebecca, 19, 26, 96
Dioptrica nova (Molyneux), 252
dissent/dissenters (*see also* Sacramental Test Act): as fanatics, 171–72; Occasional Conformity Bill, 35; occasional conformity practice, 32, 170; political restrictions

against, 32; Swift on, 33, 38, 169–72, 209; Whig, Tory party positions, 19, 20, 33, 37, 38
Dissertation on the Epistles of Phalaris (Bentley), 204
Donellan, Anne, 106
Donoghue, Dennis, 197
Downie, J. A., 35–36
The Drapier's Letters (*see also* Wood's Halfpence project): overview, 24–25, 136–37; background, 56, 105–6; *Gulliver's Travels* compared, 67; liberty defined in, 60; reward for naming the author, 25, 57, 137; symbolism in, 58; Walpole brogue event, 58
The Drapier's Letters no. 1, 56, 136
The Drapier's Letters no. 2, 136
The Drapier's Letters no. 3, 56, 136
The Drapier's Letters no. 4, 24, 57–58, 67, 137
The Drapier's Letters no. 7, 129–30, 136, 137
Dryden, John, 75, 118
Dunciad (Pope), 236
Dunkin, William, 69, 81
Dunton, John, 81

Eachard, John, 165
Earbery, Matthias, 151
economics, Swift on: context in understanding, 130; the currency system, 139, 140; (*see also The Drapier's Letters*); Dublin weavers predicament, 133, 141; emigration, 139; national bank proposal, 134–35; reputation as nationalist and, 135; solutions to Irish situation: boycott of Wood's coin, 136, economic self-reliance, 24, importing corn, 141, import-substitution proposal, 133–34; outdated positions in, 140–41, uniqueness of Irish problems, 133, 138–39
economics, Swift on (prose) (*see also A Modest Proposal*; prose, Swiftian, on economics; *The Drapier's Letters*): An *Answer to a Paper called a Memorial of the Poor Inhabitants, Tradesmen, and Labourers*, 141; *Answer to Several Letters from Unknown Persons*, 129; "Causes of the Wretched Conditions of Ireland," 138; *A Letter from a Lady in Town to her Friend in the Country, Concerning the Bank*, 135; *A Proposal for the Universal Use of Irish Manufacture*, 24, 54–56, 130, 133–34; *Proposal that all the Ladies and*

TITLE INDEX

CAMBRIDGE COMPANIONS TO LITERATURE

*The Cambridge Companion to
Edith Wharton*
edited by Millicent Bell

The Cambridge Companion to Henry James
edited by Jonathan Freedman

The Cambridge Companion to Walt Whitman
edited by Ezra Greenspan

*The Cambridge Companion to
Henry David Thoreau*
edited by Joel Myerson

The Cambridge Companion to Mark Twain
edited by Forrest G. Robinson

*The Cambridge Companion to
Edgar Allan Poe*
edited by Kevin J. Hayes

*The Cambridge Companion to
Emily Dickinson*
edited by Wendy Martin

*The Cambridge Companion to
William Faulkner*
edited by Philip M. Weinstein

*The Cambridge Companion to
Ernest Hemingway*
edited by Scott Donaldson

*The Cambridge Companion to
F. Scott Fitzgerald*
edited by Ruth Prigozy

*The Cambridge Companion to
Robert Frost*
edited by Robert Faggen

*The Cambridge Companion to
Eugene O'Neill*
edited by Michael Manheim

*The Cambridge Companion to
Tennessee Williams*
edited by Matthew C. Roudané

*The Cambridge Companion to
Arthur Miller*
edited by Christopher Bigsby

*The Cambridge Companion to
Sam Shepard*
edited by Matthew C. Roudané

CAMBRIDGE COMPANIONS TO CULTURE

*The Cambridge Companion to Modern
German Culture*
edited by Eva Kolinsky
and Wilfried van der Will

*The Cambridge Companion to Modern
Russian Culture*
edited by Nicholas Rzhevsky

*The Cambridge Companion to Modern
Spanish Culture*
edited by David T. Gies

*The Cambridge Companion to Modern
Italian Culture*
edited by Zygamunt G. Baranski
and Rebecca J. West